Wittgenstein and the Limit of Language

MW01089911

The limit of language is one of the most pervasive notions found in Wittgenstein's work, both in his early *Tractatus Logico-Philosophicus* and his later writings. Moreover, the idea of a limit of language is intimately related to important scholarly debates on Wittgenstein's philosophy, such as the debate between the so-called traditional and resolute interpretations, Wittgenstein's stance on transcendental idealism, and the philosophical import of Wittgenstein's latest work, *On Certainty*.

This collection includes twelve original essays that provide a comprehensive overview of the various ways in which Wittgenstein appeals to the limit of language at different stages of his philosophical development. The essays connect the idea of a limit of language to the most important themes discussed by Wittgenstein – his conception of logic and grammar, the method of philosophy, the nature of the subject, and the foundations of knowledge – as well as his views on ethics, aesthetics, and religion. The essays also relate Wittgenstein's thought to his contemporaries, including Carnap, Frege, Heidegger, Levinas, and Moore.

Hanne Appelqvist is Docent of Theoretical Philosophy at the University of Helsinki, Finland. Her work on Wittgenstein has been published in journals such as the *European Journal of Philosophy*, the *British Journal of Aesthetics*, the *British Journal for the History of Philosophy*, *Metaphilosophy*, and *History of Philosophy Quarterly*.

Routledge Studies in Twentieth-Century Philosophy

For more information about this series, please visit: www.routledge.com/
Routledge-Studies-in-Twentieth-Century-Philosophy/book-series/SE0438

Wittgenstein and the Limits of Language

Edited by Hanne Appelqvist

Routledge
Taylor & Francis Group

LONDON AND NEW YORK

First published 2020 by Routledge

2 Park Square, Milton Park, Abingdon, Oxon OX14 4RN
605 Third Avenue, New York, NY 10017

Routledge is an imprint of the Taylor & Francis Group, an informa business

First issued in paperback 2021

Library of Congress Cataloging-in-Publication Data
A catalog record for this book has been requested

ISBN: 978-0-8153-8501-1 (hbk)
ISBN: 978-1-03-217635-2 (pbk)
DOI: 10.4324/9781351202671

Typeset in Sabon
by Apex CoVantage, LLC

Contents

Abbreviations of Works by Wittgenstein

Published Works

BB   *The Blue and Brown Books*. Oxford: Blackwell, 1958.

BT   *Big Typescript: TS 213*. Edited and translated by C. G. Luckhardt & M. A. E. Aue. Oxford: Blackwell, 2005.

CV   *Culture and Value*. Edited by G. H. von Wright & A. Pichler, translated by P. Winch. Revised 2nd edition. Oxford: Blackwell, 1998.

LE   "A Lecture on Ethics", *The Philosophical Review*, 74 (1), 3–12 (1965), reprinted in PO, 37–44.

LW I   *Last Writings on the Philosophy of Psychology*, Volume I. Edited by G. H. von Wright and H. Nyman, translated by C.G. Luckhardt and M. A. E. Aue. Oxford: Blackwell, 1982.

LW II   *Last Writings on the Philosophy of Psychology*, Volume II. Edited by G. H. von Wright and H. Nyman, translated by C. G. Luckhardt and M. A. E. Aue. Oxford: Blackwell, 1992.

NB   *Notebooks 1914–1916*. Edited by G. H. von Wright and G. E. M. Anscombe, translated by G. E. M. Anscombe. Oxford: Blackwell, 1961.

OC   *On Certainty*. Edited by G. H. von Wright and G. E. M. Anscombe, translated by G. E. M. Anscombe. Oxford: Blackwell, 1969.

P   "Philosophy" (sections 86–93 of the *Big Typescript*), reprinted in PO, 160–199.

PG   *Philosophical Grammar*. Edited by R. Rhees, translated by A. Kenny. Berkeley: University of California Press, 1974.

PI   *Philosophical Investigations*. Edited by G. E. M. Anscombe and R. Rhees, translated by G. E. M. Anscombe. 2nd edition. Oxford: Blackwell, 1997.
Philosophical Investigations. Edited by G. E. M. Anscombe, translated by P. M. S. Hacker and J. Schulte. Revised 4th edition by P. M. S. Hacker and J. Schulte. Oxford: Blackwell, 2009.

PO   *Philosophical Occasions: 1912–1951*. Edited by J. C. Klagge and A. Nordman. Indianapolis: Hackett Publishing, 1993.

PPF   *Philosophy of Psychology: A Fragment* (Previously known as Part II of *Philosophical Investigations*), in PI, 182–244.

PR   *Philosophical Remarks*. Edited by R. Rhees, translated by R. Hargreaves and R. White. Oxford: Blackwell, 1975.

RFM   *Remarks on the Foundations of Mathematics*. Edited by G. H. von Wright, R. Rhees and G. E. M. Anscombe, translated by G. E. M. Anscombe. Cambridge Mass: MIT Press, 1983.

ROC   *Remarks on Colour*. Edited by G. E. M. Anscombe, translated by L. L. McAlister and M. Schättle. Oxford: Blackwell, 1977.

RPP I   *Remarks on the Philosophy of Psychology*, Volume I. Edited by G. E. M. Anscombe and G. H. von Wright, translated by G. E. M. Anscombe. Oxford: Basil Blackwell, 1980.

RPP II   *Remarks on the Philosophy of Psychology*, Volume II. Edited by G. H. von Wright & H. Nyman, translated by C. G. Luckhardt & M. A. E. Aue. Oxford: Basil Blackwell, 1980.

TLP   *Tractatus Logico-Philosophicus*. Translated by C. K. Ogden. London: Routledge and Kegan Paul, 1951.
         Tractatus Logico-Philosophicus. Translated by D. F. Pears and B. F. McGuinness. London: Routledge and Kegan Paul, 1961.

Z   *Zettel*. Edited by G. E. M. Anscombe and G. H. von Wright, translated by G. E. M. Anscombe. Berkeley: University of California Press, 1970.

Lecture Notes, Conversations, and Correspondence

AWL   *Wittgenstein's Lectures: Cambridge 1932–1935*. From the notes of A. Ambrose and M. MacDonald, edited by A. Ambrose. Oxford: Blackwell, 1979.

EL   *Letters from Ludwig Wittgenstein, With a Memoir by Paul Engelmann*. Oxford: Basil Blackwell, 1967.

KL   Letters to Koder, in *Wittgenstein und die Musik: Ludwig Wittgenstein – Rudolf Koder: Briefwechsel*. Edited by M. Alber. Innsbruck: Haymon Verlag, 2000.

LC   Wittgenstein, Ludwig. *Lectures and Conversations on Aesthetics, Psychology and Religious Belief*. From the notes of Y. Smythies, R. Rhees, and J. Taylor, edited by C. Barrett. Berkeley: University of California Press, 1966.

LFM   *Wittgenstein's Lectures on the Foundations of Mathematics, Cambridge 1939*. From the notes of R. G. Bosanquet, N. Malcolm, R. Rhees, and Y. Smythies, edited by C. Diamond. Hassocks: Harvester Press, 1976.

LWL   *Wittgenstein's Lectures, Cambridge 1930–32*. From the notes of J. King and D. Lee, edited by D. Lee. Oxford: Blackwell, 1980.

ML   Letters to Moore, in *Letters to Russell, Keynes and Moore.*
          Edited by G. H. von Wright, translated by B. F. McGuinness.
          Oxford: Basil Blackwell, 1974, 143–190.
M   *Wittgenstein's Lectures: Cambridge 1930–1933: From the
          Notes of G. E. Moore.* Edited by D. Stern, B. Rogers and
          G. Citron. Cambridge: Cambridge University Press, 2016.
WCL   *Wittgenstein's Whewell's Court Lectures: Cambridge, 1938–
          1941: from the notes by Yorick Smythies.* Edited by V. A.
          Munz and B. Ritter. Oxford: Wiley Blackwell, 2017.

Nachlass

WS-BNE   *Wittgenstein Source Bergen Nachlass Edition.* Edited by the
          Wittgenstein Archives at the University of Bergen under the
          direction of A. Pichler.

Acknowledgements

The idea of a collection dedicated to Wittgenstein's notion of a limit of language started to develop when I was a researcher in the Centre of Excellence *Reason and Religious Recognition* funded by the Academy of Finland and hosted by the Faculty of Theology of the University of Helsinki. In September 2016 I organized, in collaboration with Sami Pihlström and Panu-Matti Pöykkö, a conference on the theme, which brought together some of the contributors of this collection. I would like to thank Risto Saarinen, the director of the Centre of Excellence, as well as the Philosophical Society of Finland for providing financial support for that event. I am also indebted to the Turku Institute for Advanced Studies and the Helsinki Collegium for Advanced Studies for funding my work during this book project. I am especially grateful to the authors of this volume – William Child, Hans-Johann Glock, Eran Guter, Leila Haaparanta, Colin Johnston, A. W. Moore, Danièle Moyal-Sharrock, Yrsa Neuman, Sami Pihlström, Panu-Matti Pöykkö, Constantine Sandis, and Paul Standish – for their contributions. I would also like to express my gratitude to David Stern for his encouragement during the early stages of the project. I also wish to express my appreciation to Lassi Jakola for his meticulous work on the index of this volume. Finally, I thank the two anonymous referees as well as Andrew Weckenmann and Alexandra Simmons of Routledge for their feedback and support on this project. Chapter 1 of this collection, "The Bounds of Nonsense" by A. W. Moore, has been published in A. W. Moore, *Language, World, and Limits: Essays in the Philosophy of Language and Metaphysics* (OUP, 2019), pp. 56–70, and is reproduced by permission of Oxford University Press (see https://global.oup.com/academic/product/language-world-and-limits-9780198823643). Two pictures from Wittgenstein's *Nachlass* appearing in Chapter 7, "Moore's Paradox and the Limits of Language Use" by Yrsa Neuman, are printed with the permission of The Master and Fellows of Trinity College Cambridge. I gratefully acknowledge the permission to use these materials.

Introduction

Hanne Appelqvist

1. The Early View

1.1. *Logic as the Limit of the World*

In the Preface of *Tractatus Logico-Philosophicus*, Wittgenstein writes that

> the aim of the book is to draw a limit to thought, or rather – not to
> thought, but to the expression of thoughts: for in order to be able
> to draw a limit to thought, we should have to find both sides of the
> limit thinkable.
>
> (TLP, 3, see TLP 4.114)

According to the traditional interpretation of the book, this task is accomplished by presenting a theory of linguistic sense, known as the picture theory of meaning. According to this theory, every meaningful proposition is a picture of a possible state of affairs. The picturing of states of affairs requires, in turn, referential relations between the elements of the picture and the pictured and the ability of those elements to be connected with one another as the elements of the pictured state of affairs are connected (TLP 2.1514, 2.151). This structural isomorphism between the picture and the pictured is made possible by logical form shared by language and the world (TLP 2.033, 2.17). When a proposition is analyzed into its simple elements, that is, names, each name, as a constituent of the proposition, has a logical form that corresponds to the form of the object to which it refers in the state of affairs. The logical forms of objects thus ground the logical form of states of affairs as well as of the propositions depicting them. Hence, Wittgenstein writes, "Logic pervades the world: the limits of the world are also its limits" (TLP 5.61).

It follows from the Tractarian dictum, according to which meaningful propositions are pictures of possible states of affairs, that language is strictly factual. According to the *Tractatus*, all meaningful propositions are bipolar, capable of being true and capable of being false (TLP 2.21, 4.023). Moreover, in the Tractarian account, "the totality of true propositions is the whole of natural science" (TLP 4.11). Hence, when Wittgenstein sets out to draw a limit to the expression of thought, this translates into the philosophical task of setting "limits to the much disputed sphere of natural science" (TLP 4.113). However, in its attempt to draw such limits, the practice of philosophy in the *Tractatus* cannot abide by its self-proclaimed standard, namely "to say nothing except what can be said, i.e. propositions of natural science – i.e. something that has nothing to do with philosophy" (TLP 6.53). If the philosophical goal of the *Tractatus* is to delineate sense from nonsense by laying out the conditions for sense, those conditions are not among the facts expressible in language (TLP 2.172). One cannot step outside the bounds of thought to form meta-thoughts on the preconditions of sense that would themselves satisfy those conditions. Instead, Wittgenstein claims, logical form is "shown" or "displayed" in propositions (TLP 2.172, 4.121–4.122, 6.22). According to the traditional interpretation of the *Tractatus*, this is the reason why Wittgenstein declares his own propositions nonsensical (TLP 6.54).

The status of logical form as the limit of language surfaces in Wittgenstein's treatment of propositions of logic. Every imaginable state of affairs, that is, every possibility, can be expressed in language, and there are no thoughts in the technical sense of the *Tractatus* indicating bipolarity that could not be expressed by means of propositions. However, there are two limiting cases of propositions that do not fulfil the standard of bipolarity but that are not nonsensical either. These are tautologies and contradictions. Tautologies are unconditionally true, while contradictions are true under no conditions. Hence, given that they fail to "restrict reality to two alternatives: yes or no", tautologies and contradictions are senseless (*sinnlos*) (TLP 4.023). Nevertheless, as they still manifest logical form, if not empirical content, tautologies and contradictions are not nonsensical (*unsinnig*) (TLP 4.46–4.464). In Wittgenstein's view, propositions of logic are tautologies. While they do not say anything about the contingent facts comprising reality, they show "the logic of the world" (TLP 4.462, 6.22). They show the pure contentless form of language and thereby reveal its limits (TLP 6.12).

Wittgenstein's conception of the limits of meaningful language leaves the *Tractatus* itself in a puzzling position. What are we to think of the program outlined by Wittgenstein if it renders the sentences of the *Tractatus* itself nonsensical pseudo-propositions? How are we supposed to understand those sentences if they fail to say anything about reality? P. M. S. Hacker, perhaps the most prominent proponent of the traditional interpretation, argues that while the sentences of the *Tractatus* "fail to comply with the rules of logical grammar – logical syntax", they still succeed in illuminating correct insights about the relation between language and the world. The harmony between the two, necessary for sense, "is shown by the features of our means of representation" (Hacker 2000, 355, 364). For

Hacker, this means that "The *Tractatus* circumscribed the bounds of sense in order to make room for ineffable metaphysics" (Hacker 2001, 164; unless otherwise stated, the emphases in quotations are original throughout this volume). In other words, "Grammar, or logical syntax, is ineffably justified by reference to the metaphysical structure of the world" (Hacker 1986, 189; see also Hacker 2001, 152–153; Anscombe 1959; Pears 1987).

The traditional interpretation has been criticized by a group of scholars defending the so-called resolute reading of the *Tractatus*. One of the pivots of the ensuing debate has been the notion of a limit of language. Cora Diamond, James Conant, and others have argued that, instead of putting forth a general theory of meaning that entails such a limit, Wittgenstein aims at showing that there is no limit to our expressive capacities. Accordingly, for the resolute readers, there is no illuminating nonsense envisioned by the traditional interpretation. All nonsense is of the same kind, it is "einfach Unsinn", "mere gibberish" (Diamond 2000, 159; Conant 2002, 424). Hence, given Wittgenstein's statement of the nonsensicality of his own propositions we cannot so much as understand the *Tractatus* (cf. TLP 6.54). We can only let the book invite us to engage in "imaginative activity" of taking its nonsensical sentences as meaningful just to realize how they "dissolve from inside" (Diamond 1991, 158; Goldfarb 1997, 66). Cora Diamond writes:

> Are we going to keep the idea that there is something or other in reality that we gesture at, however badly, when we speak of "the logical form of reality", so that *it, what* we are gesturing at, is there but cannot be expressed in words? *That* is what I want to call chickening out.
> (Diamond 1991, 181)

Juliet Floyd connects the point explicitly to the idea of a limit, writing: "[the *Tractatus*] conjures up limits over and over again, but only in order to break them, to show them up as false limits" (Floyd 1998, 82; see also Conant 2002, 424). The resolute reading thus denies that Wittgenstein was committed to an idea of limits of language or to the corresponding distinction between saying and showing. Both notions must be thrown away together with the other nonsensical rungs of the ladder comprising the book (Conant 2002, 424; see TLP 6.54).

The obvious motivation for the resolute reading is Wittgenstein's statement about the nonsensicality of the sentences of the *Tractatus* (TLP 6.54). But there are at least two further reasons for the resolute critique of the traditional interpretation. First, the resolute readers object to the view of the *Tractatus* as prescribing a fixed logical syntax that would, in turn, limit our thought. They appeal to Wittgenstein's statement:

> Frege says that any legitimately constructed proposition must have sense. And I say that any possible proposition is legitimately

constructed, and, if it has no sense, that can only be because we have failed to give a *meaning* to one of its constituents.

(TLP 5.4733)

The point of this remark, it is argued, is that nonsense results only from our failure to use our words in a meaningful way (Conant 2002, 411–414; Diamond 1991, 196–201). One could object, however, that in the remark in question Wittgenstein talks about *possible* propositions that are indeed all legitimately constructed. For a proponent of the traditional reading, the potential failure Wittgenstein identifies in the passage is not a failure to think logically. For if a proposition (thought) did not have logical form, it would not be a possible proposition (thought) in the first place (see TLP 3.03, 5.4731). The failure in question is not logical but semantic: the possible proposition already has a logical form, but the *constituents* of the proposition as a formal structure have not (yet) been given meaning (*Bedeutung*) by being projected onto reality (TLP 3.12–3.13, 4.5; see Hacker 1986, 185).

The idea of logic as a "straightjacket", to borrow Floyd's expression, "a uniquely fixed and explicit system" imprisoning thought and speech, against which the resolute reading has reacted, may be seen as arising from the reception of the *Tractatus* as a work written primarily in the tradition of Frege and Russell (Floyd 1998, 80–81). Both Frege and Russell were looking for an ideal language cashed out in a *Begriffsschrift*, a particular syntactic system of analysis. If the *Tractatus* is read as exclusively reflecting this tradition, then we seem to be left with two options: either Wittgenstein's goal is to formulate such a system in order to limit our expression (as some formulations of the traditional reading suggest) or he outlines such a system only to reject it as nonsensical (as the resolute readers argue). Both readings run into difficulties with the text. The former view is difficult to align with Wittgenstein's claim, often evoked as evidence for the resolute reading, that "all the propositions of our everyday language, just as they stand, are in perfect logical order" (TLP 5.5563). The latter view, in treating the majority of the *Tractatus* as outright unintelligible, runs the risk of "throwing away the baby together with the bathwater", as Hacker has maintained (Hacker 2000, 369).

However, several commentators have emphasized the difference between the philosophical projects of Wittgenstein on the one hand and Frege and Russell on the other. According to them, Wittgenstein does not aim at the construction of a specific formula language of pure thought, nor does he treat logic as a discipline describing abstract entities, psychological regularities, or the most general truths about reality (TLP 4.0312, 4.441, 5.4; see Kannisto 1986, 81; Glock 1992, 1996a, 203, 1996b, 198–199; McGinn 1999, 502, 508; Moyal-Sharrock 2007, 163; Floyd 2007, 192–210). Instead, "Logic deals with every possibility and all possibilities are its facts" (TLP 2.0121). Rather than prescribing how one ought to think, logic is concerned with the necessary preconditions for any possible language.

Second, the resolute readers reject the traditional interpretation of logical form as grounded in ontology. For them, "our understanding of possibility is not ontologically based on some realm of the possible, but arises simply from our understanding of and our operating with the sensical sentences of our language" (Goldfarb 1997, 66). The resolute readers are not alone in objecting to the metaphysical interpretation of the foundation of the limits of language either. Commentators such as Peter Sullivan, Marie McGinn, and Danièle Moyal-Sharrock have defended interpretations of the status of logical form as more formal than metaphysical without, however, falling back on the resolute view of the Tractarian sentences as mere gibberish. Sullivan has argued that Wittgenstein rejects both the realist, "object-centered" explanation of the harmony between language and reality as well as its idealist counterpart that locates the necessary form of the world in the subject (Sullivan 1996). McGinn and Moyal-Sharrock have emphasized the elucidatory function of the Tractarian sentences as directing our attention to the essential in our language without the need to ground it in something absolute outside of language (McGinn 1999; Moyal-Sharrock 2007).

Some of the worries raised by the resolute readers and others against the metaphysical interpretation have been addressed also by another, long-established interpretation of the *Tractatus* that gives further weight to the notion of a limit of language by connecting the term to its arguably Kantian origin. The Kantian interpretation shares the traditional reading's interpretative commitment to what the so-called picture theory requires and implies. But by contrast to the traditional view – and in this particular respect in consonance with the criticisms of the realist reading of the *Tractatus* – the Kantian interpretation (or at least some variants of it) does not take logical form to answer to an independently established ontological order. The limits of language and of the world are determined by logical form, but this form is taken to be first and foremost the form constitutive of the very possibility of thought. In other words, possibilities of thought are not grounded in ontology, but the other way around. As Wittgenstein writes: "A thought contains the possibility of the situation of which it is the thought. What is thinkable is possible too" (TLP 3.02).

According to the Kantian interpretation, Wittgenstein's statement that "logic is transcendental" ought to be read in a specifically Kantian sense (TLP 6.13). The logic of the *Tractatus* resembles Kant's transcendental logic that deals with forms of thought that are at the same time forms of reality and has a role similar to Kant's transcendental, limiting, conditions for the possibility of experience (cf. CPR A57, P 350–365). However, by contrast to Kant, Wittgenstein does not leave any room for synthetic *a priori*, that is, for meaningful propositions about states of affairs that are true *a priori* (TLP 2.225; see Stenius 1960, 214; Hacker 1986, 22; Glock 1996a, 132, 1996b, 200). As a condition of sense, logical form is that which makes the truth and falsity of propositions possible. Hence, when Wittgenstein writes that "there is no a priori order of things", the Kantian reading takes him to refer to the contingency of facts expressible by propositions and not to logical form that grounds their possibility (TLP 5.634). This is to say that logic, as a *formal* condition of thought, is *a priori* and this is manifest precisely in the impossibility of illogical thought (TLP 5.4731). Moreover, by contrast to what Sullivan calls the "object-centered view" thus referring to the realist interpretation of the limits of language, the Kantian reading emphasizes form also in the case of objects (Sullivan 1996, 207). After all, Wittgenstein claims that objects, as the unalterable substance of the world, are form as well as content (TLP 2.024–2.0271). If this form is primarily the form of thought, as the Kantian reading argues, then the *Tractatus*'s appeal to objects as the substance of the world does not necessarily entail a commitment to an ontologically grounded limit of language. "Empirical reality is limited by the totality of objects", as Wittgenstein writes, but from the transcendental perspective the form of this reality is not independent of the form of thought (TLP 5.5561; see Kannisto 1986, 138–143).

In the Kantian reading, then, the entire project of the *Tractatus* to draw the limits of meaningful language echoes Kant's project of determining the limits of experience by reflecting the transcendental, that is, necessary and limiting, conditions for their possibility. But this just means that one does not have to run together the notions of an ideal language and that of a limit of language. Ordinary language, just as it is, is already structured by logical form that we know from our own thought. And to realize this means to realize that "*The limits of my language* mean the limits of my world" (TLP 5.6).

1.2. Subject as the Limit of the World

In the *Tractatus*, the notion of a limit is not used exclusively in relation to logic. Wittgenstein claims that there is a sense in which philosophy can talk about the self that is intimately connected to the limits of language and of the world. The philosophical self in question is not the empirical subject that we encounter among the facts of the world. Indeed, according to Wittgenstein, "there is no such thing as the subject that thinks or entertains ideas" (TLP 5.631). However, the philosophical self surfaces as a limiting condition of the world: "The philosophical self is not the human body, or the human soul, with which psychology deals, but rather the metaphysical subject, the limit of the world – not a part of it" (TLP 5.641, see also 5.632). Hacker has argued that Wittgenstein's conception of the philosophical self resembles the transcendental subject that we find in Kant's and Schopenhauer's philosophy. As pointed out by

Hacker, Wittgenstein illustrates the notion in terminology clearly reminiscent of Schopenhauer's writing. The philosophical self is not a Cartesian thinking ego, but rather the subject to whom the world is given. Hence, while everything I experience – that is, facts of the world – is *a posteriori*, *that* my experiences belong to me is *a priori*. The metaphysical subject is a limit of the world in this precise sense (Hacker 1986, Ch. 4).

In the *Tractatus*, the metaphysical subject has a prominent role in relation to two themes, namely, solipsism and ethics. According to Wittgenstein, the insight that "*the limits of my language* mean the limits of my world" shows that "what the solipsist *means* is quite correct; only it cannot be said, but makes itself manifest" (TLP 5.6, 5.62). In Hacker's reading, the route from Wittgenstein's conception of language to the solipsist's correct insight reflects the manner in which names, as the constituents of propositions, acquire their meanings. According to Hacker, propositional signs become meaningful only through the speaker's acts of intention. Hence, sense presupposes the metaphysical subject as the subject who means something by the otherwise dead propositional signs or understands them by projecting them into reality (TLP 3.11–3.13; Hacker 1986, 73–80, 100, 2001, 149). For Hacker, this is the main reason for Wittgenstein's characterization of language as "that language which alone I understand" (TLP 5.62). But if one rejects Hacker's realist interpretation of the *Tractatus* in favour of the Kantian reading, one could argue further that the solipsist's correct insight has an even more fundamental source. For if the harmony between language and reality is grounded in the necessary form of though, as some proponents of the Kantian interpretation have suggested, then the correctness of transcendental solipsism would readily follow. Language would be "my language" not merely because "by my correlating the components of the picture with the objects, it comes to represent a situation", as Wittgenstein writes in 1914, but also because the other necessary condition for sense, namely, logical form, originates with the metaphysical subject (NB, 33–34; see Kannisto 1986, 124–130).

A completely different take on Wittgenstein's treatment of the metaphysical subject is given in Sullivan's seminal article "The 'Truth' in Solipsism, and Wittgenstein's rejection of the A Priori" (1996). According to Sullivan, Wittgenstein is indeed concerned with transcendental idealism in the passages of the *Tractatus* that discuss the metaphysical subject (TLP 5.6–5.641). However, Sullivan argues, instead of yielding to the idealist temptation, Wittgenstein aims at disarming the very position along with any substantial notion of *a priori*. This is not to say that, on Sullivan's account, Wittgenstein was a realist. Rather, Wittgenstein's goal is to find a middle way between the realist and the idealist positions, which both aim at offering a philosophical justification for the harmony between language and the world by grounding it in either ontology or thought. In Sullivan's reading, Wittgenstein's project is not to give any such justification. Instead, Sullivan writes, "the notions of language and world with which 5.6 begins are the interdependent notions of formal totalities" (Sullivan 1996, 209). Accordingly, we should think of the I as an equally empty, formal notion (ibid., 211).

The other theme closely related to Wittgenstein's notion of a metaphysical subject as the limit of the world is ethics. In the *Tractatus*, Wittgenstein states that the facts of the world are contingent and therefore lack value (TLP 6.4–6.41). Accordingly, ethics cannot be expressed in language, which is in the business of stating such contingent facts (TLP 6.42). In parallel with his claim about the transcendentality of logic, Wittgenstein writes that "ethics is transcendental" (TLP 6.421). By contrast to logic, the origin of which is wanting conclusive textual evidence and subject to scholarly debate, ethics is, at least in the *Notebooks 1916*, explicitly claimed to "only enter through the subject" (NB, 79). In the *Notebooks*, Wittgenstein writes that while a thinking subject is an illusion, the willing subject is not (NB 80). Moreover, the will in question is good or evil (NB, 80; see NB, 73, 76). In Wittgenstein's account, the world is independent of the will, but this does not render ethics illusory (TLP 6.373, 5.1362). While deprived of the ability to influence the facts of the world, the willing subject can alter its limits: "If the good and the bad exercise of the will does alter the world, it can alter only the limits of the world, not the facts – not what can be expressed by means of language" (TLP 6.43).

In his remarks on ethics, Wittgenstein is again digressing the bounds of meaningful language as dictated by the *Tractatus* (TLP 6.373–6.522). While the traditional interpretation has been inclined to question whether Wittgenstein's remarks on value coherently fit into the broader framework of the *Tractatus*, the resolute reading has stressed the ethical import of the *Tractatus*, but independently of the internal evidence provided by the *Tractatus* (Hacker 1986, 105; Conant 2005, 69–70). In contrast to both, the Kantian interpretation has stressed the fact that the notions evoked by Wittgenstein in this context are the very same notions that for Kant lie outside the bounds of experience, as they arise either from practical reason or from the reflective use of the power of judgment. These notions include ethics, aesthetics, will, freedom, God, immortality of the soul, and religious faith, and the world as a whole (TLP 6.373–6.45; see Stenius 1960, 222; Moore 1987, 2007, 184–187, 2013, 251–253). For Wittgenstein, these notions comprise the "mystical" that lies beyond the limits of meaningful language.

Again, the difference between Kant and Wittgenstein results from Kant's view that, while we cannot have knowledge of free will, God, or eternity, and while attempts to establish claims to such knowledge will only lead to dogmatic metaphysics, reason can form expressible thoughts of such notions even if these do not correspond to anything in empirical reality. By contrast, for the early Wittgenstein, who limits meaningful language and thought to propositions about the contingent facts of empirical reality, the aforementioned notions must be "passed over in silence" (TLP 7; see Stenius 1960, 218). Nevertheless, in accordance with Kant, whose motivation to draw the limits of experience by reflecting their necessary, transcendental conditions was to "make room for faith" (CPR BXXX), Wittgenstein, too, claims to draw the limits of language to safeguard value. He writes to Ludwig von Ficker:

> the point of the book is ethical. . . . I wanted to write that my book consists of two parts: one of which is here, and of everything which I have *not* written. And precisely this second part is the important one. For the Ethical is delimited from within, as it were by my book; and I'm convinced that, *strictly* speaking, it can ONLY be delimited in this way.
>
> (Luckhardt 1979, 94–95)

2. The Later Views

In 1931, Wittgenstein connects the idea of a limit of language explicitly to the Kantian tradition. He writes that the "limit of language manifests itself in the impossibility of describing the fact that corresponds to (is the translation of) a sentence without simply repeating the sentence. (We are involved here with the Kantian solution of the problem of philosophy.)" (CV, 13). Wittgenstein is already distancing himself from some of the central commitments of the Tractarian view, but these words still echo the idea of logic as the inexpressible condition of sense. While every possible fact is expressible in language, we cannot step above our language to describe its formal correspondence with the world in "another language dealing with the structure of the first language", as Russell in his Introduction to the *Tractatus* had – to Wittgenstein's annoyance – suggested (TLP, xxii).

Nevertheless, by the 1930s Wittgenstein's early conception of language as a unified totality, limited by an immutable logical form and crystallized in the notion of a general propositional form that every meaningful proposition must meet, has become the target of Wittgenstein's criticism (TLP 4.001, 4.5, 5.471, 5.4711; cf. PI §23–24, 108, 114). In 1930 Wittgenstein states, still echoing the *Tractatus*: "What sort of harmony must there be between thoughts & the world? Only that the thought must have logical form; & without this it wouldn't be a thought" (M, 4:18). But now he adds: "What language must have in common is contained in rules of grammar" (M, 4:18). By contrast to the logical form of the *Tractatus*, grammar involves elements that are not purely syntactical, but incorporate features that at the outset look empirical. Moreover, the rules of grammar are not immutable, but they may be abandoned, provided that we are willing to give up the use they have made possible: "What I say of grammar (including inference) is always <u>arbitrary</u> rules: they needn't be used, but if we change them, we can't use them in this way" (M, 5:88). So even as arbitrary rules, the rules of grammar make the use of language possible.

Wittgenstein also discards the Tractarian assumption of simple objects as the termini of logical analysis and (arguably) grounding the logical form of the world (TLP 2.022). This idea, he now claims, was a digression into thinking along the lines of empirical science – a philosophical confusion that he himself had warned against (M, 5:30, 7:39, 7:88, 7:92; cf. TLP 4.111). Wittgenstein states repeatedly that the rules of grammar are arbitrary or autonomous, not answering to anything over and above grammar itself (see e.g., M, 5:87, 5:91, 6:34). Yet, in accord with the *Tractatus*, according to which "logic must look after itself", Wittgenstein still claims that the rules of grammar cannot be justified (TLP 5.473; M, 5:87). According to him,

> To rules of translation from language into reality correspond rules of grammar: & there is no possible justification for these: because any language by which we could try to justify would have to have a grammar itself: no description of world can justify rules of grammar.
> (M, 5:54)

Moreover, Wittgenstein connects the point at which justifications have been exhausted to the limit of language. He says: "Philosophy may expect to arrive at fundamental propositions. But great event to which we come is the coming to the boundary of language: there we can't ask anything further" (M, 5:28). Wittgenstein suggests that grammatical systems may be approached either "discursively", that is, as calculi that may be taught to another, or "intuitively", that is, by "taking something in as a whole at a glance" (M, 8:59). This latter perspective that "overlooks" (*übersieht*) a grammatical system as a whole limited by its constitutive rules may be seen as precursor of Wittgenstein's mature conception of the philosophical method as one that provides "surveyable representations" (*übersichtliche Darstellung*) of grammar (M, 9:33, 9:38; PI §122).

As these examples from the 1930s serve to show, Wittgenstein's rejection of central elements of his early account does not mean that the notion of a limit disappears from his imagery. Instead, it is appropriated to the new idea of grammatical systems, and later, in the *Philosophical Investigations*, to his mature treatment of concepts and language-games. Given Wittgenstein's increasingly flexible conception of grammar, the boundaries he talks about become equally flexible. Nevertheless, even in Wittgenstein's later philosophy, the idea of a limit of language is connected to themes that figure in the *Tractatus* as that which transcends the empirical. Such themes include grammar, the practice of philosophy, aesthetics, and religion. Of ethics, the later Wittgenstein remains more or less silent, except for his 1933 remark, reminiscent of the *Tractatus*'s equation between ethics and aesthetics: "Practically everything I say of 'beautiful' applies in a slightly different way to 'good' " (M, 9:18; see TLP 6.421).

According to the traditional interpretation of Wittgenstein's mature philosophy, the key goal of the *Philosophical Investigations* is to provide an account of language as a family of games, each constituted by their respective sets of grammatical rules (PI §104). The meaning of a word should not be understood as an object the name stands for, but is best characterized as the word's use in the context of a language-game (PI §43). The point of using the word "language-*game*", Wittgenstein writes, is to "emphasize the fact that the *speaking* of language is part of an activity, or of a form of life" (PI §23). The rules of language are thus not fixed or tabulated into a manual, but given in the practice of using language and transmitted by training and examples (PI §§198–199, 208–210, 355). Moreover, as the rules of language are to be found in the "customs, uses, and institutions" of a linguistic community, they are subject to change and cultural variation (PI §199). Accordingly, the idea of a limit of language becomes more flexible, historically changing, and indefinite: a riverbed ever changing with the fluctuation of water rather than a fence set up once and for all (see OC §§97–99). Wittgenstein also points out that when a limit is drawn, it is drawn for a particular purpose. Discussing the limits of concepts, Wittgenstein writes:

> For I *can* give the concept "number" rigid limits in this way, that is, use the word "number" for a rigidly limited concept, but I can also use it so that the extension of the concept is *not* closed by frontier. And this is how we do use the word "game". For how is the concept game bounded? What still counts as a game and what no longer does? Can you give it a boundary? No. You can *draw* one; for none has so far been drawn. (But that never troubled you when you used the word "game".)
>
> (PI §68)

Words are meaningful as long as they have a use in our language, and that use does not have to be fixed in advance by strict boundaries formulated by means of necessary and sufficient conditions.

In spite his new emphasis on linguistic practices and the human form of life, the later Wittgenstein still adheres to the distinction between the empirical and the grammatical (TLP 3.33, 5.552, 6.111; PI §§90, 109, 251, 295, 458). While the notions of truth and falsity apply to empirical statements and opinions, they do not apply to grammar. Rather, we take the grammatical for granted in our use of language. Indeed, it is this taking-for-granted that makes the truth and falsity of empirical propositions possible (PI §§240–241, 482; see McGinn 1999, 502, 512; Moyal-Sharrock 2007, 157). It is important to notice that, by contrast to Wittgenstein's early conception of logical form to be uncovered by analysis, the status of the grammatical as necessary does not arise from a source independent of our use of language. It is the way in which certain propositions are actually used in our language, their role in our language, that gives grammatical propositions their status as necessities: "To accept a proposition as unshakably certain – I want to say – means to use it as a grammatical rule: this removes uncertainty from it" (RFM, 170). Moreover, the status of a given proposition as either empirical or grammatical may change based on its use. As Hans-Johann Glock notes, "we can remove a sentence from the scope of empirical refutation by using it normatively rather than descriptively" (Glock 1996b, 208). This is not to say that grammar is matter of mere opinion. Wittgenstein himself makes the point explicitly by writing:

> "So are you saying that human agreement decided what is true and what is false?" – It is what human beings *say* that is true and false; and they agree in the *language* they use. That is not agreement in opinions but in form of life.
>
> (PI §241)

Without such basic agreement, taken for granted in our use of language, the possibility of making true and false statements would evaporate.

In spite of drawing their status as necessities from our use, grammatical rules provide the criteria by which we distinguish between correct and incorrect uses of words and, accordingly, between understanding and misunderstanding. The understanding of words and sentences is the ability to follow the rules constitutive of their use, manifest in the speaker's ability to justify her linguistic usages by appeal to the rules (PI §§185–242). It is not yet enough that my behaviour conforms to the rule that is constitutive of the game providing the context of the use. If I understand, then my behaviour ought to be internally related to the rule so that, for example, I can appeal to the rule in explaining my application thereof. The rule is, as the traditional interpretation given in Peter Hacker's and Gordon Baker's commentary puts it, "involved in [my] activity as a reason or part of a reason for acting thus-and-so" (Baker and Hacker 2009, 138). If this were not the case, then it would make no sense to talk about understanding, which after all is a normative notion standing in need of a criterion to distinguish it from misunderstanding. However, Wittgenstein states repeatedly that reasons come to an end. That "once I have exhausted the justifications, I have reached bedrock, and my spade is turned. Then I am inclined to say: 'This is simply what I do'" (PI §217). Here, we meet the limit of language again in the form of the bedrock that stops the chain of justification. Wittgenstein writes: "A reason can only be given within a game. The links of a chain of reasons come to an end, at the boundary of the game" (PG, 97; see also PI §§326, 482, 485). At the boundary of the game there is no further justification to be found, nor any room to meaningfully question whether one ought to follow these rules. Instead, "when I follow the rule, I do not choose. I follow the rule blindly" (PI §219).

What Wittgenstein means by the bedrock and the notion of blind rule-following has been a topic of intense scholarly discussion. As in the case of the *Tractatus*, the main points of disagreement concern the ways in which the notion of grammar and the nature of philosophy in Wittgenstein's later thought ought to be understood. Some commentators object to the traditional, "normativist" or rule-based interpretation of Wittgenstein's later philosophy just outlined. An early critic of Wittgenstein's emphasis on rules and games was Rush Rhees, who took Wittgenstein game analogy to be giving a misleading view about the nature of human communication (Rhees 1959–1960, 182). Later, proponents of the "resolute" or "therapeutic" interpretation have argued that it is in fact a mistake to attribute a rule-based account of language to Wittgenstein himself as well. Rule-bound games may be useful objects of comparison for language, to be used in "piecemeal treatment" of philosophical problems, but to take Wittgenstein to be advocating a rule-based conception of language is to fall guilty of philosophical dogmatism against which Wittgenstein warned (Kuusela 2008; Conant 2011). According to the therapeutic reading, the traditional reading mistakenly takes the philosopher's job to be to "police the borders between sense and nonsense" by tabulating rules of grammar (Morris 2006, 1). Instead, it is argued, the goals of Wittgenstein's later method are closer to psychotherapy that aims at dissolving individual confusions without any generally valid philosophical arguments or claims (Baker 2006, 109–118, 205–222).

But to align the anti-normativist interpretation with Wittgenstein's undeniable focus on rules is difficult. Wittgenstein writes in the *Philosophical Investigations* that "If rule became exception, and exception rule; or if both became phenomena of roughly equal frequency – our normal language-games would thereby lose their point" (PI §142). And even more emphatically in manuscript 164: "Following according to the rule is FUNDAMENTAL to our language-game. It characterizes what we call description" (RFM, 330). Rather than indicating a contrast between the descriptive approach in philosophy and the notion of a rule, these remarks suggest that Wittgenstein himself took description and rules to belong together. What is to be described, for a particular philosophical purpose, is a language-game, a rule-governed structure among other structures that together comprise our language (PI §108). Besides, what is sometimes highlighted as the distinctive feature of Wittgenstein's later philosophy, namely, its critical stance towards philosophical theories, is a methodological commitment present already in the *Tractatus* (TLP 4.112, PI § 109).

The necessity of taking something for granted in order to think meaningfully becomes particularly dominant in Wittgenstein's latest work, published in *On Certainty*. Here, Wittgenstein's treatment of "certainties", propositions that we treat as immune to doubt, broadens the notion of grammatical rules to cover sentences that express basic certainties of our world-view. Such basic certainties include assurance of matters that G. E. Moore treated as knowledge, for example, that "I have two hands". Wittgenstein does not accept Moore's position, given that he takes knowledge to presuppose the possibility of justification, missing in the case of basic certainties where neither doubt nor the demand of justification arises. Rather, the possibility of justifying non-basic beliefs (empirical beliefs and everyday opinions) as well as the possibility of false beliefs is grounded in our taking for granted certainties that themselves are ungrounded (see, e.g., OC §§94–95, 105, 136). According to Danièle Moyal-Sharrock, we ought to understand grammatical rules, including formulations of our basic certainties, as nonsense. Given that grammatical rules have no use *within* the bounds of a language-game, "they *have* no sense; they *determine* sense" (Moyal-Sharrock 2017, 558). In this respect, the "hinge propositions" discussed in *On Certainty* may be seen as successors of the sentences of the *Tractatus*: both are useless *in* language, as "their only use is to delineate and elucidate the correct use of language" (Moyal-Sharrock 2007, 170). Accordingly, to doubt basic certainties is "logically impossible" and amounts to "having lost the bounds of sense" (OC §454; Moyal-Sharrock 2017, 549). While we can formulate a grammatical rule for philosophical purposes, in the actual use of language they say nothing. This is why Wittgenstein writes: " 'There are physical objects' is nonsense" (OC §35).

In the *Tractatus*, the task of philosophy was one of drawing the limits of language to demarcate sense from nonsense. In the *Philosophical Investigations*, Wittgenstein writes that the task of the philosopher is to describe language games, that is, practice-laden ways of using language, without explaining or justifying them in any way (PI §§109, 124–129). The descriptive approach does not render philosophical investigation empirical, because what directs the description is a philosophical problem. Instead of phenomena, philosophical investigation is, as Wittgenstein writes, "directed towards the *possibilities* of phenomena" (PI §90, cf. TLP 2.0121). This is what makes the investigation grammatical rather than empirical (PI §187). Again, Wittgenstein connects the practice of philosophy understood as grammatical investigation to the limits of language: "The results of philosophy are the discovery of some piece of plain nonsense and the bumps that the understanding has got by running up against the limit of language. They – these bumps – make us see the value of that discovery" (PI §119). But while the mature Wittgenstein still treats the limits of grammar as that which excludes nonsense, he now emphasizes that such limits are always drawn for a particular purpose: "To say 'This combination of words has no sense' excludes it from the sphere of language, and thereby bounds the domain of language. But when one draws a boundary, it may be for various kinds of reasons" (PI §499).

In Wittgenstein's later view, then, the limits of language are reached at the boundary of a language-game, where justifications made possible by the rules constitutive of that game have been exhausted and we simply take the rules themselves for granted. At this boundary or bedrock, we can only act or else, for purposes of philosophical clarification, describe the game in question (PI §261). Particularly poignant cases of reasons coming to an end surface in Wittgenstein's later discussions of religion and aesthetics. In his lectures on aesthetics and religious belief, Wittgenstein focuses on cases where one cannot convince one's interlocutor by appeal to explicit rule-formulations. While aesthetic judgments call for reasons, the kind of reason-giving we find in aesthetics takes the form of comparisons between a particular aesthetic choice and something else, intended to guide the interlocutor to see the aesthetic phenomenon from a particular perspective. But this just means that I cannot force another to adopt my judgment by arguments: "If when I've made you see what I see, it doesn't appeal to you, there is an end" (M, 9:31).

We find a similar end in reason-giving in Wittgenstein's later discussion of religious belief. One might expect Wittgenstein to emphasize the role of the linguistic community and tradition for the possibility of religious language, given the importance placed on the linguistic community and the human form of life in his later thought. But interestingly, in his lectures on religious belief Wittgenstein discusses a gulf that may appear between a religious person and himself as somebody who does not share the "pictures" that lay down the foundation for the believer's world view (LC, 55). According to Wittgenstein, it is impossible for him to contradict the person, as he might in cases of ordinary empirical disagreements (LC, 55). Whether this means that the believer and the non-religious person "play different language-games", each limited by their own rules and hence not allowing for a translation, has been subject to debate. Those drawing on the legacy of Rush Rhees have emphasized that in spite of Wittgenstein's spatial metaphor, suggesting an unbridgeable gap between different language-games, "levels", or "planes" the disputants inhabit, the non-religious person may reasonably criticize the religious claims (Diamond 2005). Others, influenced by the more traditional interpretation have taken Wittgenstein to argue religious beliefs are "immune from falsification and from verification" and in this respect on a par with grammatical rules (Hyman 2001, 7; see Schroeder 2007, 443–445, 459; Pritchard 2018).

3. The Form and Content of This Volume

This collection brings together twelve chapters that approach Wittgenstein's notion of the limits of language from a variety of perspectives.

With the exception of A. W. Moore's chapter, "The Bounds of Nonsense", which has been published in Moore's volume *Language, World, and Limits: Essays in the Philosophy of Language and Metaphysics* (OUP, 2019), all chapters have been newly commissioned. Part I, Logic, Self, and Value in Wittgenstein's Early Philosophy, consists of three chapters that address the notion of a limit in the three roles assigned to it in the *Tractatus*: logic, the philosophical self, and ethics as limits of language and of the world. Part II, Grammar, Linguistic Community, and Value in Wittgenstein's Later Philosophy, follows the same overall pattern. It begins with four different interpretations of Wittgenstein's later treatment of the limits of language, continues to two contributions reflecting the potential limitations that arise from our anthropocentric perspective, and closes with three chapters that address themes that Wittgenstein associates with the limit of language throughout his career, namely, religion, aesthetics, and ethics.

In his chapter "The Bound of Nonsense", A. W. Moore examines the distinction between sense and nonsense in the *Tractatus*. He begins by addressing Cora Diamond's and Michael Kremer's denial of the view that, according to the *Tractatus*, all pseudo-propositions are nonsensical. Noting that such a denial, in exempting certain pseudo-propositions from the charge of nonsensicality, could exacerbate the mystery of why the pseudo-propositions in the *Tractatus* are not among those to be exempted, Moore proceeds to introduce what he calls the Principal Distinction. This is the distinction, undeniably fundamental for the project of the *Tractatus*, between truth-valued propositions (including tautologies and contradictions) and truth-valueless pseudo-propositions. Moore argues that, for Wittgenstein, our understanding of what it is for something to be a truth-valueless pseudo-proposition is not independent of our understanding of the notion of a proposition with a truth-value. Rather, a pseudo-proposition without a truth-value is an item that has the false appearance of being a proposition with a truth-value. The chapter closes with an appendix, comparing the *Tractatus*'s truth-valueless pseudo-propositions with Kant's idea of an "empty thought", indicating an interesting parallel but also an important contrast between the two.

In his chapter "Solipsism and the Graspability of Fact", Colin Johnston sets out to provide an answer to the hard question of what Wittgenstein means by stating that "*the limits of my language* are the limits of my world" (TLP 5.6). His argument begins by suggesting that the Tractarian conception of a fact is essentially Fregean: as in Frege, truth's "pride of place" dictates that a fact is at base a possible truth. This suggestion is subsequently justified by means of a thought that the subject makes no sense of content to her thinking going beyond in kind that of a truth or falsehood. This thought further includes, however, that truth is not something independent of graspability or possessability by me, a point which threatens an idealism. This threat is deflected, however, by recognising that the "me", that is the subject in question, has no content or character: there is no way of making a contrast between the subject's world and what lies outside of it, no way for the subject to find content independent of herself and accordingly content to herself.

The third chapter on Wittgenstein's early philosophy, written jointly by Hanne Appelqvist and Panu-Matti Pöykkö, discusses Wittgenstein's early ethics by comparing it with Emmanuel Levinas's ethical thought. Both Wittgenstein and Levinas claim ethics to be a "condition of the world", not explicable by reference to the empirical facts of the world (NB, 77; Levinas 1969, 204, 212). The authors argue that what motivates Wittgenstein's and Levinas's respective accounts is the characteristically Kantian contrast they identify between the absolute ethical demand on the one hand and the contingency of the facts of the world on the other. As any substantial ethical theses would only render ethics conditional, the task of the philosopher is to reflect on the transcendental grounds of the ethical demand. In this respect, the writers argue, both Wittgenstein and Levinas ought to be read as belonging to the Kantian tradition. After indicating the analogous ways in which both Wittgenstein and Levinas make use of the Kantian framework, the chapter explores the main difference between the two: while Wittgenstein's early ethics is grounded in an aesthetic, contemplative perspective on the world as a whole, Levinas famously takes the other person to be constitutive for the ethical perspective.

William Child's chapter " 'We Can Go No Further': Meaning, Use, and the Limits of Language" examines the limit of language as it appears in Wittgenstein's later philosophy. Child's point of origin is Wittgenstein's later statement about the impossibility of getting outside of language by means of language, which marks an important continuity with the views of the *Tractatus*. In Wittgenstein's later work, the idea is manifest in his denial of the possibility of general metaphysical theses about reality, of providing a linguistic characterization of the relation between language and the language-independent world, and of the possibility of teaching the use of language by means of explanations to someone who does not already master a language. Connecting these points to the debate between reductionism and anti-reductionism about meaning and rules, Child asks whether it is possible to give a substantive and non-circular explanation of what it is for someone to follow a particular rule. He argues that, while Wittgenstein ought to be read as an anti-reductionist about meaning, his point about meaning as use is not a mere pleonasm. Instead, Child argues, Wittgenstein's position entitles us to demand some account of the relation between semantic and non-semantic facts. According to Child, this relation is one of supervenience – an interpretation he substantiates by a detailed analysis of Wittgenstein's arguments presented in the *Remarks on the Foundations of Mathematics* and the *Brown Book*.

Leila Haaparanta's chapter "Frege, Carnap, and the Limits of Asserting" explores the broader philosophical context of the notion of a limit of language by relating the historical positions of Frege and Carnap to current debates on assertion. Referring to the distinction between logic as language and logic as calculus, Haaparanta argues that while Frege's conceptual notation is a calculus (in Frege's own sense of the term), it is also intended as a universal language: everything that can be thought can be also be expressed in that notation. Moreover, like Wittgenstein's early denial of the possibility of overcoming logical form in language, Frege's conceptual notation does not allow for a metaperspective from which to compare language with the world. Paying attention to Frege's discussion on different ways of justifying assertions, Haaparanta then raises the question of the legitimacy of philosophical assertions. While Frege's texts do not settle the question, in Carnap's "Empiricism, Semantics, and Ontology" we find a classic example of an argument that denies the possibility of metaphysical assertions by appeal to a kind of limit of language, namely, Carnap's notion of a linguistic framework and his distinction between statements internal and external to that framework. Haaparanta's chapter closes by proposing that Carnap's discussion of the nature of external propositions may be used as an informative point of comparison for Wittgenstein's later remarks on philosophy and philosophical assertions.

Paul Standish's chapter "On Being Resolute" addresses the notion of a limit of language against the background of the debate between resolute and traditional interpretations of Wittgenstein's thought. Here, the traditional interpretation is understood as putting forth a narrative of the early Wittgenstein as an advocate of a realist truth-conditional theory of meaning to be replaced by Wittgenstein's later, anti-realist theory of meaning given by assertability-conditions. Such a story, it is argued, not only fails to capture elements of continuity of Wittgenstein thought, but commits the early and the later Wittgenstein to the metaphysical assumption of a possibility of stepping outside of language. In doing so the traditional view "represent[s] the matter as if there were something one *couldn't* do", thus dismissing Wittgenstein's explicit warning against doing just that (PI §374). Rather than taking an explicit stance on the debate, Standish considers the inevitability of the urge to overcome the limits as well as the difficulty of returning to the ordinary, promised to serve as the cure to the urge. He does this by comparing the work of Wittgenstein and Heidegger in light of Stanley Cavell's work, the comparison leading to the acknowledgement of limits of language and of the restlessness of the desire to exceed them.

Yrsa Neuman's chapter "Moore's Paradox and the Limits of Language Use" discusses Wittgenstein's treatment of G. E. Moore's paradox, namely, the absurdity involved in the utterance "It is raining, but I do not believe that it is raining". Wittgenstein's initial response to the paradox consists in conceptual clarification of first-person and second-person ascription, intended to uncover the assumptions underlying the paradox. While some of these assumptions seem to indicate the limits of language use, Neuman argues that instead of aiming to establish or unveil rules of language to rule out the Moorean sentence, Wittgenstein's approach is sensitive to particular cases that may not follow the ordinary pattern of language use. Neuman sees this as a central feature of Wittgenstein's method, and argues that Moore's paradox emerges only when language is approached from the "cold" philosophical viewpoint without an actual context; and once a context is provided, there is nothing paradoxical about it. Accordingly, she suggests, what needs to be explained is not why the Moorean sentence fails, but our urge to philosophize about a mere piece of surface grammar.

If for the early Wittgenstein the subject of language is a formal I, the later Wittgenstein turns to the linguistic community as the subject of language. Sandis's chapter "Who are 'we' for Wittgenstein?" asks how we ought to understand Wittgenstein's frequent references to "us". Who are we who practice philosophy, who could not understand a lion if it spoke, and whose form of life finds expression in language? Sandis addresses such questions by examining Wittgenstein's later usages of "we" and its cognates. According to his analysis, the term sometimes refers to the community of philosophers, while at other times it is intended to point to language users, to average people, or a specific cultural community. Such groups ought to be contrasted, not just with that of all humans in a general sense, but also with a transcendental "we", as evoked by those interpretations that read the later Wittgenstein as a linguistic idealist.

Hans-Johann Glock's chapter "Animal Consciousness – a Limit of Language" discusses phenomenal consciousness, which is often deemed a mysterious phenomenon defying naturalistic explanation or even conceptual comprehension. Arguing against the corresponding two variants of the orthodox view, which he calls (new) mysterianism and (neo-) mysticism respectively, Glock defends a deflationist account of consciousness. Drawing in part on Wittgenstein's later discussion on mental phenomena and private language, Glock argues that the sense of a mystery that the orthodox positions attribute to phenomenal consciousness does not mark a genuine limit either of knowledge or of language but rather results from conceptual confusions. Glock develops his argument by discussing the consciousness of non-human animals, thus addressing Thomas Nagel's question "what is it like to be a bat?". According to Glock, Nagel's question can in fact be answered in an informative and reasonable way by reference to empirical findings concerning the behavioural capacities, life form, and environment of bats. The real challenge related to consciousness does not pertain to qualia, Glock argues, but to the grounds of attributing intentional states to animals. For while it is perfectly possible to ascribe some intentional states to animals based on our knowledge of animals and their behaviour, there is indeed a limit to such ascriptions, namely of determining the precise content of more complex intentional states. However, rather than pointing to ineffable animal intentionality, this limit is imposed by our undeniably anthropocentric language as applied to creatures that do not talk.

Pihlström's chapter "The Limits of Language in Wittgensteinian Philosophy of Religion" discusses the nature of religious language and belief and the way in which philosophers influenced by Wittgenstein's work, most notably D. Z. Phillips, have approached the theme. Noting the uneasiness with which the Wittgenstein tradition of philosophy of religion has regarded the metaphor of a limit in Wittgenstein's writing, Pihlström argues that instead of disarming the notion of a limit, we ought to take it as pointing to the Kantian undertones of Wittgenstein's philosophy. Indeed, he suggests, some of the arguments put forth in the Wittgensteinian tradition of philosophy of religion could be read as transcendental arguments. While religious language is not based on empirical evidence, it is still conditioned by the concrete circumstances of our lives and makes possible a response to actual human suffering. Considering the problem of evil and the way in which it has been treated in the Wittgensteinian tradition, Pihlström argues that Wittgenstein's remarks on religion provide resources for formulating a transcendental version of antitheodicy.

Guter's chapter "Measure for Measure: Wittgenstein's Critique of the Augustinian Picture of Music" discusses Wittgenstein's later remarks on music, connecting them to Wittgenstein's distinction between memory-time and information-time in his middle period. Guter argues that Wittgenstein's emphasis on public information-time as that which conditions or circumscribes memory-time sets his conception of musical expression apart from the philosophical tradition that originates in Augustine's discussion of time. Insofar as our utterances about musical experiences geared toward the order of memory-time are meaningful, they must rely on the framework of our ordinary language and its order of information-time. Guter's discussion brings to surface the particularity of expression and the aesthetically "right" in music, evoked by Wittgenstein's remarks on simultaneity and tempo in music and language. According to Guter, the musical practice and its collaborative quest for drawing in significance by means of the phrasing and re-phrasing of a musical passage to characterize it, ultimately enables distinctions between aesthetic right and wrong.

The collection closes with Danièle Moyal-Sharrock's chapter "Literature as the Measure of Our Lives", which discusses the relation between literary language and reality, thereby engaging with the debate on realism and idealism in Wittgenstein later thought. Moyal-Sharrock stresses the reality-soakedness of language, and argues that its being impacted by the extra-linguistic makes language both a *vital* and an *autonomous* force.

She argues that Wittgenstein's remarks on literature speak to the inseparability of form and content in literature. She takes her clue in Wittgenstein to argue that the language of literature does not belong to the veridical domain of discursive language but provides a qualitatively different and invaluable perspective on our lives by *showing* what cannot be *said*. That is, how we use language aesthetically to evoke what cannot be described or referred to veridically, and yet deeply generates or enhances moral and psychological understanding. In indicating how the distinction between saying and showing is reflected in Wittgenstein's later discussion of poetry and literature, Moyal-Sharrock's argument traces an important continuity between Wittgenstein's early and later views.

References

Anscombe, Elizabeth (1959) *An Introduction to Wittgenstein's* Tractatus. London: Hutchinson University Library.

Baker, Gordon (2006) *Wittgenstein's Method: Neglected Aspects*. Oxford: Blackwell.

Baker, Gordon and Hacker, Peter (2009) *Wittgenstein: Rules, Grammar and Necessity*. Vol. 2 of An Analytical Commentary on the *Philosophical Investigations*. Oxford: Blackwell.

Conant, James (2002) "The Method of the Tractatus", in Erich H. Reck (ed), *From Frege to Wittgenstein: Perspectives on Early Analytic Philosophy*, Oxford: Oxford University Press, 374–462.

Conant, James (2005) "What 'Ethics' in the *Tractatus* Is Not", in D. Z. Phillips and Mario von der Ruhr (eds), *Religion and Wittgenstein's Legacy*. Aldershot: Ashgate.

Conant, James (2011) "Wittgenstein's Methods", in Oskari Kuusela and Marie McGinn (eds), *The Oxford Handbook of Wittgenstein*. Oxford: Oxford University Press, 620–645.

Diamond, Cora (1991) *The Realistic Spirit*. Cambridge, MA: MIT Press.

Diamond, Cora (2000) "Ethics, Imagination, and the Method of Wittgenstein's *Tractatus*", in Alice Crary and Rupert Read (eds), *The New Wittgenstein*. London: Routledge, 149–173.

Diamond, Cora (2005) "Wittgenstein on Religious Belief: The Gulfs Between Us", in D. Z. Phillips and Mario von der Ruhr (eds), *Religion and Wittgenstein's Legacy*. Aldershot: Ashgate, 99–137.

Floyd, Juliet (1998) "The Uncaptive Eye: Solipsism in Wittgenstein's *Tractatus*", in Leroy S. Rouner (ed), *Boston Studies in Philosophy of Religion*. Vol. 19, *Loneliness*. Notre Dame, IN: University of Notre Dame Press, 79–108.

Floyd, Juliet (2007) "Wittgenstein and the Inexpressible", in Alice Crary (ed), *Wittgenstein and the Moral Life: Essays in Honor of Cora Diamond*. Cambridge, MA: MIT Press, 177–234.

Glock, Hans-Johann (1992) "Cambridge, Jena or Vienna? The Roots of the *Tractatus*", *Ratio* 5 (1), 1–23.

Glock, Hans-Johann (1996a) *The Wittgenstein Dictionary*. Oxford: Blackwell.

Glock, Hans-Johann (1996b) "Necessity and Normativity", in Hans D. Sluga and David Stern (eds), *The Cambridge Companion to Wittgenstein*. Cambridge: Cambridge University Press, 198–225.

Goldfarb, Warren (1997) "Metaphysics and Nonsense: On Cora Diamond's *The Realistic Spirit*", *Journal of Philosophical Research* 22, 57–73.

Hacker, Peter (1986) *Insight and Illusion*. Revised edition. Oxford: Clarendon Press.

Hacker, Peter (2000) "Was He Trying to Whistle It?" reprinted in Peter Hacker, *Wittgenstein: Connections and Controversies*. Oxford: Oxford University Press, 98–140.

Hacker, Peter (2001) "When the Whistling Had to Stop", reprinted in Peter Hacker, *Wittgenstein: Connections and Controversies*. Oxford: Oxford University Press, 140–169.

Hyman, John (2001) "The Gospel According to Wittgenstein", in R. L. Arrington and M. Addis (eds), *Wittgenstein and Philosophy of Religion*. London: Routledge, 1–11.

Kannisto, Heikki (1986) *Thoughts and Their Subject: A Study of Wittgenstein's Tractatus*. Acta Philosophica Fennica. Vol. 40. Helsinki: The Philosophical Society of Finland.

Kant, Immanuel (1998) *Critique of Pure Reason* (CPR). Translated and edited by Paul Guyer and Allen Wood. Cambridge: Cambridge University Press.

Kant, Immanuel (2004) *Prolegomena to Any Future Metaphysics* (P). Translated and edited by Gary Hatfield. Cambridge: Cambridge University Press.

Kuusela, Oskari (2008) *The Struggle Against Dogmatism: Wittgenstein and the Concept of Philosophy*. Cambridge, MA: Harvard University Press.

Levinas, Emmanuel (1969) *Totality and Infinity*. Translated by A. Lingis. Pittsburgh: Duquesne University Press.

Luckhart, C. G. (1979) *Wittgenstein: Sources and Perspectives*. Ithaca, NY: Cornell University Press.

McGinn, Marie (1999) "Between Metaphysics and Nonsense: Elucidation in Wittgenstein's *Tractatus*", *The Philosophical Quarterly* 49 (197), 491–513.

Moore, A. W. (1987) "Beauty in the Transcendental Idealism of Kant and Wittgenstein", *British Journal of Aesthetics* 27 (2), 129–137.

Moore, A. W. (2007) "Wittgenstein and Transcendental Idealism", in Guy Kahane, Edward Kanterian and Oskari Kuusela (eds), *Wittgenstein and His Interpreters*. Oxford: Blackwell, 174–199.

Moore, A. W. (2013) "Was the Author of the *Tractatus* a Transcendental Idealist?" in Peter Sullivan and Michael Potter (eds), *Wittgenstein's Tractatus: History and Interpretation*. Oxford: Oxford University Press, 239–255.

Morris, Catherine (2006) "Introduction", in Gordon Baker (ed), *Wittgenstein's Method: Neglected Aspects*. Oxford: Blackwell, 1–18.

Moyal-Sharrock, Danièle (2007) "The Good Sense of Nonsense: A Reading of Wittgenstein's *Tractatus* as Nonself-Repudiating", *Philosophy* 82, 147–177.

Moyal-Sharrock, Danièle (2017) "Wittgenstein on Knowledge and Certainty", in Hans-Johann Glock and John Hyman (eds), *A Companion to Wittgenstein*. Oxford: Wiley-Blackwell, 547–562.

Pears, David (1987) *The False Prison*. Vol. I. Oxford: Clarendon Press.

Pritchard, Duncan (2018) "Quasi-Fideism and Religious Conviction", *European Journal for Philosophy of Religion* 10 (3), 51–66.

Rhees, Rush (1959–1960) "Wittgenstein's Builders", *Proceedings of the Aristotelian Society* 60, 171–186.

Schroeder, Severin (2007) "The Tightrope Walker", *Ratio (new series)* 20 (4), 442–463.

Stenius, Erik (1960) *Wittgenstein's* Tractatus: *A Critical Study of Its Main Lines of Thought*. Oxford: Basil Blackwell.

Sullivan, Peter (1996) "The 'Truth' in Solipsism, and Wittgenstein's Rejection of the A Priori", *European Journal of Philosophy* 4, 195–219.

Part I

Logic, Self, and Value in Wittgenstein's Early Philosophy

1 The Bounds of Nonsense

A. W. Moore

There is a tripartite classification that is standardly attributed to the early Wittgenstein. According to this attribution, Wittgenstein acknowledges the following three mutually disjoint categories in the *Tractatus*:

- thoughts;
- tautologies and contradictions;
- nonsensical pseudo-propositions.

Thoughts are propositions with a sense, in other words propositions that are bipolar, or in yet other words propositions that are not only true or false but also such that, if true, they could nevertheless have been false, while, if false, they could nevertheless have been true. (See e.g., TLP 2.2–3, 4, and 4.2.) *Tautologies and contradictions* are propositions *without* a sense. They lack a sense because they lack the bipolarity that thoughts have. Although they are true or false, the true ones, namely the tautologies, are unconditionally true, while the false ones, namely the contradictions, are unconditionally false. Their lacking a sense in this very distinctive way is registered by saying that they are *senseless*, but not *nonsensical*. (See e.g., TLP 4.46–4.4611.) Finally, there are *pseudo-propositions*. These are concatenations of signs that do not belong to either of the first two categories. They are neither true nor false. And, in contrast to tautologies and contradictions, they *are* nonsensical. (See e.g., TLP 4.1272, 5.4733, and 6.53.)

Let us call attribution of this schematism to the early Wittgenstein the Standard Account. Michael Kremer and Cora Diamond have contested it.[1] They have a rival account that differs with respect to the third category. Nowhere in the *Tractatus*, they urge, does Wittgenstein commit himself to the view that, just because a concatenation of signs is to be classified as a pseudo-proposition that is neither true nor false, it must also be classified as nonsensical. The most that he does is to highlight *some* pseudo-propositions that he takes to be nonsensical (TLP 4.1272). This allows Kremer and Diamond to credit Wittgenstein with a much more circumscribed and much less draconian conception of nonsense.

Among the pseudo-propositions that Kremer and Diamond think Wittgenstein would decline to classify as nonsensical, perhaps the most interesting and the most compelling examples are those of mathematics. These count as pseudo-propositions for Wittgenstein because he takes them to be equations and therefore, on the account of equations that he proffers in the *Tractatus*, representational devices that are neither true nor false (TLP 4.241ff., 5.53ff., and 6.2). He is nevertheless quite happy to acknowledge that they have a clear, codifiable, and important use (TLP 6.211ff). It follows that they have a kind of meaning, at least on a suitably generous conception of meaning.[2] Given this, and given that Wittgenstein nowhere explicitly classifies these pseudo-propositions as nonsensical, it seems to Kremer and Diamond a needless exegetical affront to insist that this is what he would do.

They have a point. Kremer's and Diamond's alternative account certainly has considerable appeal. But it does also have at least one significant pitfall that I should like to flag. If we adopt their account, we are in danger of making a mystery, or perhaps of compounding the already existing mystery, of Wittgenstein's own avowal that the material in the *Tractatus* itself, or most of it anyway, is to be classified as nonsensical (TLP 6.54). For that material too has a use. It is a peculiar use, admittedly, and perhaps not one that is happily described – as I did describe the use that mathematical pseudo-propositions have – as clear and codifiable. In fact one of the main exegetical challenges confronting any student of this text is to determine how the use to which the material in it is to be put *should* be described. But the use in question is a use all the same. Wittgenstein has written this book with, as he indicates in his penultimate remark, a quite particular intention concerning what his readers are supposed to do with it and what they are supposed to glean from it (TLP 6.54). And if we think that he not only intends his readers to profit from the book in this way, but intends them to do so *by means of the recognition of this very intention* – which is not at all implausible – then we do not have to be all that Gricean[3] to conclude that the material in the book just does, *ipso facto*, have a kind of meaning. But why then the contrast, as far as any classification as nonsense is concerned, between this material and what we find in mathematics?

I am far from suggesting that this is an insuperable objection to Kremer's and Diamond's account. There may well be a compelling Tractarian story to be told about how the many differences between the two cases can be marshalled to justify classifying the former, but not the latter, as nonsensical.[4] But it would certainly make for a much easier exegetical life if, in accord with the Standard Account, we did not have to worry about telling any such story, but could simply accept those differences in their own terms and acquiesce in the idea that *all* this material, mathematics included, counts as nonsensical.

Which account is to be preferred, then? Perhaps neither is. Perhaps the text simply fails to settle the matter.[5] And perhaps a principle of charity affords no help either. A principle of charity would afford help only if there were more at stake here than a boring matter of terminology, and there are grounds for thinking that, at one level, there is not. On the Standard Account, the term "nonsensical" serves as a convenient sweep-up term that acts as the adjectival counterpart to the noun "pseudo-proposition" – at least relative to a suitable domain.[6] On Kremer's and Diamond's alternative account, the term "nonsensical" does additional work that allows for finer discrimination. But it would be easy enough, in the former case, to use "pseudo-propositional" instead; and it would be easy enough, in the latter case, to devise another term to do the additional work in question. And *neither* use of the term, let it be noted, is directly appropriated from ordinary language. Both accounts cast the term, at least to some extent, as a term of art – which indeed it is. This is sometimes denied. It is sometimes said that Wittgenstein uses "nonsensical" in the *Tractatus* in none other than the way in which it is ordinarily used. But insofar as there is any such thing as "the" way in which it is ordinarily used (and the same applies to "*unsinnig*", the term that appears in the original German text) this is simply false – if only because it would sound entirely natural, to an untrained ear, to call a blatant contradiction "nonsensical".

Nor, come to that, does ordinary language afford us any interesting relevant distinction between "nonsensical" and "senseless" (or between "*unsinnig*" and "*sinnlos*"). This reminds us that there is an issue about Wittgenstein's use of the term "senseless" too. Here the Standard Account can go one of two ways. Wittgenstein may be said to reserve "senseless" for tautologies and contradictions; or he may be said to apply it to *any* concatenation of signs that lacks sense, including any that is to be classified as nonsensical. Kremer's and Diamond's account, for all I have said so far, can likewise go one of two ways. They too may say that Wittgenstein uses "senseless" in the former, narrower way; or they may say that he uses it in the latter, broader way. In fact they favour the second of these.[7]

As I have already indicated, there are grounds for thinking that not much of exegetical substance hangs on this. There are grounds, more specifically, for thinking that nothing in the *Tractatus* settles the matter, that nothing of significance in the book turns on the matter, and that the matter itself concerns nothing more than which of various equally serviceable, relatively technical uses Wittgenstein assigns to a couple of terms.

This is not to deny that there are fascinating and important exegetical issues in the vicinity. (I hope that this chapter will itself bear witness to that.) It is not even to deny that the formulation of these issues is sensitive to the matter in hand.[8] It is just that, if so, this is not what makes them fascinating and important.

Do similar remarks apply to Wittgenstein's use of the term "pseudo-proposition"? Is there similar leeway in the interpretation of this term? Perhaps, on some readings of it, it denotes *some* concatenations of signs that lack a truth-value, on others others.[9] Perhaps, on some readings, it extends to concatenations of signs that *have* a truth-value, in particular to tautologies and contradictions[10] – something that is certainly the case in Wittgenstein's pre-*Tractatus* notebooks (NB, 12 and 58).

It might be said, in response to this last suggestion, that here at last the *Tractatus* is decisive, since by the time of the book itself Wittgenstein has undeniably changed his mind and settled *against* the view that tautologies and contradictions are pseudo-propositions. But in response to this response, while it is clear that by the time of the *Tractatus* Wittgenstein classifies tautologies and contradictions as propositions (TLP 4.46ff.), and while it is also clear that this represents a change of mind – since at one point in his notebooks he explicitly denies that tautologies and contradictions are propositions (NB, 58) – what is not clear is that the change of mind is a change of mind about the status of tautologies and contradictions as *pseudo*-propositions. For we cannot simply take for granted that being a pseudo-proposition, on Wittgenstein's understanding, is incompatible with being a proposition. Perhaps, in the *Tractatus*, tautologies and contradictions are both.

This is not an outrageous suggestion. To the extent that it is out of keeping with the way in which "pseudo-" (or "*Schein*" in the original German) normally functions, so be it: we can, as with "nonsensical", treat "pseudo-proposition" as a more or less technical term. Admittedly, there are contexts in the *Tractatus* where it is hard to hear Wittgenstein's use of "pseudo-", either juxtaposed with "proposition" or juxtaposed with some other noun, as anything other than privative, for instance at 4.1272, 5.461, and 5.534. But this may be a simple matter of implicature. (There are contexts in which it is hard to hear uses of "attempted" as anything other than privative either, yet this does not gainsay the fact that being an attempted overhead bicycle kick is compatible with being an overhead bicycle kick.) Moreover, there is mathematics to be considered again. When Wittgenstein tells us that what we find in mathematics are pseudo-propositions, he does not put this by saying that the *concatenations of signs* that we find in mathematics are pseudo-propositions; he puts it by saying that the *propositions* we find there are pseudo-propositions (TLP 6.2). Unless his use of "propositions" here is simply sloppy, or unless it involves some rhetorical device,[11] then it indicates not only his preparedness to countenance the possibility of propositions that are also pseudo-propositions, but his outright commitment to the existence of such things.[12]

Once we have taken seriously the suggestion that, for Wittgenstein, some pseudo-propositions are propositions, it is a comparatively small step to the more radical suggestion that, for Wittgenstein, *all* pseudo-propositions are propositions, even the ones that he would uncontentiously classify as nonsensical. There is certainly nothing on the Standard Account to preclude saying this. In fact there is some reason *to* say it. For Wittgenstein does talk about nonsensical propositions (TLP 4.003 and 6.54). To be sure, we must once again allow for the possibility that this is either sloppiness or rhetoric on his part. But is there any special reason to do so? Why should the term "proposition" *not* be used, non-sloppily and non-rhetorically, in a broad enough way to embrace both the pseudo-propositional and (if this is different) the nonsensical? Perhaps what is required of a concatenation of signs for it to be a pseudo-proposition is, not that it should appear – that is, merely appear – to be a *proposition*, but that it should appear – that is, merely appear – to have a sense,[13] or (if tautologies and contradictions do not count as pseudo-propositions) that it should appear – that is, merely appear – to have a truth-value.

Be that as it may, there is an interesting and substantive issue that has hitherto been in the background but that is now squarely in the foreground. It is an issue about the very subject matter of Kremer's and Diamond's quarrel with the Standard Account. What, harking back to the opening sentence of this chapter, was that tripartite classification supposed to be a classification *of*?[14] When I characterized the first two categories, I was explicit that each consisted of propositions of some kind. But I was deliberately non-committal about whether, between them, they exhausted the propositions. When I characterized the third category, I suggested that the overall classification was a classification of concatenations of signs. But "suggested" is the operative word. And even then there was no suggestion that it was a classification of *all* concatenations of signs. I deliberately allowed for the possibility that there are, on the Standard Account, concatenations of signs of various kinds that do not belong to any of the three categories, hence that do not even count as pseudo-propositions – the most obvious candidates being, on the one hand, perfectly meaningful concatenations of signs to which this whole discussion appears to have no application, such as questions and commands, and, on the other hand, word salads such as "Interstellar backlash carrot".[15] Subsequently, I have been cagier still, for instance when talking about the "material" in the *Tractatus*. In the light of our most recent reflections, however, the caginess appears both unnecessary and easily surmountable. There is a simple answer to the question what the tripartite classification is a classification of, and hence what Kremer's and Diamond's quarrel with the Standard Account is a quarrel about, namely: propositions.

That certainly rules out everything that we want to rule out. However, it is not unique in doing so. An equally natural alternative would be to reserve the term "proposition" for items in the first two categories, then to say that the domain as a whole consists of *apparent* propositions, with those in the third category being distinguished by the fact that their propositionhood is merely apparent. This seems to be Kremer's and Diamond's approach. At one point Kremer describes the pseudo-propositions of mathematics as "apparent propositions" (Kremer 2002, 294). Diamond, for her part, speaks in a similar connection of "proposition-like constructions" (Diamond 2011, 247). Elsewhere she speaks of "sentence-constructions" (ibid., 263).

Very well, which of these two uses of the term "proposition" (if either) do we find in the *Tractatus*?[16] Call the view that we find the first, broader use the Broad Interpretation; and call the view that we find the second, narrower use the Narrow Interpretation. We have seen reasons for adopting the Broad Interpretation. But we have also seen reasons for being suspicious of these reasons. Clearly there is much more to be said about the matter. And there is much more that has been said. Interesting and compelling arguments have been advanced both for the Broad Interpretation and for the Narrow Interpretation.[17]

My own view, as I have already intimated, is that we find at least *some* instances of the broad use in the *Tractatus*. If I am right, then the Narrow Interpretation is wrong. (I am construing each of the two interpretations in such a way that it requires uniformity of use throughout the book.) But I shall not argue for that view here. For I also believe that there is, in the Narrow Interpretation, and in the arguments for it, an insight whose exegetical and philosophical significance far exceeds that of its strict incorrectness. The choice between the two interpretations, or between both of them and some third interpretation whereby neither the broad use nor the narrow use is uniform throughout the book, appears to me to be another example of a relatively boring terminological matter which is not where the real exegetical or philosophical action is.

To see what I have in mind, note first that, *whatever* our view about this matter, we cannot deny that Wittgenstein recognizes a clear and fundamental distinction between items in the first two categories, that is to say truth-valued propositions, and items in the third category (afforced, if the Standard Account is incorrect, by such non-nonsensical items as mathematical equations),[18] that is to say truth-valueless pseudo-propositions; nor that this distinction is of critical importance to him. Call this distinction the Principal Distinction. Part of the reason why the Principal Distinction is of critical importance to Wittgenstein, as he (all but) says in the preface to his book, is that there is nothing incoherent in the idea of our drawing it. Why does this matter? It matters because drawing this distinction, with due qualifications concerning the special status of tautologies and contradictions, can serve as an unproblematical surrogate for trying to do something the idea of which *is* incoherent, though it is also of peculiar and central relevance to Wittgenstein's project, namely drawing a limit to what can be thought. This idea is incoherent because, in order to draw a limit to what can be thought, "we should have to find both sides of the limit thinkable (i.e., we should have to be able to think what cannot be thought)" (TLP, 3). It is nevertheless of peculiar and central relevance to Wittgenstein's project because it can all too easily appear to be the aim of the project, and, partly for that very reason, the attempt to do this thing provides rungs on the ladder that Wittgenstein wants us to climb and eventually to throw away (TLP 6.54). Throwing the ladder away involves acknowledging that the truth-valueless pseudo-propositions on the "far" side of the distinction that we *can* draw, and do draw, namely the Principal Distinction, do not convey anything that cannot be thought: they do not convey anything at all. This in turn helps us to see that the very idea of that which cannot be thought is itself incoherent. Here, then, is the acceptable alternative to the unacceptable project in which Wittgenstein can *appear* to be engaged, and on which, without benefit of the lessons he passes on to us, either he or we might otherwise have embarked.[19]

The insight that I believe can be found in the Narrow Interpretation is an insight into the very nature of the Principal Distinction. This is perhaps unsurprising, since it is the Principal Distinction which, according to the Narrow Interpretation, Wittgenstein marks with the term "proposition". Not that the matter is as straightforward as that. For the insight in question is also an insight into the very nature of the distinction that the *Broad* Interpretation has Wittgenstein marking with the term "proposition": the distinction between items that belong to any of the three categories and items that belong to none of them. In order not to beg questions, let us henceforth use the neutral term "sentence" to denote items that belong to any of the three categories. We can then accordingly use: "non-sentence" to denote items that belong to none of them; "truth-valued sentence" to denote items that belong to either of the first two; and "truth-valueless sentence" to denote items that belong to the third.

To see more clearly the insight that I am trying to tease out, let us begin with the sentence/non-sentence distinction, the distinction between items that lie within the domain of this discussion and items that lie outside it. What, to put it bluntly, are we talking about? What are sentences?[20]

Sentences, I submit, are those items to which truth-operations apply.[21] There is an immediate and obvious objection to this. The objection is that truth-operations apply only to items that are truth-valued; hence that this answer marks, not the sentence/non-sentence distinction, but the Principal Distinction, the distinction, within sentences, between those that are truth-valued and those that are not. But everything depends – and there is a recurring theme here – on whether "truth-operation" is to be construed in a broad way or in a narrow way. The objection holds if "truth-operation" is to be construed in a suitably narrow way. The most that can then be said of sentences in general is that they are those items to which truth-operations *appear* to apply. But "truth-operation" can also be construed in a broad way, whereby (roughly speaking) appearances are all that count.[22] And that, in a way, is the point. Sentences in general are characterized by their *appearing* to be the very thing that truth-valued sentences in particular are: truth-valued.

It follows that, even if the proposed answer to the question "What are sentences?" is correct, that answer is, in a critical sense, parasitic on the answer that we should have to give to the more specific question, concerning the Principal Distinction, "When is a sentence truth-valued?" It is only in application to truth-valued sentences that truth-operations are what they appear to be. When terms like "proposition" and "truth-operation" are construed in the broad way, they are construed as denoting items that have the appearance of those that they denote when they are construed in the narrow way.[23] The broad way of construing such expressions is a matter of psychology, the narrow way of construing them a matter of logic. And it is the narrow way of construing them that is primary. What it is for an item to *appear* truth-valued, and for the corresponding operations to appear to apply to it, is to be understood in terms of what it is for an item to *be* truth-valued, and for those operations actually to apply to it; not vice versa. *This* is the insight in the Narrow Interpretation.

One way to think of this is by analogy with the debate in the philosophy of perception about the relation between a veridical perception and a subjectively indistinguishable hallucination. According to what is sometimes called the "highest common factor" conception, the same experience is had in each of the two cases: the difference between them consists in the fact that a certain connection obtains between the experience and the world beyond it in the first case but not in the second. According to what is sometimes called the "disjunctivist" conception, there is nothing relevant in common between the two cases: all that can be said of the experience that is had in the second case, and all that needs to be said of it, is that it has the false *appearance* of being the same as that which is had in the first case. And if we describe a case in a way that leaves open which of the two it is (for instance, if we say, "He thinks he can see a dagger in front of him"), then we mean nothing more than that *either* it is the one case *or* it is the other.[24] The insight in the Narrow Interpretation is that something like the disjunctivist conception applies to the Principal Distinction. If we classify an item as a sentence – a proposition in the broad sense – then we mean nothing more than that *either* it is a truth-valued sentence – a proposition in the narrow sense – *or* it is an item that has the false appearance of being such. Sentencehood has no independent essence of its own.[25]

A caveat before I proceed. If the concept of a truth-valued sentence is what Wittgenstein calls a formal concept (TLP 4.126ff.), and if the concept of a truth-valueless sentence is *not* – both of which strike me as plausible (see, e.g., TLP 4.5ff. and 5.473ff., respectively) – then, although this lends further support to a disjunctivist conception of the Principal Distinction, it also means that my characterization of these issues has been misleading, even modulo the *Tractatus'* own commitment to the idea that *any* characterization of these issues, inasmuch as it will contain nonsense masquerading as sense, must be misleading. In particular, by framing the concern with the Principal Distinction as a concern with the question, "When is a sentence truth-valued?", I have suggested that the task at hand is to say, concerning items that satisfy one condition, namely that of being a sentence, what is required of them to satisfy a second condition, namely that of having a truth-value. But such misleadingness can, I believe, be overcome. The question "When is a sentence truth-valued?" can be recast as follows: "If, in a given situation, either signs are being used to constitute a truth or a falsehood or it falsely appears that signs are being used to constitute a truth or a falsehood, what can be said of the situation to indicate that the former is the case?" Similarly, were we to say, "Both history and mathematics involve sentences, but only history involves truth-valued sentences", our claim could be recast as follows: "In both history and mathematics either signs are used to constitute truths and falsehoods or it falsely appears that signs are used to constitute truths and falsehoods, but only in history is the former the case." With that caveat in place, I shall revert to my previous way of putting things.

Now, even without that caveat in place, it is plain that the concept of a sentence is not a tidy homogeneous concept. Apart from anything else, what we might call its "second disjunct" – the concept of a truth-valueless sentence – is not a tidy homogeneous concept. There are all sorts of ways in which an item can falsely appear to be a truth-valued sentence. The appearance can be more or less superficial, affecting a more or less extended group of people, with more or less tendency to deceive. Truth-valueless sentences may include: rubbish that two people utter to each other in an effort to fool a third person into thinking that they are exchanging metaphysical profundities; mathematical equations; the philosophical nonsense that we produce as a result of "our failure to understand the logic of our language" (TLP 4.003);

and much else besides. What Wittgenstein perhaps underappreciates, in ways that he will later rectify,[26] is the extent to which even the "first disjunct" – the concept of a truth-valued sentence – is neither tidy nor homogeneous. This criticism, if fair, cuts deep. For the untidiness and heterogeneity of the one concept, combined with the untidiness and heterogeneity of the other, surely pose a threat to the supposed clarity and fundamentality of the distinction between them: that is, the Principal Distinction. (How compelling can the appearances be while still counting as mere appearances?)

Be that as it may, there will certainly be situations in which it is *very difficult* to tell whether a given sentence is truth-valued or truth-valueless. There are deep illusions of meaning. This is something that Wittgenstein does appreciate. Indeed, as I suggested earlier, it is part of the reason why the Principal Distinction is of such importance to him. It is part of the very rationale for his writing the book.

Imagine people in such a situation. Suppose that they have produced a sentence in an attempt to say how things are. And suppose that, for very subtle reasons, their attempt is a failure. Careful scrutiny of their sentence will eventually expose it as truth-valueless, although they do not (yet) realize this and they *think* that it is truth-valued. Does the fact that they think this mean that at any rate their sentence cannot be complete gibberish; that *some* of the signs in it must have meanings, the very meanings that they have in other, truth-valued sentences? No. Here we need to recall Wittgenstein's appropriation of Frege's context principle, whereby signs have meanings *only* in truth-valued sentences (TLP 3.3).[27] Indeed signs serve as *symbols* only in truth-valued sentences, where a symbol is a sign together with a particular logico-syntactic use (TLP 3.32ff.). Or at least, this is so provided that "meaning", "symbol", and "logico-syntactic use" are themselves construed in a suitably narrow way. Again we must allow for appearances; and again, I believe, there is a broad way of construing such terms that accommodates the appearances. But the crucial point is that any relation between the use of the signs in this truth-valueless sentence and the use of those very same signs in truth-valued sentences, while it may have great psychological significance, has no logical or semantic significance whatsoever. To suppose otherwise – to suppose that the connection between signs and their meanings, or between signs and their logico-syntactic use, can be extricated from the contribution that those signs make to the saying of how things are – is to imagine an independence of the constituents of language from the saying of how things are, and indeed an independence of the constituents of reality from things' being how they are, that are quite foreign to the *Tractatus* (TLP 2.01ff.). This too is an insight of the Narrow Interpretation. In fact it is the same insight. For those connections *would* enjoy an independence of the sort indicated if the signs' "meanings" and their "logico-syntactic use" were to be originally construed in the broad way. And this would mean that it was possible to understand what it is for an item to be a symbol, in the broad sense, without understanding what it is for an item to be a symbol, in the narrow sense. In particular, it would be possible to understand what it is for an item to be a sentence without understanding what it is for an item to be a truth-valued sentence.

Still, *there are* such things as meanings, symbols, and the logico-syntactic use of signs, in their respective broad senses. Thus one constituent of a truth-valueless sentence may be identifiable as its subject, in the broad sense, another as its predicate, in the broad sense. One sign in the sentence may have speed as its designatum, in the broad sense, another motion. (Here it is worth remembering Wittgenstein's comment at 5.4733. "The reason why 'Socrates is identical' says nothing," Wittgenstein tells us, "is that we have not given *any adjectival* meaning to the word 'identical' " (emphasis in original). This comment would have no rationale unless the word "identical" had some claim to being an adjective in this sentence – the same claim that the word "Socrates" has to being a proper name there, with the individual Socrates as its designatum.) Such features of signs are admittedly superficial features of them, grounded in the psychology of those who engage with the signs. They are a matter of how the signs appear; nothing more. Even so, they are there to be acknowledged.

But *can* the way in which signs appear bear so much weight? Well, the appearances can be both extensive and elaborate. Truth-valueless sentences do not stand in isolation. It is as true of truth-valueless sentences as it is of truth-valued sentences that we are able to recognize their constituents by recognizing systematic interconnections between them and other items of the same kind.[28] If, in a given truth-valueless sentence, a given sign has speed as its designatum, in the broad sense, then there will be other sentences in which that sign likewise has speed as its designatum, in the broad sense. The *Tractatus* itself is a striking illustration of how extensive and how elaborate the appearances can be, and of how much weight they can bear,[29] even when they are false appearances.

Very well; but how far can we extend these ideas? There are some terms, notably "truth-valued" and "sense", to which I have not granted a broad use. Is there any reason why not? Could we say that the nonsensical sentences in the *Tractatus* are truth-valued, *in a broad sense of "truth-valued"*? Or that some of them have a sense, *in a broad sense of "sense"*? Hence that some of them express thoughts, *in a broad sense of "thoughts"* – a vindication, of sorts, for Wittgenstein's reference in his preface to "the thoughts that are expressed in [this book]" (TLP, 3)?

Well, as Wittgenstein himself reminds us in his later work, there is no harm in our saying what we like as long as it does not prevent us from seeing the facts (PI §79). Even so, I think it is helpful to keep the terms "truth-valued" and "sense" in reserve to be used exclusively in the narrow way.[30] For no matter how extensive and elaborate any false appearances in this area may be, and no matter how robust they may be, they can always eventually be exposed.[31] And it is convenient to have terms whose use in characterizing sentences is unambiguously of such a kind that it cannot be compromised by any such exposure in the way in which a broad use can be. As for which terms are best suited to this rôle, they are those whose use – or, more specifically, and more significantly, those whose narrow use – is pivotal in framing the tripartite classification that constituted our point of entry into this chapter (or whatever modified version of that classification is required if the Standard Account is incorrect). These include "truth-valued" and "sense". They also include "bipolar", "true", "false", and "pseudo-proposition".

The three categories of sentences that make up that tripartite classification, and the various distinctions between them, including the Principal Distinction between items in the first two categories and items in the third, are, as I have already indicated, of paramount importance to Wittgenstein in the *Tractatus*. There is therefore something pleasingly reassuring in the thought that, once the dust has settled, the familiar account of them with which we began this chapter (with whatever amendments may be required in the case of the third category – none, I am still inclined to think), remains unambiguously intact.

Appendix

In this appendix I want to compare and contrast the idea of a truth-valueless sentence with the idea, which we find in Kant, of an "empty thought".

First, a point of terminology. Kant's use of the word "thought" is broader than Wittgenstein's in the *Tractatus*. To avoid confusion, therefore, I shall retain the original German word for Kant's idea and call the items in question "empty *Gedanken*".

By a "*Gedanke*" Kant means any judgement about how things are.[32] *Gedanken* are involved in all our cognitions, where our "cognitions" are those acts or states of mind through which we entertain particular objects. The reason why our cognitions always involve *Gedanken* is that they not only require intuitions, whereby objects are directly given to us; they also require concepts, whereby we *judge*, or *think*, how the objects, as thus given, are (CPR A19/B33 and A50–51/B74–75). Kant famously puts this second requirement by saying that intuitions without concepts are blind. He puts the first requirement by saying that *Gedanken*

without content are empty (CPR A51/B75). *Gedanken* without content –
empty *Gedanken* – are thus exercises of concepts that are not related to
intuitions.

Although empty *Gedanken* cannot furnish cognitions, they are still
judgments about how things are, albeit things we know not what. And
they can still be true or false. (See, e.g., CPR Bxxv – xxvii n., Bxxixff.,
B146–149, B166 n., A253–254/B309–310, A741ff./B769ff., and A769ff./
B797ff.) In this respect they are precisely to be contrasted with the truth-
valueless sentences of the *Tractatus*. It is nevertheless apt to compare the
two because, just as truth-valueless sentences, though they have what we
could think of as a second-class status with respect to truth-valued sentences, are none the less sentences, so too empty *Gedanken*, though they
have what we could think of as a second-class status with respect to contentful *Gedanken*, are none the less *Gedanken*.[33] This in turn means that,
where there was a question in the *Tractatus* about the nature of sentences
in general, there is a question in Kant about the nature of *Gedanken* in
general. Are the answers to these questions of a piece?

It seems not. We cannot say that *Gedanken* in general are items that
appear to have content and that empty *Gedanken* in particular are distinguished by the fact that the appearances, in their case, are false. For there
is no suggestion that empty *Gedanken* do always appear to have content. Admittedly there are all sorts of illusions hereabouts.[34] For example,
there are illusions that involve merely apparent *Gedanken*, items that
appear to be judgements about how things are but that do not even get
as far as being empty such things. The most notable among these are
muddled conjectures in which *a priori* concepts that have no application
to objects given in intuition, such as the concept of the unconditioned,
are confusedly amalgamated with concepts that have application *only* to
objects given in intuition, such as the concept of the physical, the offend-
ing amalgam in this case being the concept of the physical world as an
unconditioned whole (CPR A307–308/B364–365, A418–419/B446–447,
and A740–741/B768–769). Come to that, there are cases of the very sort
envisaged: empty *Gedanken* that appear, falsely, to have content. For
instance, there are empty *Gedanken* which are grounded in the unity of
consciousness – as all *Gedanken* are – but which so exploit that unity
that they appear, falsely, to involve an intuition of the thinking subject
as an object (CPR B421–422). The point, however, is that there are also
empty *Gedanken* that appear to be just what they are.

This suggests that Kant's conception of *Gedanken* is a "highest common factor" conception; that *Gedanken*, for Kant, have their own essence
and can be divided into two categories according to whether or not they
have, in addition, content. In fact, however, there is a very significant
disjunctivist element in Kant's conception. For Kant does not believe that
we can make any real sense of *Gedanken* unless they have content (see,

e.g., CPR B148–149, A242–243/B300–301, A678–679/B706–707, and A696/B724). Our grasp of empty *Gedanken*, along with our grasp of what it is for them even to count as *Gedanken*, is extremely tenuous and parasitic on our grasp of contentful *Gedanken*. Empty *Gedanken* are to be thought of as abstracted from contentful *Gedanken* through the elimination of content and the retention of form (CPR A253–254/B309 and A408–409/B435–436). But we have no content-independent understanding of what the retention of form amounts to. That is, our understanding of what it is for *Gedanken* in general to have form is grounded in our understanding of what it is for contentful *Gedanken* in particular to have it. More specifically, it is grounded in our understanding of what it is for those *a priori* concepts that reflect the different logical forms of judgement to be applied to objects of intuition (CPR A70–83/B95–109). When we refer to the form of a *Gedanke*, then, we are indicating *either* the application of such *a priori* concepts to objects of intuition *or* an exercise of such concepts that is of the same kind as this but without any relation to intuition. By the same token, when we classify an item as a *Gedanke*, we are saying that *either* it is a contentful *Gedanke or* it is an item that has been abstracted from such in the way described. Thus, just as in the *Tractatus* sentences in general are characterized by their having the appearance of truth-valued sentences in particular, so too in Kant *Gedanken* in general are characterized by their having the form of contentful *Gedanken* in particular.

But this prompts a concern – I shall characterize it no more strongly than that, and I shall do no more in conclusion than raise it – about Kant's very notion of a *Gedanke*.[35] Given the analogy just indicated between empty *Gedanken* and truth-valueless sentences; given various further analogies that recommend themselves, such as that between the abstraction to which I have alluded in Kant and the attempt in the *Tractatus* to treat formal concepts as though they were concepts proper, an attempt that Wittgenstein expressly warns is destined to issue in nonsensical pseudo-propositions (TLP 4.126–4.1272); given how much weight the Tractarian appearances can bear; and given how tenuous Kant thinks our grasp of empty *Gedanken* is: we cannot but wonder whether the analogy between empty *Gedanken* and truth-valueless sentences should have been even closer. More specifically, we cannot but wonder whether Kant should have held that *Gedanken* in general are characterized by their *appearing* to be truth-valued judgments about how things are, while empty *Gedanken* in particular are distinguished by the fact that the appearances, in their case, are false.[36]

Notes

1. See Kremer 2002; Diamond 2011, 242, 246f., and 253, esp. n. 7.
2. In fact Kremer mounts a very persuasive case for this being the *Tractatus'* own conception of meaning: see Kremer 2002, 283ff. Cf. also RFM, Pt V,

§2, where, in keeping with 6.211 of the *Tractatus*, Wittgenstein says that what makes a sign-game into mathematics is its use outside mathematics, and then adds that this use constitutes the meaning of the signs in question. Remark 3.328 in the *Tractatus* is also relevant here.

3. Grice 1967.
4. Diamond in fact anticipates the objection and tries to tell just such a story. In Diamond (2019), p. 185, she writes,

> We need to distinguish cases like that of equations, which are [pseudo-propositions], which may look as if they are about things named in them, and which have a usefulness which is not dependent on taking them to be about those things, from cases of [pseudo-propositions] which look as if they are about things named in them (and are such that, taken in that way, they are nonsensical because they contain some sign or signs with no meaning), and which have a usefulness dependent upon both their capacity to mislead us (through their apparent aboutness) and our ultimate capacity to see through the deception. Propositions of mathematics . . . have a usefulness tied in in various ways with the functioning of . . . propositions [with a sense], a usefulness which is in no way dependent upon taking them to be a kind of failed . . . proposition [with a sense], whereas there are other propositions which are useful in particular contexts precisely through the recognition of such failure.

Cf. also ibid., 199–200.

5. That is my own view. The remark in the *Tractatus* that seems to me to come closest to settling it is 5.5303, which is at first sight very puzzling but which can certainly be made to appear less puzzling by a reading of the kind that Kremer and Diamond adopt: see esp. Kremer 2002, 294–297. Even so, I do not take this remark to be decisive. (For one thing, as Wim Vanrie has pointed out to me, it is not *obvious* that 5.5303 has anything to do with equations, which it needs to have for a reading of the kind that Kremer and Diamond adopt to be relevant to it in any way that is itself relevant.)
6. This qualification anticipates one of the main issues of this chapter.
7. See, e.g., Kremer 2002, 300; Diamond 2011, n. 5.
8. I take both Kremer 2002 and Diamond 2011 to illustrate this point.
9. But there is no reasonable reading on which it denotes *all* concatenations of signs that lack a truth-value: cf. n. 6 and see further in the main text.
10. I have chosen the word "concatenation", incidentally, rather than "combination", as a way of trying to circumvent the exegetical minefield that is TLP 4.466–4.4661 – part of whose message seems to be that we had better not unthinkingly refer to tautologies and contradictions as combinations of signs. (But see also TLP 6.124.) I hope that "concatenation" begs no questions.
11. These possibilities are certainly not to be excluded. A fake pearl is not a pearl: but it would be both natural and perfectly intelligible to say something like, "Only one of these two pearls is real; the other is fake."
12. If the pseudo-propositions of mathematics are indeed propositions, then can we say that "pseudo-", in this context, functions like "malformed", in the phrase "malformed finger" – a malformed finger being none the less a finger? That is still not quite right. A better analogy, I think, is the use of "sham", in the phrase "sham marriage". A sham marriage, though none the less a marriage, appears to be *something* that it is not. See further in the main text.
13. Cf. the previous note. And cf. NB, 9, 12, and 16. Here we find intimations of the further idea, which is not in the *Tractatus*, that the reason why (some)

pseudo-propositions appear to have a sense is that they succeed in showing something: the very thing that appears to be their sense.

14. Cf. again n. 6.
15. Not that the candidature of any of these is entirely straightforward. Concerning questions and commands, there is an issue about whether they are non-propositional. See e.g. Davidson 1984, where Donald Davidson presents a propositional account of them. Cf. also Wittgenstein's own comment, in one of his pre-*Tractatus* notes, that "judgement, command and question all stand on the same level; but all have in common the propositional form" (NB, 107, Appendix I, "Notes on Logic: 1913"). This reminds us that propositions themselves are not to be thought of as already assertoric. Concerning word salads, there is an issue about whether they are concatenations of signs. Perhaps nothing counts as a *sign* save in the context of a proposition: see e.g. TLP 3.31 and 3.32. I shall not pursue any of these complications here.
16. This is related to the issue that Peter Sullivan flags in Sullivan 2003, n. 25.
17. They have been advanced for the Broad Interpretation by (e.g.) Colin Johnston, in Johnston 2007, and by Michael Morris, in Morris 2008, §4C. Both Johnston and Morris see a priority of syntax over semantics in the *Tractatus* whereby propositions, in the relevant broad sense, have a syntactic articulation even when they are nonsensical: in particular, they contain names. Interesting and compelling arguments for the Narrow Interpretation have been advanced by (e.g.) Colin Johnston again, this time in his later essay Johnston 2017, esp. §7, and by Wim Vanrie in Vanrie (unpublished). (Johnston, in his later essay, does not address the issue explicitly in these terms, nor does he say that he has changed his mind. But he has confirmed this in private correspondence with me.) Among the most compelling pieces of evidence for the Broad Interpretation are: TLP 3.13, 3.33, 4.003, 5.4733, 6.2, 6.53, and 6.54. Among the most compelling pieces of evidence for the Narrow Interpretation are various remarks in the 3.3s of TLP, esp. 3.326, and TLP 4.5–5 and 6–6.01. Both Johnston, in his earlier essay, and Morris acknowledge TLP 3.326 as a threat to the Broad Interpretation. There Wittgenstein appears to claim that we cannot recognize a sign as having a syntactic use, nor therefore presumably as being propositional, until we have observed it being used "with a sense". Johnston explains this by construing "with a sense" in this context (a rendering of "*sinnvollen*") as itself an allusion to syntax (see Johnston 2007, §3.2); Morris explains it by arguing that Wittgenstein is talking about our most usual or most convenient way of recognizing the syntactic use of a sign (see Morris 2008, 165–166).
18. From now on I shall take this parenthetical qualification for granted.
19. For further discussion of the issues raised in this paragraph, with particular reference to Kant, see my 2019.
20. That is: what, for Wittgenstein, are sentences? What follows is exegesis. Only very indirectly shall I address the question whether his views are correct or not.
21. Cf. TLP 5.2ff. and 6ff. Cf. also Wittgenstein PI §136 and RFM Pt I, App. III, §2.
22. This enables us to characterize the sentence "$7 + 5 \neq 13$", for instance, as the negation of the sentence "$7 + 5 = 13$". Of course, it follows that, if we *simply* say, "Sentences are those items to which truth-operations apply", without any further gloss, then we shall have said something that, even if correct, is unhelpful – just as, if we simply said, "Propositions are those items to which truth-operations apply", without any further gloss, then we should have said something that, even if correct, did not thereby clarify whether we were using "proposition" in the broad way or in the narrow way. Consider in

this connection Frege's famous characterization of what he calls a "thought" as "that to which the question 'Is it true?' is in principle applicable" (Frege 1997, 362). As it stands, without some further gloss, this characterization allows for more or less broad interpretations of Frege's use of the term "thought". (I should add that I intend no criticism of Frege in saying this. In particular, I do not mean to suggest that he does nothing, elsewhere, to indicate what his intended interpretation is. That said, it is noteworthy that we find exegetical disagreement precisely on the question whether Frege recognizes truth-valueless thoughts. Michael Dummett thinks he does; Gareth Evans thinks he does not. See, respectively, Dummett 1981, Ch. 6, §4; Evans 1982, Ch. 1, §6.) Cf. also in this connection both TLP 5.5351 and PG, Pt VI, §79.

23. Cf. Diamond 2011, §4, passim.
24. See further the essays in Haddock and Macpherson 2008.
25. There is an issue about whether the disjunctivist conception of perception is incompatible with phenomenology. For phenomenology enjoins the assimilation of the two cases considered in the main text. However, anyone who thinks that there is an incompatibility here is surely forgetting the fundamental methodological tactic of phenomenology, which is precisely to bracket our normal way of understanding the world in order to focus on how things *appear*: see e.g. Husserl 1962, Ch. 3. Seen in these terms, the *Tractatus* is arguably involved in a kind of phenomenology – at least at certain points, and at least if the Narrow Interpretation is wrong.
26. Cf. PI §23 and §§134–137, and RFM Pt I, App. III, §§1–4.
27. I *take* this to be the purport of TLP 3.3. But in view of the potential ambiguity of the term "proposition", I concede that this is not straightforward and merits further discussion, which I shall not enter into here.
28. Cf. Johnston 2007, 388.
29. Enough for the Broad Interpretation to be correct? On that I pass no comment, except to say that that is a colossal weight.
30. For the record, however, I also think it is interesting to compare a broad use of "sense", should such a thing be indulged, with the use of "sense" that we find in the work of Gilles Deleuze: see esp. Deleuze 1990, passim. I say a little more about this in Moore 2012, 565–566.
31. If a sentence's lack of truth-value could *not* be exposed, then everything would behave as if it had a truth-value, and if everything behaved as if it had a truth-value, then it would have a truth-value: cf. TLP 3.3218.
32. Thus Kantian *Gedanken*, unlike Wittgensteinian thoughts, include analyticities. See respectively CPR A6/B10 and TLP 6.11.
33. John McDowell has denied this. He writes, "For a [*Gedanke*] to be empty . . . would be for it not really to be a [*Gedanke*] at all, and that is surely Kant's point; he is not, absurdly, drawing our attention to a special kind of [*Gedanken*], the empty ones" (McDowell 1994, 3–4). But, as the references given in the main text clearly show, that is exactly what Kant is doing – or at least what he takes himself to be doing.
34. The "Transcendental Dialectic" in CPR provides sustained testimony to this.
35. A crude way to express the concern would be to ask whether an exercise of *a priori* concepts that is of the same kind as an application of them to objects of intuition, but without any relation to intuition, is not disconcertingly reminiscent of a meal that is like fish and chips, but without the fish and without the chips.
36. For very helpful comments on this chapter I should like to thank Cora Diamond and Wim Vanrie. I finished the chapter before I became aware of

Bronzo 2017. I was both delighted and somewhat disconcerted to see the striking convergence of ideas. I have deliberately left my chapter intact, making no attempt to modify it in the light of Bronzo's essay. I hope that readers will find something of interest in our independent arrival at the same ideas. I should add that I have learned a great deal from Bronzo's essay, which includes much that I had not in any way anticipated.

References

Bronzo, Silver (2017) "Wittgenstein, Theories of Meaning, and Linguistic Disjunctivism", *European Journal of Philosophy* 25 (4), 1340–1364.

Davidson, Donald (1984) "Moods and Performatives", reprinted in his *Inquiries into Truth and Interpretation*. Oxford: Oxford University Press, 109–122.

Deleuze, Gilles (1990) *The Logic of Sense*. Translated by Mark Lester and Charles Stivale. Edited by C. V. Boundas. New York: Columbia University Press.

Diamond, Cora (2011) "The *Tractatus* and the Limits of Sense", in O. Kuusela and M. McGinn (eds), *The Oxford Handbook of Wittgenstein*. Oxford: Oxford University Press, 240–275.

Diamond, Cora (2019) "Wittgenstein and What Can Only Be True", reprinted with amendments in her *Reading Wittgenstein with Anscombe, Going on to Ethics*. Cambridge, MA: Harvard University Press, 171–201.

Dummett, Michael (1981) *Frege: Philosophy of Language*. Second edition. London: Duckworth.

Evans, Gareth (1982) *The Varieties of Reference*. Edited by J. McDowell. Oxford: Oxford University Press.

Frege, Gottlob (1997) "Notes for Ludwig Darmstaedter". Translated by P. Long and R. White, reprinted in Michael Beaney (ed), *The Frege Reader*. Oxford: Blackwell, 362–367.

Grice, H. P. (1967) "Meaning", reprinted in P. F. Strawson (ed), *Philosophical Logic*. Oxford: Oxford University Press, 39–48.

Haddock, Adrian and Macpherson, Fiona (eds) (2008) *Disjunctivism: Perception, Action, Knowledge*. Oxford: Oxford University Press.

Husserl, Edmund (1962) *Ideas: General Introduction to Pure Phenomenology*. Translated by W. R. Boyce Gibson. New York: Collier.

Johnston, Colin (2007) "Symbols in Wittgenstein's *Tractatus*", *European Journal of Philosophy* 15 (3), 367–394.

Johnston, Colin (2017) "The Picture Theory", in H. Glock and J. Hyman (eds), *A Companion to Wittgenstein*. Oxford: Wiley Blackwell, 141–158.

Kant, Immanuel (1998) *Critique of Pure Reason* (CPR). Translated and edited by Paul Guyer and Allen W. Wood. Cambridge: Cambridge University Press.

Kremer, Michael (2002) "Mathematics and Meaning in the *Tractatus*", *Philosophical Investigations* 25 (3), 272–303.

McDowell, John (1994) *Mind and World*. Cambridge, MA: Harvard University Press.

Moore, A. W. (2012) *The Evolution of Modern Metaphysics: Making Sense of Things*. Cambridge: Cambridge University Press.

Moore, A.W. (2019) "The Bounds of Sense", reprinted in his *Language, World, and Limits: Essays in The Philosophy of Language and Metaphysics*. Oxford: Oxford University Press, 90–104.

Morris, Michael (2008) *Routledge Philosophy GuideBook to Wittgenstein and the* Tractatus. London: Routledge.

Sullivan, Peter (2003) "Ineffability and Nonsense", *Proceedings of the Aristotelian Society Supplementary Volume* 77 (1), 195–223.

Vanrie, Wim (unpublished) "Logical Syntax and Nonsense in Wittgenstein's *Tractatus*", B.Phil. thesis, Oxford.

2   Solipsism and the Graspability of Fact

Colin Johnston

Introduction

At the start of his Tractarian discussion of solipsism, Wittgenstein sets out in two sections how the solipsist is in a certain manner correct:

5.6   *The limits of my language* mean the limits of my world.
5.62 This remark provides the key to the question, in what way solipsism is a truth.

In fact what solipsism *means*, is quite correct, only it cannot be *said*, but it shows itself.

The world is *my* world: this shows itself in the fact that the limits of *the* language (the language which alone I understand) mean the limits of *my* world.[1]

Between these two is section 5.61 which stands apart from its immediate neighbours by making no use of the first person singular, and with that by bearing no obvious connection to solipsism:

5.61 Logic fills the world: the limits of the world are also its limits.

We cannot therefore say in logic, "The world has this in it, and this, but not that".

For that would apparently presuppose that we exclude certain possibilities, and this cannot be the case since it would require logic to go beyond the limits of the world: that is, if it could consider these limits from the other side also.

What we cannot think, that we cannot think: we cannot therefore *say* what we cannot think.

The history of the passage's composition marks 5.61 as an intruder. The ancestors of 5.6 and 5.62 in the *Notebooks* have nothing intervening correlating to 5.61. And the solipsism passage of *Prototractatus* is a sentence by sentence match with that of the *Tractatus*, apart from the absence of any correlate to 5.61 whose content appears later on. (The words "This remark" at the start of 5.62 unquestionably refer not to 5.61 but to 5.6.) At some late stage of the book's composition, Wittgenstein decided that the apparently impersonal comments of 5.61, comments which had initially been placed elsewhere, should be relocated to join the first personal discussion of 5.6 and 5.62.

In this chapter, I shall seek to understand Wittgenstein's treatment of solipsism by considering first section 5.61. That will be Part 1. Subsequently in Part 2 I shall turn to sections 5.6 and 5.62. And then finally, in Part 3, I shall consider central themes of the 5.63s and 5.64s. It's not obvious up front that this strategy will be fruitful. Just because 5.61 was originally separated from 5.6 and 5.62 doesn't mean an understanding of it will be available independently of these sections. Similarly, the fact that 5.6 and 5.62 precede the 5.63s and 5.64s provides no guarantee that an interpretation can be successful which examines them in this order. But still, let's see what we can do.

Part 1: TLP 5.61

1.1

The limits of logic are the limits of the world. What does this mean?

The Tractarian world is the totality of facts (TLP 1, 1.1), and so it might be thought momentarily that by the limits of the world, Wittgenstein will mean the boundary between the facts and the non-facts, the boundary between the actual and the non-actual. Evidently, though, this is not Wittgenstein's intention. There is no concern in 5.61, or indeed anywhere in the 5.6s, with a contingent divide between what is so and what is not. The effect of Wittgenstein's talk of limits, rather, is to signal a concern with something non-contingent, namely the space comprising indifferently *both* what is so *and* what is not. It signals a concern, that is to say, with the space of the *possible*. Talk of limits has a similar effect in application also to logic or language. Here again consideration is moved away from any contingent, empirical totality of propositions – the propositions of English, say, or of Japanese – and moved on to the non-contingent matter simply of what may be said. Wittgenstein is concerned, that is to say, not with any empirically circumscribed set of propositions, but with the non-contingent space of the sayable, the space of *sense*. Wittgenstein's identification of the limits of logic and the limits of the world is, therefore, a re-expression of the Tractarian theme, familiar from elsewhere, that "what is thinkable is also possible" (TLP 3.02) and *vice versa*.

But what is this theme? Again, what does the identification mean? Let's begin towards an answer to this question by considering something Wittgenstein *doesn't* intend by the identification, namely a proposal that sense and possibility are identical *in extent*. And for this, it will be useful to talk in terms of "object-combinations". A possibility for Wittgenstein is a possible way for things to be, where in the basic, atomic case this is a possible object-combination, a possibility that certain objects combine together in a certain manner. Similarly, a sense is a thinkable way for things to be, a way things can be thought to be, where in the elementary case this is a thinkable object-combination. A thinkable object-combination, Wittgenstein thus holds, is also a possible object-combination. So expressed, however, the position is liable to be misunderstood. Specifically, it is liable to be miscast as a thesis that representability and possibility co-extend within a more general space of object-combination, a thesis held against an alternative that sense is wider in extent within that space than possibility.

A disagreement as to whether thinkability extends beyond possibility could take the form either of a disagreement about the extent of thinkability, or of a disagreement about the extent of possibility. If Wittgenstein were to hold a thesis that what is thinkable is also possible, his opponent could be someone who overestimates sense, maintaining of certain impossible object-combinations that they are thinkable. Or his opponent could be someone who underestimates possibility, maintaining of certain thinkable object-combinations that they are impossible. Either way, however, Wittgenstein's entering into a disagreement with the opponent will mean his allowing the specification of an object-combination which is not *as such* the specification of a possibility. In the case of the opponent underestimating possibility, Wittgenstein allows sense to the opponent's view that certain object-combinations are impossible. And in the case of the opponent overestimating sense, Wittgenstein himself countenances impossible object-combinations, maintaining against the opponent that such things cannot be thought. It is evident from what Wittgenstein goes on to say in 5.61, however, that the specification of an impossible object combination is not to be admitted:

> We cannot therefore say in logic, "The world has this in it, and this, but not that".
> For that would apparently presuppose that we exclude certain possibilities, and this cannot be the case since it would require logic to go beyond the limits of the world.
>
> (TLP 5.61)

There is no saying that *this* combination is a possibility, and *this*, but not *that*. For that would mean excluding certain combinations from possibility, or certain would-be possibilities from being genuine. And for this we would need logic to go beyond the limits of the world.

Not only, then, does Wittgenstein reject the idea of specifying an object-combination whilst leaving it open whether that combination is possible, he further explains that rejection as a consequence of the identity of limits between logic and the world. Transparently, we need a different understanding of that identity, one which does not construe it as a thesis about the relative extents of representability and possibility within a space of object-combinations.

1.2

Let's look back to Wittgenstein's opening remarks on the combining of objects. The notion of an object is introduced in Wittgenstein's book with the statement:

2.01   An atomic fact is a combination of objects (entities, things).

He continues:

2.011   It is essential to things that they should be possible constituents of atomic facts.

And indeed:

2.014   Objects contain the possibility of all states of affairs.

The range of possible facts, the space of possibility, is implicit within the essential nature of the Tractarian objects. This idea bears, however, two rather different understandings. It can be understood as the idea that an object's possibilities for combining in facts are a *product of* its essential nature. The object's combinatorial possibilities are grounded in its essential nature, much as the essential natures of certain geometrical shapes ground their possibilities together for tessellation. Or it can be understood as a view that the object's essential nature *consists in* its combinatorial possibilities, that the combinatorial powers are written into the object "at the start" as *constitutive* of its essential nature. In his ensuing comments, Wittgenstein repeatedly rejects the grounding picture in favour of the constitutive:

2.012   In logic nothing is accidental: if a thing *can* occur in an atomic fact, the possibility of the atomic fact must be prejudged in the thing.
2.0121 It would, so to speak, appear as an accident, when to a thing that could exist alone on its own account, subsequently a state of affairs could be made to fit.

If things can occur in atomic facts, this possibility must already lie in them.

. . .

> Just as we cannot think of spatial objects at all apart from space, or temporal objects apart from time, so we cannot think of any object apart from the possibility of its connexion with other things.
>
> . . .
>
> 2.0123 If I know an object, then I also know all the possibilities of its occurrence in atomic facts.
>
> (Every such possibility must lie in the nature of the object.)
>
> A new possibility cannot subsequently be found.

There is no having an object in view and then subsequently considering what possibilities it has for combination, no "finding out" as a "kind of accident" that *this* is a way the object can combine. Rather, what an object essentially is, Wittgenstein insists, is a possible part of facts.

It is a straightforward consequence of this conception of objects that the idea of an impossible object-combination, a combination which "goes against the natures of the entities there combining" is incoherent. Nothing is specified by "*these* objects, in *this* way" where this is not a way these can combine. On Wittgenstein's conception of an object, to speak of certain objects combining is to speak of a certain joint potential being actual. And it is immediately incoherent, immediate nonsense, to talk of potential being actual in a manner which is not an actualization of that potential. (Consider by comparison the idea of a "chess move in which a castle goes diagonally". Whilst pieces of wood can of course be physically relocated anywhere on a board, a *chess piece* is understood only by reference to its potential for *chess movement*, so that the idea is straightforwardly incoherent of a chess castle moving diagonally.) The stance expressed in 5.61 that we cannot say in logic that the world has this in it but not that, and explained there as issuing from the identity of limits between logic and the world, is thus a consequence of what appears earlier in the book as a certain priority of facts over objects. It is dictated by that priority that an object-combination is *as such* a possibility.

1.3

So there must be a close link between Wittgenstein's conception of fact and object and the identity of limits between logic and the world. With this in mind, let's ask after the source of the conception. Where does the idea come from of objects as essentially and exhaustively possible parts of facts? Why should *that* be a basic structuring of reality? Here I'm going to present what for now will appear a dogmatic account. There will be considerably more discussion as the chapter progresses.

Frege writes:

> What is distinctive about my conception of logic is that I begin by giving pride of place to the content of the word "true", and then

immediately go on to introduce a thought as that to which the question "Is it true?" is in principle applicable. So I do not begin with concepts and put them together to form a thought or judgement; I come by the parts of a thought by analyzing the thought.

(Frege 1979, 253)

This distinctive Fregean conception of logic is also, I suggest, that of the *Tractatus*. Like Frege, Wittgenstein gives pride of place to truth, and introduces a fact, or a way for things to be, or an object-combination, as that to which the question "Is it true?" has application. A fact is something which may obtain or not, and such obtaining is the matter precisely of truth. (Here and in what follows I will typically use the word "fact" non-factively to cover also possibilities which do not obtain. This use should not I hope give rise to confusion; it is present also in the *Tractatus* [see e.g., 2.1].)

It is uncontroversial of course that the obtaining of Tractarian fact is in *some* manner the matter of truth. But paralleling Frege means taking a more specific line. For one, Frege is not merely using the notion of truth to single out certain items – thoughts – in which he is interested. Rather, he is introducing the *notion* of a thought as the *notion* of something which may be true: a thought is precisely a possible truth. "The most appropriate name for a true thought," Frege says, "is a truth" (Frege 1979, 168). Similarly, I want to suggest, a Tractarian fact is not singled out merely as something whose obtaining makes for truth, something which as it happens plays a "truth-making role", as do the facts of Russell's 1910 correspondence theory. Rather, a fact is precisely a possible truth. The most appropriate name for an obtaining Tractarian fact is a truth.

More than this though, there is also the inference of Frege's second sentence quoted earlier. It follows from the pride of place he assigns to truth, Frege writes, that he does not begin with the parts of a thought and put them together to form the whole but comes by the parts of the thought only by analyzing the whole. How so?

We can imagine a view of thoughts, or facts, under which these are essentially the kinds of things to be true, essentially things for which the question of truth arises, but which nonetheless have parts arrived at independently of the whole. According to such a view, whilst the parts are in themselves quite separate from any matter of truth, the manner of their combination makes truth internal to the whole: the "self-standing, truth-independent" parts are combined in an essentially true-or-false manner to make an essentially true-or-false whole. Frege implies, however, that such a view would be contrary to his conception of logic. Why? Well, because the view proposes substance to the whole, the thought or fact, separate from the notion of truth. It is evident in Frege's drawing the inference he does, from truth's pride of place to parts arrived at only by analyzing the whole, that on his conception of logic truth has *sole* pride of place, where this means that there is no place within his theorising for *any* substance separate from truth. His theorising is in this sense nothing other than an *unpacking* of the notion of truth. So in particular no elaboration of his notion of a thought can be in view other than its unpacking as the notion of a truth or falsehood. And this means that the parts of a thought have no understanding other than as such. What a thought part is, exhaustively and from the start, is a part of thoughts.

It is for this same reason, I want to suggest, that Wittgenstein adopts his parallel conception of objects as essentially possible parts of facts. It is because he gives sole pride of place to the notion of truth, and so conceives of facts as nothing other than possible truths, that Wittgenstein comes by the parts of a fact only by analyzing the fact.

1.4

Where are we? We rejected that the identity of limits between logic and the world is a thesis that representability and possibility are identical in extent, for such a thesis would depend for its intelligibility upon something Wittgenstein sees as ruled out by the identity, namely the specification of an object-combination which is not as such the specification of a possibility. Looking for an alternative understanding of the identity, we noted that an object-combination's being as such a possibility issues from a certain conception of fact and object, a conception which is in turn, I suggested, the result of the pride of place Wittgenstein ascribes in his theorising to truth. To understand the identity of limits, this implies, we need to understand its connection to truth's pride of place. And what is necessary for *this*, I want now to say, is to put together our two uses of the word "logic". As initially introduced in connection with 5.61, logic had to do with sense, to do with representability or sayability. In context with Frege, on the other hand, logic had to do with truth. Seeing these as two sides of the same coin will complete our understanding for now of 5.61. An obtaining possibility is nothing other than a truth: this explains the identity of limits between possibility and representability, for a truth or falsehood is as such a sense, and *vice versa*.

A Fregean thought is essentially something *to be thought*, or more specifically it is essentially something to be *grasped*. But this does not mean, of course, that empirical subjects with their contingent powers and constraints are thereby internal to the nature of thoughts. That would be psychologism of a kind Frege rejects time and again. Rather, the thought's essential graspability reflects only its status as a truth or falsehood. Indeed, *it is the very same status*. Being a truth or falsehood means being something *for the understanding*, something *to be understood*, and *vice versa*. More, in being *exhaustively* a truth or falsehood, in having no substance independent of truth, the thought is *exhaustively* something for the understanding, something *wholly given to* the understanding, something for which understanding is *possession* (more on this later). And the same connection between truth and thinkability is present also in Wittgenstein. Talk of representability or thinkability does not call for Wittgenstein for consideration of representing subjects, with their psychological powers and empirical constraints. He has no more interest than Frege in such matters. Rather, the thinkability or representability in which he is interested is precisely that of a truth or falsehood.

To ascribe pride of place to truth, then, is to ascribe pride of place to the understanding, and so to representation. A fact, or way for things to be, is precisely something to be grasped. And in ascribing *sole* pride of place to truth, in allowing no substance from outside the understanding to figure within the understanding, no space is admitted for a division amongst ways for things to be between the possible and the impossible. That logic – truth, representability – doesn't merely belong to the world but *fills* the world means that possibility and thinkability, fact and sense, are one and the same. (As Wittgenstein puts it, "One can say, instead of, This proposition has such and such a sense, This proposition represents such and such a state of affairs" [4.031].) It means that an object's "metaphysical form" – that is, its essential possibilities for combining with other objects in atomic facts – is *logical* form. It means, that is to say, that the world's limits are at once those of logic.

Part 2: TLP 5.6 and 5.62

2.1

This account of section 5.61 is importantly incomplete, for no significant understanding has been provided of Wittgenstein's conception of obtaining facts as truths. So far, this point remains brute. Accounts will be considered in the work ahead, but let's turn our heads now to sections 5.6 and 5.62. As Wittgenstein presents this pair, 5.6 states the key to the question in what way solipsism is a truth, and 5.62 turns that key.

To begin, we may consider and set aside a suggestion that 5.6 is to be explained as a consequence of 5.61. The limits of language mean the limits of the world: this expresses, we have said, a theoretical stance within which no distinction is available between the possible and the sensical. Moving to 5.6 – "The limits of my language mean the limits of my world" – this might then be read as expressing a thought that no distinction is available *for me*, for the subject, between the possible and the sensical. And if that's right, an explanatory move may seem available from 5.61 to 5.6. The subject makes no distinction between the sensical and the possible because there is no such distinction to be made.

But there is a difficulty here of a kind which will recur later. Spelling out the mooted explanation, we shall have the following: There is no distinction to be made between the thinkable and the possible; so no one can make any such distinction; so in particular *I* can make no such distinction. But this must surely fail as in interpretation of 5.6, for as the reasoning goes, its "I" is the instantiation of a variable "someone", and as such will serve to pick out one of an array, or potential array, of subjects. ("No one φs" = "It is not the case that someone φs".) *The* subject has on this interpretation become *a* subject, one subject amongst (potential) others. And this can't be right, for then no move will be available to 5.62. If 5.6 is to be the basis for the solipsist's claim in 5.62 that the world is my world, its first person pronouns must match the pronoun of that claim. And whatever we are to make of "The world is my world", this patently does not express a thought that the world belongs to *a* subject, to one subject amongst possible others. (The world is Ludwig's world – lucky Ludwig!)

This reasoning may suggest that 5.6 and 5.61 must be treated as quite separate. The impersonality of 5.61 rules out, one might think, that it be understood by means of the first-personal 5.6. And understanding 5.6 by means of 5.61 involves treating its "my" as the indexical name of *a* subject, and so bars any move to 5.62. Sections 5.6 and 5.61 must therefore, it may seem, stand as independent premises within an argument for solipsism. I shall reject this conclusion in what follows, centrally by rejecting that the material of 5.61 is as impersonal as it might first appear. (Indeed, it is not as impersonal as might be suggested by this chapter's strategy of beginning at 5.61 and only subsequently considering the first person pronoun.) But it will take us a while to arrive there. Let's continue on, rather, by noting that throwing out the idea that 5.6 is a consequence of 5.61 does not mean throwing out the initial move which provided for that idea, namely the proposal to read 5.6 as expressing a thought that the subject does not distinguish between the sensical and the possible. Sticking as we may with *that* thought, let's seek a different explanatory context for it.

2.2

A division amongst senses between the possible and the merely sensical depends, we said, on the possession by a sense of truth-independent substance. Recasting this within the mind of the subject, we shall have that the subject's making a distinction amongst senses between the possible and the merely sensical – "The world has this in it, and this, but not that" – depends upon her ascribing truth-independent substance to that which she thinks. And this, I want now to suggest, she cannot do. She makes no sense of there being substance to what she thinks going beyond in kind what is available to her within her thinking – substance, that is, beyond in kind that of a truth or falsehood.

This suggestion draws on an idea of understanding as *possession*: in grasping that *p*, the subject is *possessed* of that which she understands. Where the subject understands that *p*, this is to say, she knows herself to understand that *p*, and so she knows that what she understands is that *p*. In understanding, the subject is not merely related to a certain content as Jack might be related to Jill by being taller than her. Rather, the content of the subject's understanding, and that she understands that content, is transparent to her *in her act of understanding*. This point may seem straightforward enough: the subject does not need a further act beyond her understanding that *p* in order to know herself to understand what she does. Still, it might be questioned, or at least qualified. Yes, someone might say, the subject is indeed possessed in thinking of the true-or-false content that she thinks. So much is indeed given to her merely in thinking. But there is, nonetheless, further substance to what the subject thinks, deeper substance which goes beyond in kind what is given to her *in* her thought. What is given to the subject in thought, the truth-or-falsity, is the mere tip of the sense iceberg whose full nature encompasses also the truth-independent substance of the sense's constituent objects.

The thought of 5.6, I want to suggest, is that this supposition of a "deeper content" is not something of which the subject can make sense. The subject might, perhaps, essay the idea that she is related in her thinking to objects with a life outside truth, and so a life beyond in kind that which she possesses in her understanding. She is thinking here about *this thing*. But any such idea – "I think here of *this*" – will itself be a fact whose content *available to her in thinking it* will be without truth-independent substance. For what she self-consciously thinks – what she knowingly *grasps* – will be simply another truth or falsehood. And the thought here is quite general. There is no move for the subject by which she can "get outside" her understanding in such a way as to recognise a "deeper content" to what she understands, a content going beyond in kind what she possesses in her understanding. Any such attempt at recognition will be simply another move of her understanding, and as such deliver for her only something again of the same kind.

Recognising this, the subject sees the quest for "truth-independent substance" as misconceived. The idea of fulfilling the quest is the contradictory idea of recognising something unrecognizable, of possessing something unpossessable. "I make no sense," she concludes, "of my objects, the things about which I think, having a nature which outruns in kind the nature on display for me within my thought". Or again: "The limits of my language mean the limits of my world".

2.3

Care needs to be taken in understanding this reasoning. To see why, recall our concern to avoid seeing 5.6 as an instantiation of a generalization that there is no distinction available to *a* subject, to subjects, between the thinkable and the possible. If 5.6 instantiates such a generalization, then its first person pronoun will serve to pick out one amongst an array (or would-be array) of subjects, and so cannot serve to express the solipsism in view in 5.62. (More, we suggested that such a reading would be inevitable if we tried to understand 5.6 as a consequence of 5.61.) Have we now avoided what we said must be avoided?

Well, not if the reasoning is to work as follows. First premise: I make no sense of what I think having substance going beyond in kind that which I grasp in thinking it. Second premise: what I grasp in thinking something is precisely a truth or falsehood. So conclusion: I make no sense of what I think having truth-independent substance. For insofar as the second premise here introduces a notion of truth not present in the first, the claim that what I grasp is a truth-or-falsehood will necessarily be the consequence of a generalization that what subjects in general grasp, or possess, are truth-or-falsehoods. (If the notion of truth is independent of considerations of my grasping, then the fact that what I grasp is a truth will not be explicable by reference to me, but must issue instead from considerations as to what subjects in general grasp.) And this will then infect the whole passage of reasoning: if the "I" of the second premise is the name of one of an array of subjects, then for the reasoning to run, so too the "I"s of the first premise must be the name of *a* subject. And so we shall arrive at an interpretation under which Wittgenstein's thought in 5.6 is that a certain subject, Ludwig, makes no sense of what he, Ludwig, thinks having truth-independent substance.

But this is not what the reasoning was to be. More specifically, the reasoning did not call on any independent second premise, separate from the first. To see why not, let's consider why, in understanding that *p*, the subject knows herself to understand that *p*, and so knows that what she understands is that *p*. Why by contrast does the subject not know in being taller than Jack that she is taller than Jack?

The immediate response to this is that the subject knows in the act of understanding that she so acts, because her so acting is a *determination of herself*. The subject's knowledge of her understanding is *self-knowledge* (in action) quite different in kind from any knowledge she might have of being taller than Jack. This thought of self-knowledge is not, however, the thought that because the subject's understanding that *p* is a determination of herself, she has some kind of special access to it, or has a special guarantee of knowledge. That would again involve seeing the subject as *a* subject: special access or guarantee means access or guarantee not enjoyed by *another*. ("This subject here – the 'I' subject, the one I have special access to/guaranteed knowledge of – understands that *p*.") Rather, the thought is that what is given to the subject because it is a determination of herself is given to her *essentially as* a determination of herself, essentially as herself. And this means that it is *not* given as something which might be differently known 'from another perspective' other than as herself. As the determination is known, there is no possibility of "hiving off" its first-personality to give the shape of a situation which might be known in a non-first-personal manner.

And if this is right, the subject's failure to make sense of content to her thinking going beyond in kind that which she possesses will be a failure to make sense of content to her thinking going beyond herself. What the subject possesses is essentially a self-determination, something she does: this is the basic kind of that which I possess. So where I make no sense of a content to my thinking beyond in kind that which I possess, I make no sense of what I think being of a kind which goes beyond myself. My thinking, and so what I think, is essentially a determination of myself. And this means that there are no distinct first and second premises as earlier. The thought is not that what I grasp is essentially a graspable, i.e., a truth: but what's that? Rather, it is that what I grasp is essentially something graspable *by me*. I make no sense of what I think having a deeper content different in kind from that which I possess, but no external or impersonal characterization is now to be given of that which I possess: a truth, a possibility, whatever. Rather, it is fundamentally *as something I possess*, as something I grasp, that I grasp something. And what I make no sense of is content beyond *here*: I make no sense of content beyond possessability by me.

The reasoning of the last sub-section is thus run entirely in an undistanceable first person, in a first person which is not, and cannot be, the instantiation of a third-personal generalization. There is no thought present here that I make no sense of what a certain subject – the "me subject" – thinks having content outrunning that which is given to her – that is, to me – in thinking. Rather, I make no sense of what *I* think outrunning that which *I* possess. Or again, the limits of *my* language mean the limits of *my* world.

2.4

Section 5.6 provides the key to the truth in solipsism, and in 5.62 Wittgenstein presents the turning of this key as more or less effortless. We are given only this:

> The world is *my* world: this shows itself in the fact that the limits of *the* language (the language which alone I understand) mean the limits of *my* world.
>
> (TLP 5.62)

An obvious point for the interpreter to focus on here is Wittgenstein's apparent identification of the limits of *the* language with the limits of the language which alone I understand – an identification, it would seem, between the limits of *the* language and the limits of *my* language. This identification certainly promises to take us to the solipsist's conclusion.

If the limits of *my* language mean the limits of *my* world (5.6) and the limits of *the* language mean the limits of *the* world (5.61), then if the limits of *my* language are *the* limits of the language we shall have both that the limits of the language mean the limits of my world and that the limits of the world mean the limits of my world. The world will be my world. Indeed, identifying the limits of the language and the limits of my language is surely not only sufficient but also necessary for the solipsist's conclusion. Without this, we shall have only identities with the first person pronoun on both sides, or on neither side (see Sullivan 1996, 195).

There is good reason, however, to reject this perspective from which the understanding and justification of a "cross-identification" appears the crucial matter for interpretation. For as Wittgenstein presents to his reader, the "cross-identification" of language and my language discernible in 5.62 is *not* the key to solipsism. Indeed, it is not even *a* key, an additional key to work alongside that of 5.6. Rather, 5.6 is *the* key, and what identification there is to be found in 5.62 of language and my language is something indicated only in passing by means of parenthesis. Taking this presentation seriously provides, moreover, a rather different perspective. On the one hand section 5.6 is, Wittgenstein says, *the* key: nothing substantially new is adduced in 5.62. On the other hand it is quite right that we arrive at solipsism only by means of a claim that the language is my language. So it must be that this claim is already present in section 5.6.

In fact, the presence in 5.6 of an identity between language and my language is the central point we made in the last sub-section in response to the concern of impersonality, the concern that the subject of 5.6 is *a* subject. If there were an independent notion of truth in play in 5.6, so that it is as such a truth or falsity that I grasp something, then a very good question would indeed arise of why the limits of *my* language, the range of truth and falsity that I think, the possibilities for truth and falsity contained in the objects about which I think, should be the limits of *the* language, the possibilities for truth and falsity in general. I may make no sense of a *deeper* content to that which I possess in thinking, no sense of truth-independent substance. But how am I to rule out the possibility of *wider* content? How am I to rule out, that is, the possibility that what I think is a proper sub-space only of the space of truth and falsity? Here we do indeed need an extra premise that the language is my language, that language does not extend beyond mine, and it is very hard to see where this premise might come from. Once we recognise, however, that 5.6 does *not* draw on an external notion of truth, that its notion of truth is not something independent of graspability by me, then we may recognise a single key whose turning is as straightforward as Wittgenstein suggests.

It is as something I possess that I possess something, and the thought of 5.6 is that I make no sense of what I think having substance independent of this, independent of its possessability by me. As we have emphasized enough, however, the phrase "possessability by me" does not instantiate a variable "possessability by x". Rather, it is an essentially first personal idiom. Possessability by me precisely does not, then, implicate the idea of a potentially wider space of possessability simpliciter (possessability by *a* subject), a potentially wider space of truth-or-falsity. Rather, the truth-or-falsity in play in 5.6 is essentially linked to me, it means as much as: a determination of me. It is already present in 5.6 that language is my language, that the limits of language mean the limits of that which I understand.

And so the key is indeed effortlessly turned. I make no sense of that which I understand having truth-independent substance – an obtaining fact is a truth. And truth means as much as possessability by me. So the space of possible fact is nothing other than the space of that which I may possess: the space of my determinations. The world is my world.

Part 3: TLP 5.63s and 5.64s

3.1

We previously rejected the possibility of an inference from 5.61 to 5.6. Attempting such a move would mean treating the subject as *a* subject, and so preventing any arrival in 5.62 at an engaging solipsism. It might now seem, however, that we have given an explanation in the opposite direction, from 5.6 to 5.61. The subject makes no sense of content to her thinking going beyond in kind that which she possesses in thinking. This was our understanding of 5.6. And it is this, it might now seem, which explains truth's pride of place. "Truth" means precisely that which the subject possesses. And with no sense being made of substance beyond such truth, substance beyond the subject, the rejection of truth-independent substance expressed in 5.61 becomes a consequence of 5.6.

Carefully understood, this view is I think correct. But care is indeed needed, for the position may seem alarmingly idealist. Truth and logic, it may seem, have become a mere reflection of me, the subject. The nature of truth is explained by reference to that of the subject. The core message of what Wittgenstein goes on to say in the 5.63s and 5.64s is that no such reflecting or explaining is in fact in play. There is no such idealism. Truth is not founded in the subject.

3.2

The central delivery of this message is through Wittgenstein's treatment of the metaphor of the eye and its visual field.[2] He writes:

5.633   *Where in* the world is a metaphysical subject to be noted?
         You say that this case is altogether like that of the eye and the field of sight. But you do *not* really see the eye.

And from nothing *in the field of sight* can it be concluded that
it is seen from an eye.

5.6331 For the field of sight has not a form like this:

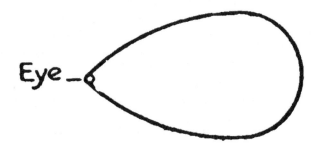

Wittgenstein doesn't reject the comparison outright between the eye and
its visual field and the subject and its world, and he doesn't endorse it outright either. His principle concern is rather to repudiate a certain understanding of the metaphor, an understanding embodied in a tendency to
draw the picture of 5.6331.

There are two things wrong with the picture, Wittgenstein says. First,
it places the eye within the visual field. This is an obvious mistake: the
visual field is constituted by that which is seen by the eye, and the eye
does not see itself. Or moving the mistake across to the subject and its
world, the subject is not something within its world, an empirical object
discernable there amongst others (c.f. 5.631). The subject is not something I speak or think about, an element of content for me. Or again: *the*
subject is not *a* subject. Rather, the subject is that whose range of determinations constitute its world. Or as Wittgenstein now puts it, "I am
my world" (TLP 5.63). In saying this, though, we threaten to run into
the second mistake Wittgenstein identifies with the drawing of the visual
field. "From nothing in the field of sight," Wittgenstein writes, "can it
be concluded that it is seen from an eye" (TLP 5.633). But insofar as the
field and the eye are two sides of the same coin, surely *everything* in the
field provides an inference to the eye!

The inference from the field to the eye is indicated in the picture of
5.6331 by the field's having a boundary whose shape focuses in on a certain point, the position of the eye. And reflecting the apparent necessity
of such an inference is the fact that there is surely nothing wrong with
this shape. In drawing a visual field, we surely *must* draw a line whose
shape draws in towards the position of the eye. But still, Wittgenstein
says, this is *not* the form of the field of sight. How so? These problems are
I think set here by Wittgenstein as parallel: how can I *not* be concluded

from my world, and how can the eye *not* be concluded from its field? And a key message within this pair of sections, a key point of Wittgenstein's introduction of the metaphor, is that these parallel questions have parallel responses.

Whilst we can fuss about the exact position of the eye vis-à-vis the boundary when we draw the visual field, there is no getting away from the fact that insofar as we are drawing a visual field, we shall be drawing something which sets the location of the eye and in doing so speaks of the eye. And this is not something Wittgenstein wants to deny. His point is not that there is something wrong with the picture, that the picture needs to be changed so as to remove the suggestion of an inference from field to eye. His point is rather that the artist makes a mistake *in drawing a picture at all.* There is, Wittgenstein is saying, *no* picture to be drawn of the visual field. We can of course draw *a* visual field, an eye with a line showing the boundary of those things within its range. And insofar as this is a generic picture as opposed to a picture of a particular eye and its particular field, we can if we like call it a picture of *the* visual field. Crucially, though, and this is I think Wittgenstein's central point, any such drawing will necessarily involve a *distancing* by the artist of the eye. The visual field, that is to say, will necessarily not be drawn *from the perspective of the drawn eye* but from a *different* perspective, from a position outside the eye. Or again, in drawing the eye and its field, the artist necessarily *looks down on* them. Any attempt to avoid such looking down, to draw the field from perspective the eye, must fail: there is simply no drawing possible here, no lines the artist can make on the paper (see Sullivan 1996, 198).

An inference from its field to the eye is avoided, I'm suggesting, only by refusing to offer any drawing, where this is equivalent to refusing to treat the eye at a distance. And transferring across the metaphor, the thought will be that an inference from its world to the subject is avoided by recognising that such an inference depends upon a distancing of the subject. But why, we may still ask, should this be true? The subject is indeed undistanceable: we have talked enough about that. But merely invoking the visual field metaphor is hardly an *explanation* of there being no inference to the undistanced subject, for there is as yet no ground for accepting the metaphor's application. Indeed the question remains addressed of how, if the subject is her world, there *could* be no inference from the world to the subject.

3.3

Let's reapproach to think in terms of content, loosely conceived. A drawing of the visual field is made with lines. And these lines have *meaning*, they *indicate something*: they express *content*, and so *difference*. Here, this stuff, is in the field; there, this other, is not. Such a drawing is immediately available of the distanced eye and its field: distancing the eye and its field means, precisely, seeing something from a distance, and so having material for a drawing. And the converse is also true: having something to draw, finding content to the eye and its field, means distancing the eye. Lines can be drawn, content found, only from a perspective other than that of the eye. Following the metaphor, the thought will then be that the undistanced subject and her world will as such be empty of content. And with this thought we find an answer – though perhaps an enigmatic one – to the question how there is no inference from the world to its subject. There is no inference because there is no content to which an inference can be made, or indeed content *from* which an inference can be made. The subject is indeed the internal unity of her world, the unity of truth, but the undistanced unity is an *empty* unity, a unity without contrast.

The idea of the contentless subject is evident in the following section 5.634. The field of sight's not having the pictured form "is connected," Wittgenstein writes, "with the fact that no part of our experience is also a priori" (TLP 5.634).

> Everything we see could also be otherwise.
> Everything we describe at all could also be otherwise.
> There is no order of things a priori.
>
> (TLP 5.634)

Where I am my world, any content *to me* would be an *a priori* necessity *for me*, content given to me merely in thinking. In thinking, the subject's determinations are given to her as such. So any content her determinations possess as such would be content to her world, that is content to the world, given to her merely in thinking. The subject would know merely in thinking that the world has *this* general character, the character of herself. But there is, Wittgenstein is insisting, no general character to the subject and her world. And so there is no such knowledge, no such *a priori* order.

Still, though, we are merely following a metaphor. So far, that is to say, the emptiness of the subject, and so the non-existence of an inference to the subject, is the product only of the transferal across the metaphor of the idea that there is nothing to be drawn of the field from the perspective of the eye. But why, we can ask again, should the metaphor apply? Well here we need I think to look back to 5.6. The application of the metaphor of the eye and its field in the 5.63s is not the development of a substantially new perspective for Wittgenstein; rather, the applicability of the metaphor is implicit already within the fact that the limits of my language mean the limits of my world.

Finding content to the subject and her world means making a contrast between the subject's world and "not the subject's world", a contrast between the subject's world and what lies outside that world, outside the range of determinations known to the subject in being so determined. It means, that is to say, being in position to say that the subject's world has this in it, and this, but not that. As rehearsed in Part 1, however, saying that the world of possibilities has this in it but not that depends upon finding possibility-independent substance to the world. And similarly saying that the subject's world has this in it but not that will depend upon finding substance to the subject's world independent of the subject, substance to the subject's determinations independent of their being the subject's determinations. Our previous elaboration of 5.6 centrally involved, however, the idea that finding content independent of herself is precisely what the subject does *not* do. I make no sense of the supposition that what I think outruns in its content that which I possess in thinking: the limits of my language mean the limits of my world. The subject makes no sense of substance *beyond* herself. But this means at the same time, we're now underlining, that she makes no sense of substance *to* herself. Finding no substance *beyond* the subject means at the same time finding no substance *to* the subject. The undistanced subject of 5.6 is thus as such an empty subject.

3.4

Wittgenstein expresses this thought in 5.64 by saying that "the I in solipsism shrinks to an extensionless point". More fully he writes:

5.64 Here we see that solipsism strictly carried out coincides with pure realism.
    The I in solipsism shrinks to an extensionless point and there remains the reality co-ordinated with it.

And with this, the solipsism story of the *Tractatus* is effectively closed. So where are we?

At the start of this third part of the chapter, we entertained the thought that in explicating truth by reference to the subject, the solipsist has cast truth as a reflection of the subject, that the solipsist has explained the nature of truth, the nature of sense, by reference to that of the subject. And this is indeed precisely what would have happened if there were content to the solipsist's I. "Sense is what *I* make sense of", "A possibility is a determination of *this*, of *me*" – said with appropriate emphases. But this is not what has happened. Indeed, it *cannot* be what has happened, for such an explanation would immediately undermine itself. Where substance is ascribed to the subject, substance is imputed beyond the subject, with the result that there will be no pride of place for the subject, and so no pride of place for truth. Section 5.61 will thus have been not explained but falsified.

Our reasoning in Part 2 did not entail, however, an explanation from the nature of the subject to that of truth: it merely ruled out that truth be independent of the subject. It is as something I possess, as a determination of myself, that I think something. And I make no sense of content beyond here, of content independent of possessability by me. From here truth will indeed need to be explained as possessability by me. But this explanation will not be of a substantial nature by reference to a substantial explanans, an idealist explanation of the nature of truth by reference to that of the subject and her powers, for in making no sense of content beyond the subject, I at the same time make no sense of content to the subject. What we shall have, rather, is an explication of truth as identical, in its emptiness, to the subject. As Wittgenstein puts it, we shall have not an idealism but a coincidence of solipsism with pure realism. The suggestion in solipsism of an idealism, of an explanation from the subjective, from what is given to and so belongs to the subject, to the objective, to what is characterized by truth, is illusory. Rather, solipsism, thought through, coincides with realism. Truth's pride of place does not derive from a deeper pride of place of the subject, but is underived. It *is* the pride of place of the subject.

From Part 1 we wanted an understanding of truth's pride of place. By the end of Part 2 we arrived at a suggestion that this is explained as reflecting something more fundamental than truth, namely the subject. And in Part 3 we have seen this mooted explanation collapse as incoherent. In recognising this collapse, however, we at the same time gain the proper understanding of what would be explained. Truth's pride of place is not mere dogma. Nor is it explained by reference to something else, the subject. Rather, it is to be understood in its coincidence with the subject. The necessity of truth's pride of place is to be understood in its identity with the fact that thought makes no sense of content outside itself.

Notes

1. I shall throughout be using the Ogden translation of the *Tractatus*.
2. My discussion here is heavily influenced by Sullivan 1996.

References

Frege, Gottlob (1979) *Posthumous Writings*. Oxford: Blackwell.
Sullivan, Peter (1996) "The 'Truth' in Solipsism, and Wittgenstein's Rejection of the A Priori", *European Journal of Philosophy* 4 (2), 195–219.

3 Wittgenstein and Levinas on the Transcendentality of Ethics

Hanne Appelqvist and Panu-Matti Pöykkö

Feeling the world as a limited whole – it is this that is mystical.

(TLP 6.45)

The conditions for the world as a whole should not be confounded with the laws regulating things inside the world.

(Levinas 2008, 93)

1. Introduction: The Gulf

According to Kant, the domain of nature and the domain of freedom are separated from one another by an "incalculable gulf" (CPJ 5:176). Nature is determined by laws of nature and is the proper object of empirical knowledge. The domain of freedom, by contrast, is governed by the moral law, which is the *a priori* principle constitutive of pure practical reason, independent of the empirical domain. From the perspective of theoretical reason, nature remains a mere mechanistic aggregate of facts, where no empirical intuition corresponding to freedom, presupposed by morality, can be found. Hence, Kant claims, while we can think about freedom, we cannot have knowledge of it. This is because knowledge, in the strict sense of the *First Critique*, requires both concepts and empirical content (CPR xxviii; CPR A545–547).

However, the human being is capable of thinking of herself not only as an empirical creature subject to natural laws, but also as the legislator of her own ends (G 4:412). These ends are answerable to the moral law, which the subject finds in her own practical reason as the necessary condition of agency (G 4:429, CPrR 5:29).[1] Moreover, the absolute demand of the moral law leads one to expect that nature itself may be hospitable to our moral ends even if nothing in nature as the object of knowledge suggests that this is possible. Accordingly, Kant's goal is to build a bridge between the domains of nature and freedom. For Kant, this amounts to the task of showing that we have the right to judge the world to be purposive for our moral goals even if that judgment fails to meet the requirements of cognition (CPJ 5:176).

This chapter begins from the assumption that this Kantian picture of the place of the human being as an object of empirical knowledge and as the subject of moral agency is the immediate background of thought for both the early Wittgenstein and Levinas.[2] Both assume that the world of facts is contingent, while the ethical demand is absolute – a position which immediately gives rise to the question of the grounds of that demand. Both respond to the question by stating that ethics is transcendental. Instead of grounding the absolute demand of morality on empirical facts, including psychological facts, they claim that ethics is a "condition of the world" (NB, 77; Levinas 1969, 204, 212).[3] In this chapter, we address the question of how this statement ought to be understood. We will argue that, just as the stage-setting of the problem, the solutions provided by Wittgenstein and Levinas respectively reflect the influence of Kant's philosophy, yet go beyond the view Kant himself prefers.[4]

2. Wittgenstein: The World as Pictured and as Felt

In the *Tractatus*, Wittgenstein defines the world as the "totality of facts" (TLP 1.1). These facts are contingent, devoid of value, and independent of the subject's will (TLP 6.41, 6.373). In these respects, Wittgenstein account of the world resembles Kant's domain of nature taken as the object of empirical knowledge. However, while Kant grants that we can conceptually formulate the moral law that is the *a priori* principle grounding the good will, Wittgenstein denies this possibility. According to him, "It is impossible to speak about the will in so far as it is the subject of ethical attributes. And the will as a phenomenon is of interest only to psychology" (TLP 6.423). Moreover, given that no contingent fact as a possible content of a meaningful proposition has value, "it is impossible for there to be propositions of ethics" (TLP 6.42).

One of the paradoxical features of Wittgenstein's early philosophy is that, in spite of his denial of value-laden facts and ethical propositions, Wittgenstein does not abandon the distinction between good and bad willing. In the *Notebooks*, he mentions the good and bad will of the subject as one of his unquestionable starting points when addressing the question about the purpose of life (NB, 73; see TLP 6.43). While the picture theory of meaning entails the impossibility of meaningfully talking about the purpose of life, moral obligation, or the good will, the *experience* of one's life as meaningful and of an absolute ethical demand are not illusions for Wittgenstein (see Moore 2013, 521–253). Like the inexpressible logical form, which is the necessary condition for the possibility of sense, ethics is strictly ineffable (TLP 2.18, 6.13, 6.42). But for Wittgenstein, this ineffability just reflects the status of ethics as transcendental rather than empirical (TLP 6.421).

What we are suggesting, then, is that Wittgenstein's *Tractatus* may be read as incorporating a radicalized version of Kant's demarcation between the domains of nature and freedom. For Wittgenstein, the relevant contrast lies between the world of contingent facts on the one hand and the "sense" [*Sinn*] or "purpose" [*Zweck*] of that world on the other (TLP 1.1, 6.41; NB, 72–73). He writes:

> The sense of the world must lie outside the world. In the world everything is as it is, and everything happens as it does happen: *in* it no value exists – and if it did exist, it would have no value.
>
> If there is any value that has value, it must lie outside the whole sphere of what happens and is the case. For all that happens and is the case is accidental.
>
> (TLP 6.41, italics in original)

Introducing the notions of value and sense of the world, these words also bear an echo of the opening lines of the *Tractatus*, where Wittgenstein defines the world as "all that is the case", determined by "the totality of facts" (TLP 1, 1.1). What is typically treated as the main import of the *Tractatus*, namely, the picture theory of language, treats the possibility of picturing such facts. According to this account, meaningful propositions are pictures of possible states of affairs, where true propositions correspond to existing states of affairs, namely, facts. Hence, every meaningful proposition has empirical content (TLP 2.12, 4.5).[5] As argued by Erik Stenius and A. W. Moore, the Tractarian limits of meaningful language may in this respect be compared with the limits that Kant draws for cognition that presupposes sensible intuitions as well as concepts (Stenius 1960, 214–226; Moore 2013, 250–250; CPR B75).

Like Kant, Wittgenstein, takes the world of facts to be the object of empirical inquiry. According to him, "the totality of true propositions is the whole of natural science" (TLP 4.11). Moreover, he claims, "the proper method of philosophy would really be the following: to say nothing except what can be said, i.e., propositions of natural science" (TLP 6.53). As the sense of the world lies "outside the world", it cannot be found among the accidental facts of the world, nor treated by philosophy insofar as we adopt what Wittgenstein claims to be its proper method (TLP 6.41). Yet, Wittgenstein adds paradoxically that natural science is "something that has nothing to do with philosophy" (TLP 6.53; see TLP 4.111). And he famously claims that the propositions of the *Tractatus* ought to be recognized as nonsensical by anyone who understands him (TLP 6.54). Hence, if philosophy is understood in the broader sense suggested by these remarks and as employed by Wittgenstein himself, then the problem of the sense of the world, while nonsensical by the lights of the picture theory of meaning, assumes a different role in the context of Wittgenstein's early thought.

As suggested by TLP 6.54, the picture theory of meaning itself can hardly be taken to consist of statements of facts. Expressing the key idea of this theory, Wittgenstein writes, "What any picture, of whatever form, must have in common with reality, in order to be able to depict it – correctly or incorrectly – in any way at all, is logical form, i.e., the form of reality" (TLP 2.18). But logical form is not a fact or a collection thereof: as indicated by TLP 2.18, it is a condition for picturing. Accordingly, it cannot be expressed in language: "Propositions cannot represent logical form: it is mirrored in them" (TLP 4.121). As we do not have access to a viewpoint outside of language or thought, logical form is known "from within", as the form constitutive of the possibility of thought, manifest or displayed in it (TLP, 3; TLP 2.172). This view is expressed later in the book by the following words: "Logic is not a body of doctrine, but a mirror-image of the world. Logic is transcendental" (TLP 6.13).

A point often left without explanation is that, in the *Tractatus*, Wittgenstein uses the notion of transcendentality to characterize ethics as well as logic (TLP 4.121, 6.421). In his 1916 *Notebooks*, Wittgenstein expresses the connection in a Kantian fashion, in terms of conditions. He writes: "Ethics does no treat of the world. Ethics must be a condition of the world, like logic" (NB, 77). The Kantian interpretation of the *Tractatus* typically understands Wittgenstein's statement of logic as a condition of the world as follows. Without the logical forms of objects as the constituents of facts, the facts themselves would fail to have structure, which Wittgenstein takes to be essential for something to be a fact (TLP 2.03–2.033). The same holds for propositions and thoughts that are also facts (TLP 2.141, 3, 3.14–3.141). Finally, without logical form propositions would fail to picture facts, given that a shared form between the picture and the pictured is a necessary condition for picturing (TLP 2.18, 4.06). In fact, like Kant's pure concepts of understanding that have an *a priori* relation with the objects of the phenomenal world, thought and reality are, in the *Tractatus*, claimed to have an *a priori* relation (TLP 3.02, 4.122, 5.4731; cf. CPR A80).[6] But for Wittgenstein, *thoughts* always have the general form of "This is how things stand"; and how things stand is contingent and hence irrelevant for ethics (TLP 4.5, 6.41). How, then, should we understand Wittgenstein's claim of ethics as transcendental? How could ethics condition the world of contingent facts so that the world appears as having sense?

Restating the irrelevance of facts for ethics, Wittgenstein writes, "We feel that even when all *possible* scientific questions have been answered, the problems of life remain completely untouched" (TLP 6.52, italics in original). In this remark, expressed by Wittgenstein by reference to a *feeling*, the problems of life indicate the sense of the world or – what Wittgenstein claims to be the same – the sense of life (NB, 73; TLP 5.621).[7] In this context, the term "sense" does not indicate "what a picture represents" as it does in the case of pictures (including propositions), but is better understood as the meaning of life or the world seen as valuable (TLP 2.221). In the *Notebooks*, Wittgenstein uses the term "purpose" interchangeably with "sense", opening the relevant discussion by asking, "What do I know about God and the purpose of life?" (NB, 72).[8] A little short of a month later he writes: "To believe in God means to understand the question about the sense of life" (NB, 74). Combining these remarks with the *Tractatus*'s point about the sense of the world lying outside the world, one might draw the conclusion that Wittgenstein's proposed answer to the problem of life is religious faith. That the case is less straightforward is shown by Wittgenstein's further remarks, according to which God is simply another name for the sense of the world, that "to believe in God means to see that the facts of the world are not the end of the matter", and that "to believe in God means to see that life has a sense" (NB, 73–74). Rather than religious faith traditionally conceived, the import of these remarks is a repeated confirmation that the factual perspective on the world, substantiated by the picture theory of meaning, is not exclusive.

In the *Tractatus*, Wittgenstein connects the problem of life to ethics, aesthetics, and religion, namely, those fields of philosophy that in Kant's account fall outside the bounds of theoretical philosophy. However, by contrast to Kant who only denies the possibility of cognition of freedom and eternity, Wittgenstein denies the very sensicality of propositions or *thoughts* about value (CPR A254–255, B xxv – xxix; TLP 4.023, 4.06; see Moore 2013). Instead, the term he typically uses in the context of value is "feeling" (see, e.g., TLP 6.43, 6.45; NB, 74, 86; LE, 7–8). The difference between Kant and Wittgenstein boils down to Wittgenstein's rejection of any expressible *a priori*, manifest in his treatment of logic as well as ethics. While Kant's position still allows the conceptual formulation of pure concepts of understanding that ground the possibility of empirical cognition, for Wittgenstein, logical form as the condition of sense is strictly ineffable and only shows itself (TLP 2.172, 4.121). The same ineffability applies to ethics: for Kant the moral law as the *a priori* principle of practical reason is expressible by the different formulations of the categorical imperative, whereas Wittgenstein states "It is clear that ethics cannot be put into words. Ethics is transcendental" (TLP 6.421). And yet, he writes, "There are, indeed, things that cannot be put into words. They *make themselves manifest*. They are what is mystical" (TLP 6.522, italics in original).

The reason for Wittgenstein's denial of ethical propositions is twofold. First, he limits the realm of meaningful language and thought to the picturing of contingent facts. Second, he holds that by contrast to contingent facts ethics is absolute. In accordance with Kant, who argues that the moral law must exhibit apodictic necessity, that is, the kind of normative force that resides in the mere form of the principle independently of empirical considerations, Wittgenstein claims that ethics cannot be grounded on anything contingent (TLP 6.41). In his 1929 "Lecture on Ethics", Wittgenstein states: "No state of affairs has, in itself, . . . the coercive power of an absolute judge" (LE, 7). The suggestion clearly is that ethics ought to have such a power. Wittgenstein illustrates the point by comparing relative value statements, reducible to facts, to a road that will lead to an arbitrarily predetermined end. Should one reject the end, there would be no point in using the road. But an absolute value judgment ought to determine "the absolutely right road", "the road which everybody on seeing it would, with logical necessity, have to go, or be ashamed for not going" (LE, 7). The road itself would, as it were, present its necessity with an absolute normative force that is self-evident.[9]

In the *Tractatus*, Wittgenstein writes:

> When an ethical law of the form, "Thou shalt . . ." is laid down, one's first thought is, "And what if I do not do it?" It is clear, however, that ethics has nothing to do with punishment and reward in the usual sense of the terms.
>
> (TLP 6.422)

In the usual sense of the terms, rewards and punishments are factual events. Hence, explaining the normative force of the ethical demand by reference to them will fail to meet the absoluteness or "fundamentality" Wittgenstein attaches to ethics (see NB, 79). In 1929, Wittgenstein states that he can express his *feeling* of ethics only by a metaphor, namely, that "if a man could write a book on Ethics which really was a book on Ethics, this book would, with an explosion, destroy all the other books in the world" (LE, 7). It seems, then, that if there were ethical laws, these would have to exhibit the kind of necessity that Kant attributes to the categorical imperative. However, for Wittgenstein, no meaningful proposition is true *a priori*; and the only propositions that are necessarily true, namely tautologies, are true only in virtue of saying nothing about reality (TLP 2.225, 4.461, 6.375). This means that, by contrast to Kant whose categorical imperative is capable of determining which empirical actions are in conformity with the moral law, Wittgenstein's insistence on the inexpressibility of ethics effectively blocks any connection between ethics and specific states of affairs. For Wittgenstein, "the only necessity that exists is *logical* necessity", and *that* will not help us in uncovering the "coercive power" of ethics (TLP 6.375, italics in original; LE, 7).

Nevertheless, we believe that Wittgenstein's alignment of ethics with logic as "conditions of the world" ought to be taken seriously, as it points to the best available model for understanding transcendentality of ethics (NB, 79; TLP 6.13, 6.421). In our reading, the operative notion of transcendentality is Kantian in both cases, indicating the necessary conditions for the possibility of kinds of judgment and also, arguably, evoking a connection to the metaphysical subject as the seat of those conditions. To be sure, the source of logical form necessary for the possibility of picturing is subject to scholarly debate. Some take it to originate in reality, i.e., in the forms of objects, which Wittgenstein claims to be the unalterable substance of the world (TLP 2.021ff.; Hacker 1986, 23n; Pears 1987, 8; Glock 1997, 296). Others reject the very question as misguided, arguing that Wittgenstein's goal is to disarm any attempt to justify the formal relation between thought and the world (Sullivan 1996). The Kantian interpretations of the *Tractatus* that draw their inspiration from Erik Stenius's 1960 commentary typically lean towards the idealist answer: the origin of logical form that guarantees the formal unity of thought and reality, is the metaphysical subject (TLP 5.63–5.633). It is not only that it would be difficult to explain logical necessity by reference to contingent facts of the world. The Kantian interpretation is further supported by Wittgenstein's insistence on the impossibility of illogical thought, which is a natural outcome if the form of thought precedes the form of reality (TLP 5.4731, 3.02; see Kannisto 1986, 148–153).

Granted, Wittgenstein argues that, when understood in factual terms, there is no such unified entity that we could rightfully call a "subject". The empirical subject is just an aggregate of facts and, Wittgenstein claims, "a composite soul would no longer be a soul" (TLP 5.5421). Whatever subject empirical investigation may uncover, it fails to do the philosophical work of making thoughts the subject's own (TLP 5.542). However, like Kant who rejects the Cartesian conception of the self but proceeds by introducing the idea of a formal, transcendental subject, to whom the phenomenal world is given and who is somehow responsible for the unity of that world, Wittgenstein writes:

> Thus there really is a sense in which philosophy can talk about the self in a non-psychological way.
> What brings the self into philosophy is the fact that "the world is my world".
> The philosophical self is not the human being, not the human body, or the human soul, with which psychology deals, but rather the metaphysical subject, the limit of the world – not a part of it.
> (TLP 5.641)

Wittgenstein's identification of the metaphysical subject with the limit of the world means that the subject cannot be isolated by means of empirical investigation any more than logical form can. In the *Notebooks*, Wittgenstein describes the subject as a "presupposition" [*Voraussetzung*] of the existence of the world, thereby aligning the subject with the other two "conditions of the world", ethics and logic (NB, 79). If read through the lens of Kant's philosophy, the philosophical self is the vehicle of the world's unity, displayed in the forms of thought and in the forms of facts – a view suggested by Wittgenstein's claim about the world being "my world" as the origin of the very notion of a metaphysical subject (TLP 5.641; see CPR B131–136).

Now, the only role for the metaphysical subject in its "theoretical capacity", as we would like to call it, seems to be to "picture facts". The metaphysical subject "shrinks to point without extension, and there remains the reality co-ordinated with it" (TLP 5.64). It thus looks as if the subject were nothing but a passive mirror of evaluatively neutral facts, inviting the interpretation of the metaphysical subject as equal with logical form (Kannisto 1986, 150). If this were the exclusive role of the metaphysical subject in Wittgenstein's early view, then the inexpressibility or ethics would amount to denial of value. Voicing the concern in 1916, Wittgenstein writes,

> can we conceive of a being that isn't capable of Will at all, but only of Idea (of seeing for example)? In some sense this seems impossible. But if it were possible then there could also be a world without ethics. (NB, 77)[10]

However, and again in accordance with Kant's position, the metaphysical self does not encounter the world solely from the perspective of meaningful thought. The subject is also a willing subject, and *this* is what renders the world meaningful or purposive. Wittgenstein writes: "If the will did not exist, neither would there be that centre of the world, which we call the I, and which is the bearer of ethics. What is good and evil is essentially the I, not the world" (NB, 80). Hence, whatever the correct view on the source of logical form may be, Wittgenstein is quite explicit about the relation between the metaphysical subject and *ethics*: "Good and evil only enter through the *subject*. And the subject is not part of the world, but a boundary of the world" (NB, 79; see Moore 1987, 132).

But how are we to distinguish between the good and the evil, if the facts of the world are devoid of value and the denial of conceptually expressible ethical principles has blocked even the possibility of a conformity between the moral demand and certain empirical actions still available for Kant? Besides, if the willing subject is not a part of the world, then how can it interact with that world – a difficulty for Kant as well (see CPJ 5:176)? Wittgenstein, clearly aware of this problem, bites the bullet. He writes: "The world is independent of my will" (TLP 6.373). And continues: "Even if all we wish for were to happen, still this would only be a favour granted by fate, so to speak: for there is no *logical* connexion between the will and the world, which would guarantee it, and the supposed physical connexion itself is surely not something that we could will" (TLP 6.374, italics in original).

Interestingly, Wittgenstein's initial response to the question of the subject's interaction with the world evokes the notion of the limit of the world. While the will is impotent with respect to facts, Wittgenstein claims that there is a difference in the world corresponding to the good or evil will, manifest in a shift in the limits of the world and experienced as happiness or unhappiness:

> If the good or bad exercise of the will does alter the world, it can alter only the limits of the world, not the facts – not what can be expressed by means of language.
>
> In short the effect must be that it becomes an altogether different world. It must, so to speak, wax and wane as a whole.
>
> The world of the happy man is different from that of the unhappy man.
> (TLP 6.43)

This remark should not be understood as claiming that ethics is a matter of feeling happy in the empirical sense of the term. Psychological states are, for Wittgenstein, as insignificant for ethics as any other facts (LE, 6). The happiness Wittgenstein talks about is rather a state of "agreement" or "harmony" between the transcendental will and the world: "In order to live happily I must be in agreement with the world. And that is what 'being happy' *means*" (NB, 75; see NB, 78). The agreement between the will and the world is brought about by the subject's attitude to that world and manifests in a change in the limits of the world (NB, 78).[11] But the question remains, if the grounds for the harmony between the will and the world cannot be found *in* the world nor expressed conceptually, then whence does the absolute demand of morality derive its force?

While his rejection of conceptually expressible ethical principles distances his position from Kant's moral philosophy, in our view Wittgenstein's way of treating ethics as absolute and transcendental still draws on Kant's core idea of locating the foundation of ethics in an *a priori* principle. In Kant's account, the goodness of the will means that the will, that is, pure practical reason, is determined solely by its own *a priori* principle revealed by transcendental reflection of the necessary condition for the possibility of practical deliberation. Our proposal is that, in accordance with this strategy, Wittgenstein treats ethics as transcendental – and as such on a par with logic – but as grounding a perspective on the world that is distinct from the perspective grounded by logic. However, while logical form is given to us as the *a priori* form of our thought, the perspective of ethics is grounded in an *a priori* form of feeling. The perspective of ethics shows the world as a happy world by bringing the will into a harmony with the otherwise evaluatively neutral facts; it shows the world as having sense or purpose that arises from the *a priori* form of willing itself.

3. Levinas: The Other as an Object and as an Absolute

The Kantian tension between contingent facts and the absolute ethical demand, which in our reading motivates Wittgenstein's early ethics, is similarly at work in Emmanuel Levinas's philosophy. Levinas joins Wittgenstein in thinking that life acquires sense or value only against the ethical demand. In *Autrement qu'être ou au-delà de l'essence*, Levinas writes: "Responsibility is what first enables one to catch sight of and conceive of value" (Levinas 1991, 128). By "value" or "the ethical", Levinas does not refer to moral, aesthetic, religious, and other evaluative judgments, which he takes to depend on their historical and cultural contexts. By contrast, the ethical is that which gives meaning to our engagement with the world and grounds specific evaluative judgments.

In striking parallel with Wittgenstein's way of connecting ethics with the sense of life and expressing that connection by reference to God (NB, 72–74), Levinas writes:

> Sense is the very fact that being is oriented, that there is Action or Life. Sense is the sense of life. To have sense is to be related to that which gives sense to life. What gives sense to life is above life. To be above life is what makes the whole of life oriented towards the other [*lui*]. To be oriented = to act and to reach [*agir et aboutir*] (it is not a game). To be completely oriented is to act without seeking simultaneity with the act's success (seeking simultaneity with the act's success is not to be oriented). That towards which being is absolutely oriented = the Infinite. . . . But God is unrevealed – in order for the renunciation of recompense not to be compromised. Sense demands simultaneously that action's success is guaranteed but that all recompense – all simultaneity – is denied. Hence it demands a God that is not revealed or is revealed in ingratitude: the face of the Other [*Autrui*].
>
> (Levinas 2009, 3, translation by Pöykkö)

This passage plays with the double meaning of the French word *sens* which, like the German *Sinn*, means both sense and direction or orientation. Ethics gives sense to life, but also orients me towards the other who commands me to acknowledge her uniqueness and vulnerability, to respond for and to her. At the outset, Levinas's emphasis on the other marks a grave difference between him and Wittgenstein. This is because, for Wittgenstein, the fundamentality of ethics entails that ethics is possible even if "there is no living being but myself" (NB, 79). However, while treating the other as the source of absolute value, originally enacted by the relation to the other, ethics would obligate me absolutely even if I did not interact with others (Levinas 1998a, 53).

The quoted passage highlights another fundamental feature of Levinas's ethics, namely, that the ethical obligation is absolute and without recompense. Ethics is neither measured by its results, nor grounded in any end. If ethics were thus grounded, then my responsibility would be "in calculations of deficits and compensations, in cost accounting. It would be subordinated to thought" (Levinas 2003a, 27). Here, "thought" indicates aboutness, i.e., an intentional relation to objects, states of affairs [*Sachverhalte*], or empirical facts as objects of knowledge that are always mediated by language as the "Said" (See Levinas 1991, 47, 1969, 69, 210).[12] As such, "thought" evokes a call for explanation and rational justification. But for Levinas, ethics is more fundamental than rational justification. While the other person is, in one sense, a contingent object of thought, my ethical orientation towards her treats her as absolute. The ethical relation between the subject and the other conditions the possibility of sense and value, and by doing so gives the other a transcendental rather than empirical status. In our reading, Levinas's term "face" [*visage*] points to the other in the latter, transcendental capacity (Levinas 1969, 202, 1998a, 111–112, 2000, 185–189).

As indicated by his criticism of the Hegelian historicist view, Levinas contrasts the ethical demand with natural and historical facts. According to Levinas, Hegel takes the value of the other to be determined by the position she occupies in a systematic conceptual whole to which she belongs, namely, the historical unfolding of the Spirit. Levinas writes: "Philosophers have ended up worrying about the meaning of history in a way a shipping company worries about weather forecasts. Thought no longer dares take flight unless it can fly straight to the haven of victory" (Levinas 1990, 226). By contrast to Hegel, Levinas takes history to be value-neutral and incapable of providing a standard of valuation: "nothing, no event in history can judge a conscience" (ibid., 23). Valuation presupposes a distinction and "discord between events and the good", unavailable for the Hegelian view (Levinas 1969, 246; see Batnitzky 2006, 78). Moreover, by collapsing the distinction between historical events and value, the Hegelian view promises a (theodical) victory, whereas for Levinas the ethical life cannot be based on promises. For just like Wittgenstein, Levinas assumes that the ethical obligates the subject unconditionally, without a promise or hope of a reward.

For Levinas, the standard of valuation is the ethical obligation itself (Levinas 2003a, 29–38). And the only available seat for this standard "is a free being who judges history instead of being judged by it" (Levinas 1997, 227; see Levinas 1969, 240–247). This is to say that the obligation is always presented to the individual subject, to *me* that is. In accordance with Kant and Wittgenstein, Levinas rejects the Cartesian conception of a substantial subject: "There is *nothing* that is named *I*. The I is said by him that speaks" (Levinas 1991, 56). Yet, Levinas argues that the subject is individuated by the unnegotiable and unshareable ethical responsibility. The relevant *I* is not an object, but that unique ethical subject on whose shoulders the entire moral weight of the world rests: "The self is a sub-jectum; it is under the weight of the universe, responsible for everything" (Levinas 1991, 116; see ibid., 112, 114; Morgan 2007, 155–160, 219–227; Drabinski 2001, 167–219; Salanskis 2015, 21–27).

Levinas's account of the subject as individuated by responsibility and as free to judge history resonates with Wittgenstein's words: "What has history to do with me, mine is the first and only world. . . . *I* have to judge the world, to measure things" (NB, 82). While Wittgenstein's concern is not related to Hegelianism, the core idea for both Levinas and Wittgenstein is that ethics forces the subject to take a personal stance on the world or on the other as that which is presented to the subject as an ethical challenge. For Levinas, the person who responds to the absolute ethical demand is liberated from her contingent surroundings and is able to see herself as unique (Levinas 1991, 121–129). Similarly, Wittgenstein connects ethics with the unique position of the subject: "Only from the consciousness of the *uniqueness of my life* arises religion – science – and art" (NB, 79, italics in original).

For Wittgenstein, psychological states are irrelevant for ethics because they are facts and as such contingent. Similarly, Levinas rejects moral sentimentalism because empirical states can never meet the absoluteness of the ethical demand: "my substitution to the other is the trope of a sense that does not belong to the empirical order of psychological events, an *Einfühlung* or a compassion which, by virtue of this sense, signify" (Levinas 1991, 125, translation modified, italics in original). As noted by Chalier, Levinas's reasons for criticizing the sentimentalist tradition are Kantian: both Kant and Levinas "are reluctant to trust efforts to defend man's spontaneous compassion or sympathy. Nothing is less sure, they say, and no ethics can rely on the partiality of individual impulses, even generous ones, without running the risk of injustice" (Chalier 2002, 25; cf. CPrR 5:118). While pragmatically useful in relating to others, compassion and love cannot ground moral obligation given their partiality and contingency. This point underscores the nature of the ethical relation: my relation to the other is not founded on empirical sentiments or interactions but on a more fundamental responsibility that alone can give those facts their value.

While Levinas does not approach the distinction between facts and value in explicitly Kantian terms, his position is clearly indebted to Kant. By reference to the distinction between being and the ethical, between ontology and ethics, Levinas writes:

> We shall retain from Kantianism a sense that is not dictated by a relationship with being. It is not accidental that this reference comes from morality, which to be sure, is said to be rational on account of universality of the maxim. It is not accidental that this way of thinking about meaning beyond being is the corollary of an ethics.
> (Levinas 2000, 65, translation modified; see also ibid., 57–77 and
> Levinas 1991, 129)

This remark expresses Levinas's commitment to the transcendentality of ethics in the previously discussed Kantian sense of treating the necessary condition for the sense of life.[13] Ethics is transcendental, "provided that 'transcendental' signifies a certain priority: except that ethics is before ontology. . . . It is a transcendentalism that begins with ethics" (Levinas 1998b, 90).[14] Given that ethics precedes ontology, no inquiry into the nature of things will give us an account of the ethical obligation (Levinas 1969, 42–48; see also Levinas 1985, 96–97, 1998a, 152–171, 1991, 99–109, 2000, 181–182; Fagenblatt 2004, 14–20). Echoing the Kantian reflective turn from facts to their possibility, Levinas states: "My task does not consist in constructing ethics; I only try to find its meaning" (Levinas 1985, 90).

Finally, for Levinas, the transcendentality of ethics means that ethics is "ineffable" or "unsayable"; it escapes the Said (cf. Levinas 1991, 7, 44).[15] If we try to "say" the ethical, we will only end up providing reasons for the ethical obligation; and doing *that* will inevitably distort the nature of the ethical as a non-conditioned condition for the sense of life. To ask for the grounds of my obligation is to already step out of the ethical relation. Instead of being grounded in reason, reason itself is grounded in the ethical: the subject's relation to the world is primarily ethical, where the ethical conditions also theoretical knowledge. Hence, even though he endorses the Kantian view of the primacy of practical philosophy, Levinas rejects Kant's attempt to provide a rational foundation for morality. According to him, by providing theoretical reasons for the obligation, Kant ends up "saying the unsayable". Interestingly, however, Levinas acknowledges that expressing "the unsayable" may turn out to be necessary in philosophy, even if this is always a "betrayal of the unsayable" (Levinas 1991, 162) – a betrayal not unlike that we find in the *Tractatus* that fails to comply with the method of saying "nothing except what can be said" (TLP 6.53).

4. Wittgenstein: Seeing the World From the Right Perspective

Wittgenstein's statements about the independence of the world of the will, the location of value in the willing subject not part of the world, and the contingency and resulting lack of value of facts leave slim resources to make sense of the will's ethical relation to the world. In the *Notebooks*, Wittgenstein struggles with the apparent gulf between the will and the world:

> Is it possible to will good, to will evil, and not to will?
> Or is only he happy who does *not* will?
> "To love one's neighbor" would mean to will!
> But can one want and yet not be unhappy if the want does not attain fulfilment? (And this possibility always exists.)
> Is it, according to common conceptions, good to want *nothing* for one's neighbor, neither good nor evil?

> And yet in a certain sense it seems that not wanting is the only good. . . .
>
> Here everything seems to turn, so to speak, on *how* one wants.
>
> It seems one can't say anything more than: Live happily!
>
> (NB, 77–78, italics in original)

As the passage shows, rather than explaining the good will by establishing a connection between the will and the world by reference to an expressible ethical principle that determines what facts may or may not be in conformity with it, Wittgenstein focuses solely on the internal character subject's will. And instead of characterizing the will as a power to influence the world, he writes, "The will is an attitude of the subject to the world" (NB, 87).

In the *Tractatus*, Wittgenstein writes about the ethical attitude to the world as follows: "To view the world sub specie aeterni is to view it as a whole – a limited whole. Feeling the world as a limited whole – it is this that is mystical" (TLP 6.45). Interestingly, in Kant's philosophy, the world as a limited whole is a notion that falls outside the bounds of cognition together with the notions of purpose, freedom, and God. However, in the *Third Critique* Kant argues that there is a non-conceptual yet normative judgment that shows the world-whole as purposive for our moral ends so that the demand of the moral law and nature may appear to be in a harmony. Kant calls this type of judgment reflecting, contrasting it with determining judgments that subsume sensible intuitions under concepts and yield empirical cognition. Rather than grounded in concepts, reflecting judgments are based on a feeling that arises from a disinterested contemplation of the form of the object, where that contemplation is governed by the *a priori* principle of the power of judgment itself. For Kant, the paradigm example of a merely reflecting, non-conceptual judgment is the judgment of beauty, which does not ascribe properties to its object but instead claims that the form of the object has a necessary relation to one's subjective, disinterested pleasure. Hence, in the Kantian tradition, a judgment based on a feeling may have normative force independently of the realm of conceptual thought (CPJ 5:179–186, 5:211, 5:236; see CPrR 5:124).

In accordance with Kant's way of connecting the judgment of beauty and the world-whole's purposiveness for our moral goals by grounding both in the reflecting power of judgment, Wittgenstein connects aesthetics and ethics by reference to a *sub specie aeternitatis* attitude. In the *Notebooks*, he writes: "The work of art is the object seen *sub specie aeternitatis*; and the good life is the world seen *sub specie aeternitatis*. This is the connection between art and ethics" (NB, 83, italics in original). Wittgenstein describes the perspective shared by ethics and aesthetics as one that sees the world *or* an ordinary object – not *in* time and space – but "*together with* time and space" (NB, 83, italics in original). His example is the experience of contemplating a stove:

If I have been contemplating the stove, and then am told: but now all you know is the stove, my result does indeed seem trivial. For this represents the matter as if I had studied the stove as one among the many things in the world. But if I was contemplating the stove *it* was my world, and everything else colourless by contrast with it.

(NB, 83, italics in original)

What renders the stove meaningful for the contemplating subject is the form of the perspective that underlies both ethics and aesthetics.[16] In addition to setting aside *knowledge* of the stove as a complex fact in the world, an integral feature of the perspective is the endorsement of the subject's inability to influence facts. The perspective is, as Wittgenstein writes, without fear and hope; i.e., fear of death and suffering as well as hope of acquiring the things for which one wishes. In short, the attitude characteristic of valuation takes a form of disinterested contemplation of an object or the world as a whole (NB, 73–75). The first instance, i.e., seeing the stove as a "my world", as a limited whole "together with space and time", thus fits Kant's account of pure aesthetic judgments. The second instance takes the whole world, that is, one's life, as the object of similar contemplation, thereby showing it as purposive (cf. TLP 5.621; NB, 73).

It should not come as a surprise, then, that in the *Tractatus* Wittgenstein states that "ethics and aesthetics are one" (TLP 6.421). If read against the background of the evidence of the *Notebooks*, ethics and aesthetics are one in that both aesthetic and ethical "judgments" (seeing the stove as one's world, seeing the world as a limited whole) spring from the same disinterested perspective of contemplation, capable of rendering the subject's world meaningful or happy:

Is it the essence of the artistic way of looking at things, that it looks at the world with a happy eye?
Life is grave, art is gay.
For there is certainly something in the conception that the end of art is the beautiful.
And the beautiful *is* what makes happy.

(NB, 86, italics in original)

Especially these final remarks may give the impression of moral nihilism, where in the face of the lack of value in the world, one ought to just enjoy pretty things and savor the pleasurable experiences drawn from them. Such a reading would be misguided due to a failure to acknowledge the absoluteness of ethics as one of Wittgenstein's unquestionable starting points. It would also fail to do justice to Wittgenstein's claim of the transcendentality of ethics, given that the pleasures thus understood would be mere contingent, empirical events. But if Wittgenstein's remarks on value are read against the Kantian background, as we have done, then the *sub specie aeternitatis* attitude is no less normative than a conceptually grounded thought. After all, the entire argument of Kant's analytic of the beautiful is aimed at showing that, while the judgment of beauty is based on a subjective feeling of pleasure, it nevertheless succeeds in making a justified claim to necessity. This is because it relies on the *a priori* principle of formal purposiveness as the principle that allows us to see actions, objects, states of mind, and even the world-whole as purposive (CPJ 5:220).

What we are suggesting, then, is that Wittgenstein's answer to the problem of life, i.e., the problem of seeing one's life as meaningful or purposive in spite of its objective lack of meaning or purpose, relies on a similar idea of formal purposiveness. The purposiveness in question is not an objective property of the facts of world that could be expressed by propositions, but the formal condition for the possibility of seeing sense or purpose in that world and as such as ineffable as logical form grounding meaningful language. In the ethical attitude, the world is judged not by reference to concepts but by reference to a feeling, where the feeling arises from a disinterested and non-conceptual contemplation of the form of the world as a whole. In this respect, the subject's ethical relation to the word resembles Kant's account of the judgment of beauty that judges the purposiveness of the object by relating the representation of the form of the object to the subject's feeling rather than by means of concepts to the object itself (CPJ 5:203).

Recall Wittgenstein's original question, "What do I know about God and the purpose of life?" (NB, 72). He responds as follows:

> Dostoievsky is right when he says that the man who is happy is fulfilling the purpose of existence.
>   Or again we could say that the man is fulfilling the purpose of existence who no longer need to have any purpose except to live. That is to say, who is content.
>
> (NB, 73; see TLP 6.521)

When the subject adopts the disinterested, contemplative perspective on the world, she does not look at the world as an aggregate of contingent facts without sense and purpose but sees the very same totality of facts from a perspective that shows it as a limited whole and as such as meaningful or purposive (NB, 74). Seeing the world as a limited whole brings the subject's will into harmony with the world and thereby renders the subject's world a "happy world" (TLP 6.43). The happiness in question is not factual, empirical happiness, but mere harmony between the transcendental will of the subject and the world given to her:

> What is the objective mark of the happy, harmonious life? Here it is again clear that there cannot be any such mark, that could be *described*.

> This mark cannot be a physical one but only a metaphysical one, a transcendental one.
>
> > (NB, 78, italics in original)

So given that the requirement of empirical content for the possibility meaningful language blocks the route to a conceptual explanation of the grounds of that harmony, Wittgenstein turns to aesthetic judgment in his elucidation of the harmony between the will and the world. In doing so, he relies on a notion of aesthetic judgment that resembles Kant's account of the judgment of beauty as a non-conceptual judgment that judges its object by feeling and yet manages to make a justified claim to necessity. Most importantly, in its appeal to the aesthetic judgment, Wittgenstein's resolution of the original tension between the world of facts and the sense of the world, characteristic of the *Tractatus*'s position, echoes Kant's strategy in his attempt to build a bridge between nature and freedom by reference to the judgment of beauty.

Now, one may ask whether the solution succeeds in doing justice to Wittgenstein's unquestioned starting assumption about the absoluteness of ethics, which ruled out the possibility of expressing ethical laws in meaningful language. That Wittgenstein himself thinks that it does is revealed by his remark:

> And if I *now* ask myself: But why should I live *happily*, then this of itself seems to me to be a tautological question; the happy life seems to be justified, of itself, it seems that it *is* the only right life.
>
> > (NB, 78, italics in original)

The appeal to the notion of a tautology here is significant. While not a tautology in the technical sense of the *Tractatus*, indicating necessary truth at the expense of empirical content, the claim that I ought to live happily, i.e., adopt such an attitude that will establish agreement between my will and the world, seems to have the kind of necessity that Kant attached to his *a priori* principles. But instead of taking his lead from conceptually grounded necessity, Wittgenstein places the normative pull of ethics on the form of the feeling that aesthetics and ethics, in his view, share.

5. Levinas: The Sense of Being

The absence of the other from Wittgenstein's early view should not mask the structural similarity between Wittgenstein's and Levinas's views of ethics as orienting the subject towards something presented as a challenge. Wittgenstein's ethical subject faces the *world* as "something that is already there" (NB, 74). For Wittgenstein, the mere existence of the world is not sufficient for ethics, for it is only in my relation to the world – when

I see the world as an "aesthetic miracle" – that the possibility value arises (NB, 79, 86, see TLP 6.44). For Levinas, the subject faces *another person*. But in the ethical relation one does not approach the other person as a mere empirical object. While the other is also an empirical being, as the source of absolute value she assumes a transcendental status: "But the epiphany of the Other bears its own significance, independent of the signification received from the world. The Other not only comes to us from a context but signifies itself, without that mediation" (Levinas 2003a, 31; see also Levinas 1969, 177–178).

Why, then, should I take the moral demand upon myself? According to Levinas, "No one is good voluntarily" (Levinas 1991, 11). As natural beings, we are disposed to prioritizing our own life over that of others: "A being is something that is attached to being, to its own being. That is Darwin's idea. The being of animals is struggle for life. A struggle for life without ethics" (Levinas 2003b, 172). This is what Levinas calls the "Law of Being", which is the defining mode of being for all natural entities, guided by interest. However, if the human life is nothing but individualistic self-affirmation driven by interest, then it is a constant state of struggle and war without sense. However, Levinas writes, "with the appearance of the human – and this my whole philosophy – there is something more important than my life, and that is the life of the other" (Levinas 2003b, 172).

In *Totalité et infini*, Levinas defines ethics as being put into question by the other, which gives rise to the moral conscience. One is called to justify one's own freedom, which is limited by the other person:

> Moral conscience welcomes the Other. It is the revelation of a resistance to my powers that does not counter them as a greater force, but calls in question the naive right of my powers, my glorious spontaneity as a living being. Morality begins when freedom, instead of being justified by itself, feels itself to be arbitrary and violent.
>
> (Levinas 1969, 84)

Being called into question arouses a consciousness of "guilt" insofar I realize that I am not an innocent spontaneity, but that in my natural concern for my own being I have already taken space away from others. I am always already a possible usurper (Levinas 1969, 83).

For Levinas, the acknowledgement of one's guilt means "awakening" or "sobering up" (Levinas 1998b, 15–32). Especially in his notes from 1950s and 1960s, Levinas calls such awakening an ethical attitude (see Levinas 2009, 459, 476). The awakening indicates a turning away from selfishness to "ethical consciousness", to seeing my world as a world conditioned by the other and hence as something to be shared, to be given to others. Hence, to sober up is to realize that I am driven by an illusory sense of freedom and readily fall into a comforting yet deceptive state of "good conscience". Levinas speaks of the *vigilant I*, awakened by the vulnerability and mortality of my neighbour, giving rise to the acknowledgment of one's responsibility for the other. The ethical awakening thus takes the form of embracing a specific attitude towards other human beings (see, e.g., Petitdemange 2003, 331).

The unconditioned ethical obligation to give from one's own without hope of a recompense should guide our everyday dealings, whether theoretical, practical, or political. Hence, when Levinas claims that ethics is a fundamental dimension of human life, he is not only making a descriptive phenomenological observation, but a normative one. Ethics as the transcendental condition for the possibility of sense must guide and serve as a standard. Acknowledgement of the endless responsibility, Levinas writes, "justifies being by that which assures it" (Levinas 1998b, 177). That ethics "justifies" being means that it is the standard against which being is measured; that ethics "assures being" means that it is the ground of being. Accordingly, to be ethically awakened is to acknowledge the fundamentality of the ethical and to treat it as a standard, which is precisely what the ethical attitude means. Levinas writes:

> I am not saying that the human being is a saint, I'm saying that he or she is the one who has understood that holiness is indisputable . . . the ideal of holiness is what humanity has introduced into being. An ideal of holiness contrary to the laws of being.
>
> (Levinas 1998a, 109–114)

So for Levinas, ethics is unreasonable and "disinterested" (See Levinas 2003b, 172; Levinas 1991, 8). Ethics is unreasonable because it is contrary to my natural mode of being and because it requires everything, including self-sacrifice. It is disinterested because the subject is forced to set aside her personal interests, to "always empty oneself anew" (Levinas 1991, 92). One might think that the centrality of the other and the demand to care for the other introduces an interest into Levinas's picture. However, insofar as there is an interest, it does not concern my own being: "The fear for another as a fear for the death of a neighbor is my fear but it is in no wise a fear for me" (Levinas 1998b, 176). Rather, to embrace the ethical, disinterested attitude is to see the world as something I must give to the other without a promise of recompense. And to see the world in this way is to see it as having sense.

Both Levinas and Wittgenstein thus connect ethics with a way of seeing the world. In conversation with Friedrich Waismann, Wittgenstein reportedly noted that people have felt a connection between ethics and the existence of the world and expressed the connection as follows: "God the Father created the world, while God the Son (or the Word proceeding from God) is the ethical" (Waismann 1965, 16). Levinas addresses the connection in one of his Talmudic Readings, discussing a passage from the Tractate Shabbat (88a–88b) that asks, why the Earth trembled in fear and then become calm when the Law was given (cf. Psalm 76:9). Levinas locates the answer in Resh Lakish's interpretation of Genesis 1:31. According to Resh Lakish, the earth was afraid because its fate was decided: in creation, God made a covenant with the world, namely, that as long as His Will is fulfilled, the world will exist. Hence, the calm was due to the consent given by Israel to follow the Law. For Levinas, this means that the ethical (the Law) is the sustaining principle of the whole of creation; that is, the ethical is the condition of the world (Levinas 1969, 204, 212).

For Levinas, "The world is here so that ethical order has the possibility of being fulfilled. The act by which the Israelites accept the Torah is the act which gives meaning to reality. To refuse the Torah is to bring being back to nothingness" (Levinas 1994, 41). This means that evil is nothing but a chaotic state meaninglessness devoid of value. The choice given by God between Law or nothingness becomes in Levinas's work a choice between sense and senselessness, between ethics and mere being. To consent to the ethical demand, then, is to give priority to ethics over being, to acknowledge absolute value, which is irreducible to how the world is and which gives sense to being itself. As Levinas writes: "Being has sense. The sense of being, the sense of creation – is the realization of the Torah [ethics]" (ibid., 41; translation modified). But it is not enough for Levinas to merely recognize the priority of the ethical. I must also realize *my* responsibility by keeping the world from falling into chaos. As God brought order into to primal chaos (*tohu-va-bohu*) through his creative action, it is *my* responsibility to continue to enact the work of creation by maintaining the ethical order. And this just is the task of ensuring that the world has sense.

The ethical attitude is to see the world in the right way, as normatively oriented from the start, governed by an ethical order whose fulfilment guarantees the world sense. In this respect, Levinas comes close to Wittgenstein, for whom ethics sees the world *sub specie aeterni*, as a limited whole and as such meaningful. However, by contrast to Wittgenstein, whose description of the view from eternity has an aesthetic, contemplative character, for Levinas, the perspective of eternity is the perspective of the ethical obligation to and for the other. Importantly, neither Wittgenstein nor Levinas refer to eternity as a *transcendent* realm. Levinas commends Kant on the idea that orientation in thinking is to direct oneself towards that which exceeds the limits of knowledge, towards a *beyond* which cannot be said *to be*. However, as ethics requires renouncing any recompense, Levinas rejects Kant's conception of the highest good as saying too much. He asks, "Are we entering a moment in history in which the good must be loved without promises . . . a time when the only right to reward would be not to expect one" (Levinas 1999, 109). In this respect Levinas, like Wittgenstein, takes ethics to contain its own reward and connects that reward with the sense of life (Levinas 1998b, 131–134; TLP 6.422; see Plant 2005, 119–120).

6. Conclusion

We have argued that both Wittgenstein and Levinas ought to be read as endorsing the divide between the domains of nature and freedom, which lies at the core of Kant's practical philosophy. For both, the relevant contrast lies between the world of facts and the sense of that world. Moreover, both respond to the philosophical challenge arising from the divide by appealing, in part, to resources provided by Kant's philosophy. The most important affinity between Wittgenstein and Levinas is that, in spite of granting a need for a transcendental foundation for ethics, they reject the possibility of a conceptual or rational explication of that foundation. Any foundation for ethics – whether given by reference to facts or to a conceptually expressible principle – will only make ethics conditional. Instead, for both, ethics is a condition of the world. The absolute ethical obligation, which the subject finds in herself independently of the facts of the world, is the necessary condition for the possibility of the world's sense.

Moreover, Wittgenstein and Levinas come together in denying the availability of a reward for the ethical orientation – or rather, as both claim, that the reward resides in the ethical relation itself. This is to say that both Wittgenstein and Levinas take Kant's initial confirmation of a break between morality and its reward reflecting the gulf between nature and morality to its extreme. Accordingly, the hope of a just distribution of happiness according to moral worth that Kant presents as grounded in practical reason, becomes extremely thin: for the subject, the ethical demand holds no other promise but her ability to transcend the contingency of the world and see it as having sense – a promise that still has a characteristically Kantian ring.[17]

Notes

1. For Kant, the moral law is the principle of universalizability of one's maxim: insofar as something is a reason for me, it ought to be a reason for everyone else as well, for otherwise it would not make sense to talk about reasons in the first place. Accordingly, the universalizability principle is a principle constitutive of agency understood as responsiveness to reasons (G 4:421, see Allison 1990, 204–205).
2. Our goal is not to defend a historical claim of actual influence, but to indicate those substantial affinities between Wittgenstein and Levinas that we see as fruitfully illuminated against the background of Kant's philosophy. Our argument relies on the Kantian interpretation of the philosophical goals of the *Tractatus* defended and developed by, for instance, Stenius 1960; Kannisto 1986; Glock 1992, 1997; Moore 2013; Appelqvist 2013, 2016, 2018. The most accessible account of the philosophical connections between

Levinas and Kant is Chalier 2002; see also Cohen 2010; Basterra 2015; Frangeskou 2017.

3. Our argument relies on the material of *Notebooks 1914–1916* and Wittgenstein's 1929 "Lecture on Ethics". While we acknowledge the drawbacks of this approach, in our view the *Tractatus's* scarce remarks on value can be understood only if read against the background of Wittgenstein's more substantial discussions on the theme.

4. On the Kantianism of Wittgenstein's early view of the world of knowledge and ethics, see Moore 1987. For comparisons between Levinas and Wittgenstein from the viewpoint of the resolute reading of Wittgenstein's early philosophy, see, e.g., Øvergaard 2007; Morgan 2007.

5. Here, we rely on Kannisto's interpretation according to which even false propositions have been projected onto a specific place in reality (see TLP 3.12; Kannisto 1986, 66–68).

6. On the transcendentality of logic in the *Tractatus*, see Kannisto 1986; Glock 1992; Appelqvist 2016.

7. The identification of the world and life is unsurprising if the *Tractatus* is read as a work committed to transcendental idealism. In that framework, the formal unity of the world and thought is grounded in the metaphysical subject as the vehicle of the *form* shared by thought and reality. Such a view may be seen as underlying Wittgenstein's remark: "The world is *my* world: this is manifest in the fact that the limits of *language* (of that language which alone I understand) mean the limits of *my* world" (TLP 5.62).

8. Wittgenstein's reference to the world's *purpose* resonates with Kant's terminology in the *Critique of the Power of Judgment*. There, Kant introduces the distinction between the determining (cognitive) and the reflecting (aesthetic) perspectives on the world: the first sees the world as an aggregate of facts, the latter sees objects, actions, states of mind, and the world as purposive (CPJ 5:179–181, 20:217–218). While the latter perspective does not amount to knowledge, Kant takes it to strengthen one's hope in highest good, namely, in God's existence and the purposiveness of the world for our moral efforts.

9. In terms of their relative and absolute normative forces, Wittgenstein's contrast between relative and absolute value judgments corresponds to Kant's contrast between hypothetical and categorical imperatives (see G 4:414).

10. This phrasing is distinctly Schopenhauerian, raising the contrast between Will and Idea (see Hacker 1986, 87–90). At the same time, Wittgenstein's position differs from the Schopenhauerian view in that, while for Schopenhauer all willing is problematic, Wittgenstein endorses the Kantian distinction between *good* and *bad* willing. Most importantly, as noted by Glock, Schopenhauer's influence does not help in explaining Wittgenstein's characteristically Kantian concern with the necessary, formal conditions of experiencing or depicting reality (see Glock 1999, 425–432).

11. Accordingly, Wittgenstein's evocation of happiness as a manifestation of good will does not directly conflict with Kant's rejection of happiness as the guiding principle of morality (G 4:417–419; 442). Given the contemplative quality of the subject's attitude to the world, happiness as "agreement" or "harmony" is more akin to the disinterested pleasure Kant identifies as the experience characteristic of a judgment of beauty (CPJ 5:211).

12. In Levinas's terminology, the "Said" is the register of intentional thought. Narrowly, the Said is any proposition that says something about the world and inner worldly objects. More broadly, the Said is the register of all that can be asserted and thought insofar as this is taken to include the meaning-constitutive intentional relation between the subject and the world.

By contrast, the "Saying" is the immediate openness toward the other. It is not yet linguistic and it is irreducible to the Said. The Saying does not point to a transcendent domain outside the phenomenal world, but to my concrete relation with another. According to Levinas, the Western philosophical enterprise has been exclusively interested in the Said without willingness or ability to "think" the Saying (the unsayable, the ineffable). Levinas's own project is to uncover the Saying, covered up by the Said (this is called "reduction"). Yet, pure Saying, as unsayable, cannot be said, thus making the attempted reduction a never-ending task. When the Saying is described, it is introduced in to the register of the Said. Thus, the philosopher's task is to continuously "unsay" that which is said about the Saying. (See Levinas 1991, 43–45, 181; Morgan 2007, 300–323; Franck 2008, 213–220.)

13. Following Morgan 2007, we read Levinas as committed to transcendentalism in the sense in which transcendentality refers to the necessary conditions for the possibility of different types of judgments. Alluding to Kant's philosophy in his 1935 essay on the philosophical strength of Maimonides's thought, Levinas writes: "For the first time, and with luminous lucidity, Maimonides separated the laws of a thinking that takes the world as an object from principles of thought relating to the conditions of the world. For the first time he put a stop to the impulse of reason to apply notions borrowed from the world to that which is beyond the world. For the first time he glimpsed what one calls, six centuries later, the critique of pure reason" (Levinas 2008, 94). For criticisms of transcendental readings of Levinas, see Bernasconi 2005; Shaw 2008, 133–176.

14. For transcendental readings of Levinas, see de Boer 1997, 1–32; Morgan 2007; Salanskis 2015, 9–43.

15. While we are not suggesting that Levinas's notions of fact, sayability, and ineffability are identical with those of Wittgenstein, the parallels are striking.

16. For a more detailed argument to this effect, see Appelqvist 2013.

17. Parts of the Wittgenstein sections of this paper were presented at the Åbo Academi Philosophy Seminar on March 5 2018 and at the Stirling Early Analytic Group on April 23 2019. Appelqvist would like to thank the participants of these events, especially Lars Hertzberg, Martin Gustafsson, Colin Johnston, Michael Potter, and Peter Sullivan, for their comments and critical remarks. We would also like to thank Jean-Michel Salanskis, Georges Hansel, and Michael Roubach for their valuable feedback on an earlier version of this paper.

References

Allison, Henry (1990) *Kant's Theory of Freedom*. Cambridge: Cambridge University Press.

Appelqvist, Hanne (2013) "Why Does Wittgenstein Say That Ethics and Aesthetics Are One and the Same?" in P. Sullivan and M. Potter (eds), *Wittgenstein's Tractatus: History and Interpretation*. Oxford: Oxford University Press, 40–58.

Appelqvist, Hanne (2016) "On Wittgenstein's Kantian Solution of the Problem of Philosophy", *The British Journal for the History of Philosophy* 24 (4), 697–719.

Appelqvist, Hanne (2018) "Wittgenstein on the Grounds of Religious Faith: A Kantian Proposal", *The European Journal of Philosophy* 26 (3), 1026–1040.

Basterra, Gabriela (2015) *The Subject of Freedom: Kant, Levinas*. New York: Fordham University Press.

Batnitzky, Leora (2006) *Leo Strauss and Emmanuel Levinas: Philosophy and Politics of Revelation*. Cambridge: Cambridge University Press.

Bernasconi, Robert (2005) "Rereading *Totality and Infinity*", in C. E. Katz (ed), *Emmanuel Levinas: Critical Assessment of Leading Philosophers*. London: Routledge, 32–44.

Chalier, Catherine (2002) *What Ought I Do?* Translated by J. M. Todd. Ithaca and London: Cornell University Press.

Cohen, Richard (2010) *Levinasian Meditations: Ethics, Philosophy, and Religion*. Pittsburgh: Duquesne University Press.

de Boer, Theodore (1997) *The Rationality of Transcendence: Studies in the Philosophy of Emmanuel Levinas*. Amsterdam: J.C. Gieben.

Drabinski, John E. (2001) *Sensibility and Singularity*. New York: SUNY Press.

Fagenblatt, Michael (2004) "Lacking All Interest: Levinas, Leibowitz, and the Pure Practice of Religion", *The Harvard Theological Review* 97 (1), 1–32.

Franck, Didier (2008) *L'un-pour-l'autre: Levinas et signification*. Paris: PUF.

Frangeskou, Adonis (2017) *Levinas, Kant and the Problematic of Temporality*. London: Palgrave Macmillan.

Glock, Hans-Johann (1992) "Cambridge, Jena or Vienna? The Roots of the *Tractatus*", *Ratio* 5 (1), 1–23.

Glock, Hans-Johann (1997) "Kant and Wittgenstein: Philosophy, Necessity and Representation", *International Journal of Philosophical Studies* 5 (2), 285–305.

Glock, Hans-Johann (1999) "Schopenhauer and Wittgenstein: Language as Representation and Will", in C. Janaway (ed), *The Cambridge Companion to Schopenhauer*. Cambridge: Cambridge University Press, 422–458.

Hacker, Peter (1986) *Insight and Illusion*. Revised edition. Oxford: Clarendon Press.

Kannisto, Heikki (1986) *Thoughts and Their Subject: A Study of Wittgenstein's Tractatus*. Acta Philosophica Fennica. Vol. 40. Helsinki: The Philosophical Society of Finland.

Kant, Immanuel (1997a) *Critique of Practical Reason* (CPrR). Translated and edited by M. Gregor. Cambridge: Cambridge University Press.

Kant, Immanuel (1997b) *Groundwork of the Metaphysics of Morals* (G). Translated and edited by M. Gregor. Cambridge: Cambridge University Press.

Kant, Immanuel (1998) *Critique of Pure Reason* (CPR). Translated and edited by P. Guyer and A. Wood. Cambridge: Cambridge University Press.

Kant, Immanuel (2000) *Critique of the Power of Judgment* (CPJ). Translated by P. Guyer and E. Matthews. Edited by P. Guyer. Cambridge: Cambridge University Press.

Levinas, Emmanuel (1969) *Totality and Infinity*. Translated by A. Lingis. Pittsburgh: Duquesne University Press.

Levinas, Emmanuel (1985) *Ethics and Infinity*. Translated by R. A. Cohen. Pittsburgh: Duqesne University Press.

Levinas, Emmanuel (1990) *Difficult Freedom: Essays on Judaism*. Translated by S. Hand. Baltimore: John Hopkins University Press.

Levinas, Emmanuel (1991) *Otherwise Than Being or Beyond Essence*. Translated by A. Lingis. Dordrecht: Kluwer Academic Publisher.

Levinas, Emmanuel (1994) *Nine Talmudic Readings*. Translated by A. Aronowicz. Bloomington and Indianapolis: Indiana University Press.

Levinas, Emmanuel (1997) *Difficult Freedom*. Baltimore: The John Hopkins University Press.

Levinas, Emmanuel (1998a) *Entre Nous*. Translated by M. B. Smith and B. Hershav. New York: Columbia University Press.

Levinas, Emmanuel (1998b) *The God Who Comes to Mind*. Translated by B. Bergo. Stanford: Stanford University Press.

Levinas, Emmanuel (1999) *Alterity and Transcendence*. Translated by M. B. Smith. London: The Athlone Press.

Levinas, Emmanuel (2000) *God, Death, and Time*. Translated by B. Bergo. Stanford: Stanford University Press.

Levinas, Emmanuel (2003a) *Humanism of the Other*. Translated by N. Poller. Chicago: University of Illinois Press.

Levinas, Emmanuel (2003b) "Paradox of Morality: Interview with Emmanuel Levinas", in Robert Bernasconi and David Wood (eds), *Provocation of Levinas: Rethinking the Other*. London: Routledge, 168–180.

Levinas, Emmanuel (2008) "The Contemporary Relevance of Maimonides" (translated by M. Fagenblatt), *Journal of Jewish Thought and Philosophy* 16 (1), 91–94.

Levinas, Emmanuel (2009) *Carnets de captivité et autres inédits*. Paris: Éditions Grasset & Fasquelle.

Moore, A. W. (1987) "Beauty in the Transcendental Idealism of Kant and Wittgenstein", *British Journal of Aesthetics* 27 (2), 129–137.

Moore, A. W. (2013) "Was the Author of the *Tractatus* a Transcendental Idealist?" in P. Sullivan and M. Potter (eds), *Wittgenstein's* Tractatus: *History and Interpretation*. Oxford: Oxford University Press, 239–255.

Morgan, Michael (2007) *Discovering Levinas*. Cambridge: Cambridge University Press.

Øvergaard, Soren (2007) "The Ethical Residue of Language in Levinas and Early Wittgenstein", *Philosophy and Social Criticism* 33 (2), 223–249.

Pears, David (1987) *The False Prison*. Vol. I. Oxford: Clarendon Press.

Petitdemange, Guy (2003) *Philosophes et philosophies du XXe siècle*. Paris: Le Seuil.

Plant, Bob (2005) *Wittgenstein and Levinas: Ethical and Religious Thought*. London: Routledge.

Salanskis, Jean-Michel (2015) *Le concret et l'idéal: Levinas vivant III*. Paris: Klincksieck.

Shaw, Joshua (2008) *Emmanuel Levinas on the Priority of Ethics*. New York: Cambria Press.

Stenius, Erik (1960) *Wittgenstein's* Tractatus: *A Critical Study of Its Main Lines of Thought*. Oxford: Basil Blackwell.

Sullivan, Peter (1996) "The 'Truth' in Solipsism, and Wittgenstein's Rejection of the A Priori", *European Journal of Philosophy* 4, 195–219.

Waismann, Friedrich (1965) "Notes on Talks with Wittgenstein", *The Philosophical Review* 74 (1), 12–16.

Part II

Grammar, Linguistic Community, and Value in Wittgenstein's Later Philosophy

4 "We Can Go No Further": Meaning, Use, and the Limits of Language

William Child

Is it possible to give a substantive, non-circular account of meaning and rule-following – an account that explains what it is for someone to use a word with a particular meaning, or to follow a particular rule, in terms that do not employ the concept of meaning or the concept of following a rule? Naturalists and reductionists about meaning and rules think it is possible to give such an account. Anti-reductionists, by contrast, hold that facts about meaning and rules are basic and *sui generis*; they cannot be reduced to, or explained in terms of, non-semantic, non-rule-involving facts. Where does Wittgenstein stand in this debate? And is he right? I shall argue that Wittgenstein is an anti-reductionist about meaning and rule-following, and that anti-reductionism is the correct view to take.

Section 1 shows how the issue of reductionism and anti-reductionism about meaning and rules relates to the idea of the limits of language as it figures in Wittgenstein's post-*Tractatus* writings. Section 2 presents a framework for assessing the interpretative debate between reductionist and anti-reductionist readings of Wittgenstein. Section 3 argues that we cannot settle that debate on the basis of Wittgenstein's general, methodological opposition to reductionism. Section 4 presents an important argument for anti-reductionism from *Remarks on the Foundations of Mathematics*. Section 5 considers some putative evidence of reductionism about meaning in the *Brown Book* and offers an alternative, anti-reductionist interpretation. Section 6 explores the nature of Wittgenstein's anti-reductionism. It argues, first, that Wittgenstein accepts that semantic and normative facts supervene on non-semantic, non-normative facts and, second, that at many points his treatment of meaning and rules is not confined to the kind of pleonastic claims that are often taken to define non-reductionist, or quietist, positions. Section 7 concludes.

1. The Limits of Language

The idea of the limits of language is a central theme in the *Tractatus*. Wittgenstein writes in the Preface that "the aim of the book is to draw a limit to thought" and explains that it is "only in language that the limit can be drawn" (TLP, 3). The discussion of solipsism begins with the claim that

"*The limits of my language* mean the limits of my world" (TLP 5.6, italics in original) and goes on to explore the implications of that claim. Elsewhere, we are told that philosophy "must set limits to what can be thought; and, in doing so, to what cannot be thought", and that its way of setting those limits is to "signify what cannot be said, by presenting clearly what can be said" (TLP 4.114, 4.115). And so on. By contrast, there are few comments in Wittgenstein's post-*Tractatus* work that explicitly mention the limits of language. But there are some. And they express a theme that runs through Wittgenstein's later work and marks an important point of continuity with his earlier writings. We can sum up that theme in a slogan from 1930: we "cannot use language to get outside language" (PR, 54).

The general idea behind that slogan is that thought and description take place within a system of concepts, categories, and standards: which is to say, within language. We cannot get outside language and think about or describe the world in a way that does not employ the concepts, categories, and standards that are built into language. So there are limits to what we can use language to do. I will mention three applications of that idea.

First, Wittgenstein insists that we cannot use language to advance general metaphysical claims about reality. As he puts it: "Time and again the attempt is made to use language to limit the world and set it in relief – but it can't be done" (PR, 80; BT, 315). "Us[ing] language to limit the world" would be using it to make a general restrictive claim about the nature of reality: a claim to the effect that reality comprises only some subset of the general kinds of fact that we ordinarily take it to include. Wittgenstein's basic objection to any such view is that, in order to "limit the world" in this way, we would need a language with which to distinguish what is genuinely part of reality from what we ordinarily but mistakenly take to be part of reality. But there is no such language: no special, philosophical language that captures the world as it really is and can be used to make our restrictive claims. (As Wittgenstein puts it elsewhere, "philosophy doesn't use a preparatory language" [RFM, 392].) The point of this *Philosophical Remarks* claim, that we cannot use language to limit the world, is essentially the same as the point Wittgenstein makes in the *Tractatus* when he writes: "we cannot say in logic, 'The world has this in it, and this; but not that' " (TLP 5.61).

Second, Wittgenstein claims that we cannot use language to characterize a connection between language, on the one hand, and the world as it is in itself, independent of language, on the other hand. As he puts it:

> The limit of language manifests itself in the impossibility of describing the fact that corresponds to (is the translation of) a sentence without simply repeating the sentence. (We are involved here with the Kantian solution of the problem of philosophy.)
>
> (CV, 13, 10.2.1931)

If we ask what fact corresponds to the sentence "p", Wittgenstein thinks, the only possible answer is "the fact that p".[1] So though we can if we want conceive of meaning or representation in terms of a relation between sentences and facts (or possible facts), the relation in question is, in an important sense, a relation within language. For the facts to which sentences correspond are themselves shaped by, and individuated in terms of, linguistic categories.

Third, Wittgenstein claims that the impossibility of using language to get outside language means that "in a certain sense, the use of language is something that cannot be taught":

> Suppose I have said to someone "A is ill", but he doesn't know who I mean by "A", and I now point at a man, saying "This is A". Here the expression is a definition, but this can only be understood if he has already gathered what kind of object it is through his understanding of the grammar of the proposition "A is ill". But this means that any kind of explanation of a language presupposes a language already. And in a certain sense, the use of language is something that cannot be taught, i.e. I cannot use language to teach it in the way in which language could be used to teach someone to play the piano. – And that of course is just another way of saying: I cannot use language to get outside language.
>
> (PR, 54)

No one could be taught to speak and understand a first language by being given an explanation of how she must use words in order to speak that language. For she could not understand the explanation unless she already understood a language: the language in which the explanation was given. By contrast, she could be taught to play the piano by being given an explanation of what she must do in order to play the piano. To understand that explanation, she must already understand the language in which it is given. But she need not already be able to play the piano. The underlying point here is the same as the point that Wittgenstein makes in the early sections of *Philosophical Investigations* and the *Brown Book* when he insists that the acquisition of one's first language cannot depend on a process of ostensive definition or explanation but must instead involve ostensive training.

Now what, if anything, do these observations about the limits of language have to do with the debate between reductionism and anti-reductionism about meaning and rules? In RFM, Wittgenstein writes: "what the correct following of a rule consists in cannot be described *more closely* than by describing the *learning* of 'proceeding according to the rule'"; "we can go no further" (RFM, 392). The point of saying that "we can go no further" than that in describing what the correct following of a rule consists in is that we cannot give an informative, non-circular explanation of what it is to follow a rule correctly. That is a clear state-ment of anti-reductionism. It also states a limit of language: a limit to what we can use language to do. We can put the point in a way that brings out the connection between our two themes – anti-reductionism and the limits of language – by adapting the formulation Wittgenstein uses in CV 13: "The limit of language", we might say, "manifests itself in the impossibility of describing what the correct following of a particular rule consists in without simply employing an expression of that rule."[2]

But it is one thing to make such a claim of anti-reductionism. It is another thing to justify it: to explain what reason there is for thinking that "we can go no further" than Wittgenstein says. We will take up that question in Section 4.

2. Meaning and Use

Wittgenstein says that "the meaning of a word is its use in the language" (PI §43).[3] How are we to understand that idea?

Many commentators take Wittgenstein to be advancing a kind of reductionism about meaning. On that reading, the point of the idea that meaning is use is to explain semantic facts about words (the fact that the word "red" means *red*, for instance) in terms of non-semantic facts about them (the fact, for example, that people who have been through the nor-mal training will, in appropriate circumstances, by and large produce the word "red" in response to red things). According to Michael Dummett, for instance, when Wittgenstein describes the use of language,

> what is described is the complex of activities with which the utter-ances of sentences are interwoven; and . . . the description does not invoke psychological or semantic concepts, but is couched entirely in terms of what is open to outward view.
>
> (Dummett 1978, 446)

Paul Horwich takes the same view; Wittgenstein's "examples of the meaning-constituting uses of words", he writes, "are never couched in semantic or intentional terms" (Horwich 2012, 112). And Paul Snow-don, in a recent paper, offers a similar interpretation, arguing that Witt-genstein advances a broadly reductive or constitutive form of naturalism about meaning and rule-following (Snowdon 2018).

Other commentators, by contrast, understand Wittgenstein as an anti-reductionist about meaning and rules. They agree that, for Wittgenstein, "there can be nothing more to an expression's having a certain meaning than its being used in a certain determinate way" (Stroud 2012, 26). But they maintain that the notion of "use" in this context has to be under-stood in semantic or intentional terms; a description of the use of an expression that "suffices to fix its meaning" must itself "employ the idea of meaning" (ibid., 27). So all we can say about the way in which use determines meaning is this: the word "red" means *red* because we use it to mean *red*; the words "add 2 each time" mean *add two each time* because they "are used by us to mean that two is to be added each time" (ibid., 27); and so on.[4]

Which of these interpretations of Wittgenstein's conception of meaning and use is correct? In addressing that question, I shall focus on two important strands in his remarks. On the one hand, there is clear evidence of anti-reductionism in Wittgenstein's work. In particular, there are his explicit general statements of quietism and of opposition to reductionism. And there is his insistence on the impossibility of giving any non-circular account of what, say, following a particular rule consists in. On the other hand, he does not adopt the crudest or most militantly anti-reductive position. In the first place, he does not think that facts about meaning are completely independent of non-semantic facts about use; on the contrary, he has things to say about the relation between semantic facts on the one hand and non-semantic facts on the other. In the second place, when he raises questions about the difference between following a rule and merely conforming to a rule, or about the circumstances under which it is right to translate a word of a foreign language in a particular way, he does not give merely pleonastic answers but aims to say something genuinely informative. To understand Wittgenstein's position, we need to understand the relation between these two strands in his work: the combination of anti-reductionism about meaning and rules with a willingness to describe the phenomena in a way that is not wholly pleonastic.

That combination of views is nicely expressed in a passage from RFM: "Don't demand too much, and don't be afraid that your just demand will dwindle into nothing" (RFM, 383). The passage comes in the context of a discussion of mathematics and the relation between mathematical propositions and empirical facts. But the point Wittgenstein is making applies equally to our case. On the one hand, we should not demand a reduction of semantic facts to non-semantic facts. On the other hand, we are entitled to demand some account of the relation between semantic and non-semantic facts; and we should not be afraid that the only thing to say about that relation will be something entirely trivial and pleonastic.[5]

3. Wittgenstein's Anti-Reductionist Metaphilosophy

It might be thought that the question, whether Wittgenstein's account of meaning and rule-following is a form of reductionism, is easily settled in the negative – and against such interpreters as Dummett, Horwich, and Snowdon. For doesn't Wittgenstein state explicitly and repeatedly that philosophy should reject all forms of reductionism? He says, for example, that "it can never be our job to reduce anything to anything, or to explain anything. Philosophy really *is* 'purely descriptive'" (BB, 18). And he expresses a similarly anti-reductionist message when he speaks approvingly of "That marvellous motto, 'everything is what it is and not another thing'" (LC, 27).[6] So, it will be said, there is no question of Wittgenstein's offering an account in which facts about meaning and rule-following are reduced to, or constructed from, non-semantic, non-normative facts. To offer such an account would be to ignore his own injunction that it is not the job of a philosopher to reduce anything to anything. And it would fly in the face of his insistence that meaning and rule-following are what they are and not other things.

The prominence in Wittgenstein's work of such statements of anti-reductionism plainly carries some weight. But we cannot rest the whole case for an anti-reductionist reading of Wittgenstein's view of meaning and rules on these general disavowals of reductionism. For we cannot tell, at this level of generality, where Wittgenstein himself would draw the line between an objectionably reductionist view and an acceptable, non-reductionist view. Suppose you are giving a naturalistic account of meaning of the kind that Dummett and others attribute to Wittgenstein, in which a sign's having the meaning it does is explained in terms of its role in a complex pattern of non-semantic behaviour. And suppose that, in your view, that account of meaning is a piece of common sense: a statement of what we all ordinarily acknowledge when we free ourselves from philosophical prejudices. Then in giving your naturalistic account, you will not see yourself as reducing facts about meaning to something else. On the contrary, you will take yourself to be giving a descriptive account of meaning, as Wittgenstein requires. And you will think that any supposed features of meaning that cannot be accommodated within your naturalistic account are not genuine features of meaning at all; that they are artefacts of a bad philosophical picture of meaning. We know from Wittgenstein's general methodological stance that he will reject any position about meaning or rule-following that he takes to conflict with our common-sense understanding of the phenomena or to involve reducing semantic and normative facts to something else. But without knowing precisely what he takes to be part of that common-sense understanding, we cannot tell which specific views he would regard as being unacceptably revisionary or reductionist.

I think Wittgenstein does reject the kind of reductionist naturalism about meaning and rule-following that is suggested by interpreters like Dummett, Horwich, and Snowdon. But to establish that point, we have to examine the details of his discussion of rules and meaning. There is no quick way of defending an anti-reductionist interpretation by appeal to his general statements about philosophy.[7]

4. An Argument for Anti-Reductionism

In RFM 392–393, Wittgenstein gives a clear statement of anti-reductionism about rules. And he offers an argument in favour of that position. What is the argument? Is it a good argument?

Wittgenstein writes:

> A language-game, in which someone calculates according to a rule and places the blocks of a building according to the results of the calculation. He has learnt to operate with written signs according to rules. – Once you have described the procedure of this teaching and learning, you have said everything that can be said about acting correctly according to a rule. We can go no further. It is no use, for example, to go back to the concept of agreement, because it is no more certain that one proceeding is in agreement with another, than that it has happened in accordance with [the] rule. Admittedly going according to a rule is also founded on an agreement.
>
> To repeat, what the correct following of a rule consists in cannot be described *more closely* than by describing the *learning* of "proceeding according to the rule". And this description is an everyday one, like that of cooking and sewing, for example. It presupposes as much as these. It distinguishes one thing from another, and so it informs a human being who is ignorant of something particular. (Cf. the remark: Philosophy doesn't use a preparatory language, etc.)
>
> For if you give me a description of how people are trained in following a rule and how they react correctly according to the training, you will yourself employ the expression of a rule in the description and will presuppose that I understand it.
>
> (RFM, 392–393; translation
> slightly adjusted)

Paragraph 2 of that passage contains a clear, anti-reductionist message: "what the correct following of a rule consists in cannot be described *more closely* than by describing the *learning* of 'proceeding according to the rule'". That repeats a claim made in paragraph 1: "Once you have described this procedure of teaching and learning, you have said everything that can be said about acting correctly according to a rule. We can go no further." But what reasons does Wittgenstein have for saying this? What stops us from "going further" and giving a non-circular, constitutive account of what it is to act correctly according to a rule?

It is important first to be clear about what exactly it is that Wittgenstein is saying cannot be reductively explained. When he talks about "what the correct following of a rule consists in", and about "acting correctly according to a rule", what is he referring to? We need to distinguish between two kinds of question: (a) questions about *rules themselves* (e.g., the question, what one must put after "1000" in order to act in accordance with the rule *add* 2); and (b) questions about what it is for a person to *follow* those rules (e.g., the question, what makes it the case that someone who puts "1002" after "1000" is following the add-2 rule, rather than merely conforming to it). Wittgenstein's concern in RFM 392–393 is predominantly with questions of type (a) rather than questions of type (b). He is concerned with the question, what it takes for an act to accord with a particular rule, rather than the question, what it takes for someone to be following that rule rather than merely conforming to it. But there is every reason to think that he has a similarly anti-reductionist approach to answering (b)-type questions.

Now what reason does Wittgenstein give for the anti-reductionist position he articulates in RFM 392–3? What prevents us describing what the correct following of a rule consists in more closely than by describing the learning of "proceeding according to a rule"? Paragraph 3 ("For if you give me a description of how people are trained in following a rule . . .") offers an answer to that question. But how exactly does that passage count in favour of anti-reductionism?

It might be suggested that Wittgenstein is making essentially the same point in this passage that we saw him making in the passage from PR 54 that I quoted in Section 1 above. His point there was that "any kind of explanation of a language presupposes a language already"; so we cannot use language to teach a language to someone who does not already have one. Someone might read paragraph 3 of RFM 392–393 in a similar way, as offering the following argument. "If you give me a description of what it is to follow a rule correctly, you will employ expressions of rules in your description. I can only understand your explanation, therefore, if I already understand the expressions of rules it contains. And I can only do that if I can already follow rules. So there cannot be a description of what it is to follow a rule correctly that could be used to teach someone how to follow rules in the first place. For if she cannot already follow rules, she will not understand the explanation."

That argument, however, does not show that it is impossible to give a reductive explanation of what it is to follow a particular rule correctly: of what it is to act correctly according to that rule. For consider. Suppose for the sake of argument that there was some correct, non-circular, reductive account of what it is to follow a particular rule correctly: say, an account on which what counts as following the rule correctly at a particular step is defined in terms of the responses given by the majority of people who have been through a certain training.[8] And suppose we agree that in order to understand that account, we would already have to be able to follow rules.[9] It follows that we couldn't use the reductive account to teach someone how to follow rules in the first place. But that would not prevent it being a successful reductive account. The requirement for a reductive account of rules is that it should explain what counts as following a given rule correctly in terms that do not simply presuppose it. There is no requirement that it should be something that could be used to impart the ability to follow the rule to someone who could not already follow any rules.[10]

However, it is a mistake to read the argument of RFM 392–393 paragraph 3 in the way just sketched. Wittgenstein is indeed offering an argument against the possibility of a reductive account of what the correct following of a rule consists in. But his argument is different. His fundamental claim is that the only way to specify what it is to follow a particular rule correctly is to use an expression of that very rule. That is a point he makes in many places. For example:

> How does one describe the process of learning a rule? – If A claps his hands, B is always supposed to do it too. Remember that the description of a language-game is already a description.
>
> (RFM, 320)

His point is this. When I describe the process of learning a particular rule, I must say what it is that the learner is learning to do. That requires me to say what counts as acting correctly according to the rule she is learning. In the current case, we can suppose that the rule B is learning is this: "Whenever A claps a rhythm, clap the same rhythm". Call that "the Clapping Rule". What counts as acting correctly according to the Clapping Rule? The obvious answer is this: whenever A claps a rhythm, clapping the same rhythm. Wittgenstein's point is that, although that answer is true, it does nothing to explain *what it is* to clap the same rhythm as A; it simply takes that for granted. And, he thinks, the same will be true for any other answer we might give. The only way of describing what counts as acting correctly according to the Clapping Rule is to employ some expression of the Clapping Rule itself. As we put it earlier: the limit of language manifests itself in the impossibility of describing what following a particular rule consists in without simply employing an expression of that very rule. It is impossible to give a non-circular, reductive account of what it is to act correctly according to a particular rule.

That is the argument that Wittgenstein articulates in paragraph 3 of the passage from RFM 392–3. It is also the argument that he offers in paragraph 1, where he says "It is no use . . . to go back to the concept of agreement, because it is no more certain that one proceeding is in agreement with another, than that it has happened in accordance with [the] rule".[11] Suppose someone offers an account like this: What it is to follow the Clapping Rule correctly in a particular set of circumstances is to behave in a way that agrees with the way A has behaved in those circumstances. As before, that claim is true. But it does not explain what it is to follow the Clapping Rule in terms that do not presuppose it. For what it is for B's behaviour to *agree with A's behaviour* is no simpler or more basic than what it is for B's behaviour to be *in accordance with the*

Clapping Rule. We cannot use the idea of agreement to give a reductive explanation of what correctly following the Clapping Rule consists in.

These remarks of Wittgenstein's state an anti-reductionist view: the only way of specifying what it is to follow a particular rule correctly is to employ an expression of that very rule. But does he offer an argument for that claim; or does he simply assert that it is true? In other passages, he mentions a range of possible reductive accounts that someone might consider. For instance:

> The question arises, what we take as [the] criterion of going according to the rule. Is it for example a feeling of satisfaction that accompanies the act of going according to the rule? Or an intuition (intimation) that tells me I have gone right? Or is it certain practical consequences of proceeding that determine whether I have really followed the rule?
>
> (RFM, 319)

Each of those suggestions ("a feeling of satisfaction", "an intuition", "certain practical consequences") points to a candidate reductive account: an account that aims to spell out what it is to act correctly according to a particular rule in terms that do not presuppose it. But Wittgenstein thinks that all of these accounts are obviously unsatisfactory. In the first place, they get the extension of the rule wrong. Acting with a feeling of satisfaction, for example, is neither necessary nor sufficient for acting in accord with a rule: we sometimes have feelings of satisfaction when we fail to act correctly according to the rule we are trying to follow; and we do not always have feelings of satisfaction when we succeed in following the rule correctly. And similarly for the other proposals. In the second place, the candidate accounts go wrong by making it an empirical issue what counts as applying the rule correctly in a particular case. As Wittgenstein puts it, if one of these proposals were correct:

> it would be possible that 4 + 1 sometimes made 5 and sometimes something else. It would be thinkable, that is to say, that an experimental investigation would show whether 4 + 1 always makes 5.
>
> (RFM, 319)

But those things are obviously not possible and not thinkable. That is to say, these reductive accounts fail to capture the internal or conceptual character of the connection between a rule and what counts as acting correctly according to the rule. And, Wittgenstein thinks, the same problems will arise for any other reductive account.[12] Admittedly, he does not offer a proof that there could be no successful reductive account. But anti-reductionist positions can rarely be established by proof. The anti-reductionist can demonstrate the inadequacy of particular reductionist proposals by producing counter-examples. Beyond that, however, the case for anti-reductionism must rest on the plausibility of the claim that the failure of those particular proposals is symptomatic of a general problem with any reductionist proposal. And, of course, the anti-reductionist must stand ready to consider other reductionist accounts if they are proposed, and to show how they fail.

As I have said, the topic of the anti-reductionist considerations Wittgenstein offers in RFM 392–393 is what I called the (a)-type question: what it is to act correctly according to a given rule. Someone might accept that we cannot give a reductive answer to that question, but maintain that we can nonetheless give a non-circular, reductive answer to the (b)-type question: what it is to *follow* a particular rule, rather than merely acting in accordance with it. That is a possible position in logical space. But, as I read him, it is not Wittgenstein's position. His approach to the (b)-type question is as resolutely anti-reductionist as is his approach to the (a)-type question.[13]

5. Language-Games in *The Brown Book*

I have claimed that, when Wittgenstein says that the meaning of a word is its use in the language, the notion of use has to be understood in an anti-reductionist way. As I have noted, however, many commentators disagree. And the language-games described in the *Brown Book* are sometimes cited as evidence of Wittgenstein's treating the relation between meaning and use in broadly reductive terms. So I want to consider a representative *Brown Book* example that might seem to support a reductionist reading of Wittgenstein. I shall show how it can be accommodated within the anti-reductionist interpretation I am advocating.

Wittgenstein writes:

> Consider this language game: A sends B to various houses in their town to fetch goods of various sorts from various people. A gives B various lists. On top of every list he puts a scribble, and B is trained to go to that house on the door of which he finds the same scribble, this is the name of the house. In the first column of every list he then finds one or more scribbles which he has been taught to read out. When he enters the house he calls out these words, and every inhabitant of the house has been trained to run up to him when a certain one of these sounds is called out, these sounds are the names of the people. He then addresses himself to each one of them in turn and shows to each two consecutive scribbles which stand on the list against his name. The first of these two, people in that town have been trained to associate with some particular kind of object, say, apples. The second is one of a series of scribbles which each man carries about him on a slip of paper. The person thus addressed fetches say, five apples. The first scribble was the generic name of the objects required, the second, the name of their number.

What now is the relation between a name and the object named, say, the house and its name? I suppose we could give either of two answers. The one is that the relation consists in certain strokes having been painted on the door of the house. The second answer I meant is that the relation we are concerned with is established, not just by painting these strokes on the door, but by the particular role which they play in the practice of our language as we have been sketching it. – Again, the relation of the name of a person to the person here consists in the person having been trained to run up to someone who calls out the name; or again, we might say that it consists in this and the whole of the usage of the name in the language-game.

(BB, 172)

On one reading, this passage and others like it show Wittgenstein taking a broadly reductive approach to meaning. His idea, on this interpretation, is that a sign's being the name of something – a house, a person, a kind of fruit, a number – consists in the existence of an appropriate pattern of non-semantic behaviour involving that sign. Thus, when Wittgenstein describes "the usage" of the name, he avoids characterizing that usage in semantic terms. He does not talk about such actions as using a scribble as *the name of* a particular person, or using it to *call someone "NN"*, or to *say something about* someone. On the contrary, he confines himself to describing simple, non-semantic actions and interactions between people. It is, on this reading, the role of a sign in such patterns of simple, non-semantic behaviour that is constitutive of its being used as a name.

If we accept that interpretation of the *Brown Book* passage, there is a question about how far the reductive account is supposed to go. Wittgenstein's description of the use of the scribbles includes such phenomena as people *calling out* words, *running up to* someone, *addressing themselves to* other people, *fetching* apples, and so on. Those characterizations may be non-semantic. But, on the face of it, they are not non-intentional; for *calling out* words, *running up to* people, and the rest are intentional actions. So if Wittgenstein is gesturing at a reductive account of meaning, the reduction in question will be a limited one; it will not yield an account of facts about meaning in non-intentional terms.

In my view, however, the *Brown Book* passage is not proposing a reductive account of meaning at all. What Wittgenstein is describing in this example is not our language but a simpler and more primitive language-game. In our community, there are facts of these kinds: someone's saying that someone is such-and-such; someone's calling someone "NN"; someone's using the sign "NN" as a person's name; and so on. In the *Brown Book* language-game, by contrast, there are no semantic facts of that kind: the pattern of sign-involving activity that Wittgenstein describes is too basic and primitive to be a practice of giving and using names. So, though he describes the scribbles as "names" in the context of the example, they are not what we would call "names". But they play a role in the simple language-game that is analogous to the role of names in our language. So we can use the simple language-game to make a point about the relation between signs and things that is equally true of the relation between names and objects in our language. In particular, the point of the example is that the relation between a sign and a thing is not constituted by anything "static": a scribble being painted on a house; the fact that someone has been trained to run up when a particular sound is called out; and so forth. Rather, it essentially involves something "dynamic": the role of the scribble in the whole practice of the language-game.[14] Wittgenstein makes that point in connection with the primitive, scribble language-game. But the point applies equally well to the relation between a full-blown name in our language and the thing or person whose name it is. The simple language-game is introduced as a way of making that point about our language.

That way of understanding the *Brown Book* passage fits well with what Wittgenstein says about the role of language-games in his method:

> Our clear and simple language-games are not preliminary studies for a future regimentation of language – as it were, first approximations, ignoring friction and air resistance. Rather, the language-games stand there as *objects of comparison* which, through similarities and dissimilarities, are meant to throw light on features of our language.
>
> (PI §130)

The scribble example is a "clear and simple language-game". Wittgenstein is not offering it as a preliminary stage in a prospective full account of language. He is not suggesting that we can build up from the simple case to give an account that shows how the relation between name and object in our language is constituted by a sufficiently complex pattern of the kinds of simple, non-semantic action that he describes. Rather, he is using the scribble example as an "object of comparison" to make a point about the simple case that is true of our language, too. Seen in that light, the scribble example offers no evidence in favour of the suggestion that Wittgenstein takes a reductionist view of meaning and use.

6. Supervenience and the Avoidance of Pleonasm

I have argued that Wittgenstein is an anti-reductionist: facts about meaning, rules, and rule-following, he thinks, are *sui generis*; they cannot be reduced to, or explained in terms of, facts about anything else. On the other hand, however, he does think that there is a close relation between semantic and normative facts on the one hand, and lower-level, non-semantic and non-normative facts on the other; if the lower-level facts were very different, then the semantic and normative facts would be different, too. And Wittgenstein aims to say something substantive and non-pleonastic in response to constitutive questions about meaning and rules. These latter aspects of his treatment distinguish his view from the simplest, most flat-footed kinds of anti-reductionism. How should we understand this element of his position?

6.1 Supervenience, Rules, and Meaning

Though Wittgenstein is clearly opposed to attempts to reduce facts about meaning and rule-following to more basic facts, he is equally clear that there is an important relation between semantic and normative facts, on the one hand, and facts characterized in non-semantic, non-normative, terms on the other hand. For instance:

> What if we said that mathematical propositions were prophecies in *this* sense: they predict what result members of a society who have learnt this technique will get in agreement with other members of the society? "25 × 25 = 625" would thus mean that men, if we judge them to obey the rules of multiplication, will reach the result 625 when they multiply 25 × 25. – That this is a correct prediction is beyond doubt; and also that calculating is in essence founded on such predictions. That is to say, we should not call something "calculating" if we could not make such a prophecy with certainty. This really means: calculating is a technique. And what we had said pertains to the essence of a technique.
>
> (RFM, 192–193)

One message of that passage is that the existence of a practice of calculating requires the existence of a pattern of empirical regularities in behaviour, non-normatively characterized. If it weren't true that people who have been through the normal training in calculation, and have been accepted as competent in multiplication, by and large give the result "625" when asked what 25 × 25 equals, there would be no practice of multiplying in our community.[15]

It is natural to express Wittgenstein's view in terms of supervenience. Facts about rule-following cannot be reduced to, or explained in terms of, non-normative facts about people's behaviour; but they do supervene on such non-normative facts. That is to say, two worlds cannot differ with respect to facts about rule-following without differing in some non-normative respect; and if two worlds are alike in all non-normative respects, they must also be alike with respect to all the facts about rule-following. In the same way, semantic facts cannot be reduced to, or explained in terms of, non-semantic facts; but they do supervene on non-semantic facts.[16]

6.2 Supervenience and Common-Sense Psychology

We can reach the same understanding of Wittgenstein's position from a different direction, by considering the picture of the nature and status of common-sense psychology that he offers in *Last Writings on the Philosophy of Psychology* volume II.

Wittgenstein presents common-sense psychology as a *sui generis* scheme of description and explanation: a scheme that we all use when we talk and think about ourselves and others. And, he thinks, we should accept such talk at face value and understand it on its own terms. In his words:

> I look at this language-game as autonomous. I merely want to describe it, or look at it, not justify it.
>
> (LW II, 40)

The descriptions and explanations of common-sense psychology cannot be reduced to, or correlated with, or explained in terms of, those of the physical sciences. But that does nothing to undermine them or to threaten their truth. For common-sense psychology does not depend for its legitimacy on the possibility of any such reduction or correlation. It is, as Wittgenstein says, autonomous.

At the same time, he insists that the truth of psychological descriptions and explanations does not require the existence of anything that is not provided for by the physical sciences. "Mental", as Wittgenstein puts it, "is not a metaphysical, but a logical, epithet" (LW II, 63). Physical investigation could in principle give a complete account of the physical make-up of a person, and of the physical processes that take place within a person and produce the movements of their body, including the movements involved in speaking: an account that did not mention thoughts, intentions, experiences and so on.[17] But the possibility of such a physical account does not undermine the descriptions and explanations of common-sense psychology. For common-sense psychology does not depend on the assumption that human behaviour is produced by non-physical mechanisms; it is compatible with accepting that human beings are exhaustively composed of physical matter.

What emerges from Wittgenstein's comments about the status of common-sense psychology is the following picture. On the one hand, common-sense psychology is a *sui generis* scheme for describing and explaining the behaviour of human beings. It cannot be reduced to, or correlated with, the physical scheme. On the other hand, common-sense psychology does not introduce any distinctive, non-physical ontology. If we fix all the physical facts, we fix all the facts, including the facts of common-sense psychology – and the facts about meanings and rules. That way of putting things would not normally be associated with Wittgenstein. But, I think, it is completely faithful to his views. And it is of a piece with the ideas about supervenience sketched in 6.i.

6.3 Anti-Reductionism Without Pleonasm

A third way of approaching the character of Wittgenstein's anti-reductionism is to consider how he responds to his own constitutive questions about rules and meanings.

What does it take for someone to be *following* a rule rather than merely *conforming* to a rule? Wittgenstein's response to that question is not simply to say, pleonastically, that what it takes for someone to be following a particular rule is, precisely, for them to be following that rule. He tries to say something more informative than that. We can illustrate the point with an example. Wittgenstein writes:

> Let us consider very simple rules. Let the expression be a figure, say this one:
>
> $$| - - |$$
>
> and one follows the rule by drawing a straight sequence of such figures (perhaps as an ornament).
>
> $$| - - || - - || - - || - - || - - |$$
>
> Under what circumstances should we say: someone gives a rule by writing down such a figure? Under what circumstances: someone is following this rule when he draws that sequence? It is difficult to describe this.
>
> If one of a pair of chimpanzees once scratched the figure $| - - |$ in the earth and thereupon the other the series $| - - || - - |$ etc., the first would not have given a rule nor would the other be following it, whatever else went on at the same time in the minds of the two of them.
>
> If however there were observed, e.g., the phenomenon of a kind of instruction, of showing how and of imitation, of lucky and misfiring attempts, of reward and punishment and the like; if at length the one who had been so trained put figures which he had never seen before one after another in sequence as in the first example, then we should probably say that the one chimpanzee was writing rules down, and the other was following them.
>
> (RFM, 345)

The behaviour of the chimpanzees can be described in terms that do not presuppose that a rule is being given and followed; the first chimpanzee scratches the figure $| - - |$ in the earth and the second scratches the series $| - - || - - |$ etc. If that is just a one-off occurrence, Wittgenstein says, no rule has been given or followed. When it happens in the right kind of context, however, we do have a case of giving and following a rule. But what exactly are the circumstances under which we should say that a rule is being given and followed? The simplest anti-reductionist response would be to say merely that the circumstances under which we should say that a rule is being given and followed are just those in which people (or chimpanzees) are participating in a practice of giving and following rules. But that is not what Wittgenstein says. Instead, he tries to say something genuinely illuminating and non-pleonastic about what it takes for there to be a custom of giving and following such rules, and what it takes for two people (or chimpanzees) to be participants in such a practice. In particular, he suggests that the existence of a practice of following rules involves the existence of a whole pattern of rule-involving activity. Some of the activities he mentions in RFM 345 are particular to the situation of learning: instruction, showing how, imitation, etc. Others are more general: reward and punishment, for instance. But the most basic feature of rule-following, which is implicit in all the activities Wittgenstein mentions, is that giving or following rules involves *treating* or *understanding* actions as being correct or incorrect. The idea of understanding an action as correct or incorrect is no more basic than the idea of following a rule itself.[18] So Wittgenstein's comments do not promise a reductive account of what it is for people (or chimpanzees) to be giving and following rules. But they do offer genuine illumination by describing, in non-reductive terms, the kind of complex structure of activities that he takes to be required if something is to count as an instance of giving or following a rule.[19]

We can see the same features in Wittgenstein's non-reductionist treatment of the relation between meaning and use. At one point in the *Brown Book*, Wittgenstein imagines an objection to some of the cases he describes:

> It is an important remark concerning this example and others which we give that one may object to the description which we give of the language of a tribe, that in the specimens we give of their language we let them speak English, thereby already presupposing the whole background of the English language, that is, our usual meanings of the words. Thus if I say that in a certain language there is no special verb for "skipping", but that this language uses instead the form "making the test for throwing the boomerang", one may ask how I have characterized the use of the expressions, "make a test for" and "throwing the boomerang", to be justified in substituting these English expressions for whatever their actual words may be. To this we must answer that we have only given a very sketchy description of the practices of our fictitious languages, in some cases only hints, but that one can easily make these descriptions more complete.
>
> (BB, 102)

The "more complete" descriptions would spell out how the words or phrases in question are used, in a way that explained why, or how, they have the same meanings as the relevant English expressions. Thus:

> whether a word of the language of our tribe is rightly translated into a word of the English language depends upon the role this word

plays in the whole life of the tribe; the occasions on which it is used, the expressions of emotion by which it is generally accompanied, the ideas which it generally awakens or which prompt its saying, etc., etc. As an exercise ask yourself: in which cases would you say that a certain word uttered by the people of the tribe was a greeting? In which cases should we say it corresponded to our "Goodbye", in which to our "Hello"?

(BB, 103)

We can say, of course, that a word of an unfamiliar language corresponds to our word "Goodbye" just in case it is used by speakers of that language in the same way that we use the word "Goodbye": or, more simply, if it is used by those speakers to mean *Goodbye*. But can we get beyond pleonastic statements like that? Can we spell out, in non-semantic, non-intentional terms, exactly how the word "Goodbye" is used in our language and, therefore, how a word in another language must be used in order to be rightly translated as "Goodbye"? There is nothing in Wittgenstein's discussion to suggest that we can. But he does think that, when we consider particular cases, we can say something to justify particular assignments of meaning in a way that respects the constraint of anti-reductionism whilst going beyond the kinds of pleonastic formulation just mentioned.

We can illustrate that point with another part of the same discussion. Wittgenstein imagines a case in which "the men of a tribe are subjected to a kind of medical examination before going into war". An examiner puts them through tests involving various physical activities: skipping, lifting weights, etc. Wittgenstein asks what justifies translating some expression of these people's language by the English expression "Go through the test for throwing the boomerang". He offers the following as the kind of account that would justify such a translation:

The examiner uses orders for making the men go through the tests. These orders all begin with one particular expression which I could translate into the English words, "Go through the test". And this expression is followed by one which in actual warfare is used for certain actions. Thus there is a command upon which men throw their boomerangs and which therefore I should translate into, "Throw the boomerangs". Further, if a man gives an account of the battle to his chief, he again uses the expression I have translated into "throw a boomerang", this time in a description.

(BB, 102)

In that passage, Wittgenstein does not say merely that what justifies translating an expression by the English words "go through the test for throwing the boomerang" is that people use it to mean *go through the test for throwing the boomerang.* He does something to unpack what it takes for an expression to be used with that meaning: pointing to the kinds of feature that would in fact be appealed to by an anthropologist or a radical interpreter in coming to understand an unfamiliar language. Thus, he stresses that the expression contains a form of words that is an ingredient in a range of different orders; and that it contains another form of words that is used for the action of throwing boomerangs in descriptions as well as commands. But there is no suggestion in those comments that we could explain what it is for an expression to mean "throw a boomerang" in entirely non-semantic, non-intentional terms. Indeed, Wittgenstein simply helps himself to the semantic notions of an expression's being "used for" a certain action, and of an expression's being used in a "command" and in a "description". It is true that he then goes on to say something more about the kind of circumstances that would justify the judgement that a particular expression is "used for", or refers to, the action of throwing a boomerang; he mentions the fact that, when the expression is used in a command, it is followed by people throwing their boomerangs. But that fact does not come close to supplying a reductive account of meaning; the fact that the utterance of an expression is regularly followed by people throwing boomerangs is neither necessary nor sufficient for it to mean "throw a boomerang". Similarly, he goes on to say something about what it takes for an utterance to be a command or a description:

> what characterizes an order as such, or a description as such, or a question as such, etc., is – as we have said – the role which the utterance of these signs plays in the whole practice of the language.
>
> (BB, 102–103)

But there is no indication that the distinctive role that characterizes an utterance as an order, or a description, or a question can be specified in wholly non-semantic, non-intentional terms.

The picture of the relation of meaning and use that we get from this *Brown Book* discussion is this. What it takes for an expression of a language to have a given meaning is for it to be used in a particular way. The relevant way of using the expression cannot be spelled out in wholly non-semantic, non-intentional terms. Nonetheless, we can say something more about the meaning-constituting use of an expression than simply to repeat the pleonastic formulation that, for an expression to mean, say, "Goodbye" is for it to be used to mean *Goodbye*. That is the point that emerges from Wittgenstein's reflections on what would justify us in translating an unfamiliar expression by a particular English word or words. His view of the relation between meaning and use, like his view of rule-following, is an anti-reductionist one. But it is not the crudest kind of anti-reductionism. Facts about meaning and rules are not completely independent of non-semantic, non-normative facts; on the contrary, they supervene on them. And we are not confined to making pleonastic claims when we say how a word must be used in order to have a given meaning, or when we describe the conditions under which someone counts as following a rule.

7. Conclusion

I have argued that Wittgenstein's position about meaning and rules combines anti-reductionism with a willingness to go beyond merely pleonastic statements about meaning and use or about rules and rule-following. That message may seem uncontroversial. But neither element is universally accepted and both deserve emphasis. The anti-reductionist nature of Wittgenstein's treatment needs emphasis because some readers continue to see his view of meaning and rules as a form of reductionism.[20] And it is equally important to emphasize the non-pleonastic nature of his treatment, and his acceptance that facts about meaning and rules are grounded in, and supervene on, non-semantic, non-normative facts. One reason why some philosophers reject anti-reductionism about meaning and rules is the thought that, unless some form of reductionism were true, the existence of meaning and rules would conflict with a reasonable, naturalistic view of the world; it would imply the kind of Fregean non-naturalism that Wittgenstein plainly rejects. But that thought is mistaken. Wittgenstein's treatment shows how facts about meaning and rules can be grounded in non-semantic, non-normative facts without being reducible to, or explicable in terms of, anything non-semantic or non-normative.[21]

Notes

1. Wittgenstein's simple statement of the point is a bit too simple. For in cases of synonymy or analytic equivalence, we can pick out the fact that corresponds to a given sentence without repeating that very sentence. We can say, for instance, that the fact that corresponds to the sentence "John is a bachelor" is the fact that John is an unmarried man. The same is true when we use one language to talk about another. That complicates Wittgenstein's point, but it does not undermine his fundamental intuition.
2. For a related discussion of the limits of language theme in Wittgenstein's post-*Tractatus* writings, and its relation to his anti-reductionism about meaning and rules, see Stroud 2012.
3. Wittgenstein restricts this "explanation" to "a *large* class of cases of the employment of the word 'meaning'" (PI §43). We can focus on that class of cases, leaving aside those to which Wittgenstein's explanation is not intended to apply.
4. For other statements of Stroud's anti-reductionism about meaning, see Stroud 2000, ix, 130, 91–92. For other anti-reductionist readings of Wittgenstein on meaning and use, see McGinn 1984; McDowell 1984; Child 2011, 101–104, 114–121. Boghossian 1989 advocates anti-reductionism about meaning as the best response to Kripke's Wittgenstein; he does not take a stand on Wittgenstein's own position.

5. For a similar message, see RFM, 323 b-c.
6. For other well-known statements of anti-reductionism, see, e.g., PI §§124, 126.
7. See Snowdon 2018, 23–25 for similar remarks, with which I am broadly sympathetic.
8. I do not suggest that this form of communitarianism is a plausible account of what the correct following of a rule consists in. I state it only for the sake of argument.
9. That assumes that using words involves following rules. It seems clear that Wittgenstein accepts that assumption: "Following according to the rule is FUNDAMENTAL to our language-game. It characterizes what we call description" (RFM, 330).
10. See Ginsborg 2011a, 163–166 for related considerations against an argument for anti-reductionism about meaning and understanding that she plausibly ascribes to Stroud.
11. Wittgenstein puts the point in epistemic terms ("it is no more *certain* . . ."). But I take his fundamental point to be constitutive rather than epistemic.
12. Notice the close relation between these two arguments against reductive accounts and the main arguments that Kripke's Wittgenstein gives against dispositional analyses of meaning: that our dispositions are finite and include dispositions to make mistakes; and that no dispositional account can capture what Kripke calls the normative dimension of rules and meaning. (See Kripke 1982, 22–37)
13. I offer some support for this claim in Section 6.iii below.
14. For the idea that meaning requires something dynamic, not something static or stationary, see, e.g., PG, 55, 100, 149; LFM, 184.
15. For similar passages, see, e.g., RFM, 325, 327, 355.
16. For discussion and defence of this supervenience claim, and its attribution to Wittgenstein, see Child 2019.
17. For this point, see, e.g., LW II, 31, 36, 40.
18. I disagree here with Hannah Ginsborg, who argues that there is a primitive way of taking a performance to be appropriate in its context, which is independent of any prior grasp of meaning or rules (see Ginsborg 2011a, 2011b, 2012). She appeals to this "consciousness of . . . primitive appropriateness" (2011b, 248) to offer a "partly reductionist" explanation of facts about meaning and rule-following (2011b, 230). I hope to discuss this interesting proposal elsewhere.
19. This paragraph is based on Child 2019, 212–214.
20. As noted earlier, Horwich 2012 and Snowdon 2018 are recent examples. Ginsborg also suggests that Wittgenstein's account is not a fully anti-reductionist one.
21. Earlier versions of this material were presented at the conferences "Wittgenstein and the Limits of Language" at the University of Helsinki in 2016 and "Wittgenstein: The Place of Normativity in a Naturalistic World" at the University of Ottawa in 2018. I am grateful to the participants on those occasions for very helpful comments and discussion.

References

Boghossian, Paul (1989) "The Rule-Following Considerations", *Mind* 98 (392), 507–549.
Child, William (2011) *Wittgenstein*. Abingdon: Routledge.

Child, William (2019) "Meaning, Use, and Supervenience", in J. Conant and S. Sunday (eds), *Wittgenstein on Philosophy, Objectivity, and Meaning*. Cambridge: Cambridge University Press, 211–230.

Dummett, Michael (1978) *Truth and Other Enigmas*. Cambridge, MA: Harvard University Press.

Ginsborg, Hannah (2011a) "Inside and Outside Language: Stroud's Nonreductionism About Meaning", in J. Bridges, N. Kolodny and W-H. Wong (eds), *The Possibility of Philosophical Understanding: Reflections on the Thought of Barry Stroud*. Oxford: Oxford University Press, 147–181.

Ginsborg, Hannah (2011b) "Primitive Normativity and Skepticism About Rules", *Journal of Philosophy* 108 (5), 227–254.

Ginsborg, Hannah (2012) "Meaning, Understanding and Normativity", *Proceedings of the Aristotelian Society Supplementary Volume* 86 (1), 127–146.

Horwich, Paul (2012) *Wittgenstein's Metaphilosophy*. Oxford: Oxford University Press.

Kripke, Saul (1982) *Wittgenstein on Rules and Private Language*. Oxford: Blackwell.

McDowell, John (1984) "Wittgenstein on Following a Rule", *Synthese* 58 (3), 325–363.

McGinn, Colin (1984) *Wittgenstein on Meaning*. Oxford: Blackwell.

Snowdon, Paul (2018) "Wittgenstein and Naturalism", in K. Cahill and T. Raleigh (eds), *Wittgenstein and Naturalism*. Abingdon: Routledge, 15–32.

Stroud, Barry (2000) *Meaning, Understanding, and Practice: Philosophical Essays*. Oxford: Oxford University Press.

Stroud, Barry (2012) "Meaning and Understanding", in J. Ellis and D. Guevara (eds), *Wittgenstein and the Philosophy of Mind*. Oxford: Oxford University Press, 19–36.

5 Frege, Carnap, and the Limits of Asserting

Leila Haaparanta

1. Introduction

In contemporary philosophy, there is much discussion on what assertions are and how they can be distinguished from sayings. The distinction between thoughts or propositions, judgments, and assertions has a long history. I will not go through its various phases in this paper. However, I take Gottlob Frege's distinction between thoughts, judgments, and assertions into account, because it is an important background for a number of contemporary theories of assertion. This paper applies the debate on assertions to the texts of three late nineteenth century and early twentieth century classics, namely, Frege, Rudolf Carnap, and Ludwig Wittgenstein. The focus is in Frege and Carnap, but a few comments on the similarities between their views and Wittgenstein's remarks are made in the last section. This paper is not a study of asserting and assertions in general; instead, it seeks to analyze the three philosophers' views on philosophers' assertings and philosophical assertions. Those assertions can be – and have been – compared with scientific theses and arguments and the limits set by scientific assertions. For example, if one claims that philosophy is a branch of science, one proposes the metaphilosophical view that the requirements set to scientific asserting also apply to philosophical asserting. This paper neither defends nor challenges that view.

Like the discussion about the distinction between thoughts, judgments, and assertions, the discussion about limits has a long history in philosophy. Kant sought to draw the limits of knowledge and experience, and Wittgenstein's *Tractatus* is a study of the limits of language, as a number of philosophers, especially those starting from Erik Stenius's work on Wittgenstein's *Tractatus*, have emphasized.[1] In this paper I pose the question about limits in more pragmatic terms, precisely because I discuss the limits set to linguistic acts labelled as assertings. In the second section, I will give a short overview of contemporary theories of assertion, which provides important background for my argument. I will then move to Frege's views, primarily to two aspects in his philosophy. The first is his idea of universal language, the second is his view of permissible ways of justifying propositions. A peculiar feature of Frege's distinction between various ways of justifying propositions presented in his *Grundlagen der Arithmetik* (1884) is the lack of an explicit view on philosophical assertions. Frege's requirements for the justification of various types of judgments provide an illuminating point of comparison with the requirements that Carnap sets for assertions and the limits he draws for asserting. I will discuss Carnap's view on metaphysical and other philosophical assertions and pay special attention to his distinction between internal and external assertions as presented in his "Empiricism, Semantics, and Ontology" (1950/1956).

At the end of the paper, I will compare Carnap's distinction between internal and external assertions with Wittgenstein's views on philosophy in the *Philosophical Investigations* and on philosophy, knowledge, and certainty in *On Certainty*. I will suggest that there is a connection between Frege, Carnap, and Wittgenstein in that the three philosophers give norms for assertion and those norms set limits to philosophers' assertings. This is not to say that Wittgenstein developed theories, such as a theory of assertion or a theory of what philosophy is. Nor do I wish to argue that there is a particular epistemic norm of assertion that Frege, Carnap, and Wittgenstein propose and defend. The main idea is rather to read Carnap's papers on metaphysics and linguistic frameworks in terms of contemporary theories of assertion and to suggest a point of view from which one can find connections between Carnap's "Empiricism, Semantics, and Ontology" and Wittgenstein's thoughts about knowledge and certainty around 1950. This paper is not an effort to make the historical context and possible factual connections explicit or to show that one philosopher has actually been influenced by an earlier one, although that is precisely what could be done in the case of the three philosophers. For example, there is the debate between various interpretations of Wittgenstein that is visible in P. M. S. Hacker's criticism of James Conant's study of the relations between Carnap and Wittgenstein (Conant 2001; Hacker 2003). I will not choose a side in these debates. Instead, I start with the contemporary debate on assertions, which arguably has its roots in the three classics, and try to reveal a few aspects of Frege's, Carnap's, and Wittgenstein's positions that, perhaps, would go unnoticed if we did not look at their texts in terms of later developments in philosophy.

2. Contemporary Theories of Assertion

Much of contemporary theorizing on assertions begins with Frege's distinctions made in his *Begriffsschrift* (1879). There Frege distinguishes between a thought (*Gedanke*) and a judgment (*Urteil*), which is an acknowledgment of the truth of a thought (BS, §2). The distinction is also shown in his conceptual notation by means of two different strokes, the horizontal content stroke and the vertical judgment stroke. In his later writings, for example, in his "Einleitung in die Logik" (1906), Frege pays attention to the distinction he made in 1879. He emphasizes the fact that he gave a sign to the assertoric force that is hidden in the word "is", when we make an assertion (NS, 211; PW, 194). In "Meine grundlegenden logischen Einsichten" (1915), he writes: "In language assertoric force is bound up with the predicate" (NS, 272; PW, 252). The word "assertoric force" is a translation for Frege's "Behauptungskraft". For Frege, the judgment stroke or the assertion sign is the sign for "it is the case that . . ." or "it is true that . . .". It is something that makes an utterance into an assertion. Assertions (*Behauptungen*) are overt expressions of judgments. When we judge or assert, when we use assertoric force, we intend to take the step from the mere thought or the sense (*Sinn*) of a sentence to its truth-value, which we thus claim to be the True.

Contemporary theories of assertion start with the distinction between a proposition and asserting a proposition and thus assume that the distinction can be made by giving the specific features of assertions that distinguish assertions from mere sayings. Jessica Brown and Herman Cappelen, who give an overview of various theories of assertion, point out that much of contemporary discussion "focuses on the idea that assertion is governed by a norm that imposes epistemic requirements on appropriate assertion" (Brown and Cappelen 2011, 1). A prime example is Timothy Williamson's theory (1996, 2000), which argues that assertion is governed by the knowledge norm, which says that "one must: assert p only if one knows that p".[2]

Apart from Williamson's theory, which proposes the knowledge norm, there are other normative theories, of which some propose the norm that "p" would be true, others the norm that there would be warrant for "p", and still others the norm that the speaker would believe that p, for the constitutive norm for the assertion "p". There are also theories that do not evoke any norms, but rather refer to the causes of sayings, such as the speaker's intentions and beliefs concerning the hearer's beliefs. Moreover, there are theories that distinguish assertions from mere sayings by reference to the effects that assertions have on what is presupposed in conversation or on background assumptions. There is also a theory close to the normative theories, proposed by Robert B. Brandom (1994). Brandom argues that assertions are individuated by commitments and entitlements and that asserting brings in rights, permissions, and obligations. John MacFarlane (2011) has identified four main accounts of assertion, which are called the constitutive rule account, the attitudinal account, the common ground account, and the commitment account.[3] These correspond to the types of theories that were listed earlier. Herman Cappelen (2011) has proposed a debunking view, according to which "assertion" is primarily a philosophical term that can be used to pick up many kinds of things, but that such picking is always conventional. His view is perhaps close to what Wittgenstein would propose at least in his later writings (see, e.g., PI §§22, 68, 112–116).

Whether the distinction between mere sayings and assertions can be made in everyday discourse, it is something that philosophers have tried to preserve in scientific as well as in philosophical discourse. The topic of this paper is whether philosophical assertions survive the test of normative theories of assertion. The theories in which I am interested here are precisely normative ones, primarily those that propose epistemic norms for assertion. They include various versions of knowledge norms as well as norms that require the speaker to have justified or warranted beliefs that what is said is true. Brandom's view can also be included in normative theories because of its deontic vocabulary. Breaking the norm of assertion does not mean that one fails to assert. Instead, one who breaks the norm exposes oneself to blame, because one is under the norm when one asserts. However, if speakers never succeeded in following the norm when making certain kinds of assertions, for example because following the given norm is impossible in the case of those assertions, then I would say that they do not even succeed in making those assertions. My question in this paper is what kinds of norms philosophers have set for their own assertions and whether those norms can ever be fulfilled.

3. Frege and Transcendental Philosophy

As noted previously, Frege distinguishes between thoughts, judgments, and assertions. His conceptual notation is meant to be a universal language, in which thoughts – in fact, all that can be thought – can be expressed. In the "Preface" of his *Begriffsschrift*, Frege emphasizes that he wants to put forward both a *calculus ratiocinator*, that is, the rules of logical inference, and a *lingua characterica*, which is the term that he uses for Leibniz's *lingua characteristica* and which was also used by Adolf Trendelenburg. Frege refers to his article on Leibniz's idea of universal language and its developments before and after Leibniz in his *Begriffsschrift*.[4] The universal language Frege presents is a genuine language, which carries contents. It is also meant to be a calculus, a tool that could be applied to various purposes, to arithmetic and to the sciences, for example, to make thoughts and the chains of inference explicit. Still, the conceptual notation is also a genuine language, as Jean van Heijenoort (1967), Warren Goldfarb (1979), and Jaakko Hintikka (1979, 1981) have argued in their seminal articles. These interpreters and the interpretational tradition building on their work have given a detailed exposition of the division between calculus and language and construed it as a means for distinguishing two traditions in modern logic and in the philosophy of language during the last 150 years.

The basic idea proposed by van Heijenoort and others is that Frege's conceptual notation is meant to be universal in the sense that it speaks about all that there is and does not allow any metaperspective from which one could give a semantic theory to the language or compare language and the world. Frege does criticize the correspondence theory of truth, precisely because in his view the theory requires that we should be able to step beyond the limits of language to compare language and the world ("Der Gedanke", KS, 344). Moreover, he does not have any systematic semantic theory, even if he has views on meaning, most prominently his distinction between sense (*Sinn*) and reference (*Bedeutung*). The structure of conceptual notation mirrors the structure of what is not language, such as the categories of objects and functions.[5] In these respects, Frege's work may be seen as preceding some of the ideas developed in Wittgenstein's Tractatus (see TLP, 3; TLP 2.174, 6.13). The distinctions that Frege makes on the level of senses mediate between language and the objects and functions to which linguistic expressions refer. Still, the items that mediate cannot be named as senses; if we talk about them in language they turn into objects. That also happens to functions; if we talk about functions, including concepts, they lose their role as functions and become objects.[6]

van Heijenoort and others argue that, in addition to the view of logic as language, there is another line in the history of logic, namely, the view of logic as calculus, supported for example by Boole, Peirce, Schröder, and Tarski, which considers logic as a reinterpretable calculus and which allows a metaperspective from which one can develop a systematic theory of meaning and truth. The division between the two traditions, that of logic as language and that of logic as calculus, has turned out to be a fruitful interpretational model. However, in Frege's own terms, his conceptual notation is intended as both language and calculus, but calculus in a different sense from what the interpreters have proposed. Nevertheless, the division that is made from the point of view of later developments in the twentieth century helps us see in the classics of modern logic features that could not have been seen clearly by Frege's contemporaries. Still, the way in which the distinction between language and calculus is understood varies if we, say, start from Leibniz's ideas and then move to Frege and his contemporaries and further to the logicians and philosophers in the twentieth century. No matter how we evaluate these interpretational debates, we may say that Frege's conceptual notation is meant to be a formula language of pure thought, an intuitive representation of the forms of thought, and a presentation of the limits of thought. The way in which he describes it in the *Grundgesetze* (1893) is as follows:

> Any law that states what is can be conceived as prescribing that one should think in accordance with it, and is therefore in that sense a law of thought. This holds for geometrical and physical laws no less than for logical laws. The latter then only deserve the name "law of thought" with more right if it should be meant by this that they are

the most general laws, which prescribe universally how one should think if one is to think at all.

("Vorwort" in GGA I, in Künne 2010, 68–69; "Preface,"
GGA I, in Beaney 1997, 202–203)

The same question concerning the interpretational approaches and methods of interpretation arises if we try to evaluate Frege scholarship more generally. Many philosophers, perhaps most notably Michael Dummett (1973, 1981), have taken Frege to be primarily a philosopher of language and a major contributor to the linguistic turn in philosophy. Ignacio Angelelli (1967) linked Frege to the Aristotelian or Scholastic tradition, and Eike-Henner W. Kluge (1980) regarded Frege as a metaphysician who proposed a list of general metaphysical categories. Especially in the 1980s, Hans Sluga (1980) and a few others considered Frege as an epistemologist. Sluga argued that one must pay special attention to Frege's German, particularly his Kantian background. What I have emphasized, but will not argue here, is that in order to understand the philosophy of Frege's conceptual notation, one should consider the links between Leibniz, Kant, and Adolf Trendelenburg, particularly his notes on Ludwig Benedict Trede's "Sprachlehre" (1811), and consider the views of Frege as well as Wittgenstein against that historical background.[7] After metaphysics returned to the analytic tradition as what we now know as analytic metaphysics, a pressing interpretational question has been whether Frege contributed to metaphysics, and if he did, what kind of contribution he made. A. W. Moore (2012) has argued that Frege's philosophy was not "making sense of things", but was "making sense of sense", which became a focal topic in the analytic tradition after Frege. Still, Moore includes Frege in his work on metaphysics, because he regards Frege's contribution as an important preparation for analytic metaphysics. I have argued elsewhere that Frege's analysis of the concept of being was, if not a contribution to metaphysics, then at least a contribution to metametaphysics (Haaparanta 2019).

This paper poses the problem somewhat differently. My question is what Frege thought about philosophical, including metaphysical, assertions. Frege's conceptual notation is transcendental at least in the minimal sense that it contributes to defining the limits of what can be thought, as argued earlier. Frege does not make direct metaphysical assertions in his texts. However, he criticizes those who do not acknowledge the independence of numbers and other abstract objects from the human mind. It seems as if he were a Platonist, but he nowhere makes the direct claim that numbers exist independently of the human mind. What he does argue is that the whole mathematical practice loses its meaning if we do not acknowledge the realm of numbers. This is the argument presented in the *Grundlagen*, and later extended to cover other abstract objects such as thoughts, namely, an argument about the acknowledgment or the recognition, as Michael Beaney translates the word "Anerkennung", of a "third realm". Frege writes:

> A third realm must be recognized. Anything belonging to this realm has it in common with ideas that it cannot be perceived by the senses, but has in common with things that it does not need an owner so as to belong to the contents of his consciousness.
>
> ("Der Gedanke", in Künne 2010, 101; "Thought", in Beaney 1997, 336–337)

Whether we consider Frege as a Platonist or a transcendental philosopher, his universal language aims at defining the limits of what can be thought and further of what can be judged and asserted, that is, judged in overt language.

4. Frege on Justification

Further limits for judging and asserting are proposed by Frege in the *Grundlagen*, where he considers the distinctions between syntheticity, analyticity, apriority, and aposteriority. For Frege, these distinctions concern the justification for making a judgment (*die Berechtigung zur Urteilsfällung*), not the thought or the content of the judgment (*Inhalt des Urteils*). According to Frege, when we use these concepts, we speak about different ways of justifying the taking to be true of a proposition (*Satz*). Instead of the word "Urteil", Frege begins to use the word "Satz" and characterizes the four concepts by means of different ways of justifying and even proving propositions. On his characterization, a proposition is analytic if we only rely on general logical laws and definitions in its proof. If we have to make use of truths which are not general logical truths but belong to a special field of knowledge (*ein besonderes Wissensgebiet*) in proving a proposition, the proposition is synthetic. For Frege, a truth is *a posteriori*, if it is not possible to give a proof for it without referring to facts (*Tatsachen*); for him, facts are truths which cannot be proved and which are not general, because they contain claims about particular objects. In Frege's view, a truth is *a priori*, if in its derivation nothing else is needed than general laws that do not need a proof and that cannot be proved (GLA §3).

Besides stating that the distinctions between analyticity, syntheticity, apriority, and aposteriority concern the ways of justifying a judgment, Frege points out that if there is no justification, it is not possible to draw those distinctions. What Frege means seems to be the requirement that, while we do not need to have the justification ready at hand, it has to be in principle possible to give a justification and we need to know how that would be done. Hence, on his view, we can determine into which of the four categories a judgment falls if we know the way in which the judgment can be justified. The alternatives are logical laws and definitions, general laws which belong to a special field of knowledge, and sense perception. Frege does not tell us into which category or categories of justification metaphysical or other philosophical judgments and assertions belong. If he thinks that philosophical judgments and assertions can be characterized by reference to the four concepts, he would probably take them to be analytic *a priori* and hence comparable to the judgments of arithmetic, or synthetic *a priori*, comparable to judgments of geometry. His own philosophy of mathematics is antipsychologistic, and therefore it is very likely that he would not vote for the alternative that philosophical judgments and assertions are synthetic *a posteriori*. However, we may only speculate on the alternatives; Frege himself does not help us here. He emphasizes the need to clarify language as one and indeed the first task of philosophy, but what else he would count as philosophy is not clear on the basis of his writings. However, he regards it as important to distinguish between different ways of justifying judgments or give proofs, which give the speaker the permission to judge and assert. If there is no justification, the judgment cannot be classified in terms of the four concepts, but in view of philosophy the very fact that there is no justification is more worrying. For if there is no justification, we should not make the judgment in the first place. That is, however, something that Frege does not claim; he does not argue that there are no metaphysical or other philosophical judgments or assertions.

In his writings in 1924 and 1925, Frege returns to different sources of knowledge, mentioning sense perception, the logical source of knowledge, and the geometric or spatio-temporal source of knowledge (NS, 294 and 298). He approves of logical knowledge, which is knowledge of a specific realm of logical objects, such as thoughts. Arithmetical knowledge is not logical knowledge for him anymore; instead, it has its origin in the spatio-temporal source of knowledge. These later writings raise the same problem as his earlier writings, but in that context the only source for philosophical knowledge could be the logical source of knowledge. What naturally remains as an alternative is that there is no such thing as philosophical knowledge that could be traced back to any of the sources of knowledge Frege mentions. But this would entail that there are no such things as philosophical judgments or assertions which would be as it were on the same level with logical, mathematical, or scientific assertions.

5. Carnap on Metaphysics

In recent years, after the rise of analytic metaphysics, there has been much discussion on Rudolf Carnap's critical attitude towards metaphysics or what can be called his overcoming of metaphysics. Matti Eklund (2013), for example, describes the current debate on Carnap by distinguishing between pluralist and relativist approaches. According to the pluralist view, there are many different possible languages, and one and the same sentence may have different meanings and get different truth-values in different languages (Eklund 2013, 231). Hence, if Carnap were a language pluralist, then what he called frameworks are languages or fragments of languages (ibid., 232). Carnap himself points out in the footnote of the 1956 version of "Empiricism, Semantics, and Ontology" that the term "framework" is in the 1950 version used for the system of entities, while in the 1956 paper it is used for the system of linguistic expressions only (Carnap 1956, 205). The relativists, for their part, argue that Carnap's frameworks are like perspectives or outlooks (Eklund 2013, 233). What that means is that the propositions that sentences express are true or false only relative to frameworks.

Vera Flocke (2018) does not regard relativism as a serious interpretational alternative, but she also raises critical arguments against the pluralist interpretation (Flocke 2018, 15–18). She proposes that Carnap's frameworks are systems of rules for the assessment of statements. She argues further that the pragmatic external statements that Carnap discusses in his paper, namely, statements about which framework one should adopt to be contrasted with internal statements within that framework, express dispositions to follow particular rules of assessment. On her view, pragmatic external statements are noncognitive, because they merely express those dispositions. She argues that this feature makes it possible to compare Carnapian noncognitivism about ontology with norm-expressivism in metaethics (Flocke 2018, 2). Giuseppina D'Oro (2015) compares Carnap and Collingwood and argues that Collingwood's distinction between propositions and presuppositions resembles Carnap's distinction between internal and external assertions. Darren Bradley (2018) emphasizes the connection between Carnap's criticism of metaphysics in the late 1920s and in the 1950s. He defends the thesis that Carnap's "Empiricism, Semantics, and Ontology" does not bring anything new to Carnap's criticism of metaphysics, because the argument against metaphysics was presented already in 1928, both in *Der logische Aufbau der Welt* and in the short article titled "Pseudo-Problems in Philosophy". Bradley claims that Carnap takes the problem of metaphysics to lie in the fact that there is no evidence that could support metaphysical assertions. Therefore, what Carnap later calls external assertions and which are made by metaphysicians, are not genuine assertions.

The terminology varies in Carnap's texts and translations. As noted, Frege used the terms "Urteil", "Satz", and "Behauptung", the latter of which has been translated as "assertion", and "behauptende Kraft", which has been translated as "the assertive or assertoric force". Carnap uses the word "assertion" in the 1950 and 1956 papers. When I discuss metaphysical and other philosophical assertions, I will use the word "assertion" in connection with both Frege and Carnap, because the requirement of giving grounds or justification is present in both cases.

For Frege, asserting is more than forming a meaningful content, whereas for Carnap, meaning and assertability are more closely connected. That is at least the case in his criticism of metaphysics in 1920s and in the 1930s.

Carnap presents his arguments against metaphysics and accordingly against metaphysical assertions in his papers "Scheinprobleme in der Philosophie" (1928), "Von Gott und Seele, Scheinfragen in Metaphysik und Theologie" (1929), "Die alte und die neue Logik" (1930), "Überwindung der Metaphysik durch logische Analyse der Sprache" (1931), and "On the Character of Philosophic Problems" (1934), published in *Scheinprobleme in der Philosophie und andere metaphysikkritische Schriften* (2004). Moreover, as previously mentioned, he discusses metaphysics, especially metaphysical assertions, in "Empiricism, Semantics, and Ontology", which is an important article in view of the topic of this paper. The fate of metaphysics in logical empiricism is well known.[8] In his "Überwindung der Metaphysik durch logische Analyse der Sprache" (1931) Carnap seeks to show that there are serious problems already in metaphysical language, hence, also in the claims that metaphysicians make. In his papers in the late 1920s and in the early 1930s, Carnap is concerned about the meaningfulness of philosophers' assertions, but in the 1950 paper he presents the problem as a problem of justification. However, there is no radical difference between the papers of the two periods; while the tolerance towards various languages is a key idea in the later article, the criticism against metaphysical language, problems, and assertions is basically the same. Like the earlier articles, the 1950 and 1956 papers take the possibility of giving evidence as the guarantee for meaningfulness: if it is impossible to give evidence in order to solve a problem, the problem is a pseudo-problem and the suggested answers are not assertions. The problem Carnap sees in what are regarded as metaphysical assertions is that they are not constituted by the norms by which assertions ought to be constituted. Therefore, they are not assertions.

In his articles in 1929 and 1931, Carnap gives examples of pseudo-problems. One of them is the question "Does God exist?" Carnap argues that because the question has no link to what can be experienced in perception, there is no way of meaningfully talking about God. He writes: "Alles, von dem man überhaupt sprechen kann, muss sich auf von mir Erlebtes zurückführen lassen", and argues that every statement (*"Aussage"*) must be connected to perceptions; otherwise it lacks sense (*"ist sinnlos"*) (Carnap 2004, 58–59). On Carnap's view, the question "Does a human being have a soul in addition to her body?" contains meaningful words, but the question as a whole lacks sense. Examples of sentences that lack sense because of problems in the combination of words include the sentence "Caesar is a prime number" and the sentence "Caesar is and", which fail as combinations, although for different reasons, because the former, unlike the latter, is syntactically correct. A famous example is naturally Martin Heidegger's sentence "Das Nichts nichtet". Carnap points out that such statements as "God exists" or "There is a god" would be false to earlier antimetaphysicians, because there is no such object of possible sensuous perception; Carnap himself sees precisely the same problem in the statements, but for that reason he further argues that the statements are meaningless (Carnap 1931, 232).

In his "Empiricism, Semantics, and Ontology", Carnap considers philosophers who ask the question "Are there numbers?" He writes: "They might try to explain what they mean by saying that it is a question of the ontological status of numbers; the question whether or not numbers have a certain metaphysical characteristic called reality . . . or subsistence or status of 'independent entities'" (Carnap 1956, 209). The problem Carnap sees in the philosophers' question is that they have not given a formulation of their question in terms of common scientific language and thus have not given their question or to the possible answers any cognitive content. Given that there is no cognitive content in the questions or in the proposed answers given by metaphysicians, Carnap argues that there are no metaphysical beliefs, assumptions, or assertions (ibid., 208). The criticism of metaphysics in "Empiricism, Semantics, and Ontology" is based on the distinction between internal and external assertions. Carnap states: "Whoever makes an internal assertion is certainly obliged to justify it by providing evidence, empirical evidence in the case of electrons, logical proof in the case of prime numbers" (ibid., 218). Hence, to use the terminology of contemporary theories of assertion, one who asserts is under an epistemic norm; that is, assertion is governed by a specific warrant rule, which requires that one should be able to bring in evidence, either empirical evidence or logical proofs. The two types of justifying judgments are also mentioned in Frege's *Grundlagen*, as we noted earlier, but Frege also includes synthetic judgments *a priori* in his list. Carnap also advises his reader to be cautious in making assertions, but tolerant in permitting linguistic forms (ibid., 221).

In his article of 1956, Carnap distinguishes between questions that are internal to the linguistic framework and questions that are external to that framework (ibid., 206). The assertions made within the framework have cognitive content. In everyday language, for example, the spatio-temporally ordered system of observable things and events is accepted, and we are permitted to make assertions about those things; such assertions can be given cognitive content by referring to perceivable evidence (ibid., 206–207). By contrast, the question concerning the reality of the thing or world itself is a metaphysical and an external question, which cannot be given the required cognitive content. Therefore, metaphysical assertions never follow the epistemic norm of assertion. Because they never follow that norm, there cannot be such assertions.

Carnap's distinctions are even more complex than the basic distinction between internal and external questions. He argues that we choose a framework for practical reasons. Therefore, the question like "A there (really) space-time points?" can be read as an internal question, although the answer to it is analytic and trivial. Alternatively, it can be read as an external question, but as such it is a practical question and asks for a choice instead of an answer which would be an assertion (ibid., 213). Hence, what this means is that instead of normal internal assertions and external philosophical assertions, which are not assertions at all in Carnap's analysis, there are external choices made on the basis of practical considerations concerning, for example, the usefulness or fruitfulness of the framework. If, say, the number language of mathematics or the space-time point language of physics is chosen, the external practical question demanding a choice, such as "Should we choose the space-time point language?" turns into an internal question, to which there is a trivial answer once the choice is made. For Carnap, the frameworks are something that are accepted or rejected, not something that could be theoretically justified. Instead, once a framework is accepted, its "furniture" can be described, but those descriptions do not require justification as their support in the way normal internal assertions do. Moreover, Carnap allows what he calls extrasystematic explanations, marginal notes, and hints that help us to learn the linguistic framework which is constituted by a system of rules (ibid., 211).

Carnap's external assertions – if there were such assertions – would be such as "There is a world outside language", "There are universals", or "Numbers exist". The concept of reality may be used as an internal concept, but then it is an empirical and scientific, not a metaphysical concept. If the description of a chosen framework consists of assertions, it does not consist of assertions in the demanding sense of introducing new information to the discussion that has not been there already. Still, we might think that it reveals something that has been hidden or gone unnoticed for those who live within the chosen framework. As a set of internal assertions, the description of the linguistic framework with its entities is given justification in the peculiar sense that it is the mutually accepted framework.

In the terminology used in contemporary theories of assertion, norms of assertion can be broken and one may be blamed for doing that. This is also what can happen in the case of Carnap's internal, but not in the case of his external assertions. One who makes an internal assertion may defend her thesis by referring to evidence, either perceptual evidence or logical rules and definitions, or even by referring to the linguistic, hence also ontological, frameworks that are mutually accepted, such as the existence of numbers in arithmetic. But external assertions arising from nowhere, outside all frameworks, have no grounds to which the asserter could refer in making her assertion. They are not constituted by any norms and they do not bring in any obligations to give justifying evidence for one's assertions.

6. Wittgenstein and the Limits of Asserting: A Few Remarks

In the *Philosophical Investigations*, Wittgenstein remarks:

> Philosophy must not interfere in any way with the actual use of language, so it can in the end only describe it.
>
> (PI §124)

He also states:

> The name "philosophy" might also be given to what is possible *before* all new discoveries and inventions.
>
> (PI §126)

His view of philosophical theses is captured by the following remark:

> If someone were to advance *theses* in philosophy, it would never be possible to debate them, because everyone would agree to them.
>
> (PI §128)

It would certainly not make justice to Wittgenstein or Carnap to argue that there is a close affinity with Carnap's "Empiricism, Semantics, and Ontology" and Wittgenstein's statements in what is called his later philosophy. Still, there are a number of well-known connections between Wittgenstein's *Tractatus* and Carnap's early philosophy, as well as several similarities between Carnap's 1956 article and Wittgenstein's earlier as well as later work. I do not wish to make any strong claims about these connections. However, what Wittgenstein writes in the passages quoted here can be expressed in Carnap's terms by saying that if philosophy has any task, it is to describe our linguistic framework. In some cases, Carnap would say that we choose the framework; as for everyday thing language, that would not be a correct characterization.

I argued that Carnap is concerned about the lack of cognitive content of metaphysical assertions; for that reason, he cannot even allow them the status of assertions. In *On Certainty*, Wittgenstein is interested in how the expression "I know" is used in language (OC §90). That interest also reveals his concern about epistemological questions and about the traditional problem of scepticism. It is not only the late period, but his earlier philosophical work as well, that is relevant in view of epistemology, even if he does not propose any epistemological theories.[9] What is also important in his remarks in *On Certainty* is that he considers the epistemic grounds for assertings, particularly for philosophical assertings.

In *On Certainty* Wittgenstein discusses the so called Moore sentences like "I know that this is my hand" or "I know that the world has existed before my birth". For him, the correct use of "I know" presupposes the possibility to justify the presented claim in one way or other, by bringing in evidence, perceptions, reasons, and the like. It also presupposes the possibility to doubt whether the claim is true, and to be mistaken about what is argued. We cannot use the word "to know" correctly where doubt and error are excluded; on the other hand, "the game of doubting" presupposes certainty (OC §§115, 116, 360, 446). What this also means is that, on Wittgenstein's view, we can *assert* that p only if we can meaningfully assert that we know that p. For Wittgenstein, there are what Carnap would call internal assertions, and to use the terminology of normative theories of assertion, they are constituted by epistemic norms. There are no norms for what Carnap would call external assertions, such as metaphysical assertions. On that point, Wittgenstein would agree. He writes:

> I am sitting with a philosopher in the garden; he says again and again "I know that that's a tree", pointing to a tree that is near us. Someone else arrives and hears this, and I tell him: This fellow isn't insane. We are only doing philosophy.
>
> (OC §467)

If we read the remark in Carnap's terms, we may say that there is no assertion, because the philosopher's saying has no cognitive content, that is, there is no way of justifying it within the language-game. We can also read the passage in terms of contemporary discussion on assertions, and conclude that the speaker fails to comply with the epistemic norm of assertion. For Wittgenstein, this is the fate of all philosophical sayings, insofar as they seek to be more than descriptions of the language-game that is being played. Wittgenstein writes:

> All testing, all confirmation and disconfirmation of a hypothesis takes place already within a system.
>
> (OC §105)

7. Conclusions

I argued that Frege's language is language with conceptual contents.[10] The step from sense to reference is the step from conceptual content to truth, and that is precisely the step from mere thoughts to judgments. In order to take that step, one must have a justification for what is judged to be true, hence, also to what is asserted. Frege gives a list of acceptable ways of justifying contents, but he does not tell us how to deal with philosophical assertions. Carnap argues in the 1920s and the 1930s that metaphysical assertions lack sense, because they do not have cognitive content, and for that reason they are not assertions at all. In the 1950s, he takes a more tolerant attitude towards various linguistic frameworks, but again argues that there is no role for philosophers who wish to make assertions about what the world is really like. However, once a linguistic framework is chosen on pragmatic grounds, it can be described within the framework. I suggested that there is a link between Carnap and Wittgenstein. On Wittgenstein's view, what philosophers take to be topics for their debates, such as the existence of the external world, is something that is certain, not something that can be known. Hence, it is not possible to make the assertion that the external world exists, because such a saying is not governed by what contemporary theorists call the epistemic norm of assertion. For Carnap, assertions are possible only within a linguistic framework; for Wittgenstein, they are possible only within a language-game. I argued that Wittgenstein rejects traditional philosophical assertions for the same reason as Carnap. The reason is that they are not constituted by the given, restrictive epistemic norms.[11]

Notes

1. See, for example, Stenius 1960; Kannisto 1986; Pihlström 2004, 2006; Appelqvist 2016.
2. Williamson 2000, 238–269.
3. MacFarlane 2011, 80; Goldberg 2015, 9–10.
4. Frege, BS, "Vorwort", and "Über den Zweck der Begriffsschrift", BS (1964), 98. Also see Trendelenburg 1867. Cf. Haaparanta 1985, 11.
5. See Frege 1892a.
6. See Frege 1892a, 1892b. I have argued earlier that these features give support for the thesis that Frege fits in with the universalist tradition. See Haaparanta 1985, 35–44.
7. See Haaparanta 1985, 2012.
8. See Carus 2007; Uebel 2004.
9. See, for example, Kober 1996.
10. For the inferentialist interpretation of Frege's conceptual content, see Brandom 1994, 2000.
11. I am very grateful to Hanne Appelqvist for her useful comments on this chapter.

References

Angelelli, Ignacio (1967) *Studies on Gottlob Frege and Traditional Philosophy*. Dordrecht: Reidel.

Appelqvist, Hanne (2016) "On Wittgenstein's Kantian Solution of the Problem of Philosophy", *The British Journal for the History of Philosophy* 24 (4), 697–719.

Beaney, Michael (ed) (1997) *The Frege Reader*. Oxford: Blackwell.

Bradley, Darren (2018) "Carnap's Epistemological Critique of Metaphysics", *Synthese* 195 (5), 2247–2265.

Brandom, Robert B. (1994) *Making It Explicit: Reasoning, Representing & Discursive Commitment*. Cambridge, MA: Harvard University Press.

Brandom, Robert B. (2000) *Articulating Reasons: An Introduction to Inferentialism*. Cambridge, MA: Harvard University Press.

Brown, Jessica and Cappelen, Herman (2011) "Assertion: An Introduction and Overview", in J. Brown and H. Cappelen (eds), *Assertion: New Philosophical Essays*. Oxford: Oxford University Press, 1–17.

Cappelen, Herman (2011) "Against Assertion", in J. Brown and H. Cappelen (eds), *Assertion: New Philosophical Essays*. Oxford: Oxford University Press, 21–47.

Carnap, Rudolf (1931) "Überwindung der Metaphysik durch logische Analyse der Sprache", *Erkenntnis* 2, 219–241. Arthur Pap's translation "The Elimination of Metaphysics Through Logical Analysis of Language", in A. J. Auer (ed), *Logical Positivism*. Glencoe: The Free Press, London: George Allen & Unwin, 1959, 60–81.

Carnap, Rudolf (1950/1956) "Empiricism, Semantics, and Ontology", originally published in *Revue Internationale de Philosophie* 4, 20–40, revised and reprinted in R. Carnap (1956) *Meaning and Necessity: A Study in Semantics and Modal Logic*. Second edition. Chicago: University of Chicago Press, 205–221.

Carnap, Rudolf (2004) *Scheinprobleme in der Philosophie und andere metaphysikkritische Schriften*. Edited by von Thomas Mormann. Hamburg: Felix Meiner.

Carus, A. W. (2007) *Carnap and Twentieth-Century Thought: Explication as Enlightenment*. New York: Cambridge University Press.

Conant, James (2001) "Two Conceptions of *Die Überwindung der Metaphysik*: Carnap and Early Wittgenstein", in T. G. McCarthy and S. C. Stidd (eds), *Wittgenstein in America*. Oxford: Clarendon Press, 13–61.

D'Oro, Giuseppina (2015) "Unlikely Bedfellows? Collingwood, Carnap and the Internal/External Distinction", *The British Journal for the History of Philosophy* 23 (4), 802–817.

Dummett, Michael (1973) *Frege: Philosophy of Language*. Cambridge, MA: Harvard University Press.

Dummett, Michael (1981) *The Interpretation of Frege's Philosophy*. Cambridge, MA: Harvard University Press.

Eklund, Matti (2013) "Carnap's Metaontology", *Noûs* 47 (2), 229–249.

Flocke, Vera (2018) "Carnap's Noncognitivism About Ontology", *Noûs*, early view available at https://doi.org/10.1111/nous.12267.

Frege, Gottlob (1879) *Begriffsschrift, eine der arithmetischen nachgebildete Formelsprache des reinen Denkens* (BS), in Frege, Gottlob (1964) *Begriffsschrift und andere Aufsätze*. Edited by I. Angelelli. Hildesheim: Georg Olms, 1–88.

Frege, Gottlob (1884) *Die Grundlagen der Arithmetik: eine logisch mathematische Untersuchung über den Begriff der Zahl* (GLA). Breslau: Verlag von W. Koebner, reprinted in *The Foundations of Arithmetic/Die Grundlagen der Arithmetik*. Translated by J. L. Austin. Basil Blackwell, Oxford, 1968.

Frege, Gottlob (1892a) "Über Begriff und Gegenstand", *Vierteljahrschrift für wissenschaftliche Philosophie* 16, 192–205, reprinted in KS, 167–178.

Frege, Gottlob (1892b) "Über Sinn und Bedeutung", *Zeitschrift für Philosophie und philosophische Kritik* 100, 25–50, reprinted in KS, 143–162.

Frege, Gottlob (1893) *Grundgesetze der Arithmetik, begriffsschriftlich abgeleitet, I. Band* (GGA I). Jena: Verlag von H. Pohle.

Frege, Gottlob (1918) "Der Gedanke, eine logische Untersuchung", *Beiträge zur Philosophie des deutschen Idealismus* I, 58–77, reprinted in KS, 342–362.

Frege, Gottlob (1967) *Kleine Schriften* (KS). Edited by I. Angelelli. Darmstadt: Wissenschaftliche Buchgesellschaft, Hildesheim: Georg Olms.

Frege, Gottlob (1969) *Nachgelassene Schriften* (NS). Edited by H. Hermes, F. Kambartel and F. Kaulbach. Hamburg: Felix Meiner Verlag.

Frege, Gottlob (1976) *Wissenschaftliche Briefwechsel* (BW). Edited by G. Gabriel, H. Hermes, F. Kambartel, C. Thiel and A. Veraart. Hamburg: Felix Meiner Verlag.

Frege, Gottlob (1979) *Posthumous Writings* (PW). Translated by P. Long and R. White. Oxford: Basil Blackwell.

Goldberg, S. C. (2015) *Assertion: On the Philosophical Significance of Assertoric Speech*. New York: Oxford University Press.

Goldfarb, Warren D. (1979) "Logic in the Twenties: The Nature of the Quantifier", *Journal of Symbolic Logic* 44, 351–368.

Haaparanta, Leila (1985) *Frege's Doctrine of Being*. Acta Philosophica Fennica. Vol. 39. Helsinki: The Philosophical Society of Finland.

Haaparanta, Leila (2012) "On 'Being' and Being: Frege Between Carnap and Heidegger", in L. Haaparanta and H. J. Koskinen Heikki (eds), *Categories of Being: Essays on Metaphysics and Logic*. Oxford: Oxford University Press, 319–337.

Haaparanta, Leila (2019) "Frege on 'Es gibt', Being in a Realm and (Meta)Ontology", in F. Kjosavik and C. Serck-Hanssen (eds), *Metametaphysics and the Sciences, Historical and Philosophical Perspectives*. London: Routledge, 81–98.

Hacker, P. M. S. (2003) "Wittgenstein, Carnap and the New American Wittgensteinians", *Philosophical Quarterly* 53 (201), 1–23.

Hintikka, Jaakko (1979) "Frege's Hidden Semantics", *Revue Internationale de Philosophie* 33, 716–722.

Hintikka, Jaakko (1981) "Semantics: A Revolt Against Frege", in G. Fløistad (ed), *Contemporary Philosophy*. Vol. 1. Martinus Nijhoff: The Hague, 57–82.

Kannisto, Heikki (1986) *Thoughts and Their Subject: A Study of Wittgenstein's Tractatus*. Acta Philosophica Fennica. Vol. 40. Helsinki: The Philosophical Society of Finland.

Kluge, Eike-Henner W. (1980) *The Metaphysics of Gottlob Frege: An Essay in Ontological Reconstruction*. The Hague, Boston and London: Martinus Nijhoff.

Kober, Michael (1996) "Certainties of a World-Picture: The Epistemological Investigations of *On Certainty*", in H. Sluga and D. G. Stern (eds), *The Cambridge Companion to Wittgenstein*. Cambridge: Cambridge University Press, 411–441.

Künne, Wolfgang (2010) *Die Philosophische Logik Gottlob Freges, Ein Kommentar*. Frankfurt am Main: Vittorio Klostermann.

MacFarlane, John (2011) "What Is an Assertion?" in J. Brown and H. Cappelen (eds), *Assertion: New Philosophical Essays*. Oxford: Oxford University Press, 79–96.

Moore, A. W. (2012) *The Evolution of Modern Metaphysics*. New York: Cambridge University Press.

Pihlström, Sami (2004) *Solipsism: History, Critique, and Relevance*. Acta Philosophica Tamperensia. Vol. 3. Tampere: Tampere University Press.

Pihlström, Sami (2006) "Shared Language, Transcendental Listerners, and the Problem of Limits", in S. Pihlström (ed), *Wittgenstein and the Method of*

Philosophy. Acta Philosophica Fennica. Vol. 80. Helsinki: The Philosophical Society of Finland, 185–221.

Stenius, Erik (1960) *Wittgenstein's Tractatus: A Critical Exposition of Its Main Lines of Thought*. Oxford: Basil Blackwell.

Sluga, Hans (1980) *Gottlob Frege*. London: Routledge and Kegan Paul.

Trendelenburg, Adolf (1867) "Über Leibnizens Entwurf einer allgemeinen Charakteristik", in A. Trendelenburg (eds), *Historische Beiträge zur Philosophie, Dritter Band: Vermischte Abhandlungen*. Berlin: Verlag von G. Bethge, 1–47.

Uebel, Thomas (2004) "Carnap, the Left Vienna Circle, and Neopositivist Antimetaphysics", in S. Awodey and C. Klein (eds), *Carnap Brought Home: The View from Jena*. Chicago and La Salle: Open Court, 247–277.

van Heijenoort, Jean (1967) "Logic as Calculus and Logic as Language", *Synthese* 17, 324–330.

Williamson, Timothy (1996) "Knowing and Asserting", *The Philosophical Review* 105 (4), 489–523.

Williamson, Timothy (2000) *Knowledge and Its Limits*. New York: Oxford University Press.

6   On Being Resolute

Paul Standish

Suppose someone comes to you to ask for advice about pursuing a career in a university philosophy department. Maybe you will give them some idea of the teaching commitments and of expectations regarding research. Maybe you will warn about current under-funding. Maybe you will want to reassure them that the academic life is, nevertheless, still very agreeable. But really you should do nothing of the sort, not at least if you want to follow Wittgenstein. Rather your advice should be simply "Don't do that." There is something shameful about an academic life in philosophy. Better to become a gardener or to work in a factory making nuts and bolts.

Suppose though that what you are asked about is not a career in philosophy but rather about how to pursue the subject, perhaps by someone who already feels pursued by the subject. Then your tone will be different, and you will say, following Wittgenstein, "Go the bloody hard way!"

The strange English swear-word "bloody" had a curious fascination for Wittgenstein. It was in his letters to Gilbert Pattison, especially, that he indulged in a kind of jocularity, giving himself licence to use the word in eccentric and original ways, often signing off "Yours bloodily". My own early attempt to find out why, in some contexts, this word caused such dismay led to the explanation that it was a contraction of "By our Lady", and hence obviously blasphemous. But this etymology is now generally doubted. The force of the word derives possibly from natural human anxiety about the letting of blood and, more probably, from a fear of menstruation.

"Go the bloody hard way," "go the bloody rough way" – this is phrasing that Rush Rhees heard recurrently from Wittgenstein, and it is invoked prominently in writings of Cora Diamond and James Conant. It intimates a conception of philosophy that takes it to be inherently difficult, not to be amenable to formulaic responses, and to require a commitment such that its pursuit cannot be separated from the way one lives one's life as a whole. It underlines the sense of philosophy as not only a form of enquiry but a matter of the will, a testing of one's resolve. This, of course, provides an entrée to considering my title phrase: on being resolute. And obviously this is prompted by the prominence in Wittgenstein studies these past two decades or so of so-called "resolute readings".

I

"Resolute reading" has become the favoured term for that line of interpretation associated with the "new Wittgenstein," in which works by Diamond and Conant function as central points of reference. While the term originates in remarks by Thomas Ricketts, it was first set in print in Warren Goldfarb's review article "Metaphysics and Nonsense: On Cora Diamond's *The Realistic Spirit*". The provenance of this thinking is explained elegantly by Alice Crary in her introduction to *The New Wittgenstein*, co-edited with Rupert Read and published in 2000. A significant line of interpretation of the later Wittgenstein, she explains, takes it that he sees the aim of philosophy as therapeutic, a term he himself provides. The more distinctive feature of resolute reading is its attributing of such an aim also to the *Tractatus*, at least in some degree. Interpretation of this kind turns very much on the significance that is attached to the later sections of that work. So we find, for example, "Philosophy aims at the logical clarification of thoughts. Philosophy is not a body of doctrine but an activity" (TLP 4.112), which might be taken as an early move in a series of propositions that reorient the reader in relation to the significance of the text's earlier pages: they are in tension with what this same text appears to have claimed ("the final solution of the problems", no less), but they align with the recognition, expressed in the concluding words of the Preface, of "how little is achieved when these problems are solved". The series extends through the statement that "Logic is not a body of doctrine, but a mirror-image of the world" (TLP 6.13), to the claim that "The sense of the world must lie outside the world" (TLP 6.41), and to the assertion that "So too it is impossible for there to be propositions in ethics. Propositions can express nothing that is higher." And, thus, almost finally to:

> My propositions serve as elucidations in the following way: anyone who understands me eventually recognises them as nonsensical, when he has used them – as steps – to climb up beyond them. (He must, so to speak, throw away the ladder after he has climbed up it.)
>
> He must transcend these propositions, and then he will see the world aright.
>
> (TLP 6.54)

Philosophy, then, is not a matter of developing doctrines or theories: it is an activity. And, finally, "what we cannot speak about" (TLP 7) does not refer to an ineffable X towards which silence might be an appropriate form of approach, but rather does not *refer* at all: it turns out attention back towards what we do in the words we use.

This is to find a degree of continuity in Wittgenstein's work that so-called "standard" interpretations deny. To express things in this way, however, is to fall short of what resolute reading is said to achieve. The new Wittgenstein takes issue not only, most provocatively, with the way that the *Tractatus* is commonly understood but also, more subtly, with standard readings of the *Investigations*. This also needs to be explained.

Standard readings claim that the *Investigations* turns on the picture theory of meaning advanced in the *Tractatus* with the doctrine of meaning-as-use: the meaning of a word is fixed not by an act that connects it with features of reality but by the part it plays in what we do – that is, its place in the language-game, its characteristic grammar. It is the grammar of the expression that determines the possibilities of its combination with other words and hence what we can do with it. Whether or not an utterance makes sense is determined by grammar. As Crary puts this:

> The most well-known version of this narrative runs as follows: in the *Tractatus* Wittgenstein advocates a *truth-conditional* theory of meaning which has the characteristic form of *realism*, and later on he embraces a theory of meaning as consisting in *assertibility-conditions* which has the characteristic features of *anti-realism*.
>
> (Crary and Read 2000, 2, italics in original)

Such an understanding of the *Investigations*, associated for instance with Michael Dummett, Saul Kripke, and David Pears, is itself sometimes taken to be therapeutic: it is intended to "cure" us of the ambition of providing a metaphysical explanation and to regularise our thinking according to the rules of grammar. The avoidance of metaphysics is achieved by confining enquiry to consideration of assertibility conditions.

But such standard interpretations of the later philosophy, so the New Wittgensteinians claim, "*utterly fail to capture its therapeutic character*" (Crary and Read 2000, 3). They fail because in giving up the picture theory and the full-bloodied objectivity that it promised, they maintain the assumption that such objectivity depends upon features of reality that transcend thought and speech. Put differently, it depends upon an implicit stepping outside of language on our part even if that attempt results only in a sense of our failure so to do. Failure to achieve the external perspective, the stepping outside of language we took ourselves to need, results in a ceding of authority to the rules of grammar and obedience thereto. Hence, its anti-realism. The proponent of the new Wittgenstein will then take these realist and anti-realist interpretations as locked into the same metaphysical presuppositions and perhaps as, in some degree, depending upon one another.

Let us pause to acknowledge that the account thus far is likely to have sounded alarm bells in the minds of some readers. Surely, it will be objected, too much is being rolled together here. The difference across the range of these "standard" readings is being obscured. What, in particular, of the place of more specifically Kantian readings? The orientation in a Kantian reading is idealist rather than realist: this opens prospects of finding continuity of a kind between the early and the later work but in a way differently articulated from that proposed by resolute readers. It is a live question for Kantian readers whether resolute readers betray a lack of attention to the varying accounts of Wittgenstein's early conception of philosophical method. It is not as if standard readers such as Peter Hacker ignore the tension between what the *Tractatus* claims to be "correct method" and what Wittgenstein himself does in this text. Furthermore, the several quotations gathered earlier are already redolent of a certain Kantianism, especially insofar as they hold to the clear distinction between statements of facts and philosophical propositions that are the outcome of some kind of transcendental reflection. As Hanne Appelqvist puts this:

> I cannot describe the form of language if that form is a necessary condition for language to make sense in the first place. Just as spatiality cannot be represented spatially but is displayed in spatial constructions, the form shared by language and reality is displayed in language and not expressible by it.
>
> (Appelqvist 2016, 704)

She relates these remarks to Wittgenstein's "Propositions cannot express logical form; it is mirrored by them. . . . Propositions show the logical form of reality" (TLP 4.121). There are important questions here, especially concerning the Kantian reader's claim that this distinction (that is, between the empirical and the logical/grammatical) is sustained in the later Wittgenstein.

For the proponents of the new Wittgenstein, in any case, such refinements do little to alter the problem. The alternative that they espouse is resolutely to turn away: they resist the truth-conditions approach and the warranted-assertability approach identified respectively in the early and the later work in standard interpretations, seeking to displace both with a perspective that is both realist and anti-metaphysical. The readings they seek often take the following paragraph from the *Investigations* as of signal importance:

> The great difficulty here is not to present the matter as if there were something one *couldn't* do. As if there really were an object, from which I extract a description, which I am not in a position to show anyone. – And the best that I can propose is that we yield to the

temptation to use this picture, but then investigate what the *application* of the picture looks like.

(PI §374, italics in original)

Not to think there is something one cannot do: it is precisely thinking that there *is* that is the metaphysical impulse behind the standard reader's anti-realism. And this impulse can readily be allied to a tendency, fostered by a non-resolute reading of the *Tractatus*, to interpret that text as gesturing towards something ineffable but substantial. This would be to reveal not only what is alleged to be the latent mysticism in the work but also the impossibility, as we saw, of ethics' being put into words. In this light, the nonsensical and what cannot be said now seem to incorporate a plural range of significance for human beings, and the idea that some things cannot be said but can be shown works powerfully with this assumption. The mystical and the ethical, as well in fact as those meta-level propositions that do not provide a picture of the world but rather purport to describe *how* propositions picture the world, are all to be classed as non-sensical. Yet this variety of significance is something resolute readers will staunchly oppose, sometimes under the rubric of "nonsense monism" or "nonsense austerity". On a resolute reading, an expression is nonsense where no use for it has been found, and in the light of this criterion there is no reason to differentiate what may seem verbal gestures towards some ineffable truth from gibberish. The cogency claimed for the lack of differentiation here will be misunderstood, so the argument goes, if it is thought in terms of *psychological* plausibility: the therapy intended is that we be released from the illusion that we mean something when in fact we mean nothing.[1]

Having sketched the principal tenets of each of the two sides to the argument, I want to refer briefly to three responses to the prominence of the debate in Wittgenstein studies. While it has thus far been necessary to consider the *Tractatus* in order to set the scene, in what follows my attention is focused predominantly on the *Investigations* and on the consequences of a resolute response to that work.

First, Genia Schönbaumsfeld's "A 'Resolute' Later Wittgenstein" expressly takes issue with Conant's "mono-Wittgensteinianism" as well as with the account of "nonsense austerity" offered in Stephen Mulhall's work. She provides a sharp analysis especially regarding nonsensicality, as well as a parting-shot against the suggestion that Wittgenstein thought that philosophical problems were "existential" or "personal" problems (Schönbaumsfeld 2010, 666). It is difficult to read this piece, however, as she might well agree, without some sense that the arguments are sometimes passing one another by, which in turn must be a plea for greater clarity. The note of exasperation in the article surely says as much. The possibility of a more existential or personal reading is both opened and ironized in the Kierkegaardian pastiche with which Conant frames his lengthy defence of "mild mono-Wittgensteinianism" (Conant 2007), and certainly the melodrama of existential engagement is partly stilled by the emphasis on the kicking away of the ladder as a matter requiring not once-and-for-all conversion but continual patience of thought. Whatever the provocations of ardent articulations of mono-Wittgensteinism, Conant ends his essay with the suggestion that the central motivation of resolute reading "*can* be to improve upon existing accounts of the discontinuity in Wittgenstein's philosophy" (Conant 2007, 111, italics in original).

In a symposium with Pascuale Frascolla, Martin Gustafsson provides a brief survey of the debate.[2] He draws attention to a key aspect of the positions developed by Conant and Diamond: "that any sign can have various intelligible uses, and that a sign can be given a new meaningful employment even without prior stipulation" (Gustafsson 2011, 205). Standard readers reject such a view on the grounds "(a) that to give a sign a new meaning is always already a linguistic affair, and (b) that the possibility of linguistic innovation is therefore by necessity parasitic on the linguistic resources that are available before the innovation is made" (ibid. 205). But this reasoning, Gustafsson tries to show, rests on a false dichotomy. It presupposes the idea that

> linguistic innovation must be conceived *either* (1) as dependent on established usage in such a way that this established usage allows us to draw the limits of intelligible innovation *before* particular innovations have actually been made and put to use in concrete circumstances, *or* (2) as completely independent of established usage, in such a way that the intelligibility of an innovation might have nothing at all to do with how language has been used before, being the product instead of some mysterious, non-linguistic meaning-giving act of the speaker.
>
> (ibid. 206)

We shall return to the question of innovation later. But Gustafsson is motivated also by a concern about the debate that may already have become apparent in what I have said so far. This is that the debate runs the risk of sounding like a local dispute and that, in consequence, it may be playing its part in confirming in the minds of at least some "lay" philosophers their sense of the marginal and perhaps somewhat esoteric appeal of Wittgenstein's work. In spite of these reservations, Gustafsson enters a qualified plea for resolute reading as offering the greatest potential to demonstrate Wittgenstein's wider significance and importance.

Hilary Putnam, himself a contributor to Crary and Read's *The New Wittgenstein*, is taken to be a friend to this position, especially in virtue of his interpretation of Wittgenstein's philosophy of mathematics, and his endorsement of a realist, non-metaphysical position. But Putnam also has expressed concern about the nature of the contemporary debate, worrying that it has come to seem somewhat self-involved and parochial, to the detriment of Wittgenstein's reception in the wider world of philosophy. If it is indeed the case that philosophy is to be understood as merely therapeutic, in the subjective sense of the term, and to some extent in defiance (or denial) of the history of philosophy with its more systematic concerns, then the view attributed to Wittgenstein does seem to run the risk of becoming irrelevant to people who take the subject up for its own sake. If Wittgensteinians now find themselves to be marginalised in that subject, to some extent they have themselves to blame.[3]

In the remainder of this paper I shall offer my own reflection on this position. I speak as someone who is institutionally marginalised from the philosophical mainstream but who is convinced of the wider significance of Wittgenstein's work.

II

> I constantly find new puzzles. (I've thought about this for years, constantly ploughed these fields.) I would not be justified in saying: "Let's talk no more about it."
>
> (WCL, 196)

The debate provoked by the new Wittgenstein has produced subtle and complex argument, and in some respects it has realised new standards of exegesis. Reference to the "*Tractatus* wars" (which, according to the account presented in the preceding section, must be taken to extend into the "*Investigations* wars") has, however, encouraged the impression that there must be two factions battling it out and that each holds a rival "position". In the reiteration of these ideas, shorthand expressions such as "nonsense austerity", "mono-Wittgensteinianism", "therapy" or "resolute reading" itself have advertised the differences with a boldness that belies the subtlety of the commitments embraced. The significance of this seems especially striking if one considers the alleged provenance of new readings – that is, the writings of Rush Rhees, Hidé Ishiguro, and Stanley Cavell, none of whom can readily be understood well in terms of the holding of "positions". I take it that the holding of positions is perilously close to the advancing of theories or doctrines, and further that too strenuous a disavowal of metaphysics may bring problems beyond what one has bargained for.

One consequence of the hardening of views into positions is that the tensions within Wittgenstein's texts are obscured. Of course the tensions within the *Tractatus* are not ignored: indeed how to read the relation between the picture theory it apparently advances and the "framing sections", as well as a series of apparently self-undermining remarks, beginning somewhere in the 4s, is the nub of the question that divides resolute from standard readers. And they are generally sharply divided. The

Investigations, by contrast, is amenable to less systematic a response, and here it is sometimes the case that the garnering of textual support for one position or the other fails to work with the dialogical tensions within paragraphs, tensions that are rendered most obviously by interactions with the interlocutor but also more subtly by shifts of tone, prompted often by variations in punctuation. These are tensions Wittgenstein works *with* rather than simply seeks to resolve. Sometimes, as we shall see, they arise not just between voices but from the extraordinary, even surreal nature of the examples that are used (a primitive builder tribe, a lion that speaks, a parrot with understanding, and a rose with no teeth) and from an overt straining of the language itself ("THIS is supposed to be produced by a process in the brain!" (PI §412), say, and "Milk me sugar" [PI § 498]).

We considered earlier the central importance to resolute readings of the claim, PI §374, that "The great difficulty here is not to present the matter as if there were something one *couldn't* do." Let us juxtapose this against the following, now familiar extract from remarks recorded by Friedrich Waismann – this one from 30 September 1929:

> To be sure I can imagine what Heidegger means by being and anxiety. Man feels the urge to run up against the limits of language. Think for example of the astonishment that anything at all exists. The astonishment can be expressed in the form of a question, and there is no answer whatsoever. Anything we might say is a priori bound to be mere nonsense. Nevertheless we do run up against the limits of language. Kierkegaard too saw that there is this running up against something and he referred to it in a fairly similar way (as running up against paradox). This running up against the limits of language is ethics. I think it is definitely important to put an end to all the claptrap about ethics – whether intuitive knowledge exists, whether values exist, whether the good is definable. In ethics we are always making the attempt to say something that cannot be said, something that does not and never will touch the essence of the matter. It is a priori certain that whatever definition of the good will be given – it will always be merely a misunderstanding to say that the essential thing, what is really meant, corresponds to what is expressed (Moore). But the inclination, the running up against something, indicates something. St Augustine knew that already when he said: What, you swine, you want not to talk nonsense! Go ahead and talk nonsense, it does not matter.
>
> (Waismann 1979, 68–69)

Are we to read this acknowledgement of the urge to run up against the limits of language, or Augustine's recognition of the need to talk nonsense, as simply opposed by PI §374? It is true that the latter was written a decade or so later, but then in 1947 we find Wittgenstein echoing

Augustine's phrasing: "Don't *for heaven's sake*, be afraid of talking non-sense! But you must pay attention to your nonsense" (CV, 56, italics in original). Is it perhaps that the urge to run up against the limits is the temptation, and the advice not to think that there is something you can-not do is the cure? Or is it the case that as human beings we need both? The issue here is how far things are to be resolved, and how far resolute-ness is directed to this.

But how curious are the connections and connotations of "resolute" and its cognates! The noun "resolution" suggests clarity, perhaps the high resolution that might be thought to characterize a perspicuous representa-tion, an *Übersicht*. To resolve difficulties can be simply to solve problems, even sometimes to resolve differences through compromise. So is philoso-phy then to seek solutions? If there are to be solutions, Wittgenstein tells us, they will come as the result not of new information or a new discovery, but rather of closer attention to our grammar. Sometimes the problem will be dissolved. Here again, however, we are faced with temptation:

> [Philosophical problems] are solved through an insight into the workings of our language, and that in such a way that these work-ings are recognized – *despite* an urge to misunderstand them. The problems are solved, not by coming up with new discoveries, but by assembling what we have long been familiar with. Philosophy is a struggle against the bewitchment of our understanding by the resources of our language.
>
> (PI §109, italics in original)

So with these urges to be resisted, temptation is foregrounded once again, and resoluteness becomes identified more directly with the idea of an unswerving will. To the contemporary Anglophone philosophi-cal reader, however, a curious further echo may be apparent, which will take us back to Wittgenstein's acknowledgement of Heidegger's notion of anxiety: Heidegger's translators chose the term "resoluteness" for that supremely important virtue, *Entschlossenheit*, which is called for from Dasein in the face of its finitude. This is described precisely as a "reticent self-projection upon one's ownmost Being-guilty, in which one is ready for anxiety" (Heidegger 1962, H. 297). The calculated resonance in Hei-degger's text of *Entschlossenheit* with *Erschlossenheit*, which translates as "disclosedness", points to a kind of realism that is perhaps not so far from the realistic spirit.

The darker note that is sounded here, regarding anxiety and finitude, leads to the main thrust of what I want to consider in the remainder of this paper, and this has three aspects. In the first place, I shall consider how the relation to the metaphysical is to be understood in Wittgenstein's later work. In the second, I ask how far contemporary articulations of the new Wittgenstein depart from the work that apparently inspired them, in respect of which I shall have most to say about Stanley Cavell. In the third, and with the main focus on the limits of language, I turn more directly to Heidegger.

Wittgenstein and Metaphysics

Certainly, the later Wittgenstein is widely understood as anti-metaphysical. While it would be wrong simply to deny this, I wonder about the confidence with which it is asserted. The reason for concern has to do not only with how far such an understanding is accurate but with how therapeutic readings are to be understood. My sense is that there is a danger of being dismissive here, which the hardening of views into positions may encourage, as may uncritical, perhaps complacent adherence to PI §374 ("The great difficulty here is not to present the matter as if there were something one *couldn't* do" – italics in original). In any case, if one attends to what follows this opening sentence in the paragraph, one finds first a subjunctive picturing of the illusion this might imply ("As if there really were an object"), followed by the proposal in response that "we yield to the temptation to use this picture, but then investigate what the *application* of the picture looks like" (PI § 374, italics in original). The picture is not to be so quickly or confidently excised. Consider then these remarks of Rush Rhees about Wittgenstein's views:

> From 1931 onwards, anyway, I do not think he was calling on his pupils to *renounce* metaphysics; no more than he would have called on any people to renounce magic. But he did want to bring them to see what metaphysics is, and in this way to free them from the special hold which it has on you when you feel that "this is the only way it *can* be". He would try to free anyone from the idea that magic is some sort of rival to science – either an inferior or a superior one.
> (Rhees 2006, 262–263, italics in original)[4]

One version of a therapeutic reading might run as follows: if we can stop running up against the limits of language, then we will no longer be burdened by the idea that there is something we cannot do.[5] And if one symptom within philosophy of running up against the limits of language is scepticism, it will follow that the dissolving of the sceptic's questions will figure as an important stage in the overcoming of the disease. Then, because we have been restored to the ordinary, because we have achieved peace, philosophy can come to an end. Our therapy will be complete, and metaphysics will truly be overcome.

It is worth attending to a much-quoted paragraph, selective reading of which has been taken to endorse such a therapeutic view:

> We don't want to refine or complete the system of rules for the use of our words in unheard-of ways.

For the clarity that we are aiming at is indeed *complete* clarity. But this simply means that the philosophical problems should *completely* disappear.

The real discovery is the one that enables me to break off philosophizing when I want to. – The one that gives philosophy peace, so that it is no longer tormented by questions which bring *itself* into question. – Instead, a method is now demonstrated by examples, and the series of examples can be broken off. – Problems are solved (difficulties eliminated), not a *single* problem.

There is not *a* philosophical method, though there are indeed methods, different therapies, as it were.

(PI §133, italics in original)

The selective reading I have in mind accentuates the achieving of clarity and the complete disappearance of the problems, with philosophy achieving peace. It loses sight of the opening assertion that it is *not* our aim to complete the system of rules, just as it underplays other qualifiers in the lines that follow.[6] An over-zealous therapist might be drawn to such a view.

Plainly, however, as we saw earlier, such a therapy does not chime well with Rhees's claims. Wittgenstein releases his pupils from a debased kind of scientific thinking; and then this running up against the limits of language can be understood better, in the light, for example, of his remarks about magic and religion. But what is at stake in his use of this term "magic"? This is clarified helpfully by the several examples he discusses in his "Remarks on Frazer's *Golden Bough*" (PO, 118–155). Frazer is condemned for the manner of his interpretation of the practices he observes in more "primitive" societies, where he mistakes something like a religious ritual – for example, a practice to mark the adoption of a child – for bad science: he has the narrowness of vision that one expects to find in an English country parson.

The monological way of thinking of the anthropologist, in Wittgenstein's description, is an instance of the one-tracked thinking that Wittgenstein has in his sights elsewhere. A philosophical version of this vice, which is found in the sciences also, involves the idea that thinking involves addressing puzzles and that puzzles admit one solution. In his early setting of the scene for the parable of the fly-bottle, Wittgenstein remarks of the fly: "The stronger the wish to get out, the harder it is for it to get out. (It is fascinated by one way of trying to get out.)" (WCL, 7). The puzzle for the philosopher provokes "one reaction – of looking for the solution". But, Wittgenstein responds, "If you wanted to let [the fly] out, you'd have to surround this (the glassy surface of the fly catcher) by something dark. As long as there is light there, the fly can never do it" (WCL, 196.) Pursuing the analogy further, he writes:

If I am puzzled philosophically, I always darken that which seems to me light, and try frantically to think of something different. The point is you can't get out as long as you are fascinated. The only thing to do is to go to an example where nothing fascinates me. First of all, it is not at all clear that this will help every fly. What happens to work with me doesn't work with him (Professor Moore) – works with me now, and may not work with me tomorrow.

There are always new ways to look at the matter.

(WCL, 196)

Wittgenstein lets the fly out of the fly-bottle, language is returned to the ordinary, philosophy achieves peace, but only for it all to start up again, and this continually so. When one reads that "we don't want to refine or complete the system of rules for the use of words in unheard-of ways" (PI §133), it is wise to set the remark against the background of Wittgenstein's massive constructivist turn in relation to mathematics. It is this turn that in the end gives impetus to Wittgenstein's growing sense of what it is to know how to go on and to what "complete clarity" might be. This clarity is achieved by a shutting of the eyes that is offensive to what appears as the intellectual conscience but that gives voice to the human. *Meine Augen sind verschlossen. Ich bin entschlossen.* Intellectual limitedness is, then, to be displaced by a picture of human finitude. But this is a finitude that does not rest without inviting a contrast to itself.

Cavell and the Threat of Scepticism

A thoroughgoing therapeutic approach would not accord with the account of the *Investigations* offered by Cavell. What would it be like to live without the threat of scepticism? Cavell rejects the familiar idea that the *Investigations* provides a refutation of the sceptic. It is not exactly that this should be denied but rather that it misses the point. This is that Wittgenstein's treatment of scepticism demonstrates not an epistemological but an existential truth, and we might readily think of this as a manifestation of running up against the limits of language. Hence, Cavell draws attention to the restlessness in the text, which, he finds, articulates this aspect of the human condition. This he describes variously as the human being's failure to acknowledge what she ordinarily knows and as the human compulsion to call into question the conditions of its own existence. Why else would the *Investigations* go on so long? Why else does Wittgenstein not solve the problem and leave well alone? There are methods, there are therapies, but there is no end to philosophy, nor to the restlessness of the human condition.

When the sceptic asks "But if you are *certain*, isn't it that you are shutting your eyes in face of doubt?" (PI, 236, italics in original), Cavell phrases his response specifically in terms of a kind of resolve:

The skeptic insinuates that there are possibilities to which the claim of certainty shuts its eyes; or: whose eyes the claim of certainty shuts.

It is the voice, or an imitation of the voice, of intellectual conscience. Wittgenstein replies: "They are shut." It is the voice of human conscience. It is not generally conclusive, but it is more of an answer that it may appear to be. In the face of the skeptic's picture of intellectual limitedness, Wittgenstein proposes a picture of human finitude. (Then our real need is for an account of this finitude, especially of what it invites in contrast to itself.)

His eyes are shut; he has not shut them. The implication is that the insinuated doubt is not *his*. But how not? If the philosopher *makes* them his, pries the lids up with instruments of doubt, does he not come upon human eyes? – When I said that the voice of human conscience was not generally conclusive, I was leaving it open whether it was individually conclusive. It may be the expression of resolution, at least of confession. "They (my eyes) are shut" as a resolution, or confession, says that one can, for one's part, live in the face of doubt. – But doesn't everyone, everyday? – It is something different to live *without* doubt, without so to speak the threat of scepticism. To live in the face of doubt, eyes happily shut, would be to fall in love with the world.

(Cavell 1979, 431, italics in original)

The juxtaposition of intellectual to human conscience is one move in resistance to the flight from the ordinary, a flight manifested here in part in our failure of acknowledgement of the other. Indeed, on the previous page Cavell says no less than that "The crucified human body is our best picture of the unacknowledged human soul" (Cavell 1979, 430). And in the Festschrift for Cora Diamond, in a piece relating to J. M. Coetzee's *Elizabeth Costello*, he more or less says that the wounded human body is a picture of the human soul – taking the woman's body, the body that must bleed, as the soul's better exemplification (Cavell 2007).

The seriousness inherent in these remarks – one might say, their sense of the tragic dimension to a human life and of the manifestation of this in human expressiveness – is something that Cavell finds to be painfully absent in much moral philosophy: both in its tendencies, even commitments, towards abstraction and in its professed investments, cautious and pinched as they often are, in ordinary language philosophy. In "Performative and Passionate Utterance", he writes:

But if what I have been aiming at is indeed some fragment of a view of expression, of recognizing language as everywhere revealing desire . . . this is because the view is meant in service of something I want from moral theory, namely a systematic recognition of speech as confrontation, as demanding, as owed . . ., each instance of which directs, and risks, if not costs, blood.

(Cavell 2005, 187)

So then it must seem abrupt, to say the least, to turn from such poignant aphorism and to consider the prominence in *his* work of the idea of the ordinary, especially the ordinary to which Wittgenstein repeatedly returns. But Cavell differentiates between the "actual ordinary" and the "eventual ordinary". Think of the actual ordinary as what is there, the world into which we came as children, and with which for a time we enjoyed a kind of animal intimacy, and later the world we mostly take for granted. But what we come to, as time progresses, is never quite the same as it was, and characteristically our experience is marked by patterns of separation and return. Return to the ordinary, including the return that is appealed to recurrently in the *Investigations*, is not something that can be simple. In a sense there can be no simple *return*, for what you return to will not be the same as what you left. The ordinary you return to will then be an ordinary encountered with a sense both of new possibility and of intimacy lost: natural or animal absorption gives way to a kind of exile, iconically figured as the exit from Eden; but exile is also the condition of imagination and opening to the new. On the epic scale, think of Ulysses or the Ancient Mariner, who return marked by the trauma of what has happened. Think also, more prosaically, of the way that we stay with the same relationships, though they cannot – and should not – stay the same. Think of the way that we stay with ourselves. On the small scale, think of the piecemeal steps that Wittgenstein takes in returning an expression to its home in the language-game. By implication and by extension, and in view of the very nature of the signs that human beings are, language cannot stay the same.

This breaching of our natural condition comes especially and inevitably with language, and hence with exposure to the rules that shape our society's practices. But following a rule does not rule out new departures from that rule, and in the learning of language this is so from a remarkably early stage. Gustafsson quotes Cavell's extended riff on the word "feed", where "feed the cat" connects with "feed the meter", and so to "feed in the film" and "feed his pride" (Cavell 1979, 181). In another example Cavell considers the young child learning the word "pumpkin", which must presumably be connected with "pumping" and perhaps with "Mr Popkin" who lives next door (Cavell 1979, 176–177). These are associations that depart from the word's apparent immediate use, indeed that extend beyond immediacy itself, opening the way most crucially for imagination. The child experiments with the words she acquires, sometimes meaningfully, sometimes aimlessly, and hits upon new associations and possibilities for the word. In fact, if we can accept that this generally is how words are, then the way we use them acquires a sharper edge of responsibility, for they will shape possibilities not only for ourselves but for our community too. If this is right, there is an exposure in our use of words, an opening onto vast possibilities of meaningfulness, but there is a poignancy in language's breaching of the immediate, of animal intimacy.

The ordinary to which we return, this eventual ordinary, is an ordinary that is marked.

Around the middle of the period of sixteen years that it took Cavell to write *The Claim of Reason*, he produced a short book on *Walden*, Thoreau's experiment in writing and living. It is in response to that book's consideration of how we can bring it about that we live by our own determination that Cavell again speaks of resolve. We live by fate, Thoreau says, because we are "determined not to live by faith" (I, 15). We must learn to live well with the fact that we are looking for something we seem to have lost. *Walden* returns continually to questions of finding, trust, and interest, and of transformation, weighing their necessities and adumbrating what we might think of as a realistic spirit. "What they come to", Cavell writes,

> is the learning of resolution. This is what will replace our determination, or commitment, to fate, to the absence of freedom. It is not a matter of doing something new, of determining a course of action and committing ourselves to it, as to jail (II, 5) or to an asylum. Resolution has to do with stillness and with settling (a "clearing", he sometimes calls it). The summary of the writer's learning this is told in his myth of winter, by what happens to him on the ice. It is there that he finds the bottom of the pond and it is in winter that the owls prophesy and the fox awaits his transformation.
>
> (Cavell 1982, 99)

Why is this a matter of resolution? Resolution is, first of all, identified with freedom, understood as a replacement of fate: we are not born free, we are fated and thrown into particular circumstances; but we can place ourselves differently and, hence, gaining distance on fate, re-place it within our lives. And resolute action will depend not upon the *drama* of action so much as on a kind of withdrawal and, what might more fashionably now be called, centering. Resolution is found visually also in the crystalline clarity of the pond in winter, its "clearing" suggesting a kind of enlightenment, as well as anticipating the clearing between the trees made by the foresters that so drew Heidegger's attention.

Thoreau's building of his house in the woods might be seen as an enacted meditation on the building-dwelling-thinking that Heidegger a century later will thematise (Heidegger 1975/1954a). Heidegger's coupling of, or rather his weakening of the boundaries between, these words – the title of his lecture, *Bauen Wohnen Denken,* has no punctuation – is intended to suggest what might, in a different idiom, be thought an internal relation between these concepts and activities. But it is more than that: to speak, to think, is a kind of *poiesis*, and hence it is – minimal though this will for the most part be – a kind of construction or building. What it constructs is the place wherein we dwell, and without dwelling, building would not make sense. And that place *becomes* a place, rather than, say, a space determined on a grid-lined map, through coordinates of human connection, where meaning is constituted out of a remembering and projection, the purposiveness characteristic of human practices. It is surely far from incidental in importance that the tribe that Wittgenstein asks the reader to imagine in the second paragraph of the *Investigations* is one whose members are builders; and it is of pointed significance that the progressive difficulty in imagining this scene has to do with the absence of recognisably meaningful practices – that is, of those qualities of building, dwelling, and thinking that might ordinarily be taken for granted.

For all the coincidences between Thoreau's and Heidegger's themes and landscapes, however, their worlds are in the end set out of kilter: by a contrast between the eschatological drama of Dasein's being-towards-death and the different time-scheme of Thoreau's fox awaiting its transformation. The dispersal of the drama in the latter and its dispelling of heroic eschatology are found in the attention given to the seasonal sloughing of identity and the rhythms of diurnal and monthly change. Thoreau bathed every day in the pond, and it was, he testifies, a religious exercise. This dispersal or permeation is caught also in words of Martin Luther that Cavell takes as epigraph to *The Senses of Walden*:

> For all our life should be baptism, and the fulfilling of the sign, or the sacrament, of baptism; we have been set free from all else and wholly given over to baptism alone, that is, to death and resurrection. This glorious liberty of ours, and this understanding of baptism have been carried captive in our day.

Thoreau's vision of this fulfilling of the sign of baptism is nothing like the heroic destining of a person or a people, symbolised by the flow of the River Ister, as Heidegger, reading Hölderlin, finds this (Cavell 2005); it is rather a kind of instilling, symbolised by the stillness of Walden Pond and realized in the daily practice of washing and cleansing.

Instilling achieves a fidelity to the way things are, here, at this time, involving the observance of a daily regime that is, or can become, something other than dull mechanical routine. The vibrancy and validity of this are born not only of familiarity but also out of an acceptance of and receptivity to the strangeness in the familiar. In the end, however, and contrary to popular readings of Thoreau, it is not this particular place, Walden Pond, that is the heart of the matter: what is more important is the possibility, or perhaps the principle, of this combination of particular attachments (regimes of living attuned to them, acceptance of their finitude, commitments drawn by experience) with a readiness for departure – before, as it were, they fossilise or perhaps come to be romanticised or to parody themselves. Moreover, as Cavell puts this in this late paper, the manner of Thoreau's leaving of Walden demonstrates what Freud calls the work of mourning, letting the past go, giving it up, giving it over, giving away the Walden it was time for him to leave, without nostalgia, without a disabling elegiacism. Nostalgia is the inability to open the past to the future, as if the strangers who will replace you will never find what you have found. Such a negative heritage would be a poor thing to leave to *Walden's* readers, whom its writer identifies, among many ways, precisely as strangers.

(Cavell 2005, 217–218)

Thinking of the *topos* of the everyday, in which the paradox of the strange in the familiar is played out, as a possible site of meeting of Heidegger not only with Thoreau but with Wittgenstein, Cavell writes that it is "a place from which it can be seen both why Heidegger finds authenticity to demand departure and why Wittgenstein finds sense or sanity to demand return" (Cavell 1995, 163). The strange finds its place in Heidegger's *Unheimlichkeit*, but the idea of the stranger is mostly alien to *Dasein's* being-with-others – a manner of being suggestive of something held in common or, in Emmanuel Levinas's caustic remark, reminiscent of marching together. Cavell alludes also to a contrast between the journeying home or being homebound that exerts so strong a gravitational force in Heidegger's thought and the *sojourning* emphasised in Thoreau, where one is to live each day, everywhere and nowhere, as a task and an event (Cavell 2005, 229). Unlike the ideas of "mineness" and belonging that recur in Heidegger, there is here some sense of an essential immigrancy of the human, of an incoming or invention that depends upon reception, of something coming from outside. We return to ourselves as through a condition of estrangement, as though we have still to arrive at our words. Education, the education of grownups of which Cavell speaks (Cavell 1979, 125), requires our discovery of our immigrancy to ourselves.

Cavell has sometimes seen himself as working within the tear in philosophy that develops in the wake of Kant, and any comparison of Wittgenstein and Heidegger must perforce take up threads in the fabric of philosophy left hanging by this. My own discussion has focused on an English word, "resolute", in relation to two philosophers, both of whom wrote in German, and the problematics and possibilities of translation this exploits might be said also to be tangled amongst such threads. But where, in the end, does this connection take us? What does it show of the limits of language?

Where Word Breaks Off: Heidegger and the Limits of Language

It is obvious that, insofar as Heidegger might be said to arrive at ways of thinking congruent with Wittgenstein's, the lineage and context of his thought is very different – untrammelled by the kind of discussion that burdens standard and resolute readers. Space prevents examination of that lineage or of the development of Heidegger's ideas, regarding the limits of language. But in their later form they are focused most explicitly and intensely in his discussions of German poetry, especially that of Hölderlin and of the early twentieth-century poets Rainer Maria Rilke, Georg Trakl, and Stefan George.[7] Let me move directly to a high point in these discussions, his consideration of George's poem *Das Wort* (1928).

The poem comprises seven two-line stanzas. The first three present the poet-narrator as a traveller returning to his country and bringing with him wonderful strange things. At the border the ancient norn, goddess of fate and surely figuring here as a source of poetic inspiration, retrieves names from her well and bestows them on these new things. In the second set of stanzas (stanzas 4 to 6), the pattern is repeated: the poet-narrator returns with "a prize so rich and frail", but on this occasion the norn is unable to find any suitable word. This lays the way for the final stanza where the poet renounces the expectation of naming established in the first part of the poem.

Das Wort

Wunder von ferne oder traum
Bracht ich an meines landes saum

Und harrte bis die graue norn
Den namen fand in ihrem born –

Drauf konnt ichs greifen dicht und stark
Nun blüht und glänzt es durch die mark . . .

Einst langt ich an nach guter fahrt
Mit einem kleinod reich und zart

Sie suchte lang und gab mir kund:
"So schläft hier nichts auf tiefem grund"

Worauf es meiner hand entrann
Und nie mein land den schatz gewann . . .

So lernt ich traurig den verzicht:
Kein ding sei wo das wort gebricht.[8]

What is it that is being renounced (*versichten*)? In the first place, it may seem that this is an acknowledgement of the ineffable: there is a thing that the poet-narrator presents to the norn, and this turns out to be something she cannot name. The wistful tone of the poem pulls the reader towards this sense of mystery, hence reinforcing, contra Wittgenstein (PI §374), the idea that there is genuinely something one cannot do. But there is good reason to reject this interpretation: the last line states clearly that in the absence of language, no thing can be; and this absence is less ethereal than visceral (*das wort gebricht*) – the rupture of a breaking off or breaking down. A less hasty reading produces a second, more promising possibility: this is both to acknowledge a limit of language and the need to resist the urge to exceed that limit. This would not be to "police" language but to acknowledge the co-dependency of language and world. Such a reading requires elaboration, however, in two related respects, regarding what the poem says (and cannot say), and regarding the background to its saying.

The Originary Word

First, an indication of what it is that the norn cannot name is provided by the title of the poem. As Jussi Backman phrases this: "The treasure for which there is no word is the *word itself* in its essence as language" (Backman 2011, 63–64, italics in original). Developing this thought and drawing a parallel with Wittgenstein, he paraphrases: "the limits of the poet's country are the limits of his language" (ibid., 63). Herein lies a problem, I think, in that if the border the poet-narrator crosses is that of a country, then the task of the norn comes to seem more like translation. While that in itself would raise interesting questions, it is surely right to see the fabulous, quasi-mythical nature of the description as suggesting something different. Taking it as an allegory makes world rather than country the crucial reference point. This is the world as ordinarily understood, shaped by the range of ordinary human practice, and manifesting itself in the familiar ways. It is on this that the sciences depend and out of this that they are developed. Heidegger conceives of world as realised through the mutual appropriation of Dasein and things by way of language. The word that makes this possible cannot be captured in a name, and it cannot be grasped in a theory or given formal definition. "[T]he becoming speakable of things," as Backman succinctly expresses this, "is itself unspeakable" (ibid., 64). I take it that the sense of this unspeakability stands in some kind of parallel to the thought expressed by Appelqvist, as we saw earlier, that "I cannot describe the form of language if that form is a necessary condition for language to make sense in the first place" (Appelqvist 2016, 704). Unspeakability, however, does not rule out the possibility of an "indirect encounter with this essence by drawing our attention to the way discoursing takes place *from* and *on the basis of (von)* language" (Backman 2011, 65, italics in original). This is not only what the poem attempts but what Heidegger, in some of his writings, aims to provide.

Backman speaks of a "resignation" in the poet-narrator's response (in the last two lines), but he is careful to qualify the negative force that is felt in the poem and its translation. The way here is opened by judicious reference to Heidegger's development of the idea of *Gelassenheit* (letting-be, releasement), which suggests a kind of letting-go:

> "[R]eleasement" does not mean simply a passive submission to a higher, divine will; it is "beyond the distinction between activity and passivity".[8] Like the concept of "resolve" (*Entschlossenheit*) in *Being and Time*, "releasement" rather signifies a release from an exclusive concentration on things as present and a receptivity to their contextual background, which the later Heidegger calls *Gegen* or *Gegnet*, "region" or "country" – that against which (*contra, gegen*) things are encountered as present.
>
> (ibid., 65)[10]

If the poem helps in the acknowledgement of the background, an idea that will be developed further shortly, a stronger but more contentious point can also be pressed. This is that the breakdown of the word, according to Heidegger, occasions an awareness of the word *as event*, awareness that depends upon receptivity. Any idea of the essence of language must have nothing to do with imagining its essential properties or defining features: language is not to be theorised in that way. As Heidegger puts this, there can be no "philosophy of language". Yet, to open the way to this *experience* of language would itself be a matter of significance for philosophy, even, he contends, its new beginning (Heidegger 2004, 47). Preposterously perhaps but pressing this point further, Heidegger rephrases the last line of George's poem as: "An 'is' arises where the word breaks down." It is precisely at this limit of language that awareness of the event of language, its bringing of things into being, is potentially realised. And this is, to quote Backman further,

> a transition from metaphysics to another beginning – a transition that opens up a new experience of the "is", of Being itself in its full dimensionality. The new realm disclosed by the breakdown is the uncontrollable background dimension of meaningfulness on which we ultimately depend, even though the full extent of this dependency is yet to be elaborated in Western thought.
>
> (Backman 2011, 66)

Words, in the becoming speakable of things, set limits that in their turn can be both limiting and enabling. Words by their very nature cut and divide. It may, on occasion, be a matter of pain that this is what they do. But how else should they define and make sense? The limits they embody are enabling where they open possibilities of thought or practice, pathways that extend in untold possibilities of projection. Words enable us to converse and think, but their limits can become limitations where they settle into habitual patterns, sometimes through the natural human acquiescence in inauthenticity, and sometimes through educational deficit or political repression. Such deficits and repressions are limitations of what the world can be. And no word can be without its background of context and support.

The Background as Context, Earth, Support

The background needs to be understood in two ways. First, the contextual background presents an aspect of what one cannot do: whatever is said or done depends upon a background, and this, insofar as it is to remain background, cannot be directly described. This background comprises the range of practices and circumstances against which our more consciously focused activity shows up. Plainly, the acknowledgement of the significance of the background is a key feature of Wittgenstein's later writings, as it is of Heidegger's philosophy, from the phenomenological elements of *Being and Time* to the foregrounding of language in the later lectures. It is also the case that the breakdown of a line of reasoning – the frustration of expression, and dead-ends and aporia in dialogue – may occasion an experience of that background, perhaps its direct exposure and, hence, its being made foreground. Acknowledgement of this necessary background (and recognising the limit that it constitutes on what can be said) weighs heavily against the impulse in philosophy towards metaphysics. The contexts that Wittgenstein draws attention to are piecemeal and various, much as the contexts referred to in the phenomenology of *Being and Time* are of ordinary human scale and as the deference to language in Heidegger's later lectures is diverse. Both can work to resist the insistence of the voice that says "This is how it must be." This is a discipline of thought that constitutes something like a renunciation.

But the background has a further dimension, which is more difficult to describe, and this is thematised more directly in Heidegger than in Wittgenstein. It can be seen in the light of what Heidegger calls "earth", a term that is brought into play with "world". The relationship is evoked, for example, in "The Origin of the Work of Art".[10] If world is realised through the *poiesis* of the word and the work of art, earth remains the support that neither word nor art can reach. The material support to the painting, for example, the paper or canvas or board, is not something that the work can depict, not without relying upon a further support – as in the material support of the kind of painting that depicts, from behind the artist's back, the easel, the canvas, the palette, brush, and paint, the marks that have been made, and, still further away, the scene that is being depicted by the pictured artist. The support, like the background referred to earlier, recedes as it is approached, refusing direct representation.

The support extends into earth as what is already there, unnamed, before *poiesis* brings things into the world, and as what must remain in that way. Heidegger writes: "The earth appears openly cleared as itself only when it is perceived and preserved as that which is by nature undisclosable, that which shrinks from every disclosure and constantly keeps itself closed up" (Heidegger 1975, 47). Earth cannot be directly described, but it can in this way be acknowledged.

Whereas the contextual background is such that there could be a shift of focus (bringing forth one aspect and hiding another, in what might be thought of as a semantic shift), background of support, the earth in Heidegger's terminology, cannot be brought into view.

Pictures and Words: The Grace of Language

Wittgenstein's proposal that we yield to the temptation to use the *picture* – that "there is an object there from which I derive its description" and that I do this to "investigate what the *application* of the picture looks like" (PI §374)) – needs to be related to the seriousness with which he came to take pictures and the compelling influence that they can have. This applies especially to religious pictures and their part in the kind of self-examination to which the human being is inclined. Stephen Reynolds (2013) finds a Lutheran aspect in this that he connects with the call of conscience in Heidegger. Neither philosopher believes that it is necessary first to establish the existence of God and then to decide whether to lead a religious life. For both, it is the way one lives one's life that comes first, and in both cases there is a sense of being called. Resoluteness now becomes something like a readiness for the call of conscience (in Heidegger) and for the way a picture commands (Wittgenstein). In both cases there is an eschewal or renunciation of any attempt to seek explanation for this in a transcendent being. Transcendence lies within the *possibilities* of the way of life, the affordances of which are words and pictures. Contrary to the heroically burdened image of authenticity, the picture of resoluteness that now emerges points to a kind of passivity, which is rightfully a receptivity. What was said here about *Gelassenheit* needs to be understood as relating to the nature of language itself. Words *give* in that they are not ultimately fixed in meaning but available for projection into further contexts. So, then, grace can be seen as a quality of language itself. It may be tempting to some to put this in terms of a contrast with the tendencies of science and technology towards fixing and controlling, But this would itself be a partial arresting and perhaps a perversion, at least a limitation, of science and technology themselves, which in turn depend upon this openness of thought to new possibilities. Thinking requires the receptiveness to allow new thoughts to come to mind.[12] And sometimes we shall be disturbed, cut and divided, by those thoughts.

Over interpretation

> If you stand right fronting and face to face to a fact, you will see the sun glimmer on both its surfaces, as though it were a cimeter, and feel its sweet edge dividing you through the heart and marrow, and so you will happily conclude your mortal career. Be it life or death, we crave only reality.
>
> Thoreau, *Walden*

> "Be bloody, bold, and resolute."
>
> *Macbeth*, IV.i.85[13]

In this discussion, I have been wary of broaching the many texts of Heidegger relevant to this book's main theme in view of the shifts of critical register that such disparate styles require, within and between Heidegger and Wittgenstein. I have moved the discussion from Wittgenstein to Heidegger by way of Cavell. Cavell was reading and teaching Heidegger in the 1960s at the same time as he was developing his creative, penetrating response to the *Investigations*. Thoreau, about whom Cavell wrote his "little book", *The Senses of Walden* (1972), in a six-week period in roughly the middle of the sixteen years that he was writing *The Claim of Reason* (1979), can reasonably be described as developing, as we saw, themes of building-dwelling-thinking *avant la lettre*. The route I have taken serves, I hope, to lay the way for this moment in Heidegger's late lectures (there where the danger of a "disabling elegiacism" is greatest),[14] this moment where he considers George's *Das Wort*, and to enable reasonable reception of its consideration of the limits of language.

As I have acknowledged, my own discussion has exploited the connotations of the English word, "resolute", in relation to philosophers who wrote in German. If this needs further apology, it is surely to the point that the preponderance of the debate to which my discussion relates has, in fact, been in English. Have I pressed the matter too far? Have I relied too much on the strength of a word and, hence, indulged in over-interpretation? In a wide-ranging survey of the literature, Silver Bronzo records early criticism to the effect that "resolute reading" has always been a problematic term because of its implicit moral connotations, connotations that hinder "a dispassionate adjudication of the debate", and the suggestion that it be replaced by "a more neutral expression", say "therapeutic reading" or "austere reading" (Bronzo 2012, 47). My own inclination has been rather towards the view that the discomfort caused by those moral connotations might be the means whereby the arguments might have most purchase. In the light of Wittgenstein's acknowledgements of the wider ethical dimensions that motivate his philosophy, it seems difficult and in fact wrong to resist connotations that this central term prompts.

Understanding of the limits of language in Wittgenstein and Heidegger is evident also in their respective (changing) styles of expression. The wariness that they shared of the encroachments of science and technology, the sense of cultural decline, and the suspicions of academic philosophy in its dominant incarnations inclined them to belief in attention to language as a source of recovery. Notwithstanding considerable differences in their approaches, there is in their work a common sense of language as giving something, providing something beyond what can be rationally calculated or fully anticipated: there is a grace to language that is revealed where there is receptiveness in the thinker.[15] Both philosophers were in certain respects culturally conservative in their taste, yet both were innovative in what they wrote. But when one compares the discursive density of *Being and Time* and the sometimes painfully nostalgic style of Heidegger's late lectures, not to mention his own poetising, with the austere stylistic modernism of the *Tractatus* and the remarkable dialogic experimentation of the *Investigations*, the contrast seems clear. Differences in temperament and sensibility are surely evident here, yet both philosophers are committed to finding a means of expression that rises to the substance of what they have to say. This in itself is a reflection of resolve.

I began by recalling the sense of humour in Wittgenstein, and the deeper irony that can go with this, qualities that seem for the most part to have escaped Heidegger. Wittgenstein's fascination with the word "bloody" – his mischievous amusement over this English swear-word but also his use of it in affirming the need to go the bloody hard way (neither of which one can imagine in Heidegger's expression) – resounds with a seriousness about philosophy and a sense that it too can risk, if not cost, blood.[16]

Notes

1. Of course, the alarm bells may ring again for the Kantian reader, who will insist that logical form and the metaphysical subject are transcendental and not matters of *substance*. Yet it is not clear how far this disclaimer embraces what is intended in the phrase "whereof one cannot speak" (TLP 7).
2. Martin Gustafsson's contribution to *Rileggere Witgenstein di James Conant e Cora Diamond* (Rereading James Conant and Cora Diamond's Wittgenstein) is entitled "L'importanza di essere resoluti" (The importance of being resolute). Quotations that follow are from Gustafsson's original unpublished English text, not from the published Italian version (Gustafsson, 2011).
3. See, for example, Putnam's remarks when interviewed by Naoko Saito and myself (Saito and Standish 2014).
4. The *Appendix: On Wittgenstein* is adapted from a letter to M. O'C. Drury dated 7 November 1965.
5. Once again, it might be said that, on the Kantian reading, the emphasis in the idea of limits is not on the inability to do something (underscored by the resolute account) but rather on the recognition of the status of what lies at the limit, namely that it is not on a par with ordinary empirical statements.
6. For further discussion of this paragraph, in conjunction with §89, see David Stern (2004, 130–131) and Cavell (1995, 1996), both of whom draw attention to the ways that sentences within these paragraphs carry a degree of

ambiguity: they point towards both "fighting the fantasy" and "granting it", in Cavell's phrase.

7. It is an interesting coincidence that Trakl was one of the main beneficiaries of Wittgenstein's generosity when he gave away a substantial part of his fortune.
8. A variety of translations of the poem into English can be found at: http://bill knottblog.blogspot.com/2013/12/das-wort.html. Accessed on 20 July 2019.
9. See Heidegger, "Conversation on a Country Path about Thinking", in Heidegger 1966/1959, 54–55.
10. See Heidegger, "Conversation on a Country Path about Thinking", in Heidegger, 1966/1959, 81.
11. For a thoughtful recent discussion, see Stephen Mulhall (2018–2019).
12. For an interesting discussion, see Williams (2018).
13. These are the words of the Second Apparition that the witches conjure for Macbeth: "Be bloody, bold, and resolute; laugh to scorn the power of man, for none of woman born shall harm Macbeth" (IV.i.85). It is the apparition of a bloody child, and what is conjured is a dream of immunity from the human condition.
14. In "The Turning", much of Heidegger's discussion reiterates phrasing from Hölderlin's *Patmos* to say that there where the dangers of Enframing are greatest, the saving power grows. "Disabling elegiacism" is Cavell's expression, as we saw earlier.
15. Anthony Rudd has commented on what he sees as a Romantic modernism in both Heidegger and Wittgenstein, associating this with the resistance to scientism that they undoubtedly shared, with the move towards a re-enchantment of the world, and with their stylistic innovations.
16. An earlier version of part of this chapter was presented to the British Wittgenstein Society in 2013. I am grateful to those present for their response and criticisms. I thank Suzy Harris for comments on earlier drafts. Hanne Appelqvist is thanked for her meticulous editing and helpful comments and suggestions.

References

Appelqvist, Hanne (2016) "On Wittgenstein's Kantian Solution to the Problem of Philosophy", *British Journal of the History of Philosophy* 21 (4), 697–719.

Backman, Jussi (2011) "The Transitional Breakdown of the Word: Heidegger and Stefan George's Encounter with Language", *Gatherings: The Heidegger Circle Annual* 1, 54–73.

Bronzo, Silver (2012) "The Resolute Reading and Its Critics: An Introduction to the Literature", *Wittgenstein-Studien* 3 (1), 45–80.

Cavell, Stanley (1979) *The Claim of Reason: Wittgenstein, Skepticism, Morality, and Tragedy*. Oxford: Oxford University Press.

Cavell, Stanley (1982) *The Senses of Walden*. Chicago and London: University of Chicago Press.

Cavell, Stanley (1995) "Notes and Afterthoughts on the Opening of Wittgenstein's *Investigations*", in his *Philosophical Passages: Wittgenstein, Emerson, Austin, Derrida*. Oxford: Blackwell, 125–186.

Cavell, Stanley (1996) "The *Investigations*' Everyday Aesthetics of Itself", in S. Mulhall (ed), *The Cavell Reader*. Oxford: Blackwell.

Cavell, Stanley (2005) *Philosophy the Day After Tomorrow*. Cambridge, MA: Harvard University Press.

Cavell, Stanley (2007) "Companionable Thinking", in A. Crary (ed), *Wittgenstein and the Moral Life*. Cambridge, MA: MIT Press, 281–298.

Conant, James (2003) "On Going the Bloody Hard Way in Philosophy", in John Whittaker *(ed)*, *The Possibilities of Sense*. Basingstoke: Palgrave Macmillan, 85–129.

Conant, James (2007) "Mild Mono-Wittgensteinianism", in Alice Crary (ed), *Wittgenstein and the Moral Life: Essays in Honor of Cora Diamond*. Cambridge, MA: MIT Press, 31–142.

Egan, David, Reynolds, Stephen and Wendland, Aaron James (eds) (2013) *Wittgenstein and Heidegger*. London: Routledge.

Goldfarb, Warren (1997) "Metaphysics and Nonsense: On Cora Diamond's *The Realistic Spirit*", *Journal of Philosophical Research* 22, 57–73.

Gustafsson, Martin (2011) "L'importanza di essere risoluti", in Rileggere Wittgenstein di James Conant e Cora Diamond, a symposum with Pasquale Fascolla, *Iride*, 1.2011, 201–210 (Italian).

Heidegger, Martin (1962) *Being and Time*. Ttranslated by J. Macquarrie and E. Robinson. Oxford: Blackwell.

Heidegger, Martin (1975/1954a) "Building Dwelling Thinking", in A. Hofstadter (trans), *Poetry, Language, Thought*. New York and London: Harper & Row, 143–163.

Heidegger, Martin (1975/1954b) "The Origin of the Work of Art", in A. Hofstadter (trans), *Poetry, Language, Thought*. New York and London: Harper & Row, 15–88.

Heidegger, Martin (1977/1962) "The Turning", in W. Lovitt (trans), *The Question Concerning Technology and Other Essays*. New York and London: Harper & Row, 36–49.

Heidegger, Martin (1966/1959) *Discourse on Thinking: A Translation of Gelassenheit*. Translated by J. M. Anderson and E. H. Freund. New York and London: Harper & Row.

Heidegger, Martin (2004) *On the Essence of Language: The Metaphysics of Language and the Essencing of the Word*. Translated by W. Torres Gregory and Y. Unna. Albany, NY: SUNY Press.

Mulhall, Stephen (2006) *Wittgenstein's Private Language: Grammar, Nonsense, and Imagination in Philosophical Investigations, §§ 243–315*. Oxford: Oxford University Press.

Mulhall, Stephen (2018–2019) "Heidegger's Fountain: Ecstasis, Mimesis and Engrossment in the Origin of the Work of Art", *Proceedings of the Aristotelian Society* 119 (2), 1–23.

Reynolds, Stephen (2013) "Heidegger's Religious Picture", in D. Egan, S. Reynolds and A. J. Wendland (eds), *Wittgenstein and Heidegger*. London: Routledge, 195–210.

Saito, N. and Standish, P. (2014) "Hilary Putnam Interviewed by Naoko Saito and Paul Standish", *Journal of Philosophy of Education* 48 (1), 1–27.

Schönbaumsfeld, Genia (2010) "A 'Resolute Later Wittgenstein'", *Metaphilosophy* 41 (5), 649–668.

Stern, David (2004) *Wittgenstein's* Philosophical Investigations: *An Introduction*. Cambridge: Cambridge University Press.

Waismann, Friedrich (1979) *Wittgenstein and the Vienna Circle: Conversation*. Edited by B. McGuiness. Oxford: Wiley-Blackwell.

Williams, Emma (2018) "Language's Grace: Redemption and Education in J.M. Coetzee's *Disgrace, Special Issue: Philosophy, Literature and Education*", *Journal of Philosophy of Education* 52 (4), 627–641.

7 Moore's Paradox and Limits in Language Use

Yrsa Neuman

1. Introduction

The philosophical tangle known as Moore's Paradox is associated with the sentence "I believe it is raining and it is not raining". Moore noted that it would be odd for a speaker to assert this proposition about herself, although it could be true that "she believes it is raining and it is not raining". He calls this tangle an "absurdity". The central tension in Moore's "absurdity" is that there is something bewildering about the fact that there seems to be a logical obstacle to asserting a sentence which is well formed and not contradictory. In an important sense, Moore's paradox concerns the limits of the use of language.

Since Moore and Wittgenstein, the paradox has been reformulated and reinterpreted many times over, sometimes to the extent that it is unclear whether what is discussed deserves to bear Moore's name at all.[1] Moreover, it is not clear whether the original problem should be called a "paradox" in the first place. Even Wittgenstein, allegedly the person who named the original tangle "Moore's paradox", considered the presence of a paradoxical feature open for scrutiny (ML, 177). In the following, I will show how Wittgenstein, by the help of grammatical investigation, makes clear that the paradox is only apparent.

In discussions of Moore's paradox, the idea that grammatical investigations render results in the form of general descriptions of language use sometimes manifests itself as the view that Wittgenstein's overarching point in these discussions is to say something important about belief.[2] In this chapter, rather than condensing descriptions of grammar into pieces of perspicuous presentation or to theories of usage of psychological concepts, I try to pay attention to how Wittgenstein actually treats and comes to terms with different sorts of limits in language use. This of course is not a theoretically innocent approach, but springs from a radical focus on methods of philosophizing.

2. Differences and Similarities of Use

Moore's own solution to the problem was to distinguish between what is asserted and what is implied by the assertion. According to him, my saying something always "implies", that I believe what I say is the case. In this way, a *sort of* contradiction between what is asserted and what is implied can be generated, a contradiction which – so Moore thought, although hesitantly – should explain the sense of absurdity.[3] While Wittgenstein got very excited about the tangle, and wrote to Moore that it is "something *similar* to a contradiction", that he had made a discovery, and should publish it, he did not agree with Moore's solution (ML, 177). Wittgenstein's remarks related to the paradox do latch on to Moore's suggested solution but continue far beyond it.[4]

In his discussions of themes related to Moore's paradox, Wittgenstein investigates and clarifies the grammar of belief expressions and ascriptions. Already a first glean on this material displays important aspects of Wittgenstein's method. This is not because of how he describes his method, but rather how he himself carries out the investigation. My contention is that rather than being a presentation of an outright alternative "solution" to Moore's paradox, Wittgenstein's treatment consists in the conceptual mapping of a territory around belief expression and ascription, which brings into view some of the assumptions which are needed for the paradox to arise. Some of these assumptions are related to transgressions of the limits of language use in different ways. In the present discussion, I understand "limits" in a broad sense, and am not concerned with the Tractarian picture of language as a whole and its limits, but limits or boundaries in language use which manifest themselves in differences and similarities of use, sometimes called rules of grammar (cf. TLP 5.6–5.62).

3. The Wittgenstein Material

The most frequently discussed section of Wittgenstein's writings on Moore's paradox is found in what was posthumously published as Part II of *Philosophical Investigations*, also called *Philosophy of Psychology, a fragment* (henceforth PPF), section x. Wittgenstein returned to the issue or its vicinity many times over the late 1940s. Hence, apart from PI, I have paid some attention to the collections of remarks published as *Remarks on the Philosophy of Psychology I* (RPP I) and *Last Writings on the Philosophy of Psychology 1 and 2* (LW I, LW II). In these latter collections, the subject matter is quite similar to that of PPF, which is unsurprising as the material published in them was used as the basis for the whole which became PPF.

The background of these published collections of remarks are a few manuscripts ranging mostly from 1946–1949. PPF was a manuscript on which Wittgenstein worked in the spring of 1949 (MS 144 in von Wright's numbering system; see von Wright 1969). This manuscript was a clear copy of a selection of remarks from 1946–1949. More than half of the remarks are from the period between October 1948 and March 1949, transferred or reworked from the two manuscripts published as LW I, and in a later versions as the typescript 229 published as RPP I. MS144 was later typed out into a typescript in which Wittgenstein added corrections by hand, and it was lost after the printing of the PI (von Wright and Nyman 1982, ix). The numbering i–xiv was added by the editors, not by Wittgenstein himself. I use the paragraph numbering introduced by Hacker and Schulte in their revised version of PI.

Wittgenstein's procedure towards more finalized work often followed the pattern described earlier: he would make notes in notebooks and then have entire notebooks or collections of remarks from them typed up. After that, he would sometimes read through the typescripts and make notes in them by hand. Then, based on the typescript, he wrote out clear copies by hand. The collections I have used had been prepared to a varying degree – the LW I material for instance, is "of a more provisional and improvised nature" (von Wright and Nyman 1982, ix) and contains more variants than RPP, as it consists of two manuscripts (MS137 and MS138). (From these papers, the editors von Wright and Nyman excluded remarks marked clearly with "II" (parallel lines) and published them in *Culture and Value*.) Apart from these published collections, I have made use of digital sources and tools for searches.[5] LW II contains an additional portion of material which Wittgenstein edited in 1948–1951 on the same themes.

These four collections of remarks all pertain to what Peter Hacker calls Wittgenstein's Philosophy of Psychology (Hacker 2010), which makes out altogether some 1900 pages (or 10%) of the *Nachlass*. Hacker summarizes the whole accurately by stating

> what we find is a painstaking *exploration* of language games with psychological concepts. Many different concepts are investigated, patterns of similarity and difference are painstakingly teased out, and conceptual connections described. The tone is tentative. We see Wittgenstein applying the methods of philosophical analysis that he had developed over the previous sixteen years.
>
> (Hacker 2010, 278)

Hacker continues

> there are numerous reflections on methodology in philosophical psychology as Wittgenstein struggles to determine his goal and to find his way. Although these writings are incomplete and unpolished, we can learn much about how he thought problems in philosophical psychology should be handled.
>
> (ibid., 278)

162   *Yrsa Neuman*

This chapter is a case study in this vein, on a share of those remarks that relate to Moore's paradox: How do different aspects of limits of language use play out in Wittgenstein's discussions of Moore's paradox? What role in the solution or dissolution of the paradox could these remarks play?

I have surveyed some of the remarks in the above-mentioned parts of Wittgenstein's *Nachlass* in which he explicitly discusses Moore's paradox, as well as the paragraphs in their vicinity, that is, in the context in which the issues are treated. (In the few cases when I refer to other parts of the material, I mention that explicitly.[6])

4. An Asymmetry in Language Use

In the PPF §§86–110 (PI II: x), Wittgenstein's discussion of Moore's paradox is framed in the more overarching discussion of "inner and outer". It appears in connection with a discussion of the relation between first and third person, of what it is to observe, to observe oneself, for example one's fear (PPF, ix), and what it is to "describe a state of mind". In the paragraphs leading up to the mention of Moore's paradox, Wittgenstein has elaborated on the way in which the relation one has to one's own behaviour is different from one's relation to the behaviour of others.

He writes:

> Moore's paradox can be put like this: the utterance "I believe that this is the case" is used in a similar way to the assertion "This is the case"; and yet the *supposition* that I believe this is the case is not used like the supposition that this is the case.
>
> (PPF §87)

In this paragraph, Wittgenstein rephrases the problematic feature in Moore's absurdity: if I said "I believe it's raining", I would *commit* to an assertion, although perhaps hesitantly. This commitment could manifest itself in action – for instance, I might reach for an umbrella when I am about to go out. Here, I might as well have said "It's raining" since the same action would follow. In this way, "I believe p" means roughly the same as the assertion "p": it has the same use. By contrast, if we *suppose* that "it's raining", the picture before us must include drops of water; however, if we 'suppose that I believe it's raining', the picture would not necessarily contain any rain at all, although perhaps a stolen umbrella.

Wittgenstein continues the train of thought:

> So it seems as if the assertion "I believe" were not the assertion of what is supposed in the supposition "I believe"!

Similarly: the statement "I believe it's going to rain" has a similar sense, that is to say, a similar use, to "It's going to rain", but that of "I believed then that it was going to rain" is not similar to that of "It rained then".

(PPF §§88–89)

Outright assertions and expressions of belief have a similar use, but this similarity comes to an end. This discontinuity we can call a limit of language: it is the end of a parallel between the uses of two utterances, of belief expression and assertion.

Having pointed at the similarity of the use of the expression "I believe" and the outright assertion and the ending of the parallel, Wittgenstein goes on to other expected and breaking parallels, such as the parallel between belief expression regarding past and future. This paragraph continues:

But surely "I believed" must say the very same thing in the past tense as "I believe" in the present! – Surely $\sqrt{-1}$ must mean just the same for -1, as $\sqrt{1}$ means for 1! This signifies nothing at all.

(PPF §89)

Hence, in the second half of the paragraph, Wittgenstein, in dialogical mode, enters a reaction in quotation marks: that surely the past and present of an expression must "say the very same thing". Immediately thereafter he enters another reaction, thereby comparing the relation of "I believe" in the past and present tense to the square root of -1 and the square root of 1 with their respective radicands (the number inside the square root), and comments "This signifies nothing at all" ("Das heißt gar nichts"). Indeed: the relation between the square roots of -1 and of 1 is merely orthographically or superficially the same: in mathematics the square root of -1 would be an imaginary number, i, by conventional extension, since the square root function (and thereby the sign, the radix) is originally defined on positive real numbers. The square root function for negative numbers works like this: the square root of 4 is 2. The square root of -4 is 2i (the imaginary number 2), it is not -2. In other words, the relation between 1 and -1 within and outside the radix is not at all "the very same thing". Rather, such a comparison would entail a serious misunderstanding of the square root sign and its "logic".

Here, Wittgenstein shows by analogy that the *expectation* that assertion and belief should work in the same way in past and present tense would be the extrapolation of the working of a rule. This rule-induced expectation on how language works lies at the foundation of the absurdity in Moore's paradox. We get a sort of contradiction, but it is only in the first person and in the present tense that this tension occurs.

Wittgenstein concludes with a kind of explanatory remark:

> Different concepts touch here and run side by side for a stretch. One does not have to think that all these lines are *circles*.
>
> (PPF §108)

To this same paragraph in RPPI, Wittgenstein had included a picture, which he omitted from PPF:

Figure 7.1 MS-137, by courtesy of The Master and Fellows of Trinity College Cambridge.

Hence, by way of contrasting and comparing, Wittgenstein brings out a limit in language use, manifested by a false expectation of symmetry.

5. Differences Between First and Third Person

Another central and recurring theme in Wittgenstein's discussions of Moore's paradox, both in PI and elsewhere, ensues in circumstances in which Wittgenstein investigates how our relation to our own words, but also to our fears and beliefs, are different from our relation to the words, fears, and beliefs of others.

For instance, in LW II Wittgenstein writes:

> I *can* not observe myself as I do someone else, cannot ask myself "What is this person likely to do now?" etc.
>
> Therefore the verb "He believes", "I believed" *can* not have the kind of continuation in the first person as the verb 'to eat'.
>
> "But what *would* the continuation be that I was expecting?!" I can see none.
>
> (LW II, 10)

Figure 7.2 MS-169, 14r, by courtesy of The Master and Fellows of Trinity College Cambridge.

He responds on the following page that if I could infer from my own utterances, the "continuation would be 'I seem to believe' " (LW II, 11). This is a kind of limit in language use, namely, that I "cannot ask [about] myself 'What is this person likely to do now?' " (LW II, 10), that "I do not draw conclusions as to my probable actions from my words" (LW II, 10f).

Later on in, there is a note along these lines:

> So it's a kind of disposition of the believing person. This is revealed to me in the case of someone else by his behaviour; and |192| by his words. And so just as well by the utterance "I believe . . ." as by the simple assertion. – Now what about my own case: how do I myself recognize my own disposition? – Here I would have to be able to do what others do – to attend to myself, listen to myself talking, make inferences from what I say!
>
> (PPF §102, cf slightly different formulation in LW II, 12)

A few pages earlier he writes:

> My own relation to my words is wholly different from other people's.
> I do not listen to them and thereby learn something about myself. They have a completely different relation to my actions than to the actions of others.

> If I listened to the words of my mouth, I would be able to say that
> someone else is speaking out of my mouth.
>
> (LW II, 9)

And in PPF:

> My attitude to my own words is wholly different from that of others.
>   I could find that variant conjugation of the verb, if only I could say
> "I seem to believe".
>   If I listened to the words issuing from my mouth, then I could say
> that someone else was speaking out of it.
>
> (PPF §§103–104)

There is a shift towards a different story here, namely, that if the grammar of belief expression and ascription functioned differently, Moore's
paradox would not arise. Then the world too – human life – would have
to be different.

From our earlier observations, drawn from the remarks quoted so far,
we see the Moorean absurdity unfold as a consequence of the failure to
observe the way we actually relate to our own words, as opposed to the
words of others. It is a failure which feeds on the expectation of grammatical unity or symmetry. It is important to note the fact that Wittgenstein does not speak about words alone, of mere *de dicto* as opposed to
de re – Moore's paradox is simultaneously a consequence of a failure to
see the way things are, the way our world works.[7]

6. Transgressions of Limits?

The differences between how we relate to our own words, our own
beliefs, our own actions, and to those of others, are differences that must
be observed in order to avoid philosophical entanglement. Nevertheless,
the failure to do so is not the sole cause of the Moorean absurdity. Nor is
this the endpoint of Wittgenstein's investigation. He counters and works
through the false expectation of grammatical unity with the help of imagined situations, but curiously does not expressly prohibit or inhibit the
use of expressions which seemingly transgress these limits. Instead, he
investigates the circumstances in which the continuations could make
sense.

> "Judging from my words, *this* is what I believe."
>
> (The same remark in PPF 105 & LW II, 11)

> (Now, it would be possible to think up circumstances in which such
> an utterance would make sense. But we are not talking about this use
> of the word "belief".)

And someone could also say "It's going to rain, but I don't believe it" if there were indications that two people were speaking through his mouth. Language games would be played here which we could imagine, to be sure, but which normally we don't encounter.

And then it would be possible for someone to say "It is raining and I don't believe it". [PPF addition: "or 'It seems to me that my ego believes this, but it isn't true'".] One would have to fill out the picture with indications that two personalities were speaking through his mouth.

(LW II, 11, see PPF §105)[8]

In a number of places, Wittgenstein returns to how "one would have to imagine a kind of behaviour suggesting that two beings were speaking through my mouth" (e.g., PPF §105). Hence, Wittgenstein uses an imaginary language game to show how different the world would have to be in order for certain of our "grammatical expectations" to be fulfilled. But he also presents or includes non-imagined situations in which no boundaries of language use are touched upon but in which the parallel between assertion and first person belief expression do not hold.

For instance, Wittgenstein provides examples of situations in which I observe myself. In PI, many of these remarks are situated in the first third of the book, in no textual vicinity of the sections on Moore's paradox which are found in last third, but in LW II they are presented immediately before these:

A thought which one month ago was still unbearable to me is no longer so today (A touch which was painful yesterday is no longer so today.) This is the result of an observation.

(LW II, 6; see PFF § 68)

This serves to show that, despite making clear statements – in a number of remarks – that we do not observe our own behaviour, the possibility of self-observation is not excluded, although it is not taken to be an ordinary course of action: "Language games would be played here which we could imagine, to be sure, but which normally we don't encounter". Here, self-observation specifically relates to such mental states as pain and grief. Again, these remarks are not an outright rejection of special uses of language or of imagined language games, but may be read as an explication and investigation of what such an extension of a language game would entail, the investigation of a possibility. Wittgenstein resists grammatical regimentation in the sense that he does not rule out certain ways of speaking (or uses of words), but views different instances of use as possibilities on a par, all eligible for investigation. In doing so, he treats language games as structures which may take different turns (cf. PI §108).[9]

The question how to understand the later Wittgenstein's results of grammatical investigations is a recurring theme in Wittgenstein scholarship which runs deep and relates to his very methodological convictions and his view of philosophy. I take the character of Wittgenstein's grammatical investigations illuminated here as a clue to the kind of aim his investigations have. Classification or final description of grammatical traits of specific psychological concepts, or a final "analysis" is not the central result of his investigation, rather it is the continuous work on the ways in which philosophers (and others too) tend to be tempted to go wrong in their thinking.

7. Moorean Sentences and Being in Order

We saw that although we are reminded that our relation to our own words, beliefs, fears, and so forth is different from our relation to those of others, Wittgenstein does not rule out the possibility for us to observe ourselves in some circumstances – even if he notes about those circumstances that "We are not talking about this use of the word belief" (LW II, 11).

What, then, is this difference between the circumstances or contexts in which we do not observe ourselves and the ones in which we may do so? Is it to be cashed out (as has been suggested) in terms of normal and abnormal or ordinary and special uses of language? And if so, is the difference to be drawn between normal and abnormal use the philosophical discovery of a boundary in language or the instituting of such a boundary? What are we to make of the cases or language games in which Moorean sentences would be alright? There are variations of an answer to be found in Wittgenstein's writings, such as his remark: "It is possible to think out a language game in which these words do not strike us as absurd", but in that case, the speaker "no longer plays the ordinary language game, but some different one" (RPPI §820).

Lawrence Goldstein (in *Clear and Queer Thinking* 1999) writes that there are cases "where Mooronic assertions are apt, just as there are instances where the utterance of a contradiction is intelligible" (Goldstein 1999, 104). (He takes split personality as an example.) He goes on: "In such instances there is some story to be told, against which background an utterance which, when viewed 'cold' or context-less looks odd, makes perfectly good sense" (ibid., 104). His answer about the difference between normal and "Mooronic" or contradictory assertions is that the latter are utterances which require explicit contexts.

As we saw, we can – as Wittgenstein himself does – think up cases in which the sentence schema could be or is used. Let me give another example where a Moorean sentence works: if I keep feeling with my hand behind my chair I may quite understandably explain to my company at the table that "I believe I have my bag with me, but I don't" (Neuman 2015, 174; 189).[10]

However, when it comes to contextlessness or utterances viewed "cold", contrary to how Goldstein sets up the dichotomy, a central characteristic of *Moorean sentences* is that they don't work although they seem to be in order. Moreover, it is when they are *void of context* that they seem to be in order: it is in the very philosophical situation in which they are held under the magnifying glass, that they *lack a context of use*. The paradoxical feature runs on the very fact that, when cold, the Moorean sentences do not *only* look odd, but they *also* look alright. At the very least, they look alright to the extent that we feel that we need to mobilize some kind of philosophical apparatus of explanation to fence them off.

My claim is that we should take it to be a central feature of Moorean sentences that they are never in order. The moment we think up a use for such strings of words, with circumstances in which they can do work, they are no longer Moorean (i.e., problematic) and we are no longer in the grip of the paradox (i.e., "we are not talking about *this* use of the word") (LW II, 11). Otherwise, we have moved on to a mere discussion of orthographical matters or psychological features of phrase meanings (surface grammar), the philosophical relevance of which would need to be established separately. When it comes to Moore's paradox, then, "If we do indeed have a use for a certain expression, then it is, logically speaking, perfectly in order", as Peter Winch writes about Wittgenstein's mature thinking (Winch 2001, 207). What needs to be explained is not why the Moorean sentence fails, but why we feel the urge to philosophize about a mere piece of surface grammar, and why we cannot let go of the puzzlement.

8. Features, Not Limitations

In my view, the work that Wittgenstein is principally doing in his treatment of Moore's paradox is this: he is issuing grammatical reminders, reminders of how language is used and not used, in order to reveal the roots of our inclinations both to get rid of the sentence and to keep it as part of our language. This is why the most suitable way out of paradox at a time of Moorean confusion would be to say "That's not the way I meant it" (PI §125): when we follow the rules of language as we see them, yet things don't go as we had assumed, we find ourselves entangled in our own rules. A reminder of actual reactions when things do not go as expected in our dealings in language is in place: "That is just what we say when, for example, a contradiction appears: 'That's not the way I meant it.' The civic status of a contradiction, or its status in civic life, that is the philosophical problem" (PI §125).[11]

So how are the limits of language used to show us the way out of paradox? Wittgenstein's treatment of Moore's paradox shows how the sentence is in order and how it is not; it brings out the grammatical bases for the paradoxical feature, namely, our false expectations. Moreover, it shows us something about how the world is by providing objects of comparison in the form of descriptions of language games of different sorts. But rather than establishing "limits" in any prescriptive sense of the term, the remarks work as reminders of features of language use, the disregard of which we require to entertain this particular confusion.

Moore's paradox is an apparent paradox in that once the assumption underlying the paradox, namely, that we cannot express the proposition about ourselves although it could be true, is clarified, then we see that the proposition does not have a use. And when it does have a use, there is nothing paradoxical about it. This is how Wittgenstein shows the way out of, or around paradox: by dissolving it.

Notes

1. Some discussions of this kind are found in Green and Williams 2007.
2. Marie McGinn sketches one grammatical feature of Wittgenstein's reflections on Moore's paradox, on the asymmetry in supposition and belief expression:

   it is not that what is asserted presupposes our gasp of what is supposed; rather what is supposed presupposes our mastery of how we operate with the word 'believe' in the language-game in which we originally learned it, and in which its employment is equivalent to asserting 'It is the case that . . .'

   (McGinn 2011, 69)

3. At the end of his manuscript, Moore discloses that he is not quite convinced that his implication actually explains why it is absurd to assert a Moorean sentence and he concludes by somewhat loosely referring to a remark by Wittgenstein that a similar situation would arise if one said "Possibly it isn't raining, but as a matter of fact it is" (Moore 1993, 211).
4. This is correctly diagnosed in McGinn 2011.
5. The digital tools used are The Bergen Nachlass Edition, BNE in Wittgenstein Source, www.wittgensteinsource.org/BFE/Ms-144_f, WittFind (Beta version November 2017) http://wittfind.cis.uni-muenchen.de/ as well as the Nachlass Transcripts online (prepared by Alois Pichler) http://wab.uib.no/transform/wab.php?modus=opsjoner.
6. As a disclaimer, my aim is not to provide a unified account of Wittgenstein's take on Moore's paradox. (Such attempts at exegetical syntheses have been made before, and they have brought out interesting aspects of Wittgenstein's discussion but not succeeded in their overall aim since Wittgenstein's material is not set for it.) The idea leading my way is rather that the point of reading Wittgenstein is going on from his work in some way, and for philosophical work in that air, exegetic completeness is not a key value.
7. The view that Wittgenstein speaks of linguistic traits only, not about how the world is, is mistaken although not uncommon, for instance expressed in Searle 1969, 148–149.
8. Wittgenstein continues the stretch of reasoning on the possibility of saying "It is raining and I don't believe it" with a sort of discovery on the assertion "I believe" (where that "I believe" is stated and does not function as a force device or prefix as in some earlier remarks): Here it does look as if the assertion "I believe" were not the assertion of what is supposed in the hypothesis

"I believe" (LW II, 11). This relates to the asymmetry in section II and to the idea of a sentence-radical in PI.

9. Beth Savickey discusses the normativity of these maps: "While Hacker contrasts description with explanation, Wittgenstein reminds us that there are many different kinds of description (PI §24). He characterizes descriptions as instruments for particular purposes (PI §291). Further, Hacker equates philosophy with the description of actual language-usage, while Wittgenstein writes that 'philosophy is not a description of language-usage, and yet one can learn it by constantly attending to all the expressions of life in the language' (LW I §121). In other words, for Hacker, the central preoccupation of the Investigations is the nature of language (Baker and Hacker 2009, 43). While for Wittgenstein, it is life (i.e. all the expressions of life in the language)" (Savickey 2014, 111).
10. See Neuman 2015 for an extensive discussion on the role of examples of this kind in relation to Moore's paradox.
11. This echoes his letter to Moore in 1944, in which Wittgenstein writes that the assertion has to be ruled out and that it is ruled out by common sense, just as contradictions are, and that it "shows that logic isn't as simple as logicians think it is. In particular: that logic isn't the unique thing people think it is" (ML, 177).

References

Baker, Gordon and Hacker, Peter (2009) *Wittgenstein: Understanding and Meaning. Part II: Exegesis §§1–84.* Second Edition. Oxford: Wiley-Blackwell.
Goldstein, Laurence (1999) *Clear and Queer Thinking.* London: Duckworth Publishing.
Green, M. and Williams, J. N. (2007) *Moore's Paradox: New Essays on Belief, Rationality and the First Person.* Oxford: Clarendon Press.
Hacker, Peter (2010) "The Development of Wittgenstein's Philosophy of Psychology", in J. Cottingham and P. Hacker (eds), *Mind, Method, and Morality: Essays in Honour of Anthony Kenny.* Oxford: Oxford University Press, 275–305.
McGinn, Marie (2011) "Wittgenstein and Moore's Paradox", in Richard Heinrich, Elisabeth Nemeth, Wolfram Pichler and David Wagner (eds), *Image and Imaging in Philosophy, Science and the Arts.* Vol. 1. Publications of the Austrian Ludwig Wittgenstein Society. Heusenstamm am Frankfurt: Ontos Verlag, 59–72.
Moore, G. E. (1993) *Selected Writings.* Edited by T. Baldwin. London: Routledge.
Neuman, Yrsa (2015) *Standing Before a Sentence: Moore's Paradox and a Perspective from Within Language.* Turku: Åbo Akademi University Press.
Savickey, Beth (2014) "Wittgenstein and Hacker: Übersichtliche Darstellung", *Nordic Wittgenstein Review* 3 (2), 99–123.
Searle, John (1969) *Speech Acts: An Essay in the Philosophy of Language.* Cambridge: Cambridge University Press.
Von Wright, Georg Henrik (1969) "Special Supplement: The Wittgenstein Papers", *The Philosophical Review* 78 (4), 483–503.
Von Wright, Georg Henrik (1992) "The Troubled History of Part II of the *Investigations*", *Grazer Philosophische Studien* 42 (1), 181–192.
Von Wright, Georg Henrik and Heikki Nyman (1982) "Editors' Preface", in *LW I*, Oxford: Basil Blackwell, ix–x.
Winch, Peter (2001) "The Expression of Belief", in T. McCarthy and S. Stidd (eds), *Wittgenstein in America.* Oxford: Clarendon Press, 195–214.

8   Who Are "We" for Wittgenstein?

Constantine Sandis

"Why can't Panama invest in Panama?" She complained . . . "Why do we have to have *Asians* do it? We're rich enough. We've got one hundred and seven banks in this town *alone*, don't we? Why can't we use our own drug money to build our own factories and schools and hospitals?" The "we" was not literal. Louisa was a Zonian, raised in the Canal Zone in the days when by extortionate treaty it was American territory for ever, even if the territory was only ten miles wide and fifty miles long and surrounded by despised Panamanians.

John Le Carré, *The Tailor of Panama*

Prologue

We might, as I am doing now, employ the first person plural "we" to invite our readers to join us in a collective form of self-consciousness, thereby narrowing, or at least concealing, the distance between author and reader. But one may equally widen the distance by using impersonal pronouns instead.[1] Wittgenstein does both in his writings, but the former approach predominates.

"If a lion could speak", Wittgenstein famously states, "we [*wir*] could not understand him".[2] But who are "we" for Wittgenstein? It is commonplace to assume that he is referring to "us humans" and, by the same token, that "a lion" stands for all non-human animals.[3] This is often found in defences of Wittgenstein's remark such as those by John Dupré (2002, 232), Vicki Hearne (1994, 160), Nancy E. Baker (2012, 63), and Rami Gudovitch (2012, 147–148). Dupré, for example, writes that the thought behind Wittgenstein's remark is that:

> since lions, and other animals, lead wholly different lives, **their** hypothetical language could make no sense to **us**.
>
> (Dupré 2002, 232)[4]

Numerous anti-Wittgensteinians share this thought that Wittgenstein's "we" refers to all humans to be contrasted with all lions, or perhaps even all (other) animals:

Wittgenstein once claimed, "If a lion could talk, we would not understand him." He seemed to assume that because the **lion's** consciousness is so different from **ours**, even if there were a spoken lion language, it would be too alien for **us** to understand. However, lions and many other animals do indeed communicate in their own ways, and if **we** make an effort to understand their communications, **we** can learn much about *what they are saying*.

(Bekoff 2007, 38)

Wittgenstein said that if a lion could speak, **we** couldn't understand a word it was saying, since the form of a **lion's** world is so massively different from **our own**. He was wrong. I know he was wrong.

(Foster 2016, 21)[5]

But while Wittgenstein's invitations to his readers are typically issued in virtue of varying assumed shared features, he never uses "us", "we", "them" (and related determiners such as "our" and "theirs") to mark a neat division between "us" humans and "them" animals. Instead, he refers to human beings in the third person (e.g., RPP II §33; cf. RPP II §§29–30) and groups "them" together with other animals (NB, 82, 84; PI §224). Invitations need not be taken up, of course. The reader may find that she can only go so far before realising or deciding that the author's "we" does not speak for her.[6] Indeed, the question of who we are is not always separable from those of who we want to be and who we want "we" to be.[7] No amount of precision on the part of the author can settle these things in advance. Nor should it. Every audience is, to a certain extent, self-selecting.

1. We Philosophers

There are numerous remarks in which the later Wittgenstein uses the pronoun "we" to refer to people engaged in philosophical activity:

> Of course, what confuses **us** is the uniform appearance of words when **we** hear **them** in speech, or see them written . . . For **their** use is not that obvious. Especially when **we** are doing philosophy!
>
> (PI §11)

The "other" which contrasts with "us" here is not a creature but the words we hear or read. Their appearance confuses "us" especially *qua* philosophers, for to be confused by them in the relevant way is part and parcel of what Wittgenstein refers to as "[t]he dogmatism into which **we** fall so easily in doing Philosophy" (PI §131):

> When **we** do philosophy, **we** are like savages, primitive people, who hear the way in which civilized people talk, put a false interpretation on it, and then draw the oddest conclusions from this.
>
> (PI §194)

Yet it is also *qua* philosophers (of a diametrically different kind) that "we" are to escape such confusions:

> The work of **the philosopher** consists in marshalling recollections for a particular purpose.
>
> (PI §127; Cf. §§52, 110)

> **Learning philosophy** is *really* recollecting. We remember that we really did use words that way.
>
> (BT §89)

Wittgenstein uses "philosophy" to refer to both a kind of malady *and* its cure viz. bad (unhealthy) and good (healthy) ways of philosophizing. When referring to the former, he sometimes distances himself and "us" from philosophers:

> When **philosophers** use a word – "knowledge", "being", "object", "I", "proposition/sentence", "name" – and try to grasp the essence of the thing, **one** must always ask oneself: is the word ever actually used in this way in the language in which it is at home? –
> What *we* do is to bring words back from their metaphysical to their everyday use.
>
> (PI §116; cf. PI §§124–128)[8]

> We are, indeed, also interested in the correspondence between concepts and very general facts of nature . . . we are not doing natural science . . . we can also invent a fictitious natural history for our purposes.
>
> (PPF §365)

There are echoes here of Nietzsche's more bombastic form of esoteric appeals to "We scholars" (BGE: VI); "We artists" (GS §59, BGE §250[9]); "we (last; good) Europeans" (GS §352; BGE §§214, 241, 267); "we incomprehensible ones" (GS §371); "we philosophers of the present and the future" (GS §372); "we modern men" (GS §375); "we northeners" (BGE §48); "we new philosophers" (WTP §988); "we few or many . . . pagans in faith" (WTP §1034); "we free spirits" (BGE §61); "we first born of the twentieth century" (BGE §214).[10] These pick out the kind of philosopher that Nietzsche thought he was, often via an (implicit or explicit) reference to his gender,[11] or the time and place in which he is writing.[12]

Both philosophers hover between speaking as if they are *alone* in opposing the old guard, and forming part of a wider "we" who practice this new method. Nietzsche thus advertises his *Human, All Too Human* as "a book for free spirits" and his *Thus Spoke Zarathustra* as a "Book for All and None". Wittgenstein likewise writes with very few specific individuals in mind, making references to the few possible readers who might understand what he was up to.[13] In his 1918 Preface to the *Tractatus*, Wittgenstein states that "[p]erhaps this book will be understood only by someone who has oneself already had the thoughts that are expressed in it – or at least similar thoughts" (TLP, 3/26).[14] Little has changed by the time of his 1945 Preface to the *Investigations*:

> It is not impossible that it should fall to the lot of this work . . . to bring light into one brain or another – but, of course, it is not likely.
>
> (PI, 4)

Wittgenstein differs from Nietzsche, in not contrasting the "we" of those philosophizing in the right way with a "they" of completely distinct *others* who have gone wrong. Indeed, the "they" which contrasts with Wittgenstein's "us" is arguably his own past self:

> A picture held **us** captive. And **we** couldn't get outside it, for it lay in **our** language, and language seemed only to repeat it to **us** inexorably.
>
> (PI §115)

If so, then PI §§115–116 is contrasting a present-tense royal "we" (referring to the author of the *Investigations*) to a past-tense royal "us" (referring to the author of the *Tractatus*). Certain remarks in the *Investigations* offer some support to this autobiographical reading:

> The real discovery is the one that enables me to break off philosophizing when I want to. – The one that gives philosophy peace, so that it is no longer tormented by questions which bring itself in question.
>
> (PI §133; cf. PI §255)

> What is **your** aim in philosophy? – To show the fly the way out of the fly-bottle.
>
> (PI §310)

Wittgenstein's uses of "we" and "us" thus serve to both unite and separate him from his earlier self. We should not exclude the possibility, however, that the scope of each indexical extends more widely to include kindred spirits:

> Philosophy is a struggle against the bewitchment of **our** understanding by the resources of **our** language.
>
> (PI §109)

So understood, Wittgenstein uses "we" to talk of philosophers both when in the grip of a misleading picture of language (PI §§11, 131, 194, 295,

303, 520, 598) and when dissolving the pseudo-problems presented by the picture (PI §§109, 127, 393; BT §89). While he sometimes refers to philosophers in the third person (PI §§309, 514), it is never in the pejorative sense in which some of his followers talk of certain kinds of philosophers as the misguided enemy whose confusions they are too enlightened to share. Wittgenstein includes himself among those who, tricked by language, are on the verge of lapsing into philosophy:

> What **we** are "tempted to say" . . . is, of course, not philosophy; but it is its raw material.
>
> (PI §244; cf. PI §38)

But "we" are also they who *rise* to a better way of doing philosophy, one that proceeds by way of observing how it is that the use of words tempts us so.

2. We Language Users

Wittgenstein writes that for "a large class of cases – though not for all – in which **we** employ the word 'meaning' it can be defined thus: the meaning of a word is its use in the language" (PI §43; cf. LW II, 38–39). Applied to the word "we" itself, this introduces a potential problem of circularity: must "we" already know how the word "we" is being used to know who the "we" who are using the word in the first place are? But the difficulty, such as it is, is not insuperable. For the question to be settled is only how Wittgenstein himself is using the word "we" in various philosophical contexts. One obvious answer is that he uses it to refer to users of language. If so, then the "we" here picks out competent users of a lexical language who are not misapplying a rule (for mere competency does not render one immune to error), with the presumption that their set includes both author and reader. His later work is replete with such uses of "we":

> **We** can put it like this: This sample is an instrument of the language, by means of which **we** make colour statements.
>
> (PI §50)

> Consider, for example, the activities that **we** call "games".
>
> (PI §66)

> If **we** are using the word "know" as it is normally used (and how else are **we** to use it!), then other people very often know when I am in pain.
>
> (PI §246)

> But would **we** really say that he feels pity? Wouldn't **we** say "It really isn't pity because he isn't acquainted with any pain of his own" –?
>
> (RPP II §28)

We would say, perhaps, of a green pane: it colours the things behind it green, above all the white behind it.

(ROC I §26; see also ROC I §§24, 25, 33, 40)

We speak of the "colour of gold" and do not mean yellow.

(ROC I §33, see also ROC §§24, 47–48)

It is tempting to think that "we" shifts from German speakers to the speakers of all the languages the text has been translated into, even in cases where Wittgenstein could not anticipate – let alone authorise – the translation. But, in contrast to phrases such as *"wir deutsch sprechen"* (see following paragraphs), none of these examples seem to exclude the typical reader of the phrase in translation. It would be far more sensible to assume that in the passages "we" includes anyone who shares the concept expressed by any German word(s) he discusses. Wittgenstein contrasts such people (viz. "us") to *other* people, whose language games are different from ours:

Now it is conceivable that **some people** might have a verb whose third person would be *exactly* equivalent to **our** "He is afraid"; but whose first person is not equivalent to **our** "I am afraid".

(RPP II §169)

This assumes the existence of a "we" which includes Wittgenstein himself, alongside others who all share certain concepts and grammatical training, including the concept expressed by the German word "wir" and the English word "we". These words are no different from others in being used in a variety of interrelated ways across contexts, including the following by his near contemporaries:

"Good" . . . if **we** mean by it that quality which we assert to belong to a thing, when **we say** that the thing is good, is incapable of any definition.

(Moore 1903, §§6–10)

Where **we** are tempted to **speak** of "different senses" of a word which is clearly not equivocal, **we** may infer that **we** are in fact pretty much in the dark about the character of the concept which it represents.

(Anscombe 1957, §1)

To maintain that good is indefinable is not to maintain that **we** cannot know what it is like or that **we** cannot **say** anything about it but only that it is not reducible to anything else.

(Ewing 1953, 89)

> [W]e might observe what words have actually been used by com-
> mentators on real incidents, or by narrators of fictitious incidents.
> However, **we** do not have the time or space to do that here. **We** must
> instead imagine some cases . . . and try to reach agreement upon
> what **we** should in fact say concerning them. If **we** can reach this
> agreement, **we** shall have some data . . . which **we** can then go on to
> explain . . . Of course, **we** shall then have arrived at nothing more
> than an account of certain ordinary "concepts" employed by English
> speakers: but also at no less a thing.
>
> (Austin 1966, 429)

Prima facie, Austin's "we" may seem to refer to English speakers. But
his works have been translated into numerous languages. One can imagine translating "by English speakers" in the last sense both literally as
"*wir englischsprachige*" and more liberally as "*wir deutschsprachige*".
But the latter "translation" would only be viable in cases (such as Austin's) in which the remainder of the phrase, as well as its wider context,
made no allusion to any non-transferable peculiarities regarding English
speakers.

The question of how the study of the use of words in a particular
language relates to the exploration of how concepts function across languages is an important one.[15] But we do not need to agree on its answer
to allow that when Austin describes how "we" use a certain word in
English he is consciously including or excluding the non-English speaker
reading in translation. That is to say, the remark need not be read either
as one which only invites the English-speaking reader to join him in a
shared consciousness, or as one which explicitly sets out to do more.

When someone (*even* a philosopher) uses the word "we", they need
not have in mind any precise parameters of its referent. As Wittgenstein
himself maintains in his discussions of meaning and intention, what we
have in mind when we use a certain word or phrase might only make
itself manifest as and when the need for precision arises (often enough,
there is no need for precision at all, see PI §70). Suppose you ask me to
clear your room and I tidy the inside of your desk. Upon finding out, you
tell me that you did not mean for me to do that, but only such things as
emptying the bin and hoovering the floor. Must the precise range of thing
you did and did not mean for me to do have flashed before your mind
when you originally asked me to clean your room? Wittgenstein asks a
similar rhetorical question, in the notes accompanying PI §70:

> Someone says to me, "Show the children a game." I teach them
> gambling with dice, and the other says, "I didn't mean that sort of
> game". In that case, must he have had the exclusion of the game with
> dice before his mind when he gave me the order?
>
> (PI, 33n.; cf. RPP II §244)

No more than one need have a precise definition of what will count as a novel when one enters a bookshop and comes out with a copy of Anthony Powell's *A Question of Upbringing*.

Appeals to what "we" say and do of the sort found in the work of Wittgenstein and others have in recent years become the target of experimental philosophy and related forms of scepticism regarding so-called "ordinary language philosophy". Thus, for example, Kwame Anthony Appiah asserts:

> If conceptual analysis is the analysis of "**our**" concepts, then shouldn't **one** see how "**we**" – or representative samples of **us** – actually mobilize concepts in **our** talk? So one strain of this work seeks to elicit and tabulate intuitions people have about various scenarios.
>
> (Appiah 2008b, VI)[16]

He elaborates, elsewhere:

> For Austin. . . . What a person knows in knowing English, say, is what every competent speaker *should* say in a certain situation; and so, being competent myself, I know what everyone else *would* say if they were competent. That is why it wouldn't matter if we found individuals who *didn't* say it: it would just show that they weren't competent. In section 21 of the *Philosophical Investigations* . . . Wittgenstein wrote: "**We** do in fact call 'Isn't the weather glorious today?' a question, although it is used as a statement." Until recently, philosophers in my tradition would have thought it impertinent to ask who the "**we**" is here, and pointless to go out and inquire of people in the street whether someone who said these words was really asking a question.
>
> (Appiah 2008, 19–20)

The old-fashioned (armchair) philosophers that Appiah berates are to be contrasted with the new (street) philosophers conducting surveys. Here is how some of the latter conceive of what *they* do, and why they consider their approach superior:

> [T]he conceptual analyst might write "in this case, one would surely say . . .," while the experimental philosopher would write, "in this case, 79% of subjects said . . ." and back her claims with statistical data.
>
> (Knobe and Nichols 2008, 4)

> [A]reas of philosophy that rely on (i) intuition-pumps and thought experiments, (ii) appeals to commonsense and pre-philosophical intuition or (iii) conceptual analysis conceptual analysis based in part

on ordinary usage . . . are ripe for investigation by experimental philosophers . . . examining these things in a controlled and systematic
way . . . there is a **shared** distrust of philosophers' (common) claims
of the general form . . . "The ordinary use of 'X' is Y," . . . based
upon armchair reflection on their own intuitions and (perhaps selective) consideration of their conversations with friends, family, and
especially students . . . methods . . . highly susceptible to well-known
biases.

(Naddelhoffer and Nahmias 2007, 125)

Leaving aside obvious questions about who "we" and "one" are for
Appiah, or who is sharing the distrust of Naddelhoffer and Nahmias,
these passages collectively incorporate a jumble of confusions, including the mistaken assumptions that (i) Wittgenstein and Austin were in
the business of offering *analyses* of concepts, (ii) such "conceptual ana-
lysts" rely on nothing more than *intuitions* under the guise of "common
sense",[17] and (iii) remarks about "what we say" are to be verified by
statistical facts about actual usage. I unravel these elsewhere in more
detail,[18] so will here focus solely on their relation to how we should view
uses of "we" in philosophy.

At times, it would appear that experimental philosophers take the
"we" of Wittgenstein, Austin, and others to be referring to *all* speakers
of a language, regardless of whether or not they use language correctly.
But it is perhaps fairer to ascribe these critics the view that there isn't a
distinction to be made here at all: meaning really just *is* collective use.
Either way, the claims of Wittgenstein and others about "what *we* ordinarily say" are not expressions of their intuitions about what a statistical
survey would reveal about the usage of native speakers (RPP II §28), but
claims describing the norms of linguistic use. To be sure, the norms grow
out of actual linguistic and non-linguistic behaviour (see ROC I §3), but
they live a life of their own. As we have already seen, the "we" in question often picks out an idealisation of *competent* speakers at their best.[19]

One could distinguish here, as David Hume does, between what *philosophers* say and what "the *vulgar*" say (both of whom misuse terms
to the extent that they fail to grasp the proper significance of any given
idea).[20] By contrast, we have seen that Wittgenstein sometimes uses "we"
to sometimes refer to philosophers (see Section 1) and other times to competent speakers (Section 2). The latter, a linguistic analogue of the proverbial "man on the Clapham omnibus",[21] should not be confused with the
"vulgar" in Hume, and neither are identical to the class of all humans.

We shall see (Section 3) that, like Hume before him, Wittgenstein sometimes uses "we" to talk of the "average" or "normal" human being. This
elusive person may overlap with the competent speaker, but Wittgenstein
is not interested in hypothesising the precise way in which she uses language, but in how her concepts might differ from those of people who are

altogether more unusual. On these he could have equally used the pronoun "one" or perhaps even the more direct "you". Indeed, the famous final sentence of the *Tractatus*[22] has been translated as both "whereof **one** cannot speak, thereof **one** must be silent" (Ogden) and "what **we** cannot speak about **we** must pass over in silence" (Pears and McGuiness). It is, however, more literally translated as reaching right up to the reader in terms of what "*you*" cannot speak of and should thus remain silent about.

The use of "we" to mean "one" is also present in Nietzsche:

> What **others** know about **us**, – What we know about **ourselves** and remember is not so decisive for the happiness of our life as **people** suppose. One day that which *others* know about us (or think they know) assaults us – and then we realize that this is more powerful.
> (BGE, 52; cf. D, 292; HATH, 428; GM, Preface)

Here the "us" refers to all individuals *qua* themselves, and the "other" to the same individuals *qua* others.[23]

3. We Normal People

Jonathan Lear puts forth the following worry about Wittgenstein's use of "we" in the sort of passages quoted in Section 1. He writes:

> "We must do away with all explanation." To whom is this injunction addressed? Who are the "we" who must do away with all explanation: we philosophers? we anthropologists? On the split-level interpretation, the injunction would be restricted to philosophers. . . . But philosophy is not so divorced from the rest of **our** lives. . . . Wittgenstein should have distinguished between the "We" and a form of life in much the same way that Kant should have distinguished the "I" from the "I think." "Form of life" is a predicate which may be predicated of various objects. We may use the term narrowly and label disparate social groups alternative "forms of life"; or we may use the term widely to mark the form of life which we all constitute. . . . Switching to the first person plural, *form of life* is a reflective concept, used by philosophers and anthropologists when they try to construct a representation of us. It is "We" as "We" appear to ourselves . . . Even if **we** represent ourselves as reflective thinkers trying to understand who **we** are, by the very nature of the anthropological stance **we** will end up with a form of life, not with what I have gestured at calling "We." . . . Who are we?! If, on the one hand, we are one group among others, then Wittgenstein's remarks about forms of life lacking justification would seem to encourage a slide toward relativism. If, on the other hand, the "We" encompasses us all, it encompasses any being who might in the widest of senses count as

one of us, then doesn't the first person plural lose its force? . . . In this instance at least, I believe there is a middle course.

(Lear 1998, 263–276)

It is striking that in a passage questioning who "we" must be for Wittgenstein Lear refers to the relation of philosophy to "our" lives, without specifying what he means by "our".[24] His own "middle course" is that of the "we" that picks out the very mindedness that is a "constitutive condition" of what occurs in any human form of life (in Wittgenstein's sense of the term). But there is nothing to rule out alien language users from philosophising.[25] Moreover, philosophy is not yet possible for toddlers and other human beings who are not competent speakers of any language. It is tempting to think we might do better and try to think of philosophy as part and parcel of the life of the average human being. But this cannot be right either, and not just because of the possibility of alien philosophers. The problem is that we cannot answer the "we" question without looking at why Wittgenstein claims that "we" should do away with explanation.

Wittgenstein is not claiming that the average human being, let alone humans as a species, must cease explaining things. Good science, after all, is often explanatory. Nor could Wittgenstein be thinking that everyone within the academy must do away with explanation, not least because he does not think of philosophy as being limited to (or even primarily connected with) activities conducted within the academy.

Philosophy is part and parcel of the lives of those linguistic beings who are ordinary users of words. But it does not follow that such beings should never attempt to explain anything. In fact, it is not clear that Wittgenstein can really think that even *qua* philosophers we are not sometimes in the business of explaining why certain things follow from other things. Indeed, he often speaks of explaining this or that himself. What Wittgenstein really has in mind is the philosopher's tendency to seek for logical or metaphysical explanations of phenomena when a mere description of how we use words will do. Whether or not the shoe fits anthropological and other investigations is an open question to be judged on a case by case basis.

Lear talks as if there is a general problem. But there is no philosophically difficult question of where "we" are meant to draw the line. "We" must do away with all explanation when engaging in a certain kind of philosophical activity and for this to be true "we" had better be the sort of creatures able to engage in such activity. For Wittgenstein, this means that "we" often picks out creatures that can use human language and be puzzled with the philosophical questions it tempts us into (Section 1). This excludes both those who are either unable to say anything or would be tempted to say very different things, because they are in some way not like "us":

What would a society of all deaf men be like? Or a society of the "feeble-minded"? *An important question!* What then of a society that never played any of **our** customary language games?

(Z §371)

Wittgenstein raises such questions time and time again, contrasting "us" with certain non-human animals, alien tribes, young infants, those who are blind or colour blind, people with differing abilities and impediments, and "mental defectives".[26] For his purposes, the lion is in many respects no different from the colour-blind person, the extra-terrestrial, or the member of some foreign tribe. The other side of this coin is that by focusing on "normal people", Wittgenstein allows that those with special abilities (be they acquired or innate) that the rest of "us" lack – be they horse whisperers or those with perfect pitch – are capable of understanding things and creatures (including one another) that "we" normal people cannot.[27]

In *Remarks on Colour*, our normality is often fixed in relation to something specific, particularly sight. While possibly relevant to certain empirical investigations, it is of little interest to his conceptual exploration of colour whether the set of normally sighted people includes those of "us"[28] who are horse whisperers, bad at hearing or spelling, left-handed, autistic, musical prodigies, mathematical geniuses, or moral monsters (ROC I §40). What is required and assumed is that they are otherwise capable of employing and sharing concepts with us:

> **We** say: "Let's imagine people who do not know this language-game." But in doing so **we** still have no conception of the life of these people in so far as it differs from **our** own. **We** do not yet know what we are supposed to imagine; for the life of **these people** is in all other ways to correspond with **ours**, and it still must be determined what **we** would call a life corresponding to ours under these new conditions.
>
> (LW II, 71e)

This would exclude a normally sighted lion, even if it could speak. "Most people" here contrasts with, for example, the "very few people" who, according to Lichtenberg, have ever "seen pure white" (ROC I §3). The former who comprise the "we" in remarks such as:

> And of course such a construct may in turn teach **us** something about the way **we** in fact use the word.
>
> (ROC I §4)

> And to whom can I describe all the things *we* normal people can learn?
>
> (ROC III §121).

These are to be contrasted with the following:

> **People** might have the concept of intermediary colours or mixed colours even if they never produced colours by mixing (in whatever sense). **Their** language games might only have to do with looking for or selecting already existing intermediary or blended colours.
>
> (ROC I §8)

> The colour-blind not merely cannot learn to use our colour words, they can't learn to use the word "colour-blind" as a normal person does.
>
> (ROC I §77; see also ROC III §§97 and 112)

> Imagine a *tribe* of colour-blind people, and there could easily be one. **They** would not have the same colour concepts as **we** do. For even assuming they speak, e.g. English, and thus have all the English colour words, **they** would still use them differently than **we** do and would *learn* their use differently. Or if **they** have a foreign language, it would be difficult for **us** to translate their colour words into **ours**.
>
> (ROC I §13; cf. ROC III §§128–9, PPF §325)

Wittgenstein continues:

> But even if there were also people for whom it was natural to use the expressions "reddish-green" or "yellowish-blue" in a consistent manner and who perhaps also exhibit abilities which we lack, we would still not be forced to recognise that they see *colours* which we do not see. There is, after all, no *commonly accepted* criterion for what is a colour, unless it is one of our colours.
>
> (ROC I §14)

Here "we" are being contrasted to both people who lack an ability "we" have and to those who have an ability "we" lack. In the context of *Remarks on Colour*, Wittgenstein's examples of such abilities are understandably ones relating to perception (usually of colour, though he sometimes employs analogies with sound). But his thoughts on the relation of language use to concepts and, in turn, concepts to abilities, should not be limited to them.

Wittgenstein sometimes talks of "mental defectives"[29] and, again, he could have also added those with extraordinary mental abilities that "we" lack. "We" then, often means "most of us". Who's counting? Wittgenstein is not in the business of providing statistical data. Rather the "most" is indicative of a typical norm that could easily change across very long periods of time (e.g., most of us are not colour-blind). In this he resembles Hume, who despite being labelled as a kind of "sceptic" always begins with a "we" and not an "I" (see Sandis 2019).

The passages from *Remarks in Colour* quoted here (written in 1950, and revised March 1951) revisit the issues raised in Ch. XI of the second part of the *Investigations* (written 1948–1949).[30] Indeed we can imagine it fitting between §325 and §326 (just before the lion remark in §327):

> **We** also say of a person that he is transparent to **us**. It is, however, important as regards **our** considerations that one **human being** can be a complete enigma to another. **One** [man] learns this when **one** comes into a strange country with entirely strange traditions; and what is more, even given a mastery of the country's language. **One** does not *understand* the **people**. (**And not because of not knowing what they are saying to themselves**). **We** can't find **our** feet with **them** [*Wir können uns nicht in sie finden*].
>
> (PPF, 235, §325)

Or indeed:

> Imagine that the people of a tribe were brought up from early youth to give no expression of feeling *of any kind* . . . an education quite different from **ours** might also be the foundation for quite different concepts . . . what interests **us** would not interest *them*. . . . "**These men** would have **nothing human** about them." Why? **We** could not possibly make ourselves understood to them. Not even as **we** can to **a dog**. **We** could not [*könnten*] find our feet with them. And yet there surely could be such beings, who in other respects were human.
>
> (Z §§383–390)

Wittgenstein's foreign tribes and peoples may be fictional, but their inspiration is not always very far away from home:

> It's important for **our** approach, that someone may feel concerning **certain people**, that he will never know what goes on inside **them**. He will never understand **them** (**Englishwomen** for **Europeans**.)
>
> (CV, 84)[31]

> "Which **foreigner** doesn't feel that way when **he** comes to England?"
>
> (TS 232/MS 135–137, 1947–1948)

> **We** tend to take the speech of a Chinese for inarticulate gurgling. Someone who understands Chinese will recognize *language* in what he hears. Similarly I often cannot discern the *humanity* in **a man**.
>
> (CV, 1)

> **We** don't understand Chinese gestures any more than Chinese sentences.
>
> (Z §219; see also LW II, 89)

This problematic othering once again betrays traces of Nietzsche, who contrasts his "we" (see Section 1) with groups such as "the Greeks" (GS §§155, 356; D §§15, 72, BGE §260), "savage tribes" (GS §147), "the Englishman" (BGE §252), "the Celts" (BGE §48), "The Chinese" (BGE §267), "the Jesuits" (BGE §48), "the Brahmins" (BGE §61), "the Jews"[32] (D §72, BGE §§61, 250), and "the first Christians"[33] (D §72), "German middle-class Protestants" (BGE §58), and, indeed, "the German(s)" (BGE §§11, 28, 246).[34]

Wittgenstein might not *always* tell the reader who "we" and "they" are quite as explicitly as Nietzsche but, *pace* Lear, he paints a reasonably clear picture across different contexts and contrasts – for better or worse. Both are far removed from the collective of *all* humans. In contrast to Nietzsche's superhuman "we", Wittgenstein's is typically that of people who are as normal as possible in the relevant respect. This meaning is easily achieved without entering into spurious metaphysical debates regarding the ontology of we-groups.[35]

Epilogue

One might find it odd that Wittgenstein seems philosophically uninterested in the first person plural, despite his fascination with the singular first person pronoun, from his early pronouncement that "the I is what is deeply mysterious!" (NB, 80) to his later scepticism about "I" referring to a "self" (PI §§404–413). Of course, "we" is not the plural of "I" (Lyons 1968, 277) but, rather, a plural term lacking first-person form (de Gaynesford 2006, 41).[36] For "we" does not amount to "I and I" (Bierce 1911/2000, 116), which only finds meaning in Rastafari vocabulary (Iyaric) signifying the oneness of two people, one of whom may, but need not, be God (said to be within all humans).[37] And what, if anything, would a chorus uttering "we think therefore we are" prove?[38]

Bernard Williams ingeniously suggests that Wittgenstein's "well-chartered moves in the later work from 'I' to 'We'" take place "*within the transcendental ideas themselves*" and that the "important element of idealism" that the later work retains helps to explain the "pervasive vagueness and indefiniteness evident in the use Wittgenstein makes of 'we'" (Williams 1974, 147). Curiously, Williams' own article begins with a quotation from TLP 5.61 in which Wittgenstein talks of what "**we** [*Wir*] cannot say in logic" and states that "**we** cannot think what **we** cannot think; so we cannot think what we cannot *say* either".[39] The fact that this is being quoted as evidence of Wittgenstein's "me" stance in the *Tractatus* betrays a peculiar downplaying of an important linguistic thread that runs throughout Wittgenstein's early and later work.

On Williams' view "one finds oneself with a *we* which is not one group rather than another in the world at all, but rather the plural descendant of that idealist *I* who was not one item rather than another in the world" (Williams 1974, 160). This reading is motivated by the thought that "we" in Wittgenstein refers to neither "our group as contrasted with other human groups" nor to "humanity" (ibid., 160). I have tried to show that while the latter contention is correct, we would be wrong to think that Wittgenstein's "we" is never the former. While there is no doubt that Wittgenstein transitions to a more practice-based philosophy in his later work,[40] we have seen that he often uses "we" to mark specific in-groups, be they united by culture, ability, philosophical disposition, or mere averageness. Not only do such groupings not require a transcendental "we", they positively forbid it. As Ilham Dilman puts it, Wittgenstein's "speakers are themselves *in* the world of the language they speak" (Dilman 2002, 86). The social worldview that this is embedded in (Section 2) is incompatible with a linguistic idealism in which the solipsistic suggestion that "the limits of *my* language mean the limits of *my* world" is simply replaced with the mass idealism that "the limits of *our* language mean the limits of *our* world" (Williams 1974, 150).[41]

Part of the explanation of Wittgenstein's apparent lack of puzzlement with "we" is that, *pace* Williams and Lear, he takes the context of each remark to render the intended referent of the term reasonably obvious. Accordingly, "we" functions as a linguistic shifter whose meaning shifts depends on the message, who is delivering it, and the context in which it is being delivered.[42] Indeed, as Julia Kursell notes, "the pronoun 'we' opens up the possibility to include or exclude the participants of a communicative situation" (Kursell 2010, 218). She illustrates this by reference to Bertolt Brecht's "*Wer aber ist die Partei?*", a song highlighting features that render "we" an important rhetorical tool in politics.[43] The song highlights the features that render "we" an important rhetorical tool. The shifter's political power is also captured by George Orwell across Napoleon's first speech towards the start of *Animal Farm*, and his second speech just over twenty pages later:

> [C]omrades. . . . We are born, we are given just so much food as will keep the breath in our bodies . . . the very instant that **our** usefulness has come to an end we are slaughtered. . . . **No animal** knows the meaning of happiness. . . . Why then do we continue in this miserable condition? . . . **Man** is the only real enemy we have . . . the only **creature** that consumes without producing.
>
> (Orwell 1945, 8–9)

> Comrades! . . . **You** do not imagine that **we pigs** are doing this in a spirit of selfishness and privilege? Many of **us** actually dislike milk and apples. I dislike them myself. . . . Milk and apples (this has been proved by Science, comrades) contain substances absolutely

necessary to the well-being of **a pig. We pigs** are brain-workers. . . . It is for *your* sake that **we** drink that milk and eat those apples.

(ibid., 32)[44]

Even the "you" of the second speech must remain a "we" of sorts in the totalitarian system in which the "I" is altogether eliminated. The best known portrayal of this is to be found in Arthur Koestler's *Darkness at Noon*:

> The hours which remained to him belonged to that silent partner, whose realm started just where logical thought ended. He had christened it **"the** grammatical fiction" [*grammatikalische Fiktion*[45]] with that shamefacedness about the first person singular which the Party had inculcated in its disciples . . . he had never yet consciously tapped the word "**I**".
>
> (Koestler 1940, 201)

The parallels between Wittgenstein and the author who would later write *The Ghost in the Machine*, named after Ryle's famous attack on the Cartesian self (itself indebted to Wittgenstein), are impossible to ignore:

> "Aren't you nevertheless basically saying that everything except human behaviour is a fiction?" If I speak of a fiction, then it is of a grammatical fiction [*einer grammatischen Fiktion*].
>
> (PI §307)

Like Nietzsche before him (see BGE §16 & WLN I-87), Wittgenstein speaks of the "I" as a kind of grammatical fiction. This is all the more true of "us", even when individuated as precisely as "Marlon Brando, Pocahontas, and me".[46]

Notes

1. I discuss the relation of "one" to "we" in Section 2.
2. PPF §327. My translation differs slightly from both the 1953 and 2009 ones, though not in ways that affect the central question of this paper. Unless otherwise noted, all attributions of the word "we" and "our" to Wittgenstein are translations of "*wir*" and "*unserer*".
3. For instance, Kipling (1894, 33) and Epstein (2005, 158). Nietzsche describes this as "the denial of the individual ('all lions are at the bottom only one lion')" (GS §99). Cf. Tyler (nd).
4. All quotations retain *italics* for original emphasis, with my own additional emphasis in bold.
5. Despite Foster's explicit dismissal of Wittgenstein, his book is an excellent illustration of Wittgenstein's ideas about what one needs to share with a foreign being in order to better understand it, and where the limits of such understanding lie.

6. See Barnes (1987, 176) who distinguishes between a royal, editorial, and conspiratorial "we".
7. Incidentally: https://whodowewanttobe.weebly.com.
8. The extent to which "the author of the *Tractatus*" (PI §23; cf. 4e, §46) is one of "us" is a moot point, as is about to become evident.
9. The 2002 translation has "artists like us".
10. The contrast between these pluralities and the "I" which dominates the section titles of *Ecce Homo* is striking (see Sandis 2019b).
11. For the problem of privileged maleness within the philosophical "we" see Naomi Scheman, who writes that "[p]art of what is distressing to many women in reading philosophical texts is the experience of taking oneself to be included in the 'we' and coming up short against the realisation that one really wasn't" (Scheman 1990, 27).
12. Peter Adamson writes that "Instead of assuming that the historical figures we study are motivated by the same philosophical worries that worry us, we need to understand why they care about each issue they raise" (Adamson 2016, Rule 7). Martin Lenz argues that this presupposes "a fair amount of unity among *us*", thereby "indexing some unified idea of a current philosophical state of the art" (Lenz 2018). Adamson replies that he was using "we" to just mean "all of us who are (aspiring or practicing) historians of philosophy" (Adamson 2018). In response, Lenz distinguishes between and indexical and a normative use of the word "we"; the former "might refer to a quite diverse set of individuals", whereas the latter picks out a certain group specified as "analytic philosophers" (Lenz 2018b). It is normative because it picks out what "we" should be interested in rather than what "we" happen to be interested in. The ambiguity is akin to that found in statements such as "we don't eat peas without fingers" (Cf. Millikan 2005, Ch. 9; Orvell et. al. 2018).
13. For Wittgenstein's personal difficulties in understanding others and being understood by them see Klagge (2011) and Sandis (2015).
14. The original Ogden translation reads "those who have themselves" (TLP, 3) and the revised Pears and McGuinnes one "someone who has himself". Katja Behrens pointed out to me that while Wittgenstein starts with the masculine "*der*" he ends with the neutral "*selbst*", which is closer to "oneself" than "himself", but that the revised translation is right to emphasize that Wittgenstein is writing in the singular. So, while this does not exclude the possibility of more than one reader who understands Wittgenstein, the expectation that pluralities doing so are very low indeed.
15. Cf. Harrison (1832), Soames (2005, 323–30), Das (2006), Deutscher (2011), Cassin (2014), and Crane (2015).
16. Appiah adds the following cute anecdote: "In the empirical spirit, I should report that, when I typed the phrase 'it would be natural to say' into Google's Book Search, it happily returned, as its top search results, passages by Gilbert Ryle, Peter Strawson, Max Black, and Bertrand Russell" (Appiah 2008b, §VII). But my own empirical research via search engines accessed from the proverbial armchair reveals that Russell (who hated anything vaguely resembling appeal to ordinary language philosophy) is not the utterer of the phrase appearing in connection with him and that high up on the search results for the phrase are situationist Gilbert Harman (1973), bio-semanticist Ruth Garrett Millikan (1994), Kantian logician Charles Parsons (1974), and evolutionary psychologist Steven Pinker (2007) who speaks of certain sentences sounding "odd to an English-speaker's ears" (33).
17. See Appiah (2008, 73).
18. See Sandis (2010).

19. In a critique of experimental philosophy, Neil Levy uses the word "we" to refer to a small, clearly defined, community: "By 'we' I mean the geographically and temporally extended philosophical community, engaged in an open-ended debate. Everyone is invited to participate in this debate, but the price of entry is hard work: only when you expose your intuitions to the best arguments and the full range of relevant cases will they count as (defeasible) evidence for and against philosophical theories" (Levy, nd).

20. Hume (1739, I.3.14, 1.4.2.30. For exegesis see Sandis 2019, Ch. 4.4).

21. A legal fiction, whose origins may be traced back to Walter Bagehot's *The English Constitution*: "[p]ublic opinion" now-a-days, "is the opinion of the bald-headed man at the back of the omnibus", representing "the ordinary mass of educated, but still commonplace mankind" (Bagehot 1867, 325–326).

22. Wovon man nicht sprechen kann, darüber muss **man** schweigen (TLP 7).

23. In a recent study, Orvell et. al. (2018) discovered that children (ages 2–10) more often interpret the second person pronoun "you" as generic (viz. referring to people in general) in normative contexts and canonical (viz. referring to the addressee) in descriptive ones. When asked, for example, "what do you do with books" or "what should you do with books" they would generally respond "you read them". By contrast, when asked "what do you *like* to do with books they tended to answer "I read them". The generic, but not the canonical "you" is replaceable with the third person singular pronoun "one". The research team informally noticed that *parents* seemed to frequently use "we" in normative contexts. It is not as easy to distinguish generic from canonical uses here, since "we" could refer to either people in general (generic) or parent and child (canonical). Once again, only the former is replaceable with "one".

24. Striking, but not unique (see Despret 2008, 123). Despite his officially transcendental position, Lear gives away that he actually thinks of "we" as all humans: "Perhaps there are Martians who speak a language which because of some kinks in our hardwiring we will never be able to recognize as such" (Lear 1998, 279–280; cf. Sagan et. al. 1978, 5–6, 14).

25. The point is made by Bernard Williams (1974, 160), though I reject his transcendental framing of it (see Epilogue).

26. Additional examples to those I will quote include ROC I §81 and ROC III §§28, 31. As we shall see, he sometimes shifts the reference of "them" to particular subsets of "normal people" such as "the Chinese".

27. Hence my claim in note 4 that Foster's book is more aligned with Wittgenstein's own views than he thinks.

28. Note how easily the context allows "us" to contrast with who "we" were in the previous paragraph.

29. ROC I §75, ROC III §118, RPP I §§179, 198, 216, 957.

30. In her Editor's Preface, G. E. M. Anscombe writes that she has left out "inner outer" material because it was "both marked as discontinuous with the text and also will appear elsewhere", namely LW II. These form a natural continuation of the themes of PPF §§301–332, which is primarily concerned with the concept of hiddenness in relation to inner/outer.

31. Whatever the personal truth, presumably one could replace "Englishwomen" and "Europeans" with any number of nouns referring to non-geographical communities such as "Catholics", "intellectuals", "scientists", "builders", "nurses", "schoolchildren", "botanists", "addicts", or "Wittgensteinians". And in each case various qualifications and further distinctions will need to be made.

32. While Wittgenstein's problematic remarks about "Jews" are in the third person, they are not intended to exclude him: "Amongst Jews 'genius' is found

only in the holy man. Even the greatest of Jewish thinkers is no more than talented. (Myself for instance.)" (CV, 18; see also CV, 13,16). Wittgenstein also offers a rather elaborate example (written between 1946 and 1947) of a "tribe that we want to enslave" (RPP I §96, cf. Z §528) that is much too close to home. For explorations of Wittgenstein's remarks concerning Jewishness see McGuiness (2001) and Stern (2001, esp. 254–262).

33. Nietzsche also refers to "Christians" across his works, but the locution is relatively rare by comparison to "Christianity" and "the Christian X".

34. Nietzsche reminds us that the names of peoples are usually terms of abuse. "The Tartars, for example, are literally 'the dogs'; that is what the Chinese called them. The 'Germans': this originally meant 'heathen'; that is what the Goths after their conversion named the great mass of their unbaptized kindred tribes" (GS §146).

35. Cf. Stekeler-Weithofer (2019, §1).

36. De Gaynesford adds: "*I* is crucially unlike the so-called 'first person plural' if, as some argue, *We* 'leaves room For anaphora and binding' [Vallée 1996, 230]" (de Gaynesford 2006, 92); for free and bound variable pronouns see Higginbotham (1980) and Franz (2018).

37. Similarly, "Me ne me" in the Twi language of Ghana can be used instead of "you and I" or "we". For recent observations of "I" metamorphosing into "we" see Sullivan (2018, 4) and P. Williams (2019, 11); cf Vallée (1996, 220ff.)

38. Cf. Stekeler-Weithofer (2019, §1). Brendan Larvor has pointed out to me a peculiar use of "we" that effectively means "the others" in contemporary journalism bemoaning something about "us". The journalist exclaims, for example, that "we" have forgotten the meaning of Christmas. Unless the article is self-flagellatory, the "we" cannot include the author who is the one pointing out what has been forgotten. If the similar-minded reader is to be flattered, it does not refer to him or her either. It is *they* – the *other*s – who have forgotten the true meaning of Christmas, but "we" (you and I: reader and author in unison) know better than that.

39. The Ogden translation is the same in all crucial respects.

40. Sami Pihlström cautiously suggests that we can see the later Wittgenstein's "we" as a "socio-pragmatic reinterpretation of the transcendental self", while remaining neutral on what Wittgenstein's own view was (Pihlström 2015, 230).

41. For two different attacks on idealist readings of Wittgenstein see Dilman (2002, esp. Chs. 3 and 4) and Mulhall (2009). As Mulhall notes, Williams' reading is deeply inspired by the neo-Kantian reading of Wittgenstein in P. M. S. Hacker's first (1972) edition of *Insight and Illusion*, which Hacker comes to rejects as "misconstrued . . . exaggerated and distorted" in the 2nd edition (1986, ix); cf. A.W. Moore (2010, 209–212).

42. Ironically, the terms "shifter" was introduced by Jakobson as an account of the first person *singular* (Jakobson 1957, 42–43), influenced by Russell's account of "egocentric particulars" (viz. indexicals) which "have a meaning relative to the speaker" (Russell 1940, 17).

43. See Brecht 1977, 28 (cf. Brecht 1998).

44. In Napoleon's second speech, "we pigs" have already begun to replace "man", except for being portray as allies rather than enemy. It is worthwhile to compare this pig's use of "man" to that of the human Mowgli in *The Jungle Book*:

> What is the good of a man," he said to himself at last, "if he does not understand a man's talk? Now I am as silly and dumb as a man would be with us in the jungle. I must speak **their** talk.

> (Kipling 1894, 58)

45. While originally written in German, the book was first published in a last-minute English translation (and subsequently in Koestler's German re-translation of the English) as the original remained lost until Matthias Weßel discovered it in the Zurich Central Library in 2015. While there are hundreds of differences between the original MS and the version published in 1940 (Scammell 2016), Weßel has confirmed to me (private correspondence) that the original manuscript of Koestler's *Sonnenfinsterni* does indeed use "grammatikalische Fiktion" (MS 298–99; Koestler 2018).

46. I presented earlier versions of this chapter at the *Wittgenstein and the Limits of Language* conference (University of Helsinki, 8–9 September 2016), the Wittgenstein Forum (University of Reading, 15 November 2016), and the *Royal Institute of Philosophy* Human Sciences Seminar (Manchester Metropolitan University, 9 February 2017). I would like to thank audiences at these events as well as, for various kinds of help, Peter Aronoff, Jonathan Beale, Katja Behrens, Anna Bergqvist, Stephen Burwood, Louise Chapman, Ann Garry, Max de Gaynesford, Susan Gelman, Hans-Johann Glock, Adrian Haddock, Andy Hamilton, Joanna Hodge, Julia Kursell, Brendan Larvor, Sami Philström, Antonio Scarafone, Severin Schroeder, Tom Tyler, and Matthias Weßel. I owe particular thanks to Hanne Appelqvist and Andrew Lugg for their invigorating conversations and characteristically insightful comments on an earlier draft.

References

Adamson, Peter (2016) "Rules for the History of Philosophy", 31 December, available at https://historyofphilosophy.net/rules.

Adamson, Peter (2018) "Comment", on Lenz (2018).

Anscombe, G. E. M. (1957) *Intention*. Oxford: Blackwell.

Anscombe, G. E. M. (1975) "The First Person", in S. Guttenplan (ed), *Mind and Language: Wolfosn College Lectures 1974*. Oxford: Oxford University Press, reprinted in her *Metaphysics and The Philosophy of Mind*. Oxford: Blackwell, 1981, 21–36, to which any page numbers refer.

Appiah, Kwame Anthony (2008a) *Experiments in Ethics*. Cambridge MA: Harvard University Press.

Appiah, Kwame Anthony (2008b) "Experimental Philosophy", *Proceedings and Addresses of the American Philosophical Association* 82 (2), 7–22.

Austin, J. L. (1966) "Three Ways of Spilling Ink", *The Philosophical Review* 75 (4), 427–440.

Bagehot, Walter (1867) *The English Constitution*. Reissue edition, 2009. Oxford: Oxford University Press.

Baker, Nancy E. (2012) "The Difficulty of Language: Wittgenstein on Animals and Humans", in N. Forsberg, M. Burley and N. Hämäläinen (eds), *Language, Ethics and Animal Life: Wittgenstein and Beyond*. London: Bloomsbury, 45–64.

Barnes, Jonathan (1987) "Teachers of Moral Prudence", *The Cambridge Review* 108, 174–177.

Bekoff, Marc (2007) *Animals Matter: A Biologist Explains Why We Should Treat Animals with Compassion and Respect*. Boulder, CO: Shambhala Publications.

Bierce, Ambrose (1911/2000) *The Unabridged Devil's Dictionary*. Edited by D. E. Schultz and S. J. Joshi. Athens, GA: The University of Georgia Press.

Brecht, Bertold (1977) *The Measures Taken and Other Lehrstücke*. London: Methuen.

Brecht, Bertold (1998) *Die Maßnahme: Zwei Fassungen*. Frankfurt: Suhrkamp.

Cassin, Barbara (2014) *Philosopher en langues: les intraduisibles en traduction*. Paris: Rue d'Ulm.

Costello, Bonnie (2019) *The Plural of Us: Poetry and Community in Auden and Others*. Princeton, NJ: Princeton University Press.

Crane, Tim (2015) "The Philosophy of Translation", *Times Literary Supplement* (28 January).

Das, Kanti Las (2006) *Philosophical Relevance of Language: A Methodological Reflection*. New Delhil: University of North Bengal.

De Gaynesford, Maximilian (2006) *I: The Meaning of the First Person Term*. Oxford: Oxford University Press.

Despret, Vinciane (2008) "The Becomings of Subjectivity in Animal Worlds", *Subjectivity* 23, 123–139.

Deutscher, Guy (2011) *Through the Language Glass: Why the World Looks Different in Other Languages*. London: Arrow.

Dilman, Ilham (2002) *Wittgenstein's Copernican Revolution: The Question of Linguistic Idealism*. London: Palgrave Macmillan.

Dupré, John (2002) *Humans and Other Animals*. Oxford: Oxford University Press.

Epstein, Richard A. (2005) "Animals as Objects, or Subjects, of Rights", in C. R. Sunstein and M. Nussbaum (eds), *Animal Ethics: Current Debates and New Directions*. Oxford: Oxford University Press, 143–161.

Ewing, A. C. (1953) *Ethics*. London: The English Universities Press.

Foster, Charles (2016) *Being a Beast*. London: Profile Books.

Franz, Paul (2018). "We vs Them", *Times Literary Supplement* 6029 (19 October), 30.

Gudovitch, Rami (2012) "What's Wrong with a Bite of Dog?" in N. Forsberg, M. Burley and N. Hämäläinen (eds), *Language, Ethics and Animal Life: Wittgenstein and Beyond*. London: Bloomsbury, 139–151.

Hacker, P. M. S. (1972/1986) *Insight and Illusion*. First and Second editions. Oxford: Oxford University Press.

Harman, Gilbert (1973) *Thought*. Princeton, NJ: Princeton University Press.

Harrison, Benjamin (1832) *The Study of Different Languages, As It Relates to the Philosophy of the Human Mind*. Oxford: Prize Essay Read in the Sheldonian Theatre.

Hearne, Vicki (1994) *Animal Happiness*. Brooklyn, NY: Harper Collins.

Higginbotham, James (1980) "Pronouns and Bound Variables", *Linguistic Inquiry* 11 (4), 679–708.

Hume, David (1739) *A Treatise of Human Nature*. Second edition, 1978. Edited by L. A. Selby-Bigge. Oxford: Clarendon Press.

Jakobson, Roman (1957) "Shifters, Verbal Categories and the Russian Verb", reprinted in his *Russian and Slavic Grammar: Studies 1931–1981*, L. R. Waugh and M. Halle (eds) (1984), to which any page numbers refer. Berlin: de Gruyter.

Kipling, Rudyard (1894) *The Jungle Book*. London: Palgrave Macmillan.

Klagge, James C. (ed) (2001) *Wittgenstein: Philosophy & Biography*. Cambridge: Cambridge University Press.

Klagge, James C. (2011) *Wittgenstein in Exile*. Cambridge, MA: The MIT Press.

Knobe, Joshua & Nichols, Shaun (eds) (2008) *Experimental Philosophy*. Oxford: Oxford University Press.

Koestler, Arthur (1940) *Darkness at Noon*. London: Palgrave Macmillan.

Koestler, Arthur (2018) *Sonnenfinsterni: Nach dem deutschen Original-manuskript*. Coesfeld: Elsinor Verlag.

Kursell, Julia (2010) "First Person Plural: Roman Jakobson's Grammatical Fictions", *Studies in East European Thought* 62 (2), 217–236.

Lear, Jonathan (1998) *Open Minded: Working Out the Logic of the Soul*. Cambridge, MA: Harvard University Press.

Le Carré, John (1996) *The Tailor of Panama*. London: Hodder & Stoughton.

Lenz, Martin (2018a) "Who Are We? Myths in the History of Philosophy (Part I)", *Handling Ideas*, 9 August, reprinted on the APA blog, 24 August.

Lenz, Martin (2018b) "On Saying 'We' Again", *Handling Ideas*, 28 August.

Levy, Neil (nd) "Experimental Philosophy: A Critique", Unpublished manuscript.

Lyons, John (1968) *Introduction to Theoretical Linguistics*. Cambridge: Cambridge University Press.

McGuiness, Brian (2001) "Wittgenstein and the Idea of Jewishness", in J. Klagge (ed), *Wittgenstein: Philosophy & Biography*. Cambridge: Cambridge University Press, 221–236.

Millikan, Ruth G. (1994) "On Unclear and Indistinct Ideas", *Philosophical Perspectives*, 8 (Logic and Language), 75–100.

Millikan, Ruth G. (2005) *Language: A Biological Model*. Oxford: Oxford University Press.

Moore, A. W. (2010) "Transcendental Idealism in Wittgenstein, and Theories of Meaning" (with new Postscript), in Daniel Whiting (ed), *The Later Wittgenstein on Language*. London: Palgrave Macmillan, 191–212.

Moore, G. E. (1903) *Principia Ethica*. Cambridge: Cambridge University Press.

Mulhall, Stephen (2009) " 'Hopelessly Strange': Bernard Williams' Portrait of Wittgenstein as a Transcendental Idealist", *European Journal of Philosophy* 17 (3), 386–404.

Nadelhoffer, Thomas and Nahmias, Eddy (2007) "The Past and Future of Experimental Philosophy", *Philosophical Explorations* 10 (2), 123–149.

Nietzsche, Friedrich (1878/1996) *Human, All too Human: A Book for Free Spirits* (HATH). Second edition. Translated by R. J. Hollingdale. Cambridge: Cambridge University Press.

Nietzsche, Friedrich (1881/1997) *Daybreak: Thoughts on the Prejudices of Morality* (D). Translated by R. J. Hollingdale. Edited by M. Clark and B. Leiter. Cambridge: Cambridge University Press.

Nietzsche, Friedrich (1883–1891/1997) *Thus Spoke Zarathustra* (TSZ). Translated by A. Del Caro. Edited by A. Del Caro and R. B. Pippin. Cambridge: Cambridge University Press.

Nietzsche, Friedrich (1885–89/2003) *Writings from the Late Notebooks* (WLN). Translated by K. Sturge. Edited by R. Bittner. Cambridge: Cambridge University Press.

Nietzsche, Friedrich (1886/1973) *Beyond Good and Evil* (BGE). Translated by R. J. Hollingdale. London: Penguin.

Nietzsche, Friedrich (1886b/2001) *Beyond Good and Evil* (BGE). Translated by J. Norman. Edited by R-P. Horstman and J. Norman. Cambridge: Cambridge University Press.

Nietzsche, Friedrich (1887/2001) *The Gay Science* (GS). Translated by J. Nauck-hoff and A. Del Caro. Edited by B. Williams. Cambridge: Cambridge University Press.

Nietzsche, Friedrich (1887b/1994) *The Geneaology of Morality* (GM). Translated by C. Dietthe. Edited by K. Ansell-Pearson. Cambridge: Cambridge University Press.

Nietzsche, Friedrich (1889/2005) *Ecce Homo: How One Becomes What One Is* (with *Other Writings*). Translated by J. Norman. Edited by A. Ridley. Cambridge: Cambridge University Press.

Nietzsche, Friedrich (1901/1967) *The Will to Power* (WTP). Translated by W. Kaufmann and R. J. Hollingdale. New York: Vintage Books.

Orvell, A., Korss, E. and Gelman, S. A. (2018) "That's How 'You' So It: Generic You Expresses Norms During Early Childhood", *Journal of Experimental Child Psychology* 165, 183–195.

Orwell, George (1945) *Animal Farm*. London: Secker and Warburg.

Parsons, Charles (1974) "The Liar Paradox", *Journal of Philosophical Logic* 3 (4), 381–412.

Pihlström, Sami (2015) "Subjectivity as Negativity and as Limit", in G. Gava and R. Stern (eds), *Pragmatism, Kant, and Transcendental Philosophy*. London: Routledge, 217–238.

Pinker, Steven (2007) *The Stuff of Thought: Language as a Window into Human Nature*. London: Allen Lane.

Russell, Bertrand (1940) *An Inquiry Into Meaning and Truth*. Edinburgh: Bishop and Sons.

Sagan, Carl, Drake, F. D., Druyan, Ann, Ferris, Timothy, Lomberg, Jon and Sagan, Nick (eds) (1978) *Murmurs of Earth: The Voyager Interstellar Record*. New York: Ballentine Books.

Sandis, Constantine (2010) "The Experimental Turn and Ordinary Language", *Essays in Philosophy* 11 (2), 181–196.

Sandis, Constantine (2012) "Understanding the Lion for Real", in A. Marques and N. Venturinha (eds), *Knowledge, Language and Mind: Wittgenstein's Thought in Progress*. Berlin: de Gruyter, 138–161.

Sandis, Constantine (2015) " 'If Some People Looked Like Elephants and Others Like Cats': Wittgenstein on Understanding Others and Forms of Life", *Nordic Wittgenstein Review* 4, 131–153.

Sandis, Constantine (2019a) *Character and Causation: Hume's Philosophy of Action*. New York: Routledge.

Sandis, Constantine (2019b) "We Philosophers", *The Philosophers' Magazine* Issue 84, 1st Quarter, 14–16.

Scammell, Michael (2016) "A Different Darkness at Noon", *The New York Review of Books*, 7 April.

Scheman, Naomi (1990/1996) "The Unavoidability of Gender", *Journal of Social Philosophy* 2 (2–3), 34–39, reprinted in A. Garry and M. Pearsall (eds), *Women, Knowledge, and Reality*. Second edition. London: Routledge, 26–33.

Soames, Scott (2005) *Philosophical Analysis in the Twentieth Century*. Vol. 2. Princeton, NJ: Princeton University Press.

Stekeler-Weithofer, Pirmin (2019) "A Hegelian Logic of 'Us': Implicit Forms and Explicit Representations of Actions and Practices", in E. Maraguat and C. Sandis (eds), *Hegel and the Philosophy of Action* (special issue of Hegel Bulletin; https://doi.org/10.1017/hgl.2019.6).

Stern, David (2001) "Was Wittgenstein a Jew?" in J. Klagge (ed), *Wittgenstein: Philosophy & Biography*. Cambridge: Cambridge University Press, 237–272.

Sullivan, H. (2018) "Never Nice? Love, Loneliness and Poetry in the Correspondence of Sylvia Plath", *Times Literary Supplement* 6031 (2 November), 3–4.

Tyler, Tom (nd) "Becoming What We Are", Unpublished manuscript.

Vallée, Richard (1996) "Who Are We?" *Canadian Journal of Philosophy* 26 (2), 211–230.

Williams, Bernard (1974) "Wittgenstein and Idealism", in G. Vesey (ed), *Understanding Wittgenstein* (Royal Institute of Philosophy Lectures 7, 1972–1973). London: Palgrave Macmillan, reprinted in his *Moral Luck*. Cambridge: Cambridge University Press, 1981, 144–163, to which any page numbers refer.

Williams, Patricia (2019) "Trembling with Thought: Immersed in the World of the Former First Lady", *Times Literary Supplement* 6045, 9–11.

9 Animal Consciousness – A Limit of Language?

Hans-Johann Glock

1. Consciousness – The Last Mystery?!

In the wake of Nagel's "What is it like to be a Bat?" (1974), there has been an almost universal consensus among philosophers and cognitive scientists that consciousness is a deeply mysterious phenomenon. Furthermore, in the philosophy of mind it is common to distinguish *intentional* and *non-intentional* or "qualitative states". The former include believing, desiring or intending; these have a "content", that is, they are directed at or about *something*: one believes that something is the case, desires an object or intends to perform an action. The latter include sensations and moods; these lack a content or object they are about, yet have qualitative or "phenomenal" aspects. Finally, the mainstream in both philosophy and cognitive subscribes to physicalism. It accepts (more or less explicitly) that only those phenomena are real that are reckoned with by natural science and in particular physics.

In combination, these three factors – Nagelian puzzlement about consciousness, the distinction between intentional and qualitative states, and naturalism-cum-physicalism – have created a striking constellation of problems and positions. Whereas intentional phenomena are supposed to be amenable to naturalist treatment, through functionalism or related physicalist theories, the indelibly subjective nature of non-intentional states with phenomenal aspects is supposed to resist such treatment.

Many cognitivist scientists talk about "the race for consciousness". And even among those committed to the physicalist project, many are at a loss about how this race is to be won. Concerning the question "How does sentience work?" the otherwise highly confident Steven Pinker writes: "Beats the heck out of me! I have some prejudices, but no idea of how to begin to look for a defensible answer. And neither does anyone else" (Pinker 2009, 146). The clearest manifestation of the widely perceived contrast between the prospects for understanding, respectively, intentional states and cognition on the one hand, phenomenal states on the other hails from Chalmers. He drew a celebrated distinction between "the hard problem of consciousness" and several "easy problems". The latter are posed by "phenomena" that "can be explained scientifically", that is, "in terms of computational or neural mechanisms" (Chalmers 1995, 201). Examples include the abilities to discriminate, categorize, and react to environmental stimuli; the integration of information by a cognitive system; the reportability of mental states; the ability of a system to access its own internal states; the focus of attention; the deliberate control of behaviour; and the difference between wakefulness and sleep. The hard problem starts out from the uncontroversial fact that sentient creatures have experiences, notably in perception. It consists in explaining the alleged subjective feel of these experiences, the qualia associated with them. According to Chalmers, this constitutes "the greatest challenge left for science".

Consciousness is held to pose a stumbling-bock to naturalism/physicalism on account of its "phenomenal aspects". Allegedly, "there is something it is like" to be in a state of consciousness. All such states are "qualitative states" characterized by certain qualitative feels or "qualia", a term coined by C. I. Lewis (1929). "Phenomenal consciousness" is the subject's awareness of these qualia. What renders the explanation of phenomenal consciousness especially taxing if not downright insoluble, in the eyes of many, is the naturalistic requirement to do so by appeal only to purely material or mechanistic phenomena, such as neurophysiological or computational operations of the brain.

It is important to note that the new orthodoxy comes in two variants, which have not been sufficiently distinguished so far. The weaker of these is known as "(new) mysterianism". It holds that (phenomenal) consciousness defies scientific explanation in particular and human understanding in general. An early illustration of mysterianism is provided by the following exchange between Herbert Feigl and Albert Einstein.

> I asked Einstein whether in an ideally perfect (of course utopian) four-dimensional, physical representation (à la Minkowski) of the universe the qualities of immediate experience (we called them metaphorically "the internal illumination" . . .) were not left out. He replied in his characteristic humorous manner (I translate from the German in which he used a rather uncouth word): "Why, if it weren't for this 'internal illumination' [i.e., sentience] the world would be nothing but a pile of dirt!"
>
> (Feigl 1967, 138; the more robust German version is quoted in Heckmann and Walter 2001, 5, yet without indication of its provenance)

The stronger variant does not yet have an official label, but is appositely characterized as "(neo-) mysticism". It diagnoses a still more serious problem; decisive aspects of phenomenal consciousness, neo-mystics insist, defy not just knowledge but even conceptual comprehension and intelligible linguistic expression.

In spite of the popularity of the Nagelian orthodoxy, there have also been dissenting voices. Among them, one can distinguish:

Reductionism (Harman, Tye) explains phenomenal consciousness and qualia in terms of intentional and therefore, by their physicalist lights, physical states.

Eliminativism-cum-instrumentalism (Dennett) denies the existence of qualia outright or regards the attribution of experiences to subjects as a mere instrument for explaining their behavioural dispositions.

Deflationism (Hacker, Hanfling) insists that consciousness is not as mysterious a phenomenon as the Nagelian orthodoxy makes out.

The dividing lines between these camps are not hard and fast. Thus Dennett strikes a deflationist chord on occasion. Nevertheless, deflationism constitutes a distinctive stance. It was inspired by Wittgenstein and Ryle. Unlike eliminativism, it does not deny the existence of consciousness or "subjective experiences" as real phenomena; unlike instrumentalism, it does not demote talk of experiences to a *façon de parler*; unlike reductionism, it does not maintain that phenomena like sensations and moods are intentional after all, nor does it regard intentional phenomena in particular or mental phenomena in general as purely physical. Instead of negating or reducing consciousness, deflationists question the orthodox *conceptualizations* of consciousness that, in their estimation, give rise to the sense of mystery and paradox. Many of the allegedly irresolvable and profound puzzles – in particular the ineffability of feelings of "what it is like" – mark conceptual-*cum*-linguistic muddles rather than limits of *either* knowledge *or* language.

This paper defends a deflationist perspective on consciousness. For purposes of illustration and as an intriguing field of application, I shall follow Nagel and concentrate on the question of what kind of consciousness non-human animals without language (henceforth simply "animals") can possess. As regards animal minds, there are two opposing stances. *Differentialists* maintain that there are categorical differences separating us from animals; *assimilationists* hold that the differences are merely quantitative and gradual. Differentialism comes in differing degrees and versions. According to extreme differentialists like the stoics and Descartes, animals are bereft of all genuinely mental properties. By contrast, according to Aristotelianism, we share sensation, emotion, and perception with higher animals. These powers form part of the soul (*psyche*), the life force possessed by all living things. On the other hand, reason, rational will, and thereby knowledge and even belief are the prerogative of humans (see Sorabji 1993). Only these intellectual or rational powers are part of the "rational soul" (*nous*), and thereby of the mind, strictly understood. From Aristotle onwards, through Kant and Hegel to Dewey, Heidegger and Gadamer, moderate differentialists granted to animals "lower" mental/psychic phenomena like sentience, affective and conative states, while denying "higher" faculties like reason. This trend continued into recent analytic philosophy. Davidson and Dummett concede animal sentience or "consciousness"; Sellars and Brandom do so for the most part, and McDowell on occasion. All of them, however, consistently balk at crediting animals with intentional states like belief.

In recent years, there has also been an opposing tendency. It dissociates the capacities for "cognition" and intentionality (knowledge, belief, desire) – hitherto regarded as "higher" – from mental connotations and reserves these for hitherto "lower" faculties such as sentience. Ironically, this trend partly derived from the so-called "cognitive revolution" that overtook the behavioural sciences from the 1950s onwards. This revolution overturned the previous behaviourist consensus that "inner" mental phenomena are difficult to investigate even in the case of humans and definitely on the index as regards animals. But although contemporary cognitive scientists pride themselves on having shed the shackles of behaviourism, they continue to look askance at mental phenomena like consciousness, which appear to defy scientific investigation because of being irreducibly private. This trend within cognitive science was reinforced mysterian and mystic doctrines wafting across from philosophy.

The mesmerisation by and mystification of consciousness has had important fallouts for the treatment of animal minds. Whereas the numerous discoveries of cognitive ethology are accepted as proof of cognition and intentional states among intelligent animals like apes, cetaceans and corvids, they are widely regarded as insufficient or even immaterial to the question of animal sentience and consciousness. In order to assess this differentialist stance, one needs to scrutinize the subjectivist picture of consciousness and experience on which it rests.

In doing so, my special focus is on whether characterising animal consciousness takes us to and beyond the limits of language. My paper also goes beyond simply applying a deflationist recipe to animal consciousness in another respect. Deflationism helps to clarify animal consciousness. At the same time, I diagnose an important *lacuna*. Concerning animals, Nagel's fateful challenge still stands. What kind of consciousness, if any, can we ascribe to "dumb" animals, given that they lack language? However, and this is the final innovation of my paper, the reasons for the challenge that animal consciousness presents run *diametrically counter* to the Nagelian orthodoxy. They concern the "intentional contents" of consciousness – what animals are conscious of, what precisely they perceive, desire, or intend – rather than the "phenomenal feels" of their perceiving, desiring and intending. What undergoing an experience is like for higher animals – its hedonic, qualitative, and "biographical" imports – is often sufficiently evident from non-linguistic behaviour. But whereas what exactly humans are conscious of and what they think *is* authoritatively captured by their sincere avowals, this is no option for non-linguistic subjects. The limits of diagnosing complex intentional states to animals are "limits of language" alright, but not because animal intentionality exists yet transcends linguistic expression. Rather, our mental concepts preclude or qualitatively restrict the application of some mental terms to animals.

2. What on Earth Are Qualia?

Few devotees of qualia are forthcoming when it comes to explaining what precisely they amount to. Many of them excuse this evasiveness by reference to their uniquely subjective character. Although they would be loath to admit this, they seek refuge in a kind of mysticism. Supposedly, qualia can be apprehended only from the subject's point of view and therefore defy linguistic characterization. Some qualia merchants try to turn this alleged ineffability to their own advantage by suggesting that the very demand for explanation betokens a failure on the part of the enquirer. In the words of Ned Block:

> You ask: What is it that philosophers have called qualitative states? I answer, only half in jest: As Louis Armstrong said when asked what jazz is, "If you got to ask, you ain't never gonna get to know."
>
> (Block 1978, 278)

Even taken half seriously, however, this excuse is feeble. In the absence of an intelligible and coherent explanation one cannot enter into a debate about qualia, but nor is there any need to do so. This dialectic lesson is brought out vividly by a (probably apocryphal) anecdote (see Crane 2002). In a lecture from the 1950s, Feigl anticipated the current debate by maintaining that although the mind must be physical, the physical explanation of qualia remains an unsolved mystery for science. Rudolf Carnap, who was in attendance, protested: "But Feigl, there is something missing from your lecture. Science is beginning to explain qualia in terms of the alpha factor." Feigl, unsettled by this intervention from the doyen of logical positivism, exclaimed: "But Carnap, please tell me: what is the alpha factor?" Carnap curtly replied: "Well Feigl, if you tell me what qualia are, I'll tell you what the alpha factor is!" To quote another admirer of Carnap, namely Quine: "Whistling in the dark is not the proper method of philosophy!"

The challenge to explain what qualia are cannot be shirked, therefore. Orthodoxy characterizes them as *non-physical*, *subjective* and *non-representational*. Beyond these general points of agreement, however, the extant explanations diverge; and some of them ignore important distinctions.[1] A preliminary clarification: "qualia" is used both for mental *episodes* such as perceptual experiences and for the alleged indelibly *private properties* of these episodes. Only the latter are contested in the debate between devotees and deflationists. Block's fairly standard characterization does not fall foul of this point. "Qualia include the ways things look, sound and smell, the way it feels to have a pain, and more generally, what it's like to have experiential mental states" (Block 1994, 514).

On the downside, Block's explanation ignores important differences between perceptual *experiences* – for instance, seeing that the sky is blue – and *sensations* such as feeling pain. First, sensations have a bodily location, yet, unlike perceptions or the senses, they are not associated with distinctive sense organs. That is, provided that sense organs are understood morphologically as more or less distinct body parts rather than purely functionally, that is, as the ensemble of physiological mechanisms that causally enable a biological function. Secondly, unlike experiences, sensations do not furnish *direct* information about the environment. Thirdly, perceptual experiences have an object and/or content, in the (as we shall see minimal) sense that we experience something – an object X, a fact that p.

As regards this object/content, the quoted explanation commits a widespread mistake. It runs together perceptible objects and their qualities – *perceptibilia* – with *perceivings* and *their qualities*. The *way the sky looks* just now is *blue*. Yet (the colour) blue is neither an experience (or a state of mind more generally) nor a property of such an experience. Rather, it is a *property of material phenomena*. Experiences themselves can be *of* a blue object or the colour blue; but to suppose that they themselves can be blue is just as egregious a category mistake as supposing that numbers can. Furthermore, having an experience of an object a as being F is not tantamount to having an experience that is F – something that does not make sense for most Fs. "My tasting of this wine is dry" makes no sense. Finally, "This wine is dry" is not a misleading or elliptic expression of "I currently experience this wine as dry" (or, more realistically, "This wine tastes dry to me"). The two concern different topics, they have different truth conditions and often different truth values; for instance, an off-dry wine typically tastes dry to a subject that has just imbibed maple syrup.

The confusion of perceptions and perceptibilia also vitiates the widespread tactic of explaining qualia by appeal to personal experiences. Anyone except a zombie, we are lectured, will know what qualia are simply "by virtue of having them". Everyone knows how strawberries taste, a siren sounds, or rotting eggs smell. But once we keep perceptions and perceptibilia apart, we lose the elusive subjective aspect that is supposed to mark out qualia. Ripe strawberries taste sweet, sirens sound shrill and rotting eggs smell of sulphur, and these are perfectly intelligible and objective features of reality. That lesson also applies to the following ostensive explanation (Beckermann 2001, 385). Take a sip of wine; afterwards suck a mint candy; then take another sip of the wine. What has changed for you on this occasion is the quale, the subjective feel of the tasting experience. However, what has changed is the way the wine tastes, or the way the wine tastes to me – sweet vs. dry, let's say. But once again, both of these are objective features of the wine. This holds even if, as Locke's doctrine of secondary qualities alleges, how the wine tastes period is just as much a relational property – a disposition to elicit experiences in sentient creatures – as how the wine tastes to me. Finally, even if having certain experiences is necessary for understanding what qualia are, it is *not sufficient*. One does not understand what negative numbers are simply by virtue of having run up a debt; and one does not understand what depression is simply by feeling depressed. A coherent explanation remains vital.

3. What Are Experiences (like)?

In sum, one needs to distinguish between sensation (feeling pain) and perception, and between perceptible properties (*a* being *F*), (perceptual) experiences of these properties (seeing that *a* is *F*), and properties of these experiences (seeing that *a* is *F* being *G*). Allowing for these contrasts, qualia can be defined as properties of experiences that their subjects are immediately aware of, namely the qualitative character of an experience, "what it is like" for the subject to undergo it. To this the Nagelian orthodoxy adds the following contentions:

1. A subject *A* is conscious or sentient if there is something it is like to be *A*;
2. An experience of *A* is conscious if there is something it is like for *A* to undergo it, if the experience feels a certain way to *A*;
3. What it is like for *A* cannot be explained by science or even expressed by language;
4. Every experience is individuated by a unique qualitative character. After all, anyone must admit that tasting wine is different from hearing music!

What difference could be greater? Yet the constitutive contrast between the two experiences is instituted simply by the difference between *tasting* and *seeing*, and the difference between *wine* and *music*. The identity of a perceptual experience – what type of experience it is – depends solely on the sense modality on the one hand, the object or content on the other. This goes for the type experience. For the token, subject and time are also constitutive. The episode of a wine tasting off-dry to Stuart Pigott at t_1 is different from the episode of the same wine tasting off-dry to Jancis

Robinson at t_2. All in all, four factors are in play: subject, sense modality, object or content and time. Fully elaborated, statements about perceptual experiences have the form

$$S \quad V\text{-s} \quad \text{that } p/X \quad \text{at } t$$

where "S" signifies the subject, "V" the sensory modality, "that p"/"X" its content or object and "t" the time the experience occurred.

But, qualia enthusiasts will demur, there can nevertheless be *additional* differences between two experiences, concerning what it is like or what it feels like to have them. This is correct, yet inadequate to vindicate the orthodoxy on phenomenal consciousness. That orthodoxy starts out from the perfectly respectable question "What is (was) it *like* for you to experience X?" But in the established discourse that gives meaning to that question, the latter allows of only three types of answers.

The first is *hedonic* – delightful, horrifying, repugnant, and so on – and concerns the subject's affective attitude towards having the experience. Tasting a corked wine is repugnant, for instance, hearing a familiar sonorous voice can be soothing, seeing the Matterhorn can be uplifting.

The second is *comparative*: just like, better, worse, and so on. Thus seeing the Matterhorn is just as impressive as seeing the Taj Mahal, feeling a very light electric discharge on the tongue feels like sucking effervescent powder, and so on. The second-order quantification that Nagel introduced – "There is something it is *like* to experience X" – makes even grammatical sense only in this second case. One cannot answer the question "What was it like to watch a performance of *Die Soldaten*?" by "It was like disturbing"; what one can say is "It was like (just as disturbing as) watching *Scenes from a Marriage*."[2] Locutions such as "It feels a certain way to experience X" are not restricted to comparisons. Yet they fall short of a third and hitherto underappreciated type of answer to the "What was it like?" question, which I call *biographical*. A subject can characterize an experience indirectly, by placing it in the context of her life, notably by telling how it affected her views, character, and activities. Watching scenes from a slaughterhouse can totally turn around one's attitude towards vegetarianism. But although seeing the suffering of the animals can feel nauseating, for example, this type of lasting impact is not captured by expressing how the perceptual evidence feels.

Such differences notwithstanding, all three types of answer to "What was it like?" questions are perfectly intelligible and potentially informative, rather than desperate attempts to convey something that defies linguistic expression, as the orthodoxy implies. That is why such answers can be given not just by the subject herself – "Experiencing X was . . ./like experiencing Y" – but also by others: "For A, experiencing X was . . ./ just like experiencing Y." That third-person use is based on the same, loosely speaking behavioural criteria as the ascription of other mental terms, whereas *A* herself can avow what her experience was like with first-person authority.

The orthodoxy also ignores that many experiences do not sport a distinctive qualitative character and cannot be compared to ones that do. There is nothing distinctive it is like to see, for instance, a blue surface. Furthermore, *different* experiences can have *the same* hedonistic or, more generally, *affective* qualities. Tasting a 1983 *J. J. Prüm Wehlener Sonnenuhr Goldkapsel Eiswein* can be just as delightful or uplifting as hearing a performance of Beethoven's *Mondscheinsonate*. Conversely, *the same* experience can have *different* affective qualities, depending on the subject's circumstances. Seeing the Matterhorn when a broken leg prevents you from skiing is anything but uplifting. Finally, a qualia enthusiast could rely on an ostensive explanation/demonstration only if he could be reasonably confident that the subjective experiences of his interlocutor *resemble his own*. But that assumption is precisely undermined by their reification of experiences as private inner objects.

The notion of experience covers a wide range of phenomena, from sensations through perceptions and moods to mental acts. Admittedly, all of them are *grammatical* subjects of affective predicates; they can be pleasant, unpleasant, and so on. Soberly speaking, however, experiences are not *bona fide* objects with affective properties, but modifications of a sentient creature. *A*'s experience of *X* being *F* is constituted by *how A experiences F*. And the qualitative character of an experience is in the first instance simply constituted by the affective attitude of the subject to *experiencing what she does*. In the second instance, the aforementioned comparative and biographical dimensions come into play. But there is no unknowable let alone ineffable dimension.

The idea that essential qualities of our experiences transcend linguistic characterization is part and parcel of the "inner/outer picture of the mind" which has dominated Western philosophy since Descartes. It portrays the mind is a private domain – an inner peep-show – to which its subject enjoys exclusive access by means of introspection, an inner gaze. As Wittgenstein pointed out, it implies that our words for sensations, perceptions and their qualities are part of a "private language". Their referents would perforce be unknowable to anybody except the individual speaker, with the result that only the latter is in a position to know what they mean and that they *cannot* be explained to anyone else. The "private linguist" maintains that he can baptize as "*S*" such a radically private sensation (impression, sense-datum, quale, pre-conceptual content) through an inner ostension ("'*S*' means *this*"). However, a ceremony of naming can only lay down standards for distinguishing between correct and incorrect uses of a term "*S*", and hence provide the latter with meaning, if it *can* be explained to and understood by others. In the absence of that option, the private linguist reaches a similar impasse to the one facing those refusing to explain what "qualia" means.

> What reason have we for calling "S" the sign for a *sensation*? For "sensation" is a word of our common language, which is not a language intelligible only to me. So the use of this word stands in need of a justification which everybody understands. – And it would not help either to say that it need not be a *sensation*; that when he writes "S" he has *Something* – and that is all that can be said. But "has" and "something" also belong to our common language. – So in the end, when one is doing philosophy, one gets to the point where one would like just to emit an inarticulate sound. – But such a sound is an expression only in a particular language-game, which now has to be described.
>
> (PI §261)

The private language argument explicitly allows that a language can be spoken or even invented by a single speaker. It merely excludes the possibility of a language that *cannot* be understood by others because its "meanings" – the objects its words are supposed to refer to – are *private in principle*. Its inference-ticket is neither a stipulation according to which the term "language" is confined to systems of communication, nor scepticism about memory. At issue is not whether the private linguist can remember what he means by "S", but whether he has managed to *endow* "S" with meaning in the first place. To this end, the putative naming ceremony would have to lay down a rule for the correct use of "S". But there is no such thing as a "non-operational rule", one that cannot even in principle be used to distinguish between correct and incorrect applications. Yet the putative definition of the private linguist is *non-operational*. The private linguist's application of "S" at t_1 is incorrigible not just at t_1; he cannot even correct it at t_2. For at t_2 nothing distinguishes the private linguist's rectifying a mistake by reference to a prior rule from his having moved the goal-post by adopting a new rule. Justification consists in "appealing to something independent", and this is *ab initio* precluded in the case of a private language. Hence there can be no private ostensive definition in which a subjective impression or quale functions as a sample.

If the private language argument is sound (as Glock 1996, 309–315 vouchsafes), it is indeed impossible to make Nagelian qualia intelligible to sceptics; but the reason is that *there is nothing to be understood*. Once qualia are discarded, however, the "hard problem of consciousness" can be cut down to manageable proportions and tackled by a divide-and-conquer strategy. To quote an illuminating formulation: "How can one explain how non-conscious parts of an organism can come together to form a subject of consciousness?" (Silberstein 2001).

The question has both a conceptual and a factual trajectory. At the conceptual level, the explanation is that our concept of consciousness is tied to criteria that can in principle be satisfied by all and only subjects with a certain body, organization, and behavioural repertoire. At the factual, scientific level, the question is how various physiological mechanisms have to combine causally to constitute a suitable vehicle of consciousness. In addition to biological/physiological phenomena, this involves information-theoretic phenomena. For instance: How much Shannon information must be processed by a brain to provide its possessor with consciousness? What biological mechanisms can sustain such a flow of information? Keep in mind, however, that the answer may depend heavily on what species, individual, or context is at issue. One can admit all this, *without* readmitting qualia or abandoning a deflationary perspective on consciousness.

4. What it *Is* Like to Be a Bat

What answer does such a perspective suggest to Nagel's famous conundrum? Here we must distinguish several "What is it like?" or, less confusingly, "How is it?" questions.

1. What is it like (for a subject *A*) to *V*? (How is it for Sonja to live in Freiburg?)
2. What is it like for *A* to be *F*? (How is it for Romi to be in the army?)
3. What is it like for a *G* to be *F*? (How is it for a woman to be in the army?)
4. What is it like for a *G* to be a *G*? (How is it for a woman to be a woman?)
5. What is it like for *A* to be *A*? (How is it for Sonja to be Sonja?)

Questions 1–3 can be posed in a nebulous manner. But they are widespread and, even as posed by philosophers, can be clarified and answered. This is done by describing experiences, circumstances and biographies of individuals, or by describing experiences, circumstances and biographies that are typically associated with being *F*. Questions 4 and 5 lack an established use, because "What is it like?" questions presuppose a *contrast class*. And those who pose questions 4 and 5 often "explain" them in a way that renders them even less comprehensible. Still, they can be given an intelligible gloss, though only by relating them to the earlier questions. To cut a long story short, to ask what it is like for Sonja to be Sonja may be a pompous way of inquiring into her life and circumstances. By the same token, to ask what it is for a woman to be a woman may boil down to asking what it is like to be a woman, and hence to asking what kinds of lives women lead. That question is intelligible enough at a linguistic level, though way too general to allow of an informative answer.

If "*F*" signifies a biological species, the answer to what it is like to be an *F*, or, if one must, for an *F* to be an *F*, is given by a description of that species' typical form of life. As a result, my answer to Nagel's question runs, only half in jest:

> Being a bat is like being a small mammal that can fly (courtesy of wings, etc.) and is furnished with a sonar detection mechanism!

That quick and dirty response can be expanded, modified, and corrected subject to empirical findings concerning the behavioural capacities, life cycle, and environment of bats. Ethology is perfectly capable of informing us about what bats can do and perceive, what they enjoy, what attracts, deters and frightens them, and so on (see Dennett 1998). Finally, the way in which bats use echo sound location is not that far removed from the way in which some blind humans have learnt to use it.

In fact, answers to Nagelian questions concerning various species of animals *are* being expanded permanently by the explosion of biological and ethological research into the cognitive, conative, and affective capacities of complex animals. These efforts are not to be confused with Charles Foster's confused – if highly publicized – attempt to find out what animals feel. Foster subjected himself to situations identical with or similar to those confronting animals of various species and engaging in behaviour that is analogous to theirs (Foster 2016). But that procedure tells us at best what it is like *for humans* to experience the conditions under which animals live and to try behaving like animals. On this point Nagel (1974, 439) is dead right.

What about specific experiences of *individual* animals? Even here we can characterize and compare their affective qualities. This is possible on the basis of four types of information. They concern:

1. The life form of the species, namely, information of the kind mentioned just now;
2. Direct behavioural characteristics, including facial expressions and bodily demeanour;
3. Indirect behavioural evidence like that explored by research into "cognitive distortion" and "cognitive biases";
4. Perhaps (neuro-)physiological phenomena, such as the level of stress hormones or the activation patterns of neural stimuli.

Of these, type 2 provides the core criteria which are constitutive of mental concepts. But these concepts require the framework of type 1, that is, of at least rudimentary familiarity with the biological background. Of particular importance is information about functional connections between the needs and vulnerabilities of animals, their environment, and their behaviour. Such generic knowledge concerning the species may play a lesser role in understanding fellow humans than in comprehending animals without language and more remote in their behavioural displays. Yet it is indispensable even in the "domestic" case. While knowledge concerning the life forms of animals is often commonsensical, derived from everyday acquaintance, it is continuous with and can be enhanced by scientific findings.

In this respect, type 1 is connected to type 4. Anatomical and physiological evidence may have started to play a role in our concepts of sensations like pain. Yet they can be misleading as regards the moods and emotions of individual specimen. For instance, levels of "stress hormones" like cortisol and pulse rate are standardly regarded as indicators of stress. However, both increase not just after experiences that are objectively harmful to an animal, and hence presumably distressing, but also during feeding and mating.

Direct behavioural evidence of type 2 carries furthest in the case of two types of animals. First, those that resemble us closely in physiology and behavioural patterns, notably primates. Secondly, those that have been bred and trained to interact with us, notably dogs. It is more difficult to get mileage out of such evidence in the case of orders that include highly intelligent species, yet are more remote from us in their behavioural manifestations. Examples include cetaceans, corvids, and cephalopods. The functionally adaptive and flexible ways in which they interact with their environment testify to their cognitive capacities and conative drives. Unfortunately, behavioural evidence offers fewer clues about the affective quality of experiences. It is here that type 3 offers a way forward. "Cognitive bias" is a label for systematic deviations, in the judgement and behaviour of a subject *A* from what is normal and/or rational, that arise from irrelevant information or emotional states. Such interfaces between cognition and emotion have been well documented in humans (Sutherland 2007). Background affective states influence, among other things, attention, memory, and decision-making. For instance, humans in negative emotional states attend to threats, retrieve negative memories, and make negative judgements about ambivalent stimuli more frequently than those who are happier.

Recently this paradigm has been extended to affect-induced cognitive biases in animals. Subjects are trained that one cue predicts a positive event and another cue predicts a less positive (negative) event; they are then presented with ambiguous (intermediate) cues.[3] According to the cognitive bias hypothesis, animals in a negative affective state will be more likely to respond to these ambiguous cues as if they predict the negative event (a "pessimistic" response) than animals in a more positive state. Recent experimental studies on a range of species, including rats, dogs, and rhesus macaques, support this hypothesis (Burman et. al. 2009). Cognitive bias holds the promise of furnishing objective measures of cognitive performance as indicators of the more elusive and less easily measured affective states that influence them. What is more, some connections between affective properties on the one hand and cognitive bias on the other are *conceptual* in the case of humans. This is obvious in the case of certain character traits and attitudes. The fact that, *ceteris paribus*, optimists regard the glass as half full whereas pessimists regard it as half empty is partly constitutive of what it is to be, respectively, an optimist and a pessimist. In an attenuated form this connection extends to emotions and moods: it is not an empirical discovery that humans tend to be more pessimistic when they are in a sombre mood or have undergone traumatic experiences. Moods and experiences that engender an upbeat outlook would not qualify, respectively, as sombre or traumatic. And there is no reason for insisting that the case of animals is *au fond* different in this respect.

5. Animal Sentience and the Inner/Outer Picture of the Mind

Having deflated the subjective aspects of the concept of consciousness, the next question is whether it allows of ascription to animals. Let us begin with sentience, more specifically pain. Ascribing to animals sensations like pain is accepted not just by empiricists like Hume and Bentham, but also by some of their opponents, notably Wittgenstein (e.g., PI §284). More importantly, there are countless philosophically informed studies of the behavioural and physiological reactions of animals to harmful stimuli (Allen 2004; Braithwaite 2010; Wild 2012). That vertebrates, at any rate, have sensations and are capable of perceiving their environment should be glaringly obvious. Nonetheless it has been contested (e.g., Harrison 1991). That animals can feel pain tends to be *doubted* especially by those who conceive of sentience in terms of *qualia*, mysterious inner goings-on accessible only to their respective owners. It has also been *denied* outright. There are three general objections to animal sentience. I label them, respectively, the *inner-outer*, *higher-order*, and *neurophysiological* objection, and shall address them in turn.

Bermond (2003) combines all three. Against the idea that their behavioural repertoire shows animals to be susceptible to pain he points out that there can be pain without pain behaviour and pain behaviour without pain. Just so. But if this were sufficient reason to disregard behaviour altogether, it would open the floodgates to a *general scepticism about other minds* rather than casting particular doubt on animal sensation. For in humans we also encounter pain without *linguistic* pain behaviour and *linguistic* pain behaviour without pain.

Furthermore, this scepticism rests on the inner/outer picture: what is private – my own mind – is better known than the public world of material phenomena and the minds of others. I can know for certain that I am in pain, yet never that others are in pain. Indeed, I am unable to communicate to others what my pain amounts to, its qualitative feel.

Wittgenstein overturned this picture. We often know that others are in pain on the basis of their behaviour. The behavioural criteria for the application of sensation terms like "pain" are partly constitutive of their meaning. Unless certain patterns of behaviour – including facial expressions, posture, and linguistic utterances – counted as manifestations of pain *in a specific overall context*, the term "pain" would not mean what it actually does. If we came across human beings who used a word lacking any connection with pain behaviour and the circumstances in which we display it – for instance, bodily injury – we could not translate it as "pain". If neuroscientists started to assert or deny that a subject is in pain, in complete disregard of her sincere avowals, they would clearly have altered the meaning of "pain". By a similar token, Putnam's fiction of "super-super-spartans" (Putnam 1975, Ch. 16) who are in constant agony without ever showing it in any way is incoherent. With a vengeance, the same goes for an even more *outré* idea that nonetheless plays a crucial role in the qualia orthodoxy, namely that there might be "zombies", creatures that are exactly like us in all observable respects – including not just behavioural dispositions but physical make-up – and yet completely devoid of conscious experience (see Hacker 2013, Ch. 1; Beckermann 2012, Ch. 12). Although our criteria for pain are defeasible, in the absence of defeating conditions and on the assumption of sincerity, doubt whether someone displaying them is in pain loses its sense (see Glock 1996, 93–97, 174–179).

6. Higher-Order Theories and Different Types of Consciousness

Bermond dismisses out of hand arguments for the presence of pain in animals, even in species that possess higher cognitive capacities. Such capacities, he avers, are no indicator of consciousness, since cognitive processes in humans such as speaking or calculating need not be conscious.

This cavil overlaps with higher-order differentialism in denying that cognition suffices for consciousness. Carruthers (1989) based his denial of animal sentience on an elaborate higher-order theory – "HOT" – of consciousness. According to HOT, "a conscious state is a mental state whose subject is aware of being in it" (Lycan 2001, 3). From this Carruthers, along with other higher-order theorists, concludes that only creatures with second-order mental states have conscious mental states. According to Carruthers, that covers only adult human beings and perhaps primates with a "theory of mind", beliefs about the beliefs of other subjects. In effect, higher-order differentialism rests on the following argument:

P_1 Sensation requires consciousness.
P_2 Consciousness is a "higher-order" capacity that requires representation of one's own mental states.

P₃   Higher-order representation requires language.
C₁   Non-linguistic subjects lack consciousness. [from P₂ and P₃]
C₂   Non-linguistic subjects lack sentience. [from P₁ and C₁]

P₂ trades on confusions surrounding "conscious" and its cognates. It is at odds with the established distinction between being in a state of consciousness – such as a state of thinking about Mary – and being conscious of such a state – such as becoming aware that one is constantly thinking about Mary. Furthermore, if P₂ is based on a stipulative definition, one which bestows a more demanding meaning on "conscious" and its cognates, then sensations simply need not be conscious in this novel sense, that is, P₁ is mistaken. Accordingly, the argument is unsound since either P₁ or P₂ fails.

This response is reinforced by taxonomies of types of consciousness.[4] At the most basic level, there are states of *mere* consciousness. Consciousness in this sense is "what vanishes every night when we fall into dreamless sleep and reappears when we wake up" (Tononi 2008, 216). It has no object and contrasts with various states of sleep and unconsciousness. It can be lost and regained, and it comes in degrees: one can be more or less conscious in this sense. Subject to this qualification, mere consciousness is a precondition of all other forms of consciousness. Organisms can be in occurrent mental states or undergo mental processes only to the extent to which they are conscious in this sense. Some of these states and processes are intentional, that is, they have an object or content, a thing, state of affairs, and so on at which they are directed. These are cases of *transitive* consciousness, consciousness of something. But other mental states and processes lack such an object. This holds not just of sensations like pain, as Wittgenstein recognized, but also of moods, as Heidegger pointed out. One might feel uneasy about classifying these as states of consciousness at all. On the other hand, they are states one is only in while being conscious, that is, they presuppose mere consciousness; and they are potential objects of self-consciousness. For these reasons I shall speak of them as states of *intransitive* consciousness.

Finally, there is *self-consciousness* or self-awareness. This is a particular variant of transitive consciousness. In it one is conscious of one's own properties. A special case of self-consciousness in this widest sense – though the one philosophers tend to be obsessed with – is consciousness of one's own *mental* phenomena (states, processes, abilities, etc.). All forms of consciousness discussed so far are *potential* objects of self-consciousness, though only for those subjects who *possess* that advanced capacity. I can be aware of being awake, of fretting about an exam, or of being depressed. But these other forms of consciousness *need not* be confined to subjects capable of self-consciousness.

Through P₂, higher-order theories elide the difference between a *state one is conscious of*, which requires a form of self-consciousness, and a first-order state of consciousness, a state *in which one is conscious*. The latter in turn could be one of three things: mere consciousness – roughly being awake; intransitive consciousness – such as a sensation or mood; or transitive consciousness. In terms suggested by Dretske (1995, 101), the error of higher-order theories consists in assuming that any state one is "conscious with", any state being in which makes a subject conscious, by virtue of which the subject is conscious, notably a state of being conscious of something, must also be a state the subject is "conscious of".

A state in which one is transitively conscious requires a certain level of attention and alertness on the part of the subject. In standard cases, however, it is *attention to the world* rather than to the subject herself. Being alert and attending to something is most straightforwardly manifest in linguistic subjects. Such subjects can express a conscious experience, as in "There is a pot of flowers on the window-sill"; they also ascribe such experiences to themselves and others, as in "I see that there is a pot of flowers on the window-sill". But intelligent animals capable of learning have their attention caught and held by features of their environment, and they can attend to these features just as acutely and alertly as humans. This is amply evident from their use of sense-organs and the behavioural dispositions and abilities that it induces in them.

On this point I agree with Hacker (2013, 47). By contrast to him (2013, 28), I allow that one is conscious of something one is intentionally attending to. Asked at a trial whether she was conscious of the blood on the carpet, an eye-witness can answer in the affirmative by saying, for instance, "Yes; I was scanning it for traces". Hacker himself accepts that what one is conscious of is "something that holds one's attention" (Hacker 2013, 24). But what a subject intentionally attends to often holds her attention. Recently, I intentionally attended to Holbein's *Bildnis des Charles de Solier* because it was extolled as a highlight of the *Gemäldegalerie* in Dresden, and it continued to hold my attention since its photographic accuracy mesmerized me. One could coherently respond that X holding A's attention is only necessary but not sufficient for A being conscious of X. But then one would need to specify what distinguishes attention-holding with and attention-holding without consciousness in a way that does not beg the question. The connection between attention and consciousness is material to the issue of animal consciousness; for it ought to be uncontroversial that animals can intentionally attend to and indeed concentrate on features of their environment in perceiving, reacting to and manipulating the latter.

Be that as it may, higher-order differentialism rests on an argument that is unsound. Furthermore, by denying sentience even to intelligent animals with proven cognitive capacities, it severs the links between cognition, intentionality, and consciousness. Genuinely cognitive processes are not exhausted by the primitive information-processing displayed by microorganisms and plants. They require at least some intentional states, notably beliefs and knowledge. In the case of most cognitive processes these include beliefs and knowledge about external objects. At the most basic level, what is required is that the subject be able to *perceive* an object or that something is the case.

As previously stated, *all* occurrent mental states presuppose mere consciousness. This holds for intentional states as well. *A* can be in an occurrent intentional state only to the extent to which *A* possesses mere consciousness. For that reason alone, intentionality requires a capacity for mere consciousness. At the same time, there are intentional states that are "unconscious" in one sense, notably cases of subliminal perception. They include not just the recherché phenomena investigated by the psychology of perception, but also humdrum cases like the one mentioned by Dennett: you are, "able to count, retrospectively . . . the chimes of the clock which you only noticed was striking after four or five chimes. But how could you so clearly *remember hearing* something you hadn't been conscious of in the first place?" Dennett asks (1991, 137–138). His answer, surely correct, is that one can hear chimes without being conscious of them. In our context, it is crucial to note three points about Dennett's example. First, that a perception is unconscious in this sense does not just mean that *A* is not aware of being in these states at the time; such absence of self- or second-order consciousness characterizes most of our mental episodes. Rather, it means that at the time *A* is not *aware of* and *attending to* the objects of its first order state. For instance, *A* may fail to react appropriately to the chiming of the clock without prompting, but be able to answer the question of how often the clock has chimed immediately and confidently. Consequently such cases do not reinstate higher-order theories; they do not imply that first-order states qualify as conscious only when accompanied by second-order states.

Secondly, that *A* did perceive the chimes is evident from her remembering retrospectively. Such memory of what one subconsciously perceived is easily manifested by human subjects capable of avowing them linguistically. But it *can* also be manifested by non-linguistic subjects at least in principle. We can readily imagine a suitably modified version of the seminal tests for episodic memory devised by Clayton et. al. (2000). Leaving aside the more demanding case of counting chimes retrospectively, a great ape could behave in a way indicating that it does not take note of the *chiming* of the clock at the time. For instance, it has been trained to react to such chiming, but fails to manifest any such reaction on a particular occasion, e.g., because the chime volume has been turned down slightly. Still, the ape later displays having heard the chiming in a problem-solving setting. Therefore Dennett's example does not furnish conceptual reasons for excluding animals from the distinction between conscious and subconscious experience of a first order kind.

Finally, unconscious perception of this kind is intentional. In our scenarios *A* unconsciously hears not just the chiming of the clock but also how often the clock has chimed, that is, that it has chimed n times. Consequently unconscious perception is not a case of cognition without intentionality. It does cast doubt, however, on the idea that occurrent intentional states require occurrent transitive consciousness. One might insist that all such states qualify as cases of transitive consciousness; but this would be a Pyrrhic victory by stipulation. The proper reaction is to concede that there are episodes of intentionality without transitive consciousness, while insisting that a subject *A* cannot have the sizable suite of intentional states required for cognition, without at least the *ability* for transitive consciousness/awareness. How could *A* be able to perceive *X* or think that *p* without *ever* being aware of *X* or that *p*?

In response one might invoke blind-sight. Blind-sighted subjects appear to perceive their environment, yet without any visual awareness either of what they see or their seeing it. Blind-sight is an intricate phenomenon posing several philosophical puzzles. But it does not constitute a clear case of perception. For in blind-sighted subjects the criteria for seeing that go together in non-pathological cases – appropriate reaction to the environment, affective response and avowal of perception – come apart due to extraordinary circumstances for which our established perceptual notions were not tailored (see Hyman 1991).

In sum, cognition implies intentionality and thereby the capacities for both mere and transitive consciousness. Accordingly, one cannot deny consciousness to higher animals without denying intentionality and cognition. Intentional states presuppose the capacity for transitive consciousness and by implication for mere consciousness or sentience. However, they do *not* require self-awareness or self-reflection. One needs to be conscious of something, yet this need not be one's own mental states.

7. Pain, Behaviour, and Neurophysiology

Considered on its own, susceptibility to pain does not even require cognitive processes and hence transitive consciousness. It only requires sentience and intransitive consciousness. It may seem, therefore, that its presence in higher animals is even less contestable than that of transitive consciousness. There is a complication, however. Genuine sentience requires more than a disposition to react to stimuli. A real sensation must be *felt* by its subject; indeed, there is no difference between having a sensation and feeling a sensation. For this reason, one must distinguish between feeling or experiencing pain and *nociception*, the mere detection of and reaction to noxious stimuli. The latter correlates damage to the body with certain forms of behaviour, yet without implying awareness. What is more, even subjects who can detect a noxious stimulus *immediately* (rather than, e.g., as a result of perceived correlation) need not be in pain strictly speaking. For such detection need not be susceptible to the hedonic or affective dimension that characterizes genuine sensations. Pain, for instance, has an aversive dimension and is felt as bad – *ceteris paribus* and *pro tanto*, given phenomena like certain kinds of masochism.

In view of this difference, higher-order differentialism can stage a comeback. By contrast to nociception, pain requires some kind of self-consciousness after all. *A* feels or experiences a mental state of *A*. But this last step is unsound. While feeling or experiencing a pain contrasts with nociception, it does not constitute a case of self-consciousness. For, as Wittgenstein argued persuasively, the subject of a pain does not stand in a genuine "representational" relation to a *bona fide* object which makes an appearance on an inner stage. At a pinch, one might say that in many cases *the subject* "represents" *bodily damage* by feeling a pain, in that this feeling informs the subject of such damage. Nevertheless, the pain is not an object that represents the damage and is in turn represented by the subject. *Feeling a pain* is simply *being in pain*; indeed, that is a corollary of the affective dimension of pain that the differentialist riposte itself trades on. A pain is no more a substance than "a mind". Unlike the latter, it is not a set of capacities either; instead, it is a *modification* of subjects with certain mental capacities, those capable not just of detecting a bodily damage, but of affective responses as well. If you wish, the bodily damage must be sensed *as* unpleasant (stinging, numbing, etc.). To that extent, the hedonic qualities that loom large in the idea of qualia play a decisive role in setting sensations apart from nociception. Unfortunately, qualia proponents see that role through a looking glass darkly. Far from being essentially private and ineffable, the affective responses to bodily damage are displayed in behaviour (notably pain avoidance), facial expressions, and bodily demeanour of sentient creatures. Being sensitive to such manifestations is part and parcel of being human, albeit a part that sceptics about other minds and qualia merchants supress.

Admittedly, though they are modifications, physical pains resemble objects in having a *location* (Hacker 2013, 266–267). I feel a pain *in* a part of my body. What is more, this use of "in" is *locative*, by contrast, for instance, to "in the mind", "in the novel", "in fact". Nevertheless it does not ascribe an *extensional location* within the physical framework of overall space-time, by contrast to locating genuine objects. Instead, it ascribes a location *in the flesh-and-blood creature* that is in pain. The pain is in my finger not in the straightforward sense in which my keys are in my pocket. By contrast to that extensional sense, it is *not* transitive: the pain is in my finger and the finger is in my trousers; yet it makes no sense to conclude that the pain is in my trousers.[5] Furthermore, even though the pain can be made to abate by interfering with my finger, it cannot be spatially removed from my finger. In short, that the pain is in the finger simply means that it is one of my fingers that hurts, rather than, for instance, one of my toes.

For higher-order differentialists, sensitivity to the environment is insufficient to prove sentience. But spare a thought for complex animals with bodily demeanour, facial expressions, sense organs, and brains resembling ours. When such animals are awake, alert and adroitly "negotiate the world" on the basis of the information provided by their senses, it makes scant sense to wonder whether they do so unconsciously. Unless this were to mean – perversely – that they might not be aware of their *own states of consciousness*. Yet the latter is by no means a prerequisite for being aware of one's environment. *Au contraire*, self-consciousness is often a distraction. Conversely, "being available to thought" – that is, being a potential object of self-awareness – is not a precondition for a mental state being conscious in the sense of intransitive or transitive consciousness, let alone of mere consciousness. To suppose otherwise is once more to confuse intransitive and transitive consciousness with self-consciousness and reflection.[6]

Let us turn to the neurophysiological objection. Bermond defends the unrestrained separability of pain and pain behaviour by reference to the alleged fact that both have different neurophysiological loci, namely, respectively, cortical and sub-cortical (Bermond 2003, 81–82). But this argument would prove too much, since it engenders scepticism about pain in other human as well. Fortunately, it proves nothing in either case. For it confuses the *de facto* separation of the physiological vehicles of the two capacities with a separation of the capacities themselves. As argued earlier, there is a conceptual connection between sensations and forms of behaviour. Even in the absence of such a connection, moreover, there can obviously be a tight causal connection between two capacities implemented in different parts of the brain.

Another neurophysiological objection is epitomized by the slogan "No brain, no pain!" Its fulcrum is the idea that feeling pain requires the possession of a neocortex. Even in animals that possess a central nervous system such as snails, noxious stimuli are translated into avoidance behaviour not through the central nervous system, but through nociceptors and localized neural centres. Such animals, the objection runs, do not feel pain.

This line of reasoning would not sustain a blanket denial of or scepticism about animal pain in general, since vertebrates sport a neocortex in which noxious stimuli are processed. What is more, by disregarding behaviour completely, this blunt version falls foul of the aforementioned fact that behavioural capacities and dispositions are at least partly constitutive of the phenomena that neuroscience seeks to explain by reference to the brain (see also Wild 2012, 119–133). A subtler version is based on the idea that "pain" signifies a "matrix" or syndrome of phenomena. This matrix includes behavioural parameters such as learning to avoid harmful stimuli and suspension of normal behaviour under impact of noxious stimuli. But it also includes neurophysiological parameters (nociceptors, brain structures analogous or homologous to human brain; neural pathways connecting the two; endogenous opioids and opioid receptors) and criteria mixing the two (analgesics show potency of reducing avoidance behaviour).

Such a matrix may well guide our current employment of "pain" not just within science, but in everyday parlance as well. The verdict it delivers concerning pain in a particular biological taxon is a list of ticks and crosses (see Segner 2012, 78); consequently it will be more or less qualified. Perhaps there can be differences in patterns that trigger a kind of sudden conceptual *Gestalt* switch even without any conceptual change having occurred. However, where precisely such a switch occurs will differ between speakers, and is hence not part and parcel of the lexical meaning of "pain". In any event, as long as the verdicts of normal members of the linguistic community are not swayed by half-digested popular science, that pattern will not include *recherché* criteria such as opioids or evolutionary homologies.

There are pains to which we do not pay attention. But there cannot be pains that are principally and deeply unconscious. Otherwise the difference between the concept of *pain* and the concept of *bodily damage* is lost. Furthermore, if nothing counted as a typical behavioural manifestation of pain in pertinent circumstances, our current concept of pain would lose its grip. Finally, the claim that the behavioural manifestations of the mental must be *linguistic* is particularly implausible with respect to sensations. For here both the occasion and the reaction – not to mention the anatomical, physiological, and neurophysiological mechanisms – are very similar in humans and higher animals.

8. The Really Hard Problem

Properly understood, consciousness poses only "easy problems" like conceptually clarifying and causally explaining phenomena like wakefulness, focus of attention and the reportability of one's mental states. Nevertheless, in one respect, Nagel's fateful challenge still stands. Animal consciousness is fraught with problems of understanding. However, the Nagelian challenge misses the most severe obstacle. The real difficulty is not answering the question

1. What is it like for an animal to be in a state of transitive consciousness?

It is rather answering the question

2. What intentional state or state of transitive consciousness is an animal in?

Regarding animals, at least, it is not question 1, standardly linked to the spectre of ineffability that may mark a limitation of language. It is rather question 2, standardly linked with the allegedly more tractable phenomenon of intentionality. The reason is that in order to answer question 2 we must be capable of specifying *what precisely* an animal believes, desires, and intends.

This may appear surprising or ironical at first. On second thought, however, it is simply a consequence of the fact that "lower" mental phenomena and properties are more easily ascribed in the absence of language than "higher" ones. This includes not just intellectual operations like reasoning but also, though to a lesser extent, intentional states like believing, desiring, and intending. We can ascribe to animals not just sensations and experiences, but also characterize these in hedonic, comparative, and even "biographical" terms. To the unblinkered eye it is obvious, for instance, that monkeys enjoy eating peanuts, and there is ample laboratory evidence that they enjoy eating peanuts more than eating cucumbers. As regards the biographic dimension, traumatic experiences can transform the behaviour and indeed character of higher animals (see Braitman 2014). This is evident for instance in those deplorable cases of bears held in captivity displaying symptoms of hospitalism.

By contrast, when it comes to determining what precisely even intelligent animals like bears think – believe, desire, and intend – we are at a loss. That, at any rate, is the conclusion of arguments pressed by Davidson and Stich. As regards specifying what a subject believes, intends and desires, natural languages are the *ultimate medium of disambiguation and explanation*. If we want to know what a linguistic subject *s* believes, the definitive answer is provided by *s*'s sincere and well-considered avowals and explanations. There is nothing more to the content of intentional states than what can be ascribed to subjects subject to the authority of their sincere avowals.

In the case of animals we can exclude exotic contents in the same way in which one can exclude alleged instances of Quinean inscrutability of reference for humans (see Glock 2003, chs. 6–7). But we cannot nail down a precise content.

> The dog, we say, knows that its master is home. But does it know that Mr. Smith (who is his master) or that the president of the bank (who is the same master), is home? We have no real idea how to settle, or *make sense of*, these questions.
>
> (Davidson 1984, 163; my emphasis)

But is this a limitation of *our language* or of *creatures without language*? My answer: it is a *limitation imposed by our language* on *creatures without language*. More specifically, it is a limit imposed by the conceptual scheme underlying our attribution of intentional states.

Ascribing intentional states makes sense only in cases where we have criteria for identifying thoughts. In Quine's memorable phrase, "No entity without identity" (Quine 1969, 23). Something must count as thinking that *p* rather than that *q*, otherwise ascriptions of thoughts are vacuous. This means that intentional states, although they need not actually be expressed, must be *capable* of being expressed. Non-linguistic behaviour can manifest a great range of such states. It can also manifest finer distinctions in their contents than Davidson and Stich allow. But there are limits to such fine-grainedness. In his last writings, Wittgenstein diagnosed an "imponderability of the mental" even for the ascription of complex mental properties to humans. For animals, that imponderability arises with a vengeance.

Even such a moderate restriction and qualification concerning the applicability of mental notions to animals invites the charge of *conceptual* anthropocentrism. We arrogantly set ourselves apart, the allegation runs, through our language, through *human* concepts rather than those of animals. However, conceptual anthropocentrism is both *inevitable* and *legitimate*. For a starter, insisting that animals might possess advanced mental capacities according to their own concepts is a *petitio principii*, since it is very much in question whether animals have concepts at all, let alone mental concepts. Secondly, the anthropocentrism charge itself relies on concepts – notably *anthropocentrism* and *concept* – which are indisputably the prerogative of humans. Indeed, without the use of such concepts the question of animal minds and the distribution question cannot be raised. There is no gainsaying that these questions are legitimate – the very attempt of debunking them would once more rely on exclusively human concepts; therefore the employment of the concepts required in formulating and addressing these questions is equally legitimate. Finally, as Davidson reminded us (albeit in a different context), "Our concepts are ours" (Davidson 1999, 19). They play a role in our cognition, serve our epistemic needs and interests, and are geared to our capacities. To that extent, *mental concepts* are anthropocentric; yet they are none the worse for that! And it does *not* follow that it is anthropocentric to insist that these concepts preclude application to non-linguistic creatures.

Notes

1. Parts of what follows are indebted to Dupré 2009 and Hacker 2013, Ch. 1.
2. One might challenge this by reference to recent slang. But in that employment the term functions as an interjection rather than a comparative adjective. It features "It was, like, awesome!" rather than "It was like awesome."
3. In a standard experimental setting, if *A* presses lever *X* after a 80Hz tone she is rewarded by highly desired food, while pressing lever *Y* after a 60Hz tone yields bland food. Subsequently *A* is offered both levers after an intermediate test stimulus, such as a 70Hz tone. The hypothesis is that in a cognitively biased animal, emotions and mood will affect the choice of levers after the test stimulus: if positive, *A* will tend to choose lever *X*, if negative she will tend to choose lever *Y*. It is tested by manipulating factors that might affect mood – for example, the conditions in which *A* is kept or specific potentially pleasant or unpleasant experiences.

4. Mine builds on Malcolm 1984 but is more elaborate.
5. This contention is not subject to the Gricean response that the conclusion is odd rather than nonsensical, since it states something obvious. For the conclusion of the parallel transitive inference "The receipt is in my wallet and the wallet is in my trousers; therefore the receipt is in my trousers" states something obvious, while making perfect sense. Eva Schmidt alerted me to the following analogy: There is a wrinkle in my sock, and my sock is in my pocket, yet there still isn't a wrinkle in my pocket. In both cases transitivity fails because "There is a wrinkle in my sock" and "There is a pain is in my finger" do not just locate, respectively, a wrinkle or a pain, but ascribe a property/modification to me and the sock respectively. Both pains and wrinkles are what Strawson (1959) called "dependent particulars", they lack the kind of independent location in objective space-time that material objects have.
6. Carruthers (2004) came round to granting that some animals possess sentience and are capable of suffering, yet without "subjectivity". Unfortunately, I have been unable to fathom what precisely that caveat amounts to.

References

Allen, Colin (2004) "Animal Pain", *Noûs* 38 (4), 617–643.

Beckermann, Ansgar (2001) *Analytische Einführung in die Philosophie des Geistes*. Berlin and New York: Walter de Gruyter.

Beckermann, Ansgar (2012) *Aufsätze Band 1: Philosophie des Geistes*. Bielefeld: Universitätsbibliothek, available at http://pub.uni-bielefeld.de/publication/2508111.

Bermond, Bob (2003) "The Myth of Animal Suffering", reprinted in Susan J. Armstrong and Richard G. Botzler (eds), *The Animal Ethics Reader*. London: Routledge, 79–85.

Block, Ned (1978) "Troubles with Functionalism", *Minnesota Studies in the Philosophy of Science* 9, 261–325.

Block, Ned (1994) "Qualia", in Samuel Guttenplan (ed), *A Companion to the Philosophy of Mind*. Oxford: Blackwell, 514–520.

Braithwaite, Victoria (2010) *Do Fish Feel Pain?* Oxford: Oxford University Press.

Braitman, Laurel (2014) *Animal Madness*. New York: Simon and Schuster.

Burman, O. H. P., Parker, R. M. A., Paul, E. S. and Mendl, M. T. (2009) "Anxiety-Induced Cognitive Bias in Non-Human Animals", *Physiology and Behavior* 98 (3), 345–350.

Carruthers, Peter (1989) "Brute Experience", *Journal of Philosophy* 86, 258–269.

Carruthers, Peter (2004) "On Being Simple-Minded", *American Philosophical Quarterly* 41, 205–220.

Chalmers, David (1995) "Facing up to the Problem of Consciousness", *Journal of Consciousness Studies* 2, 200–219.

Clayton, N. S., Griffiths, D. P. and Dickinson, A. (2000) "Declarative and Episodic-Like Memory in Animals", in C. M. Heyes and L. Huber (eds), *The Evolution of Cognition*. Cambridge, MA: MIT Press, 273–288.

Crane, Tim (2002) "The Hot Theory of Sensations", *Times Literary Supplement* (14 June), 9.

Davidson, Donald (1984) *Inquiries into Truth and Interpretation*. Oxford: Clarendon Press.

Davidson, Donald (1999) "Is Truth a Goal of Inquiry?" in U. M. Żegleń (ed), *Donald Davidson: Truth, Meaning and Knowledge*. London: Routledge, 17–19.

Dennett, Daniel (1991) *Consciousness Explained*. Boston: Little, Brown and Company.

Dennett, Daniel (1998) "Animal Consciousness: What Matters and Why?" in his *Brainchildren: Essays on Designing Minds*. Cambridge, MA: MIT Press, 337–350.

Dretske, Fred (1995) *Naturalizing the Mind*. Cambridge, MA: MIT Press.

Dupré, John (2009) "Hard and Easy Questions About Consciousness", in H. J. Glock and J. Hyman (eds), *Wittgenstein and Analytic Philosophy*. Oxford: Oxford University Press, 228–249.

Feigl, Herbert (1967) *The "Mental" and the "Physical": The Essay and a Post-script*. Minneapolis: University of Minnesota Press.

Foster, Charles (2016) *Being a Beast*. London: Profile Books.

Glock, Hans-Johann (1996) *A Wittgenstein Dictionary*. Oxford: Blackwell.

Glock, Hans-Johann (2003) *Quine and Davidson on Language, Thought and Reality*. Cambridge: Cambridge University Press.

Hacker, P. M. S. (2013) *The Intellectual Powers: A Study of Human Nature*. Oxford: Wiley-Blackwell.

Harrison, Peter (1991) "Do Animals Feel Pain?" *Philosophy* 66 (255), 25–40.

Heckmann, Heinz-Dieter and Walter, Sven (2001) *Qualia: Ausgewählte Beiträge*. Paderborn: Mentis.

Hyman, John (1991) "Visual Experience and Blindsight", in John Hyman (ed), *Investigating Psychology: Sciences of the Mind After Wittgenstein*. London: Routledge, 166–200.

Lewis, C. I. (1929) *Mind and the World Order*. New York: Charles Scribner's Sons.

Lycan, William (2001) "A Simple Argument for a Higher-Order Representation Theory of Consciousness", *Analysis* 61, 3–4.

Malcolm, Norman (1984) "Consciousness and Causality", in D. M. Armstrong and N. Malcolm, *Consciousness and Causality*. Oxford: Blackwell, 1–102.

Nagel, Thomas (1974) "What Is It Like to Be a Bat", *The Philosophical Review* 83, 435–450.

Pinker, Steven (2009) *How the Mind Works*. New York: Norton.

Putnam, Hilary (1975) *Mind, Language and Reality. Philosophical Papers Volume 2*. Cambridge: Cambridge University Press.

Quine, W. V. (1969) *Ontological Relativity and Other Essays*. New York: Columbia University Press.

Segner, Helmut (2012) *Fish: Nociception and Pain*. Bern: FOBL.

Silberstein, Michael (2001) "Converging on Emergence: Consciousness, Causation and Explanation", *Journal of Consciousness Studies* 8, 61–98.

Sorabji, Richard (1993) *Animal Minds and Human Morals: The Origins of the Western Debate*. London: Duckworth.

Strawson, P. F. (1959) *Individuals*. London: Methuen.

Sutherland, Stuart (2007) *Irrationality: The Enemy Within*. Second edition (First edition 1992). London: Pinter and Martin.

Tononi, Giulio (2008) "Consciousness as Integrated Information: A Provisional Manifesto", *Biological Bulletin* 215, 216–242.

Wild, Markus (2012) *Fische: Kognition, Bewusstsein und Schmerz. Eine philosophische Perspektive*. Bern: BBL.

10 The Limits of Language in Wittgensteinian Philosophy of Religion

Sami Pihlström

1. Introduction

The purpose of this chapter is to examine the issue of the limits of language from the point of view of Wittgenstein's (and "Wittgensteinian") philosophy of religion – that is, to raise some fundamental issues characterizing the loose Wittgensteinian tradition in this field from the point of view of the question concerning the limits of language, as it arises in Wittgenstein's own work. I am not primarily seeking to make any detailed contribution to scholarly Wittgenstein interpretation, as Wittgenstein's significance for the philosophy of religion has been extensively studied. However, I do believe that, by contrast to what some Wittgensteinians argue, the notion of a limit of language in Wittgenstein's discussion of religion ought to be taken very seriously – even if we are only aiming at a Wittgenstein-*inspired* illumination of the nature of religious language and religious belief.[1]

There is plenty of evidence for so-called Wittgensteinian philosophers' uneasiness with the limit metaphor. For instance, when D. Z. Phillips, in his editorial preface to a volume of his teacher's Rush Rhees's writings, acknowledges that the idea of "the limits of language" was important for Rhees, he continues to note that he (Phillips) himself "never could get into the simile of 'bumps and bruises' which come from striking one's head against the limits of language – and speaking of the worry or distress which belongs to philosophy in those terms" (Phillips 2006, xx; cf. PI §119, see also Rhees 2006, 222).[2] More specifically, it seems to me that Wittgensteinian philosophers of religion such as Phillips have not been fully conscious of the way in which the issue concerning the limits of language arises in the philosophy of religion as a *Kantian* issue, thereby evoking a need for a *transcendental* analysis of religious practices. Nor have they therefore sufficiently appreciated the possibility of interpreting Wittgenstein himself as a Kantian thinker in this respect, presenting something like a transcendental investigation of the conditions of religious language. Indeed, some of the core arguments characterizing Wittgensteinian philosophy of religion, identifiable in the work of Phillips, among others, can (*pace* Phillips himself) be reinterpreted as transcendental arguments.[3]

Phillips's and other Wittgensteinians' arguments also, importantly, raise the issue of *relativism* about religion, because it might seem that from the Wittgensteinian perspective one may simply reject scientific (or presumably any external) criticism of religion by pointing out that it does not follow the rules of religious language-games that are available only "from within" the religious use of language itself. As is well known, critics of such relativist views have used pejorative terms like "Wittgensteinian fideism" to highlight the unwelcome relativistic, fideistic, or even irrationalist consequences of the proposal to simply ground the meanings of religious language in the activities engaged in by people who actually "play religious language-games" or "engage in a religious form of life". If such meanings are unavailable to those who do not participate in such activities, no rational criticism of religious belief seems to be possible at all. In particular, no science-based critique of religion is relevant to the critical assessment of religion, or even strictly speaking possible, because by confusing the grammar of religious language with that of scientific language such critique does not even speak about religion in the end. Evaluating the validity of the Wittgensteinians' concerns with relativism (and related views) would require a detailed analysis of what exactly is and ought to be meant by "relativism". Instead of entering that discussion, I will directly explore the "limits of language" issue without taking any final stand on the relativism question.

This chapter will not offer any close critical reading of Phillips's or other Wittgensteinians' views, either. That would also be a task for a much more comprehensive discussion. My main aim is to offer selected insights into the way in which the Wittgensteinian approach in the philosophy of religion differs from other relevant approaches – that is, into what is truly distinctive in it in comparison to mainstream analytic philosophy of religion in particular – by emphasizing the central status of the problem of the limits of (religious) language. I will also suggest that the distinctiveness of the Wittgensteinian approach can be perceived much more clearly if we are willing to read Wittgenstein as engaged in transcendental reflection. This does not preclude us from appreciating, for example, Phillips's (and other Wittgensteinians') emphasis on the significance of literary fiction in philosophical attempts to understand religious language-use and religious problems, especially in drawing our attention to the particular and personal in religious language-use (see, e.g., Phillips 1991). On the contrary, transcendental considerations themselves can be embedded in literature (cf. Kivistö and Pihlström 2016).[4]

As an illustration of my general claims, I will toward the end of the chapter (Section 5) briefly discuss the problem of evil and suffering, suggesting that Wittgensteinians like Phillips can be taken to have offered transcendental considerations in favour of what we may call *antitheodicism*, refuting theodicies as violations of genuinely religious language-use. However, we should first (Sections 2–4) take a look at how the issues concerning limits as conditions of religious language arise in Wittgenstein's early and late philosophy as well as some "Wittgenstein-ian" views based thereupon.[5] That discussion will lead us to an appreciation of what I propose to call "the contingency of necessity" – something that will turn out to be highly relevant in the theodicy vs. antitheodicy explorations as well.

2. The Limits of Language in Wittgenstein's "Early" Views on Religious Belief

Let us begin from the way in which the "early Wittgenstein" – the author of the *Tractatus* (1921) and the brief "Lecture on Ethics" (1929) – formulates his view that religion, analogously to ethics and aesthetics, is something that cannot be put to words but is, rather, "mystical". Wittgenstein tells us that God does not make himself manifest *in* the world ("Gott offenbart sich nicht *in* der Welt", TLP 6.432), and as the limits of my language designate, famously, the limits of the (or my) world (TLP 5.6), this seems to rather straightforwardly suggest that God cannot be meaningfully spoken about in language; anything we try to say about God falls beyond the limits of language. The realm of ethics and religion simply lies beyond language and the world. The purpose of language is to describe the world, which is a collection of states of affairs ("Sachverhalte"), as Wittgenstein tells us already in the opening remarks of the *Tractatus* (TLP 1.1), and clearly God's existence is not among such worldly states of affairs but something entirely different – so different that we should not speak about God at all. Our attempts to say something about God are, rather, attempts to say something about the meaning of life or the world, or perhaps about the "problem of life" (cf. TLP 6.521). Indeed, Wittgenstein says that the *Sinn* of the world must lie outside or beyond ("ausserhalb") it (TLP 6.41) and that propositions ("Sätze") cannot express anything "higher" (TLP 6.42). What is "mystical" ("das Mystische") is not *how* the world is but *that* it is (TLP 6.44).

Thus, according to the early Wittgenstein, religion (along with ethics and aesthetics) seems to lie beyond the limits of language in a rather obvious sense. As mystical, religion belongs to the transcendent realm. This transcendence of ethics and religion is also forcefully expressed in the "Lecture on Ethics" (PO, 37–44), where Wittgenstein tells us that "absolute" ethical expressions are nonsensical attempts "*to go beyond* the world and that is to say beyond significant language" (PO, 44). The tendency of all attempts to discuss ethics or religion in language is "to run against the boundaries of language", but this "running against the walls of our cage is perfectly, absolutely hopeless" (PO, 44). Religion, or God, is something we must pass over into silence (cf. TLP 7).

However, things may be not as simple as that, if we take seriously the Kantian transcendental interpretation of Wittgenstein.[6] If religion and ethics (and aesthetics) are truly analogous in the *Tractatus*, then we should pay close attention to the fact that ethics (which is "one" with aesthetics) is, just like logic, claimed to be *transcendental* – not "transcendent". This is highly significant. Insofar as ethics is comparable to logic in providing a kind of (in itself linguistically inexpressible) transcendental structure for the empirical world that we can speak about in language, then religion must in some sense be doing the same thing. That is, for the religious person, religion may play the "transcendental" role of providing the fundamental framework through which such a person sees, or is able to see, the world in general and everything contained in it. In this sense, religion might, for the religious person, be the framework through which the significance of any worldly fact (all of which are in principle describable in language) can (perhaps only) be ultimately viewed – though this viewing itself cannot be put to words and lies beyond any sensible linguistic expression. God's being manifest not "in" the world but (as it were) somewhere else would then have to be construed *not* along the lines of God's manifestation anywhere "outside" the world – Wittgenstein's somewhat unfortunate use of the word "ausserhalb" at TLP 6.41 and his tendency to speak about ethics as "supernatural" in the "Lecture on Ethics" (e.g., PO, 40, 43) notwithstanding – but as God's being somehow "at the limit", playing a transcendental rather than a transcendent role there. There is no point beyond the linguistically describable world where God could be manifested; there is nothing there. But there is the transcendental limit making the world possible as a world of states of affairs describable in language. For the religious person, God (or, perhaps, one's faith in God, which could simply correspond to one's viewing the world as a limited whole, to a faith that sees some inexpressible – potential – meaning in the fact that there is a world at all) would be a transcendental condition for the possibility of the world itself as a world having sense, somewhat analogously to the way in which the metaphysical (transcendental) subject is claimed by Wittgenstein to be a "limit" ("Grenze") of the world instead of being a "thing" in the world (TLP 5.632).[7]

In brief, while according to Wittgenstein anything we try to say about religion (or ethics) is bound to be nonsensical in the sense that it fails to describe any states of affairs that could obtain in the world, such futile attempts are indications of something "higher", of the religious person's attempt to view the world in a certain way, with a kind of fundamental seriousness. While neither ethics nor religion that is supposedly about the ultimate meaning of life or about ultimate value can be accounted for by science and "does not add to our knowledge in any sense", our (futile) attempt to put such things into words "is a document of a tendency in the human mind which I [he tells us] personally cannot help respecting deeply and I would not for my life ridicule it" (PO, 44). From such a perspective, the fundamental flaw in (say) mainstream analytic philosophy of religion, which tends to operate in terms of realism and evidentialism in their various versions, is precisely that its representatives believe religion to be a kind of "science", something that "adds to our knowledge", something that for example science cannot add. The hopelessness of this view can be revealed by a transcendental critique that indicates the underlying mistake of confusing fundamentally different types of language-use.

3. The "Later" Wittgenstein and the "Factual Dependence" of Language-Games

This brings us to the remarks on religion by the "later" Wittgenstein – remarks that are available not so much in the main works like the *Investigations* and *On Certainty* but in brief writings and notes such as "Lectures on Religious Belief" (in LC, 53–72; WCL, 129–132), "Remarks on Frazer's *Golden Bough*" (PO, 115–155), and some remarks collected in *Culture and Value*. I won't be able to go through this material in any systematic way here. We should note, however, that one of the central metaphors now is the one of *picture* – rather than the metaphor of a limit suggesting that one might in principle (while one in practice cannot) move across some boundary dividing sense from nonsense.[8] According to Wittgenstein, the religious person "uses a picture", and "[t]he whole *weight* may be in the picture" (LC, 72; WCL, 132). Certain pictures – for the religious person, religious ones – may express our basic convictions that are as firm as anything can possibly be for us, something we are absolutely certain of (in the sense of OC) and something without which our lives would be entirely different from what they are, and perhaps inconceivable from our present standpoint. Such pictures can (though this is not Wittgenstein's own terminology) be regarded as "transcendental" precisely in the sense that using them makes a certain world – and a certain way of relating to, or viewing, the world – possible for us. They could act as the enabling conditions without which certain kinds of language-use and certain forms of life would simply not be there, or would be unavailable to us.[9]

Pictures, religious pictures included, are used by real human beings in real-life circumstances, within various contexts of using language and thus within certain forms of life. One of the most perceptive commentators on Wittgenstein, Hilary Putnam, reflecting on Wittgenstein's "Lectures on Religious Belief", emphasizes this deep connection between understanding religious discourse and understanding a human being engaging in such a discourse:

> What then is Wittgenstein saying? I believe that what Wittgenstein (in company with Kierkegaard) is saying is this: that religious

discourse can be understood in any depth only by understanding the form of life to which it belongs. What characterizes that form of life is not the expressions of belief that accompany it, but a way – a way that includes words and pictures, but is far from consisting in just words and pictures – of living one's life, of regulating all of one's decisions. . . . What Kierkegaard and Wittgenstein have in common is the idea that understanding the words of a religious person properly – whether you want to speak of understanding their "meaning" or not – is inseparable from understanding a religious form of life, and this is not a matter of "semantic theory", but a matter of understanding a human being.

(Putnam 1992, 154)

At the same time, precisely because we are here concerned with understanding real human beings in their real this-worldly circumstances, religion may be a response to *real* events of life, especially to the deepest despair or torment that individuals may feel – that is, the kind of despair Wittgenstein had in mind when he noted in a diary remark that the whole world cannot be in a more intense "distress" than a single lost soul experiencing "die höchste Not" (CV, 52, c. 1944).[10] Hence, one's use of religious "pictures" may (potentially) be such a response; indeed, this possibility of using religious pictures or other expressions as indicators of one's ultimate concern regarding suffering, meaning, the loss of meaning, or other such profound existential experiences is itself a transcendental feature of the ways in which the meanings of religious language (and religious symbols more generally) are constituted. *That* religious language *can* make such a response to existential dimensions of human life is, we might say, constitutive of the possibility of genuine religiosity, and for some (religious) people the availability of such responses may be comparable to the availability of a given language-game that makes certain actions and operations possible (rather than to the logical form of language as something that is, according to the *Tractatus*, isomorphic to the form of the world, because logic is universal while the religious perspective seems to be optional). We might put this more clearly by saying that the possibility of religious responses is grounded on a certain "picture", just as the rules of language-games in the *Investigations* make meaningful language possible.[11]

As has often been observed, the Wittgensteinian approach seems to lead to the issue of relativism and perhaps even more problematically to fideism in the philosophy of religion. The fideist maintains that religious faith can be accepted without any epistemological justification or critical examination as a basic conviction underlying all our actions; in particular, no evidential considerations are needed or even possible. Some uncritically embraced basic convictions are, arguably, needed for us simply to be able to live and act at all. A firm and certain belief (either religious or something else) – a basic conviction – cannot be justified or criticized, since there is nothing more basic, more certain, or more fundamental on the grounds of which it could be justified or criticized. There is, in the end, only the life the believer leads, the rules s/he follows "blindly" (cf. PI §219). It is thus easy to understand why Wittgenstein's *On Certainty* has been a source of inspiration for religious fideists, or has at least been taken to be such a source by their critics (cf., e.g., Nielsen and Phillips 2005). However, the relation between fideism and the very possibility of rational thought remains problematic. Arguably, fideism, at least in its extreme form, stands in an irresolvable conflict with the basic requirement of rationality, according to which we must aim at defending our beliefs against actual or potential criticism in a process of inquiry aiming at the truth. Such a defence need not be cashed out in terms of evidential considerations but may, pragmatically, invoke the ways in which religious beliefs "work" in relation to our existential worries and concerns, including the "höchste Not" that individuals could respond to by means of religious pictures. According to the extreme relativist and fideist, there may, however, be no religious truth to be achieved at all, let alone any inquiry pursuing the truth – even existential inquiry – if religion is simply a matter of "blindly" engaging in, or adopting, a form of life or a set of pictures characterizing that form of life.

Wittgenstein famously points out that the believer and the non-believer, despite the enormous difference between their ways of thinking and living (i.e., between the kinds of pictures they use), need not disagree regarding their conceptions of empirical reality at all (LC, 55). This could be taken to be an expression of relativism. The two *perspectives* on reality are so different that no genuine disagreement is possible; there is no common ground between the two parties to the debate, and therefore no genuine debate at all. This rather radical relativism may seem to be an unwelcome consequence of certain initially plausible Wittgensteinian ways of thinking emphasizing the form-of-life-embeddedness of religious language-use.

While it is certainly naïve to characterize Wittgenstein, or later Wittgensteinian philosophers of religion, as simple relativists, I do not think there is any easy and straightforward way out of this predicament. Even as insightful a reader of Wittgenstein as Putnam has, in my view, difficulties in maintaining the balance between appreciating the individual use of religious pictures as a ground of one's religious forms of life, on the one hand, and keeping the doors open for critical and rational discussion of religion, on the other. Putnam does not seem to endorse any relativist interpretation of Wittgenstein: "To say something is true in a language game is to stand outside of that language game and make a comment; that is not what it is to play a language game." (Putnam 1992, 176.) So we can "stand outside" our language-games and comment on the truth of the statements made within them. Moreover, the thought that "everything we believe is, at best, only 'true in our language game' isn't even a coherent thought", Putnam reminds us; as he rhetorically asks, "is the very existence of our language then only 'true in our language game'? So our language game is a fiction?" (ibid., 177). But then, drawing on the central insight of Wittgenstein's work, Putnam goes on to say that our language – the language by means of which we *can* say that "some things are true and some things are warranted and some things are reasonable" – rests on "trust" instead of any metaphysical foundation (ibid. 177; cf. OC §§508–509; see also Hertzberg 1994, Chapter 5). Trust sounds like a basic conviction or certainty that cannot be set into doubt through inquiry but functions as the basis of any possible inquiry that could be pursued in order to confirm or disconfirm any (other) views whatsoever.

An adequate appreciation of the Wittgensteinian approach in the philosophy of religion crucially requires a detailed philosophical reflection on these basic notions, including trust and rationality, instead of any simple fideistic declaration of the "arationality" of religious belief or any easy "language-game relativism". The issue of the limits of language is fundamental to this entire discussion and must therefore be taken seriously by anyone inquiring into these matters from a Wittgensteinian perspective (or from a perspective critical of Wittgenstein). In any event, it is highly important to maintain a critically *fallibilist* attitude to the possible changes in our basic convictions and certainties – something that Wittgenstein himself may be seen as doing in *On Certainty* by acknowledging the historical mutability of our basic certainties. While our basic convictions cannot be rejected or revised because of conflicting evidence, as the availability of any evidence presupposes such basic convictions, they may nevertheless change along with changes in our (forms of) life, including changes that require us to reconsider our responses to existential challenges of life. This is why we should take very seriously what Lars Hertzberg (1994, Chapter 2) aptly calls the "factual dependence" of language-games, something he introduces by quoting *On Certainty*:

> Certain events would put me into a position in which I could not go on with the old language-game any further. In which I was torn away from the *sureness* of the game.
>   Indeed, doesn't it seem obvious that the possibility of a language-game is conditioned by certain facts?
>
> (OC §617)

We must not, that is, set up any metaphysical barrier between our language-games and the reality in which we live and act and use language; we must not do so even when treating the limits of language as transcendental. Instead, we should, following Hertzberg, understand Wittgenstein as suggesting that our ways of speaking and living are inevitably connected with the ways the world around us factually is, though of course those ways are available to us – we can take the world to be in any way whatsoever – only from the point of view of the language-games we play within our forms of life situated in that very same world, and we cannot be committed to the world being "factually" in any particular way independently of our language. Playing language-games is not merely a matter of using language itself absolutely independently of any worldly connection. Language-games should, borrowing terms used by Jaakko Hintikka in a related though somewhat different context, be considered "outdoor games" rather than "indoor games" (cf., e.g., Hintikka 1996, 166).

On Certainty offers us a picture of language (a picture, as we have seen, highly relevant to the philosophy of religion) according to which we must rely on our "basic convictions" whose possibility of being false we cannot even conceive of (Hertzberg 1994, 48). These are beliefs or fundamental assumptions we just cannot think as mistaken, because they are not based on reasons or evidence at all, nor in need of reasons and evidence – that is, convictions we have simply learned to trust, as we have "grown into them" (ibid., 49–50). There are nevertheless facts "conditioning" even those convictions and the language-games based upon them, in the sense that "certain events" (as Wittgenstein himself says) could force us to reject such convictions (though, again, not in the sense of providing new evidence against them). When something like that happens, then our language-game changes into something different. Not the truth of what we claimed when we were playing the "old" language-game, but the very meanings of our expressions – what we can or cannot believe or claim to be true – would then change (cf. ibid., 52–55). Therefore, the limits of language would change in such situations. Those limits are not fixed once and for all, as they seem to be according to the early Wittgenstein, but they may naturally be redrawn along with rearrangements in our forms of life. It is in this sense that, as Hertzberg puts it, *On Certainty* offers us a "this-worldly" picture of language: "our language-games are tied to the actual world we live in" (ibid., 59).

In the case of religion, in particular, when such changes do take place, they are beyond any common standards regarding stable meanings or epistemic assessment. Hertzberg notes that there is a kind of "metaphysical insecurity" we have to live with when subscribing to the Wittgensteinian conception he is articulating:

> [W]e have no guarantees that the world will go on being comprehensible to us. In this regard, the insecurity of our language is a feature it shares with our ways of acting. Our ability to go on acting in this world is dependent on certain facts about ourselves, our bodies, and our environment remaining unchanged.
>
> (Hertzberg 1994, 60)

Now, I am tempted to suggest that the fact that some of us play religious language-games and engage in religious forms of life (whatever that specifically means) to a certain degree reflects the acknowledgment of such metaphysical insecurity, the permanent possibility of experiencing "die höchste Not", of finding one's soul threatened. The world could turn out to be incomprehensible to us, and it occasionally does. For instance, when faced with extreme evil and cruelty, and unspeakable sufferings, whether in our own case or in our neighbors', we might find the very comprehensibility of the world we live in to be at issue (cf. Neiman 2002; Pihlström 2014). This is one reason why we need to deal with the problem of evil and suffering in this context.

The basic message I want to drive home at this point is that the issues of relativism and fideism invoked by the late-Wittgensteinian conception of language, as applied to the case of religion, are, first, much more complex than any simple account of relativism acknowledges, and secondly, cannot be fruitfully discussed without paying due attention to the problems surrounding the limits of language. Our need to examine these problems by means of transcendental reflection is, moreover, far from subscribing to any simple theological antirealism. This is because we need to acknowledge the "factual dependence of language-games" (to use Hertzberg's terminology), as has been briefly sketched. It is in and through our living and acting in the world, our natural and social surroundings, that we (can only) give meanings to our religious (or any other) expressions, even though the world we live and act in is structured by us to any humanly meaningful shape precisely by our always already using language to structure it.

Accordingly, the limits of language become relevant as a philosophical problem in the context of this quasi-naturalist or (arguably) pragmatist understanding of religious language and its contextually constrained and historically transforming meanings.[12] In order to highlight the importance of the peculiar kind of contingency of the limits of language that nonetheless are treated as necessary for the functioning of a given language-game, we now need to take a closer look at how these topics emerge in Wittgensteinian philosophy of religion and how they are manifested in the lectures on religious belief Wittgenstein delivered in the early 1930s.

4. The Contingency of Necessity: How the Limits of Language Change

Acknowledging the factual dependence of language-games should make us recognize a closely related phenomenon, i.e., what may be called the *contingency of necessity* – adopting an expression that has been occasionally used in recent contributions to metaphysics, philosophical cosmology, and French new realism (e.g., by Quentin Meillassoux) but employed here in a somewhat different, transcendental sense. In brief, what is at issue here is that while the limits of language are manifested in, or marked by, the rules and grammar of a language-game set conditions for what is possible and impossible for us to express within that language-game (i.e., by making "moves" within it according to its grammatical rules), it seems that, given the contingent historical variability of such rules – or the historical changes in how language-games are played – there is a sense in which we have, at least potentially, a variety of different limits of language that are contingently drawn in the ways they are based on the life (with language) we lead. Our contingent form of life determines (albeit not immutably but always in a historically contextualized and therefore potentially changing manner) how we are "minded" (cf. Lear 1998), or how we draw the limits of expressibility – and this "we" (our socio-historical transcendental subjectivity, if we want to put it that way) may itself change and be reinterpreted along with such transformations of the structures of the language we use, to the extent that Lear speaks about the "disappearing 'we'" (ibid., Chapter 12).

Let us briefly examine some of Wittgenstein's formulations (as they appear in his pupils' notes) in "Lectures on Religious Belief". In those lecture notes from the early 1930s, Wittgenstein is, among other things, concerned with "*[w]hat we call* believing in a Judgement Day or not believing in a Judgement Day" (LC, 55, my emphasis). He says he "can't contradict" the person who believes. The following passage is crucial:

> In one sense, I understand all he says – the English words "God", "separate", etc. I understand. I could say: "I don't believe in this," and this would be true, meaning *I haven't got these thoughts or anything that hangs together with them*. But not that I could contradict the thing. . . . My normal technique of language leaves me."
> (LC, 55, my emphasis; see also Putnam 2012, 490)

That is, the thoughts that I (or you) have (or have not) contingently "got" determine the limits of language for me (or for us), at least regarding this particular matter at the moment. *Necessity is, then, grounded in contingency.* Whether you *can* contradict someone or not (i.e., what your *logic* is like, or what you can do, logically speaking, by using your language) depends on your contingently "having got" certain thoughts, or your leading a life that "hangs together with them". The distinction between modalities (necessity, possibility) and factual contingencies is not necessarily drawn in the way we draw it; it could be drawn in a different way. The ways in which we (contingently) do draw this distinction reflexively influence our understanding of the notions of contingency and modality themselves. Clearly, when we are engaged in a certain language-game, we treat the rules governing our operations within that game as necessary, but whenever we take a step out of the game, we realize that our playing the game in the first place is itself contingent. We could play another game and follow rules different from the ones we do follow, and then the division between the necessary and the contingent would be rearranged in our lives.

Consider some analogies. The distinction between the *epistemic* and the *non-epistemic* (e.g., regarding the notion of truth) is itself (partly) epistemic, not independent of our epistemic standpoints in drawing the distinction. Our epistemic perspective may thus have an ineliminable influence on how we view the interplay between epistemic and non-epistemic factors in our concept of truth, that is, whether we consider truth something radically non-epistemic and potentially recognition-transcendent or an idealization of epistemic notions such as rational acceptability or justification. Similarly, the ontological distinction between "real" and "virtual" reality is, as such, neither fully real nor fully virtual; these notions are interpenetrated and interdependent in our act of drawing the distinction itself.[13] Analogously, we may say that the distinction between the *natural* and the *supernatural* is relative to our concept of nature, and hence to the historical development of science (pretty much like the distinction between science and pseudoscience is itself a historical product of the way our scientific self-understanding of what science is develops). Now, what is crucial here is that it is not out of any absolute metaphysical necessity that the distinction between contingency and necessity is drawn in the way we actually draw it – or even if it were, that meta-necessity would then be (at a yet higher meta-level) contingent and would depend, reflexively, on our contingent language-use. I take this to be a vital (late-) Wittgensteinian point that must not be overlooked in any attempt to understand the grammar of language-games, religious language-games included.[14]

This is also why we need empirical understanding of contingent religious practices in order to study the philosophical issue of the limits of religious language – though here Wittgenstein himself might be worried about the risk of blurring the distinction between describing and explaining (cf. PI §109). Even so, we also vitally need philosophical (even transcendental) analysis and argument focusing on the limits of language – the conditions of what is possible within a religious way of using language – in order to appreciate the *relevance* of such empirical investigations. Theology and empirical (or comparative) religious studies seek to understand the systems and practices within which religiosity is manifested, either from within those systems and practices or from without them.[15] Such investigations are philosophically relevant in order for us to be able to understand the grounding of transcendental necessities in empirical (practical) contingencies. But a philosophical examination of the limits of language issue is, conversely, needed to guide such investigations.[16] Paraphrasing Kant, we might say that mere philosophy of religion focusing on the limits of religious language in the absence of any empirical (non-reductively naturalized) understanding of the kinds of practices people contingently engage in within such limits (i.e., the "systems" or "worldviews" they live and think within) is *empty*, while mere empirical study of religion in the absence of guiding philosophical questions and analyses is *blind*.

The lectures on religious belief by Wittgenstein primarily seek to refute the evidentialist view that evidence, or neutral rational argument more generally, is essential to the assessment of religious belief. At the same time, they contain profoundly interesting remarks on the limits of language. Consider, for example, this: "Whether a thing is a blunder or not – it is a blunder in a particular system. Just as something is a blunder in a particular game and not in another" (LC, 59). Wittgenstein's note again invokes transcendental conditions (i.e., limits), grounded in the contingent reality of a particular "system", in the fact that we do operate within that particular system, perhaps comparable to what pragmatists have often preferred to call "practice". Our having the life we do makes the necessities that appear as constitutive (grammatical) rules conditioning all possible meanings within that life possible for us.[17]

Another relevant example Wittgenstein discusses is this: " 'Seeing a dead friend,' again means nothing much to me at all. I don't think in these terms. I don't say to myself: 'I shall see so and so again' ever" (LC, 63). Again, what is essential here is *whether I contingently think in certain terms* or say to myself certain things (or not). At this point we may return to the famous remark in the *Investigations*: "Once I have exhausted the justifications, I have reached bedrock, and my spade is turned. Then I am inclined to say: 'This is simply what I do' " (PI §217). What we are able to do – what our grammar and rules enable us to do or say – depends on what we actually do, and it is in this sense that necessities and possibilities are ultimately grounded in contingency. Or so Wittgenstein seems to be arguing.

The asymmetry between the "I" and the "we" is, arguably, important here. It may be highly significant that Wittgenstein does not in passages like this speak in terms of "we" (i.e., a shared, public form of life) but in terms of "I" (i.e., in terms of what I habitually or customarily do). The "truth" in solipsism (or, according to Cavell, in scepticism) – the significance that I do not "know" but can only acknowledge that there is, for instance, an external world and other human beings in it – thus becomes relevant in this context (cf. Cavell 1979; see also Putnam 2008, 26, 2012, 489). The way *I* use certain words, or the way *I* think, may be the crucial thing here, no matter what or how others around me think. The transcendental limits of language, and hence transcendental necessities about what can be said or expressed within those limits, may constitutively depend on contingent facts about *my* using words, or having thoughts, in certain ways, comprising networks of words and thoughts hanging together. The significance for all this for philosophy of religion is enormous, but it is equally important to point out that here we in the end return to the relevance of the "first-person" (transcendentally solipsistic) picture of language Wittgenstein sketched in the *Tractatus*. The metaphysical subject disappearing into the world (cf. TLP 5.64) corresponds to the social subject of Wittgenstein's later philosophy precisely in its transcendental function.

5. Theodicy vs. Antitheodicy – and the Limits of Language Again

I want to add another twist to this discussion by commenting on one specific issue in the philosophy of religion, the problem of evil and suffering. In this context, *theodicies*, in particular, have from a Wittgensteinian perspective been regarded as unethical violations of religious language-use (even though Wittgenstein himself had little to say about this particular topic).[18] Religiously speaking, theodicies could even be criticized as superstitious or blasphemous (cf. Phillips 1977, 2004). In addition to making this general point, I now wish to suggest, more specifically, that the theodicy vs. antitheodicy issue can interestingly be approached from the point of view of the phenomenon of the contingency of necessity (as briefly characterized earlier on the basis of Wittgenstein's "Lectures on Religious Belief"). Contingent historical sufferings may motivate a response (viz., antitheodicy) that may even turn out to be transcendentally necessary by functioning as a necessary condition for the possibility of occupying a serious moral perspective at all in a certain historical (again contingent) situation – such as our post-Holocaust world.

Let us note, first, that several Wittgensteinian philosophers have argued that theodicies allegedly justifying "the ways of God to man" – that is, arguments seeking to make sense of apparently meaningless and absurd evil and suffering in God's overall harmonious plan – amount not only to ethically insensitive use of language disregarding or misrecognizing others' suffering in its pointlessness but also to conceptual confusion and pseudo-religious use of language. It is not only ethically wrong but in an important sense *meaningless* and *conceptually confused*, and thus beyond the meaning-constitutive grammar of religious language-games, to claim that others' suffering has a metaphysical or theological meaning, function, or explanation. Such a "conceptual oddness" of theodicies has been noted not only by Phillips (see, e.g., Phillips 1977, 2004) but also by Ben Tilghman (1994, 192) – who uses this very phrase – and by Stephen Mulhall (1994, 18–19), who even suggests that theodicies end up with blasphemy. In a similar vein, Andrew Gleeson (2012, especially Chapter 1), also writing against theodicies in a broadly Wittgensteinian tradition, notes that theodicies should be criticized on both moral and conceptual grounds, while Mikel Burley (2012, §5) points out that the theodicist is "so confused as to be unaware of the degree of their own insensitivity" to pain and suffering – with both moral as well as logical and conceptual dimensions pertaining to this confusion.

Here we cannot examine the possibility of arguing for a "transcendental antitheodicy" (see Kivistö and Pihlström 2016, Chapter 6), but let me offer a few observations regarding Phillips's Wittgensteinian approach in particular, in order to highlight the connection between this issue and the main topic of this paper, viz., the limits of language. The Wittgensteinian method Phillips (along with many other Wittgensteinians) subscribes to carefully looks at the actual use of language in concrete human situations and practices, instead of any *a priori* rules or principles establishing linguistic meanings. Yet, Phillips also emphasizes the general Wittgensteinian ideas that "it is only in the context of [religious] language games that belief in God has any meaning" and "concepts have their life" "only in practice, in what we do" (Phillips 1993, xi, xiii). In his criticism of theodicies, in particular, Phillips focuses on what goes wrong in the very form of the allegedly moral reasoning the theodicist engages in; he interestingly refers to the Book of Job here: "Job cannot make *sense* of his afflictions in terms of the [theodicist] arguments of his would-be comforters" (ibid., 157). While those defending theodicies try to calculate what kinds of goods or benefits might outweigh or compensate for the evils and sufferings there are, the Phillipsian-cum-Wittgensteinian antitheodicist objects to "the *concept* of calculation in this context, because it excludes *moral* concepts" (ibid., 158).[19]

Phillips argues that the truly religious reaction to the contingencies and adversities of human life does not seek to "tidy up" messy human reality or to find explanations and understandings of suffering (see Phillips 1993, 166–168). This brings us again to the issue concerning the limits of language. Genuinely religious uses of language, when addressing the problem of evil and suffering, recognize the limits of understanding and linguistic expression – not as contingent limitations that could in principle be transcended but just factually cannot be overcome by us, but as necessary limits defining the relevant language-game and therefore playing a transcendental role in constituting what is meaningful and possible for us (see ibid., 168), albeit (recognizing the "factual dependence of language-games" and the "contingency of necessity") in the end only contextually necessary limits that could in principle be redrawn as our lives change. A transcendental critique of theodicies, when formulated from a Wittgensteinian perspective along Phillips's lines, will thus crucially focus on the "grammar" constitutive of moral and religious language, that is, on the transcendentally meaning-structuring rules of the relevant language-games – rules that might, however, themselves be historically transformed. If we take seriously the Wittgensteinian line of thought (transcendentally reconstructed) according to which there can be no meaning without practice-laden, habitual, world-engaging use of expressions within public human ways of acting, or language-games, then we should also acknowledge the fact that the meanings of such expressions as "evil", "suffering", "God", "meaning", and so forth, are inextricably entangled with their use in religious language-games and thus in our forms of life. If we do take this seriously, then it is conceptually, morally, and religiously misguided to seek to provide a theodicy – or to require one.

Phillips (or the other Wittgensteinians cited earlier in this section) would hardly endorse this transcendental reconstruction of the antitheodicist argument. Certainly they need not embrace the transcendental vocabulary; that particular vocabulary is not forced on anyone developing a Wittgensteinian antitheodicy. I am merely suggesting that their way of attacking theodicies as confused responses leading us out of genuinely religious – and genuinely ethical – ways of using language can be rephrased as a transcendental critique drawing attention to the limits of (religious, ethical) language, as long as we keep in mind the fundamental contingency of the way in which those limits, and the structures of necessities and possibilities they constrain, are drawn by us. Phillips and others thus tend to slide toward something like transcendental philosophy.

In many cases, for a genuinely religious person who sincerely attempts to speak about God in a religious way, the coordinates provided by their adoption of the religious frame of reference – that is, "theology as grammar" in Wittgenstein's sense (PI §373) – function as the necessary background of any potential theological or philosophical account of evil and suffering. Any possible argument, including the atheist's argument challenging the theist to provide a theodicy by appealing to the problem of evil, will have to be evaluated against this background. The believer might point out, against both the atheist and the theist seeking to provide a theodicy, that it is strictly speaking nonsensical (i.e., beyond the meanings available in religious language-games) for human beings to try to evaluate God's motives morally, or to seek to criticize or justify them. At the moment when the theodicist begins to engage in an argument, *pro* or *contra*, regarding the problem of evil conceived as an atheist challenge, the grammar of the religious language-game will already have been violated and the relevant expressions will no longer be used in a genuinely religious meaning. Therefore, the atheist argument starting from the problem of evil does not even get off the ground due to this confusion. But those theists who try to respond to such an argument by producing a theodicy are even more confused, because they do not perceive the atheists' confusion any more than their own. Theodicies should therefore be rejected as transcendentally confused misuses of the language of "God", "evil", and "suffering". It can be suggested that one comes close to illegitimately transgressing the limits of meaningful discourse – the limits of religious language – simply in examining the problem of evil in terms of the alleged "argument from evil" and in attempting to respond to such an argument theodicistically. Both the theist and the atheist theodicists fail to use the grammar of religious language religiously and thus breach the limits of language.[20]

It is roughly in this way that I would like to suggest we can reinterpret Phillips's and other Wittgensteinians' perceptive remarks on theodicies being both morally and conceptually (or even logically) confused. The reason why these confusions are so deep is that they are transcendental in the sense of this notion that remains available in the later Wittgenstein's thought. This is the transcendentality of the constitutive (albeit historically transformable and reinterpretable) features of language-games and forms of life. It is only by violating the limits of language that the problem of evil and suffering construed as an atheist argument requiring a theodicy as a response can so much as be formulated. When we realize that such a (mis)formulation is based, precisely, on a violation of grammar, we realize that the entire business of theodicy is misconceived from the start. It is by means of a Wittgensteinian analysis of the limits of language that this point can be brought home.

However, as soon as we note all this we should re-emphasize that the grammar and meanings of our expressions may vary historically along with the changes and transformations taking place in our forms of life. The necessity of transcendental rules is based on the contingency of human life (as we saw earlier). This applies with full force to the problem of evil and suffering. Different reactions to this problem may become possible in different historical circumstances characterizing the forms of life through which the grammar of the relevant language-games is established. We may, for instance, find it necessary to examine the problem of evil and suffering after the Holocaust in a way essentially different from its pre-Holocaust articulations.[21] In the contingent historical context in which the Holocaust actually took place and will therefore permanently, ineliminably, irredeemably, be part of our human history, it may seem that certain (new) limits of appropriate religious language have been established. It is no longer possible – morally or conceptually – to approach the problem of evil by providing a theodicy. We now – after the Holocaust – can see this as a striking, violent confusion. Moreover, we can now see – after the Holocaust – that it was *never* possible, even if that was not as clearly perceivable earlier. Historical contingencies may thus ground philosophical, ethical, and conceptual necessities – and this I take to be a fundamental Wittgensteinian message that we may learn from reading not only *On Certainty* but also the lectures on religious belief quoted in the previous section.

6. Conclusion

I have not attempted to determine in any great detail what Wittgenstein himself really thought about the limits of language in relation to religion and theology. I suppose my discussion is compatible with several different interpretations of Wittgenstein – albeit not, I think, with the extreme "postmodern" or radically "New Wittgensteinian" account according to which Wittgenstein's main point is a merely ironical one about our being unable to engage in any systematic and argumentative philosophical activity at all. I have basically suggested that it makes sense to approach his thoughts from a Kantian (transcendental) perspective in order to be able to fully appreciate the special character of the kind of thought on religion that some of his most original followers (e.g., Phillips) have developed in their attempts to understand religious belief – and also to understand what it means to lose such belief as believers' forms of life change.

I will close with a brief metaphilosophical suggestion that strengthens the transcendental analysis presented in this paper but perhaps also makes it more controversial. In investigating the limits of language in the context of the philosophy of religion – Wittgenstein's and Wittgensteinian – I have repeatedly emphasized the historical contextuality and mutability of the transcendental necessities grounding the meanings possible in any language-games we may engage in. This "factual dependence", this contingency of necessity, can itself at a meta-level be regarded as a transcendental condition for the possibility of the kinds of meanings that can so much as be available to us human beings, given the kind of language-using beings we naturally are. (So we would here be dealing with yet another meta-level transcendental necessity that would itself be based on contingent facts about the ways we live our lives – and so on, potentially *ad inifinitum*.) *For us*, no firmer transcendental necessities are possible. Yet, again for us, it is necessary that our contingent forms of life do function as the background for any (contextually) necessary sets of grammatical rules that enable us to say anything definite and meaningful in any concrete circumstances of using language. We can get rid of neither contingency nor necessity, and *this* meta-level necessity (or impossibility) is again itself constitutively part of human life as we contingently know it. Any Wittgensteinian investigation of religious language and its limits should appreciate this interplay of transcendental necessities and contingencies.[22]

Notes

1. The "New Wittgensteinians", in particular, seem to dismiss the "limit" metaphor rather straightforwardly: "I think the spatial conception, the picture of boundary, is misleading here, in inviting us to take there to be something, the existence of certain limits, that explains the kinds of ways we are distant from each other, and makes possible also an explanation of the conditions for shared understanding" (Diamond 2005, 114). On "New Wittgensteinianism" generally, see Crary and Read 2000.
2. Similarly – albeit in a somewhat different tradition of reading Wittgenstein – Hilary Putnam joins Stanley Cavell in arguing that when distinguishing between what "makes sense" and what doesn't we should not operate in

terms of the distinction between what we "can" and "cannot" do. See especially Putnam 1994, Chapter 12 ("Rethinking Mathematical Necessity"),
also reprinted, for instance, in Crary and Read 2000. See also Cavell 1979.

3. Phillips, in particular, has offered numerous arguments in virtually all areas
of philosophy of religion at least implicitly invoking the theme of the limits
of language – regarding, for example, evidence in relation to religious belief,
death and immortality, religious conceptions of the soul and of God, as well
as the problem of evil, typically claiming that realist and evidentialist views
misconstrue the grammar of religious language, thus resorting to an account
of religion that seriously distorts the way in which believers themselves use
language. See, for example, Phillips 1970, 1977, 1986, 1993, 2004; cf. my
discussion of the limit between religious and pseudo-religious language-use
in Pihlström 2007, 2013.

4. One might thus suggest that the kind of particularism emphasized in literary
readings and the kind of universalism embedded in Kantian transcendental
philosophy are not necessarily incompatible. But I won't be able to argue for
this meta-level view here.

5. I am not assuming any traditional received view on the simple divisibility of
Wittgenstein's philosophy into two phases, the early and the late. For example, the "third Wittgenstein" is to be taken very seriously in this context, and
it is equally important to note the significant philosophical and methodological continuities between the "early" and the "late" Wittgenstein, perhaps
most importantly the transcendental methodology itself. My references to
Wittgenstein's "early" and "late" writings in the context of the philosophy
of religion are thus only intended to keep things relatively clear and simple;
no heavy interpretive assumptions should be read into this categorization.

6. I am here basically following Hanne Appelqvist's Kantian interpretation
of Wittgenstein, which builds upon Stenius's (1960) and Kannisto's (1986)
scholarship but emphasizes the role of aesthetics (in relation to Kant) much
more strongly. See Appelqvist's introduction to this volume as well as her
earlier work (e.g., Appelqvist 2013, 2018). On transcendental idealism in
the *Tractatus*, see also, e.g., Moore 2013.

7. For an examination of the transcendental subject in this Wittgensteinian
context (and more broadly), see, for instance, Pihlström 2016.

8. On the other hand, Wittgenstein also maintains that there is a "gulf" separating the believer from the non-believer (LC, 53).

9. Note that Wittgenstein talks variously about pictures (mostly using the German word "*Bild*"), similes, patterns, images, metaphors, analogies, and so
forth; works such as *Culture and Value* and *Philosophical Occasions* are
rich sources of material here. It is worth pointing out that in the "Lecture on
Ethics" he maintains that ethical and religious expressions seem to be "just
similes" (PO, 42). In ethical and religious language "we seem constantly to
be using similes", he says, but then again "a simile must be the simile for
something", which is not the case here: "if I can describe a fact by means of a
simile I must also be able to drop the simile and to describe the facts without
it. Now in our case as soon as we try to drop the simile and simply to state
the facts which stand behind it, we find that there are no such facts. And so,
what at first appeared to be a simile now seems to be mere nonsense" (PO,
42–43). These reservations – again regarding the limits of language – ought
to be kept in mind when we turn to the later Wittgenstein's use of the term
"picture", for instance. See also Moyal-Sharrock and Brenner 2004, Part II.

10. In a related remark in 1950 (CV, 97) Wittgenstein suggests that there are experiences of life that may educate or even force us into believing in God, but these
are not evidential experiences but for instance sufferings of various kinds. We

might suppose that such experiences may also include the kind of experience briefly discussed in "A Lecture on Ethics", namely, the experience of being absolutely safe and the one of wondering at the existence of the world.

11. This view could also be compared to Pritchard's (2018) Wittgenstein-inspired "quasi-fideism".
12. I have elsewhere argued at some length for a re-reading of Wittgenstein that links his late philosophy of language with both the Kantian transcendental tradition and the pragmatist tradition; see Pihlström 2003. For an attempt to connect broadly Wittgensteinian approaches with pragmatist philosophy of religion more specifically, see Pihlström 2013.
13. This is a case of a kind of realism being entangled with a certain kind of constructivism. I won't be able to deal with this issue here, of course.
14. This also indicates a difference between the early Wittgenstein, for whom necessities are based on a universal and unchanging logical form, and the later Wittgenstein, for whom necessities arise out of the forms of life within which we engage in various language-games.
15. Compare this to methodological controversies related to, for example, the cognitive study of religion: it seems that such methodological issues might be more fruitfully discussed if the distinction between "internal" (hermeneutic, understanding) and "external" (causally explanatory) perspectives were made more clearly.
16. Even the direction of transcendental argumentation may vary according to our perspective of inquiry, as argued in Kivistö and Pihlström 2016, Chapter 6.
17. Analogously, it could be suggested that even Kant's original transcendental philosophy, despite its formalism and apriorism, fundamentally relies on the "transcendental fact" that the human cognitive faculty is of a certain kind and has certain specific features – features that it has contingently, not out of any metaphysical necessity. For example, it is, arguably, a contingent (yet transcendental) fact about human beings and their cognition that we do not possess the capacity of intellectual intuition, even though this fact is then an element in the transcendental structure of conditions and limits constitutive of any humanly possible experience and its objects. ("Here one can only *describe* and say: this is what human life is like" [PO, 121].)
18. Wittgenstein's early reflections on happiness as a kind of harmony with the world whose states of affairs are completely value-neutral are certainly relevant to the theodicy problem, however. For some discussion of this issue, see Pihlström 2019.
19. For an extended discussion of how the Book of Job can been read in the context of Kant's 1791 Theodicy Essay (Kant 1998) as a criticism of Job's "friends'" theodicist arguments, see Kivistö and Pihlström 2016, especially Chapter 2.
20. Note that I am here (as in Kivistö and Pihlström 2016) using the word "theodicism" broadly to cover not only theistic theodicies but also the requirement that theism ought to provide a theodicy, which is something that atheists typically share when attacking theism by appealing to the "argument from evil". (Moreover, theodicism also comes in secular versions.)
21. Consider, for instance, the ways in which Jewish philosophers like Hans Jonas have found it necessary to "rethink God" after the Holocaust (cf. Pihlström 2014).
22. I am crucially indebted to Hanne Appelqvist's detailed and thoughtful comments on earlier drafts. The antitheodicist position only briefly discussed in this chapter has been largely developed in collaboration with Sari Kivistö. The topics of this paper are more comprehensively discussed in my forthcoming book, Pihlström 2020.

References

Appelqvist, Hanne (2013) "Why Does Wittgenstein Say that Ethics and Aesthetics Are One and the Same?" in P. Sullivan and M. Potter (eds), *Wittgenstein's Tractatus: History and Interpretation*. Oxford: Oxford University Press, 40–58.

Appelqvist, Hanne (2018) "Wittgenstein on the Grounds of Religious Faith: A Kantian Proposal", *The European Journal of Philosophy* 26 (3), 1026–1040.

Burley, Mikel (2012) "Contemplating Evil", *Nordic Wittgenstein Review* 1 (1), available at www.nordicwittgensteinreview.com/article/view/NWR-1_2012-Burley.

Cavell, Stanley (1979) *The Claim of Reason*. Oxford and New York: Oxford University Press.

Crary, Alice and Read, Rupert (eds) (2000) *The New Wittgenstein*. London and New York: Routledge.

Diamond, Cora (2005) "Wittgenstein on Religious Belief: On the Gulfs Between Us", in D. Z. Phillips and Mario van der Ruhr (eds), *Religion and Wittgenstein's Legacy*. Aldershot: Ashgate, 99–137.

Gleeson, Andrew (2012) *A Frightening Love: Recasting the Problem of Evil*. Basingstoke: Palgrave Macmillan.

Hertzberg, Lars (1994) *The Limits of Experience*. Acta Philosophica Fennica. Vol. 56. Helsinki: The Philosophical Society of Finland.

Hintikka, Jaakko (1996) *Ludwig Wittgenstein: Half-Truths and One-and-a-Half-Truths*, Selected Papers 1. Dordrecht: Kluwer.

Kannisto, Heikki (1986) *Thoughts and Their Subject: A Study of Wittgenstein's Tractatus*. Acta Philosophica Fennica 40, Helsinki: The Philosophical Society of Finland.

Kant, Immanuel (1998) "On the Miscarriage of All Philosophical Trials in Theodicy", in A. Wood and G. Di Giovanni (trans and eds), *Religion Within the Boundaries of Mere Reason*. Cambridge: Cambridge University Press, 15–30.

Kivistö, Sari and Pihlström, Sami (2016) *Kantian Antitheodicy: Philosophical and Literary Varieties*. Basingstoke: Palgrave Macmillan.

Lear, Jonathan (1998) *Open Minded: Working Out the Logic of the Soul*. Cambridge, MA and London: Harvard University Press.

Moore, A. W. (2013) "Was the Author of the *Tractatus* a Transcendental Idealist?" in Peter Sullivan and Michael Potter (eds), *Wittgenstein's Tractatus: History and Interpretation*. Oxford: Oxford University Press, 239–255.

Moyal-Sharrock, Danièle and Brenner, William H. (eds) (2004) *Readings of Wittgenstein's On Certainty*. Basingstoke: Palgrave Macmillan.

Mulhall, Stephen (1994) *Faith and Reason*. London: Duckworth.

Neiman, Susan (2002) *Evil in Modern Thought: An Alternative History of Philosophy*. Princeton, NJ: Princeton University Press.

Nielsen, Kai and Phillips, D. Z. (2005) *Wittgensteinian Fideism?* London: SCM Publications.

Phillips, D. Z. (1970) *Death and Immortality*. London: Palgrave Macmillan.

Phillips, D. Z. (1977) "The Problem of Evil", in S. C. Brown (ed), *Reason and Religion*. Ithaca, NY and London: Cornell University Press, 103–121.

Phillips, D. Z. (1986) *Belief, Change and Forms of Life*. Basingstoke and London: Palgrave Macmillan.

Phillips, D. Z. (1991) *From Fantasy to Faith*. Basingstoke: Palgrave Macmillan.

Phillips, D. Z. (1993) *Wittgenstein and Religion*. Basingstoke and New York: Palgrave Macmillan.

Philips, D. Z. (2004) *The Problem of Evil and the Problem of God*. London: SCM Publications.

Phillips, D. Z. (2006) "Preface", in Rhees (2006).

Pihlström, Sami (2003) *Naturalizing the Transcendental: A Pragmatic View*. Amherst, NY: Prometheus, Humanity Books.

Pihlström, Sami (2007) "Religion and Pseudo-Religion: An Elusive Boundary", *International Journal for Philosophy of Religion* 62, 3–32.

Pihlström, Sami (2013) *Pragmatic Pluralism and the Problem of God*. New York: Fordham University Press.

Pihlström, Sami (2014) *Taking Evil Seriously*. Basingstoke: Palgrave Macmillan, Pivot.

Pihlström, Sami (2016) *Death and Finitude: Toward a Pragmatic Transcendental Anthropology of Human Limits and Mortality*. Lanham, MD: Lexington Books.

Pihlström, Sami (2019) "Wittgenstein on Happiness: Harmony, Disharmony, and Antitheodicy", *Philosophical Investigations* 42 (1), 15–39.

Pihlström, Sami (2020) *Pragmatic Realism, Religious Truth, and Antitheodicy: On Viewing the World by Acknowledging the Other*. Helsinki: Helsinki University Press. Forthcoming.

Pritchard, Duncan (2018) "Quasi-Fideism and Religious Conviction", *European Journal for Philosophy of Religion* 10 (3), 51–66.

Putnam, Hilary (1992) *Renewing Philosophy*. Cambridge, MA and London: Harvard University Press.

Putnam, Hilary (1994) *Words and Life*. Edited by J. Conant. Cambridge, MA and London: Harvard University Press.

Putnam, Hilary (2008) *Jewish Philosophy as a Guide to Life*. Bloomington and Indianapolis: Indiana University Press.

Putnam, Hilary (2012) *Philosophy in an Age of Science*. Edited by M. De Caro and D. Macarthur. Cambridge, MA and London: Harvard University Press.

Rhees, Rush (2006) *Wittgenstein and the Possibility of Discourse*. Edited by D. Z. Phillips. Malden, MA and Oxford: Blackwell.

Stenius, Erik (1960) *Wittgenstein's Tractatus: A Critical Exposition of Its Main Lines of Thought*. Oxford: Basil Blackwell.

Tilghman, B. R. (1994) *An Introduction to the Philosophy of Religion*. Oxford: Blackwell.

11 Measure for Measure: Wittgenstein's Critique of the Augustinian Picture of Music

Eran Guter

> Sometimes a sentence can be understood only if it is read at the *right* tempo.
> My sentences are all to be read *slowly*.
>
> – (CV, 65)

To say that Ludwig Wittgenstein has a philosophy of music might appear as something of a misnomer. If we tend to understand the term "philosophy of music" rather narrowly as the philosophy whose job is conceptually to determine the object "music", then it would seem that there is no "philosophy of music" in Wittgenstein. I would like to suggest that Wittgenstein was after a kind of philosophic sensitivity rather than a body of knowledge, one which is best cultivated by *musizieren*, by music-making in the broadest sense, and so should we be, if we truly wish to see the value of his remarks on music. There is much to say about the extent and depth of Wittgenstein's thinking about music, which is spread across his *Nachlass*, his lectures, and other texts, both systematically and in the context of the history of ideas. Indeed, Wittgenstein should be considered as an important transitional figure from Romantic thinking about music to the modern time (Guter 2017).

Thus, in this chapter my goal is twofold: to give a detailed, contextually rich exposition of Wittgenstein's thinking about music and to flesh out the philosophic sensitivity which he wants to cultivate by means of thinking about such matters. More specifically, I trace and reconstruct Wittgenstein's understanding of the conceptual framework pertaining to musical temporality. Wittgenstein's view emerges as a sustained critique of what I propose to dub the "Augustinian picture of music". The obvious allusion to Wittgenstein's critique of "the Augustinian picture of language" (in the *Philosophical Investigations*) is more in spirit than in substance. The picture which holds us captive here is not that of language per se, but of time as a substance, or a space, or motion, all of which are internally experienced and identified. Wittgenstein's discussion is carried out in the context of his middle-period philosophizing (1929–1936).

I start by offering an overview of Augustine's account of time, as understood by Wittgenstein, and the latter's specific rejection of Augustine's notion of measuring in the mind. I then argue that Wittgenstein's sustained critique of "the Augustinian picture of music" actually sets him antagonistically vis-à-vis a venerable tradition in the philosophy of music by means of exposing and clarifying the many limitations of the language which has been used on pains of obfuscation and nonsensicality for undergirding this view of musical temporality. In the final part of my chapter, I argue that by opting to reverse the Augustinian priorities as regards temporal orders, Wittgenstein's critique underscores the philosophic importance he attributed to the very idea of the limit of language in aesthetics.

1. Memory as the Source of Time

Musical motion is perhaps one of the most fundamental, essential characteristics of Western tonal music, which is also conveniently transparent in our mundane talk about music of the kind that was so close to Wittgenstein's heart. Listening to a melody, we hear not only a beginning and an end, but also distinct motion from its beginning to its end. In such a musical unfolding, we experience the rise and fall of a melodic line, the quickening of an *accelerando*, the slowing down of a *ritardando*, the soaring of a modulation, and the coming to a halt of a perfect cadence. We even experience motion when no sound is heard, as in the occasional pregnant silences that are part of so many musical themes. Yet the idea of musical motion ultimately admits an apparent paradox. Musical motion seems to take place in the absence of anything that moves. It seems that if we are to speak meaningfully about musical motion as opposed to a mere series of acoustic changes, we must assume that it involves something that moves – to wit, tones – as well as something that does not move – a certain spatial frame, in which musical motion occurs.

The paradox of musical motion can be seen as the persistent shadow of what Wittgenstein called in the *Big Typescript* "understanding memory as the source of time" (BT, 517–518).[1] This is the idea of time as a "mental picture", rendered as the source of our cognition and the verification of our propositions – the time of which the present immediate experience is a limit, yet a limit which cannot be mapped onto a physical system (Schulte 2006, 565). This sort of "personification of time" (M, 7:108; BT, 522) was a subject of Wittgenstein's criticism in his writings and lectures in the 1930s. Wittgenstein aimed to show that what generates the tendency to reify memory-time, to render it as a substance or in spatial terms, including the very idea of measurement, is a set of false analogies, which only generate philosophical confusion. Ultimately, Wittgenstein's criticism undercuts those conceptions of music that exclusively rely on such a reification of memory-time.

The locus classicus for this picture of time is Saint Augustine's discussion of time in his *Confessions*. Book XI of the *Confessions* consists of a sustained discussion of the paradoxical nature of the flow of time. Augustine's first step is to affirm the flow of time, for without flow, there can be neither future nor past (Augustine 1948, 191). Next we learn the first immediate difficulty with the notion of time thus understood: of the triad, past, present, and future, only the present seems to exist, since "the past now is not, and the future is not as yet" (ibid., 191). Then another immediate difficulty arises: if the present bears the mark of time, that is, directional flow, it must become past; that is, the present tends not to be as it continuously flows out of existence. Importantly, Augustine links the ontology of time to time measurement. Acknowledging that we compare periods of time and measure their relative length, Augustine moves to discuss time measurement for time present (time measurement for both time past and time future drops out of consideration, since they were shown not to exist). Under the assumption concerning the flow of time, Augustine tries to close in on a "temporal atom", which cannot be divided further into future and past. Ultimately, he whittles down the time that is said to be present to a dimensionless point, which has no measurable extension (ibid., 192). Thus, Augustine portrays time as passing "from that . . . which as yet is not, through that which has no space, into that which now is not" (ibid., 195).

Against this backdrop, the problem of time measurement becomes acute. Augustine's escape route out of this paradoxical picture of time leads directly to music. In his treatise on music, *De Musica*, Augustine defines music as *bene modulandi scientia*, "the knowledge [science] of measuring well". According to Augustine, to be "well measured" musical motion must be in harmonious proportions; hence the true science of music rests in knowing these mathematical ratios which govern musical art. Musical rhythm is created in metrical terms when temporal modules of similar proportions are joined to form a verse or phrase. Most importantly, Augustine acknowledges that musical motion in the sense of rhythm is formed only when the chosen temporal modules are repeated (Waite 1980, 696).

We can easily recognize Augustine's theory of musical rhythm in book XI of the *Confessions*, as he employs musical examples in order to explain the way we measure the passing of time (Augustine 1948, 199). The measurement of time takes place in actual performance and in relative terms. The temporal units "long" and "short" do not designate absolute values but are rather grounded in comparison – the former is "long", because it is relatively longer than the latter by a fixed ratio of 2:1; and vice versa. The introduction of absolute temporal values, such as the values measured by a chronometer, upsets Augustine's conception of musical motion. Augustine contended that in music measuring the "spaces" of the temporal units "is not measuring by pages (for in that manner we measure spaces, not times), but when in uttering the words they pass by" (ibid., 199). For Wittgenstein, this contention epitomizes the philosophical confusion, which besets this picture of time. Augustine seems to have commingled the very different ways in which we measure time and space as he concluded that we measure the specious-present in our mind, as if the present is some object in front of him.

Since we seem to measure tracts of time in performance, Augustine concludes that "time is nothing else than extension; but of what I know not" (ibid., 199). However, measuring the extension of a tract of time cannot begin while it is future, before coming to existence, and until it is complete, having passed out of existence to become past. Sound can be measured only while it is sounding, for "while passing, it was being extended into some space of time, in which it might be measured, since the present has no space" (ibid., 199). Augustine's final resolution of the problem of time measurement gives priority to memory time: "do I not measure [syllables] themselves, which now are not, but something in my memory, which remains fixed. In thee, O my mind, I measure time" (ibid., 200). Since each syllable uttered, each sound voiced, is immediately past, to measure a tract of time by comparing it in the following act of annunciation to a subsequent one is made possible only through memory. Our attention – through the acts of remembering, attending and expecting – is a lasting thing that produces continuity in present experience (ibid., 195). As we sing or recite a psalm, time flows from future to past through this extended present experience, and as expectation wanes memory lengthens.

Thus, it is only when we identify the first tone as coming *before* the second tone once it is complete and the second one sounds (and by the same token, when we identify the second tone, while it sounds and later on, as coming *after* the first tone), that we can speak of musical motion. And this motion stretches between my expectation and my memory. In the words of Augustine, "the life of this action of mine is extended both ways between my memory, on account of what I have repeated, and my expectation, on account of what I am about to repeat" (ibid., 201). In other words, the paradox of musical motion can be resolved only by introducing a notion of musical time that is based on the framework of memory time.

2. Measuring Measures

Augustine's notion of time measurement captured Wittgenstein's attention in the context of his growing interests in relativity in measurement, metrology, and his fascination (beginning in 1929) with Albert Einstein's discussion of time in terms of time measurement and clock coordination (Kusch 2011, 2015). Ultimately, the core insight of Einstein's account, as Wittgenstein understood it, was that "how a dimension is measured determines what dimension it is" (MS 107, 124). Hence, if we wish to know what time is, we need to ask how it is measured. As we have seen, this is precisely how Augustine proceeds in his discussion of time in the *Confessions*.

For Wittgenstein, Augustine's search for a definition for time is a paradigmatic case of being led astray by an inclination to suppose that the sense of the word "time" is governed by exact rules. Once Augustine realizes that there are certain cases where such rules cannot be applied consistently, he moves to replace what he takes to be a mistaken definition (for example, "time is the motion of the celestial bodies") with a supposedly true definition (for example, "time is a protraction of the mind").

Wittgenstein's criticisms of Augustine's discussion of time proceed along two related strands: one pertains to the standard of exactness that is embedded in Augustine's way of speaking of time, and the other to the apparent contradiction in the grammar of the word "time" that generates Augustine's difficulties with time measurement (BB, 26). Augustine's conception of time measurement generates a puzzle, which becomes manifest also in his view of music. "Solving this puzzle," says Wittgenstein, "will consist in comparing what we mean by "measurement" (the grammar of the word "measurement") when applied to a distance on a traveling band with the grammar of that word when applied to time" (BB, 26). Wittgenstein's point is that the word "measurement" and its related standards of exactness and precision belong to the vocabulary of the physical. Augustine's conception of music as some sort of knowledge based on demonstrable data, whose subject matter are temporal units based on memory shows precisely the kind of grammatical confusion involved in any attempt to use physical vocabulary in the realm of immediate experience.

Wittgenstein suggests another formulation of the false analogy: the "river analogy". The Augustinian question "where does the present go when it becomes past?" arises most easily when we are preoccupied with cases in which there are things flowing by us – as logs of wood float down a river. We then use this simile for all happenings in time (BB, 107–108). Insofar as they are built into our language in some sense, the travel band and the river analogies seem to allure us into thinking of temporal events as fixed points or entities coming towards us as we expect them, passing us by as we experience them, and then flowing away from us as we remember them. We are then tempted to think not only that we can measure, as it were, the distance between these events, but also – as strongly suggested by the picture of the floating logs of wood – that we can measure the length of each event.

It is not hard to see how susceptible music can be to this model of time measurement. We readily accept the picture that a melody consists of audible events that we anticipate before we actually can hear them fading away into the deep recesses of our memory. The river analogy goes as far as prompting us to employ spatial concepts when we speak of tones that are heard higher or lower than others, that they occur in tandem (like two logs of wood floating side by side), or that the various voices in a contrapuntal formation pull to different directions. Moreover, the river image itself allows the analogous opening of a spatial framework in which tones are attended to as they are in themselves, as if they were floating logs of wood.

Like in case of the logs of wood that float on the river, we measure not only the relative length of the tones that pass us by, but also the intervals of silence between them. Modern musical notation provides a very clear and elaborate representation of these duration values. Furthermore, we attach such an importance to the regular flow of the "melody river" that we are genuinely surprised, at times even annoyed, when we hear that a tone arrives too late or too early. In such cases we say that our expectations were not fulfilled. Oftentimes this might be just a matter of the music being played incorrectly, and on very rare occasions among great composers this might also be a result of a miscalculation in the construction of the music. Notwithstanding, the history of Western music has witnessed the development of numerous techniques for upsetting the regular flow of musical time – from the earliest employment of *recitativo* in the 16th Century to the latest syncopated Jazz – that have risen to the highest level of artistic significance. Most importantly, we speak of a melody as something, which has a beginning and an end that demarcate a (more or less) finite number of temporal units (tones and silent intervals). Finitude is probably the most trivial yet utterly peculiar characteristic of concrete pieces of music (as opposed to whatever we may mean by "the music of the spheres", for instance).

A piece of music has a beginning and an end. At least within the realm of common compositional practice, these boundaries are *musical* boundaries, not arbitrary time indexes that merely delineate certain duration, as it is the case in John Cage's notorious piece *4:33*. It would not be unusual to observe a conductor asking the members of his orchestra during a rehearsal of a symphony to repeat the last 100 measures before its end. In such a case there will be 100 more measures and that will be the end, and indeed we might conceive of an experience which would verify these statements: a final majestic tonic chord played in full-fledged *tutti*, then silence, and then scattered clacks of bows hitting metal music stands in acknowledgment of the conductor's inspired rendition. More important yet, one would simply hear that the music reached its end. The fact that the Swiss-made hand-watch on the conductor's wrist never stopped measuring time even after the last musician has left the rehearsal hall is of no consequence here. Since we have been following measures, and since the measures came to an end, time in this sense – to wit, musical time – ceased when the symphony ended.

In his lectures in Cambridge during 1930–1933, Wittgenstein offered an elaborate discussion of the river analogy, which illuminates the strangeness of the finitude of musical time (AWL, 14). If we think about time in terms of the river analogy, and think that times ceases, then we might say that "time ceases when 'Time River' ceases". He suggests that we could drop the idea that we have the substantive "time", and just talk of the passing of logs. In this sense, "we could talk of time coming to an end, meaning that the logs came to an end".

3. The Augustinian Picture of Music

Augustine's discussion of time qua substantive gave rise to a philosophical picture of music as embodiment of "time as the source of cognition", to use Wittgenstein's words. This is a picture of music as "the personification of time": musical motion is rendered as something which is subject-centred, felt inwardly, internal to the specious present – a duration, or a flow, which is experienced as the passage of life itself, measurable only in terms of sensibilities, tensions, and emotions. That which is to be understood in, and also as music – form and expression alike – is thus patently related to such inner movement. The only real present in music is puncti-form, stretching in the mind between memory and expectation. Musical time occupies its own space, which is voluminous, complex, and variable in a way which makes it utterly unlike metrical time.

In the Augustinian picture of music, musical time is contained in the specious present, hence we rely exclusively on the conceptual framework of memory-time in order to make sense of the extent of virtual imaging backwards, to what is retained in our mind, and forwards, to what we anticipate. We can compare this patently perspectival mode of identifying the musical object (in this sort of direct experience of time) to a "searchlight", following a suggestion made by J. D. Mabbott (Mabbott 1951). The constant span of illumination of the searchlight (representing the span of the specious present) moves continuously parallel to, and along, its postulated "target" (i.e., the music) as it "illuminates" it.

The Augustinian picture of music underlies a venerable tradition in the philosophy of music, which openly attaches the paramount profundity of the art of music to its embodying of the nature of time "as the source of cognition". The general characteristics of this sort of "searchlight" conception of musical time are manifested spectacularly by distinctly different representatives of this tradition, for example, Edmund Husserl in *The Phenomenology of Internal Time-Consciousness* (Husserl 1964), Susanne Langer in *Feeling and Form* (Langer 1953) and most recently Jerrold Levinson in *Music in the Moment* (Levinson 1997).

Wittgenstein went to the heart of the Augustinian picture of music in his debunking of Augustine's contention that the word "now" is a specification of time, a name of an instance of time, a real punctiform present. This is where that picture seems to hold us captive, yet according to Wittgenstein, the error is already contained in Augustine's initial question "what is time?", which presupposes that in some sense time is made of some material (BT, 522).

Thinking about measuring time by means of the river analogy is symptomatic of our preoccupation with cases in which there are things flowing by us. The analogy leads us to render the "present moment" as one such thing. But "what does one mean by the 'present moment'"? Wittgenstein asks, "This idea is already based on a physical image, that of the stream of experiences that I'm now bisecting at a point" (BT 494). Augustine's discussion of time is an attempt to come to terms with the question "where does the present go when it becomes past?" For Augustine, the present moment leaves a kind of temporal space behind its own disappearance. This is the reason, he thought, why it can be measured presently as having occurred in the past. Wittgenstein's reaction to this is biting:

> It's strange that in ordinary life we are not troubled by the feeling that the phenomenon is slipping away from us, the constant flux of appearance, but only when we philosophize. This indicates that what is in question here is an idea suggested by a misapplication of our language.
>
> (PR, 52)

Augustine's original puzzlement concerning the nature of time is a prime example for language being seduced by substantives as it runs against its own limits. The "personification of time" arises when we extend language by only looking at language instead of using it practically (M, 7:108). Importantly, Wittgenstein says in this context, "when we hand over the reins to language and not to *life*, that's when the philosophical problems arise" (BT, 522; my emphasis).

The very idea of time qua temporal *space*, and with it the captivating idea concerning the flow of time (within that space), sidelines the way we use "time" as a temporal *ordering* of events. "It's just we've used a simile," Wittgenstein wrote, "and now the simile is tyrannizing us. In the language of the simile, I cannot move outside of the simile. Wanting to use the language of this simile to speak of memory as the source of our cognition, as the verification of our propositions, has to lead to nonsense" (PR, 49; BT, 518). Wittgenstein's point is that we need to observe a limit: we cannot apply the concept of time, i.e., the grammatical rules as they apply to physical nouns, to the world of mental imagery, where one uses a radically different way of speaking: "For 'time' has one meaning when we regard memory as the source of time, and another when we regard it as a picture preserved from a past event" (PR, 49). For instance, saying that we have perception into the past (as we do in the framework of memory-time) contradicts every concept of physical time (PR, 50).

Also, the idea of the specious present invites us to regard the future as pre-formed in some sense. This is very characteristic of the philosophies of music, which I mentioned earlier. Wittgenstein points out that "there is a point in saying future events are pre-formed if it belongs to the *essence* of time that it does not break off" (PR, 51). Yet, not breaking off is characteristic of the framework of physical time. The present in memory-time is patently slipping away from us.

One of the images, which Wittgenstein used occasionally during his middle period in order to tease out this sense of limit for our language of time, is the film-strip analogy (PR, 49–54; M, 8:49–50; BT, 494–498, 518). Wittgenstein suggested that we think about the present experience as a picture on a film-strip. There are two alternatives here: either to talk about the projected image, or else to talk about the picture on the film-strip itself. In the latter case, there are other clearly identifiable pictures preceding and succeeding it on the strip. Wittgenstein's point in this analogy is that the philosophical idea that "present experience only is real" – the crux of the Augustinian picture of music – arises from imagining events to pass before us like film in a projector, or lantern. When the image is there and seen, no other image is there and seen. Wittgenstein says "It would be all right, in case of lantern, if pointing to one picture of the film – we say 'this is the only one which is in the lantern now': and we could call this 'real'. . . . But if he pointed to screen & said 'this is only real picture' he would talk nonsense, because it has no neighbours" (M, 8:49). Wittgenstein extended the film-strip analogy also to music by imagining also a film with soundtrack. Again, the point is that what produces the music is part of the film-strip (PR, 70; BT, 496).

As Joachim Schulte points out (Schulte 2006), the film-strip analogy is closely related to the theme of solipsism in Wittgenstein's middle-period, and in an important sense for our present concern, as we shall see in the following sections. According to Wittgenstein, there are modes of talking about present experience in which we can, and sometimes ought to dispense with the word "present", just like we can sometimes do without the word "I". In such contexts (e.g., when we cannot speak of the present as opposed to past and future), the word "present" seems to cancel out simply because there is no other word, which could replace it. In such context, the word "present" does mean something bordering on something else, from which it can be limited off. Wittgenstein's upshot is very clear. At the heart of the Augustinian picture of music we might find an idea which is akin to "the picture on the screen which would illegitimately be called present, since 'present' would not be used here to distinguish it from past and future. And so it is a meaningless epithet" (PR, 54).

Wittgenstein's critique of the Augustinian picture of music is given a striking pronouncement in the context of Wittgenstein's consideration of C. D. Broad's theory of our awareness of the temporal extensity of the immediate objects of our experience (Broad 1923). Broad argued that at a given instant we are directly acquainted with a temporally extended sense datum, which occupies a short interval of time "stretching" into the past from that instant. He also argued that the sensing involved in our experience of a long musical tone and the aural sensum with which we are acquainted are both *continuous*.

Again, Wittgenstein makes a move characteristic of his middle period: distinguishing between different kinds of logical or grammatical "spaces", pointing out analogies and dis-analogies between them, and stressing that what could be said of the concepts which belong to one such space could not meaningfully be said of concepts belonging to another space. Wittgenstein's point here is that the word "continuity" belongs strictly to the vocabulary of the physical world. When we apply the physical notion of continuity to our immediate experience of a musical tone we end up precisely with a "searchlight" model of music. Wittgenstein is on record for rejecting this model in the most straightforward way:

> Can you in a continuous sound distinguish the part you are hearing at the moment and the part you remember hearing? You can hear a click, and there is no part of it which you can remember as coming before or after another part; whereas with a sustained violin note you can remember the part which has gone before. The problem then is to find an intermediate stage at which you can say that you both hear and remember.
>
> (LWL, 71)

The "intermediate stage at which you can say that you both hear and remember" is the musical specious present in which actual hearing and vivid remembering (and anticipating) coexist. According to Wittgenstein, the confusion lies in thinking that physical sound and the sense-datum are both continuous. The physical sound is continuous, but the sense-datum is not. The two experiences, hearing and remembering, are quite distinct. You can narrow down the point between where you finish hearing and where you begin remembering, but there will be no point at which you can say you both hear and remember (LWL 71–72).

Wittgenstein makes it very clear that a notion of continuity based on memory-time is nonsensical, and his argument – apparently a direct rebuttal of Broad's position – undercuts the very foundation of the Augustinian picture of music.

4. The Janus-Face of Musical Time

Wittgenstein's river analogy intimates the Janus-face of musical time. The steady pace of the traveling band or the constant flow of the river, and, at the same time, the possible unevenness in the spread of the logs of wood across the water, the differences in their relative velocity, or their varied size; and, of course, their finite number. One face speaks of *meter*: an order of time which is regular, chronometric in the sense that it is determined and verified by means of publicly observed criteria (for example, metronomes), and open-ended in the sense that it does not entail any structure. The other face speaks of *rhythm*: an order of time which is malleable in the sense that it is subservient to a musical contour, hence integral to it, admitting a mode of identification that is primarily subject-centred.

To elucidate this bifurcation, let us ponder a little the clicking of a metronome. On the one hand, the evenly spaced clicks of the metronome serve the same purpose as any other time measuring device. Set it to sixty beats per minute (bpm) and it would virtually replace any regular stopwatch (one might say, our lives are set against the resolute beating of a secret *larghetto*). Musicians use the metronome primarily to determine a *tempo*, namely, the sheer velocity in which a musical performance ought to proceed. Strictly speaking, if we play the same piece of music first *adagio* (66–76 bpm) and then *allegro* (120–168 bpm), the latter performance should take roughly half the duration of the former. Thus, the regularity of meter is essentially chronometric. On the other hand, the clicks of a metronome mark also a distinct accent, and, as David Epstein points out, it is the manner of this accent – its marked articulation, the quick onset lacking the capacity for broad expressive character – not necessarily its durationally equal spacing, that is of utmost significance to the character of beat, the primary level of meter (Epstein 1995, 29).

Yet counting has a special character in music. Following the clicks of a metronome, musicians do not count "one, two, three, four, five," and so on *ad infinitum*, but rather periodically: "One, two, one . . ." (for duple meter); "One, two, three, one . . ." (for triple meter); "One, two, three, four, one . . ." (for quadruple meter), and so on. The periodicity of musical meter gives rise to the musical measure, which is represented in modern musical notation by bar lines. However, there is nothing in the accent of the isochronal, equitonal clicks that would prompt us to parse them one way or another, and, in effect, to count "in a closed system" (see RPP I § 647). We certainly can, and do, use the metronome or any other time measuring contraptions to count at will in any of the aforementioned ways as well as in many other ways. Yet when we do count "in a closed system" following the clicks of a metronome we acknowledge a periodic accent on what we take to be the first beat of a metrical group. "The *knowledge* of metre," Wittgenstein wrote, "One who *knows* the metre, hears it differently" (RPP I § 746). Thus, the periodicity of the musical meter is informed by our knowledge of a further musical element: *pulse*. Pulse, the primary durational level of rhythm, is the complementary unit to beat with regard to meter. In contradistinction to the chronometric beat, pulse is enlivened and shaped by the wide variety of onset qualities that give rise to accent, which is, to quote from Roger Scruton, "the primary form of rhythmic emphasis, the bringing forward into consciousness of a particular *moment* in the rhythmic order" (Scruton 1997, 29).

Here we approach that which pulsates, throbs, swells, and lilts in music. By counting in musical meter, we move beyond the realm of the chronometrically measured into the realm of the rhythmically alive.

This is precisely where Wittgenstein diagnoses the kind of grammatical confusion involved in any attempt to use physical vocabulary in the realm of immediate experience. "The moment we try to apply exact concepts of measurement to immediate experience, we come up against a peculiar vagueness in this experience," Wittgenstein wrote, "But that only means a vagueness relative to these concepts of measurement. And, now, it seems to me that this vagueness isn't something provisional, to be eliminated later on by more precise knowledge, but that this is a characteristic logical peculiarity" (PR, 211). This is splendidly embodied in the performance of so-called "non-linear tempos", such as *tempo rubato*, *accelerando*, and *ritardando*. In the simplest terms, rubato performance involves a certain distortion in musical time, the expressive alteration of tempo and rhythm within a bar, a phrase, or even an entire movement. *Tempo rubato* – "stolen time" in Italian – means that time in rubato performance is robbed from one part of the music, arguably to be paid back elsewhere. An expressive quality is achieved by giving more duration to certain notes in the melodic figure and then compensating the stolen time by shortening notes in another part of the bar or phrase. Underlying this concept of rubato is the notion that a phrase played in rubato should not take more time than the same phrase played in strict time.

In Romantic rubato, the pull of expressive rubato in melody eventually overpowers the musical complex, with the result that an entire passage in all its elements – melody, harmony, and rhythm – would be drawn out of rhythmic shape as particular segments are compressed or extended in their duration. Yet which time is stolen and paid back in rubato performance? Certainly not the chronometric time of metric beat, which maintains its regular, steady, unchanging, indifferent, mechanistic pulsation throughout the rubato passage. Rather, the term *tempo rubato* refers to the temporal malleability of the musical contour, to the significantly irregular pull that leads us, or guides us – performer and listener alike – from one side of the metric chasm to the other. A successful rubato performance is quite an artistic feat. Like in a daring acrobat's act, much of its suspense and gratification lies in the prospects and the ability of the performer to land with grace and precision on the right spot, namely, the phrase end, which in its timing is simultaneous with the attack on the next phrase.

Thus, we have two aspects that are dialectically intertwined in a rubato performance: significant irregularity and precision. The former without the latter is a meaningless spasm; the latter without the former is a mere mechanical reproduction. As Scruton aptly put it, "rhythm plays with regularity, but is not reducible to it: the pulse is both counted and discounted" (Scruton 1997, 24). Rubato makes sense only on the assumption that, in a sense, the beat is measured out. In rubato performance we have a dramatic display of two different systems of time control, two kinds of time measurement, operating simultaneously, as they rapidly become dis-synchronous and thus in conflict only to realign at the phrase end (see Epstein 1995, Ch. 11). On the one hand, we have the metric control of the beat, which is precise and chronometric, and on the other, we have the contorted pulse that leads us away from the regular beat and back. These two senses of time differ significantly from one another by their respective means of verification hence by their respective means of measurement. The verification of the former rests on the regularity of any time measuring device – a metronome, a stopwatch, even steady foot tapping – while the verification of the latter rests on the recollection and anticipation of the particular phrase structure in its particular performance.

We may conclude that different musical elements – the way we perform them, express them, and in general, understand them – are geared toward two different conceptual systems of time. This amounts to saying that these different musical elements are respectively governed by different grammars. It is the clarification of this grammatical difference that is crucial in Wittgenstein's thinking.

5. Two Orders of Events

According to Wittgenstein, in a language in which there is only "before" and "after", but not past and future, "personification of time would not have occurred" (M, 7:108). So unless we are in the grip of a picture – such as the Augustinian picture of music – which persuades us to think of time as personified, we need to acknowledge that what we call "time" in our variegated language-games is rather the ordering of events. "An order could be established," says Wittgenstein, "without knowing what it was about. We might call it 'grammatical' time" (M, 8:64). Wittgenstein distinguishes between two independent orders: memory-time and information-time.

Viewed as an order or a system of reference, not as a temporal space, memory-time is the specific order of events or situations in my memory. It is not part of time in the larger sense (*große Zeit*; BT, 521). Memory is relative to the moment of time at which the remembering takes place. This means that memory-time is a now-centered system of time-references. In such a system, there is only "before" and "after", "earlier" and "later", but no "past" and "future". Wittgenstein points out, significantly, that "in my memory there is a direction from more remote to nearer, which I might call direction towards the present – which I might call "memory-present" analogous to eye in visual field" (M, 8:39). In this order it makes no sense to say of a given event that it "occurred after the present in memory-time" (PO, 112). Furthermore, the order of memory-time, when taken in isolation, cannot rely on any external criteria for time-reference or time-measurement. According to Wittgenstein, the mere internal description of my memory will not show any difference between my memory and other people's. The only difference will be relative to a public system of references, namely, information-time (M, 7:106). Memory-time can rely only on one's current memories and expectations. Yet such references do not seem to give us any direct way of measuring time-spans.

In contradistinction, Wittgenstein suggests to look at another order of events, involving the specification of time-references by means of public, observable chronology, which is implemented not only by means of chronometers and calendars, but also by means of documents, diaries, manuscripts, and other modes of making records or consulting them. Information-time is "the order in which information is got by asking different people" (AWL, 15). It is observation-time (M, 7:106), written-time (M, 8:64), narrative-time (M, 8:45), historical time (BT, 495), and the time of documents (M, 8:49). More narrowly it is also physical time (BT, 495). It is the order of the film-strip, in which "before" and "after" spell also "past" and "future" (M, 8:46). "With our language," Wittgenstein writes, "we find ourselves, so to speak, in the domain of the film, not of the projected picture" (PR, 70). Schulte makes a helpful suggestion that the game of asking for and receiving information is a variegated activity (significantly less predetermined system than physics and its applications) and that Wittgenstein's middle-period conception of information-time is pioneering in the sense that it could be taken as a move toward the rich variety of language-games in the form it is presented in *Philosophical Investigations* and in Wittgenstein's other later writings (Schulte 2006, 566). In this sense, Wittgenstein's emphasis on information-time is an attempt to resolve philosophical conundrums pertaining to an exclusive reliance on the order of memory-time, for instance, temporal solipsism (see Hintikka 1996, 242–243). For Wittgenstein, "the process of 'language' runs its course in homogeneous historical time" (BT, 495).

Wittgenstein makes it clear that "we have to give up the view that in order to speak about the immediate, we must speak about a state at a moment in time" (BT, 494). However, in our actual language there is hybrid order: "If I say: 'before' & 'after' mean something different, when you use memory as criterion, & when you use documents, I'm referring to 2 games, which are never played in their purity" (M, 9:49). If the two games (exemplifying the two orders of events respectively) are never played in their purity, then a need arises to ascertain priorities in our language: the order of information-time must be prior to the order to memory-time – a reversal of the Augustinian priorities. The reliance of information-time on public, observable criteria lends it the kind of multifarious complexity, which is familiar to us from major themes in Wittgenstein's later philosophy. This is shown by Wittgenstein's frequent use of metrological models and analogies for understanding ideas or phenomena in other domains, such as language, mathematics and the study of certainties (Kusch 2015).

As we have seen, Wittgenstein argued against Augustine's view of time measurement that the word "measurement" itself, and its related standards of exactness and precision, belong to the vocabulary of the physical world. Yet, as Martin Kusch points out (Kusch 2011; 2015), Wittgenstein gradually came to realize that "methodology" (metrology), is "a description of the activities called 'measuring', a branch of human natural history that helps us understand the concepts of measurement, precision, etc. in all their variants . . ." (MS 135, 129). The very standards of exact measurement are entrenched in social institutions, as shown, for example, by Wittgenstein's well-known discussion of the "Parisian Standard Meter", deposited in the French Archives in 1889 (PI §50; RFM, 36). To be familiar with the standard meter requires that one is "acquainted with the institution of measuring and its connexion with the standard meter" (RFM, 36). Wittgenstein's point is that in order for something to be a unit or standard of measurement, it needs to have a social status within an institution. This idea links directly with Wittgenstein's consideration of rule-following, in particular the problem of the regress of rules, that is the apparent need to deposit in the archive not only the standard for measuring, but also rules for comparing the standard with tokens of that type, and rules for using such rule, and so on infinitely (LFM, 106; see PI §201). According to Wittgenstein, the regress stops due to the fact that we establish by means of training a more or less uniform practice on the basis of what is in the archives and what is available in the institution of measuring.

6. The "Physical Ear", the "Auditory Ear" and the Aesthetically "Right"

Wittgenstein's emphasis is on "now", not as a "specification of time", a name of an instance of time, but as "ligature to reality", whereas "the reality that belongs to a symbol in this way falls under the domain of grammar" (BT, 525). His ultimate point is that we need to look at the whole language game in which the word "now" plays a role, instead of just looking at the contexts, the phrases in language in which the word is being used (BB, 108).

In music, the word "now" and its manifold preparative gestures (a deep breathing in, a meaningful glance, a nod, a thrust of the conductor's baton) prefigure musical simultaneity, which features primarily in the context of *musizieren*, of music-making in the most inclusive sense (see KL, 37; RPP I § 1130).

Wittgenstein's discussion of the word "now" (during his middle-period) is linked with his consideration of other "ligatures to reality" such as the words "here" and "this" (see e.g., BT, 523–527). In this context, he repeatedly makes the distinction between two kinds of criteria, which he dubs respectively "the geometrical eye" and "the physical eye" (e.g., BB, 63–64). The physical eye, quite simply, is the biological mechanism we use to see objects in physical space, where rays of light converge etc.; the geometrical eye is the place from which visual space is seen, which is determined by one's pointing at it. The important difference between these two "eyes" is in the way we use them to identify and verify objects. We use the physical eye to name and locate objects in physical space, while we use the geometrical eye to pinpoint the contents of our present visual experience. The former is carried out publicly by pointing to an object in the room and saying "the second book from the right on the bookshelf, the one with the blue cover", while later is carried out by ostension as we say "here!" or "this!"

Wittgenstein's point is that while the two eyes, the physical and the geometrical, usually coincide, it is conceivable that the aforementioned foci do not (see Stern 1995, 76). Importantly for our present concern, Wittgenstein quite naturally extended this distinction into the realm of musical experience: "Change of pitch or intensity does not require any 'auditory ear'. For movement of sounds what is needed is a 'system of co-ordinates' which might be called 'auditory ear'" (M, 8:35). In a way that is analogous to the distinction between the physical eye and the geometrical, we have here a distinction between two criteria for temporal location: the one is physical (hence chronometric), namely, a physical ear; the other is integral, "a system of coordinates", namely "an auditory ear". Using the physical ear we publicly measure and time sonic objects that persist in physical time by means of institutionalized devices such as clocks and metronomes, and give exact identification of temporal locations like, "it is 6:07", or "you are exactly two milliseconds off the beat" (think of Karlheinz Stockhausen's electronic music, if you like). Using the auditory ear we refer to a temporal location that is integral to the contents of our present aural experience, saying "now!" when we hear an accented beat or describing the accented beat as "sandwiched" between a preceding long interval and a following short interval, or, as in the case of a perfectly executed rubato, landing with grace and precision at the phrase end, that is, simultaneously with the attack on the next phrase. Wittgenstein maintained that while "now" is not a name for an instance of time, presupposing a privileged, independent framework for identifying objects of immediate experience (i.e., the framework of memory-time), we do need a way of expressing the phenomena of immediate experience separately from experiences of another kind (MS 113, 247–248; BT, 496).

In order not to fall prey to the image of musical experience as a kind of, say, seashell that everyone carries with him close to his ear, and to the corresponding specter of a metaphysical owner for each such seashell, we must circumscribe the grammar of the auditory ear. That is, we must acknowledge that our utterances about our musical experiences (the order of memory-time), if they are to be used meaningfully, must rely on the framework of our ordinary language (the order of information time). The upshot is this: according to Wittgenstein, the auditory ear cannot have primacy over the physical ear. To carry out its job, the auditory ear must rely on the publicly identifiable means of the physical ear.

This is Wittgenstein's reversal of Augustinian priorities, the upshot of his critique of the Augustinian picture of music. This reversed hierarchy (namely, that information time conceptually precedes memory-time), which obtains, according to Wittgenstein, between the physical ear and the auditory ear ultimately means that in music the use of the language of memory-time is subordinated to, or rather circumscribed by the language of information time. That is, our conception of musical elements – the way we perform them, express them, and in general, understand them – must acknowledge and manifest this grammatical caveat, if it is to make sense. In particular, the very notion of "measurement" and related concepts such as "precision" and "simultaneity", can meaningfully describe musical experience only if governed by the grammar of the physical ear.

However, in the context of *musizieren*, and in light of what I described as the Janus-face of musical time, this caveat is an onset for aesthetic puzzlement. As the aforementioned case of rubato performance suggests, certain expressive musical elements are geared toward the framework of memory-time while other – those responsible for clockwork execution of certain aspect of the musical performance – are geared toward the framework of information time, in particular physical time with its time-measuring devices. This bifurcation is shown in the different systems of time control that are implemented in musical performance. Wittgenstein was acutely aware of this. For him, the musical "now" is a ligature to the aesthetically "right", to a (possible) resolution of an aesthetic puzzle. In music, "now" betokens a conversation among music-makers, it belongs to a whole language-game, wherein reasons are given to the effect that one hears differently, hence one also plays differently.

Consider the following two striking passages, where Wittgenstein goes straight to the heart of the matter:

> A language, which is spoken on the beat [*im Takt geredet wird*], so that you can also speak according to the *metronome*. It does not go without saying that music could be paced, like ours, at least occasionally, by a metronome [*metronomieren läßt*]. (Playing the theme from the 8th symph. exactly according to the metronome.)
> (CV, 85, 14.11.1948; translation modified)

> The simultaneity [*Zeitgleichheit*] of the clock and simultaneity in music. They are by no means equivalent concepts. Playing strictly according to the measure [*Streng im Takt gespielt*] does not mean

playing exactly according to the metronome. But it would be possible that a certain *kind* of music should be played according to the
metronome. (Is the opening theme <of the second movement> of the
8th symphony of this kind?)

(CV 92, 30.1.1949; translation modified)

The philosophically important concept in these two passages is the German musical term "Takt", which singularly embodies the Janus-face of
musical time. The term is employed at the same time on three intricately
interrelated, yet importantly distinguishable strata pertaining to musical
time. First, it concerns the level of the beat, that which divides time into
spans of equal duration. Beats can be indicated by time-keeping devices,
such as a metronome. Second, it concerns the level of the measure, that
is, the demarcation of a certain quantity of beats according to a given
meter by means of bar-lines. The term "meter" is both a synonym for a
time signature (again, relatable to time-keeping devices), but also denotes
a structured attending to time, which allows the listener to have precise
expectations as to when subsequent musical events are going to occur.
As such, meter is an aspect of *musizieren*. Third, it concerns the realm of
rhythm, the ordered time, which is, as Wallace Berry points out, is "the
sum of a broad range of factors each of which is in some way a manifestation of pace and grouping, the former a product of relative frequencies
of events, the latter of their relative qualities and the means by which they
are unit-ordered" (Berry 1987, 305). Thus, whereas meter is a mode of
attending, rhythm is that to which we attend (Gjerdingen 1989).

In these two passages, Wittgenstein underscores the grammatical
difference between the two faces of musical time: the "now" of the
physical ear, and the "now" of the auditory ear. For the physical ear,
the word "now" is used most significantly to synchronize and calibrate
actions as well as time-measurement devices. Measuring devices, such
as clocks and rulers, can be rigid and reliable when we continuously
update and calibrate them against each other. According to Kusch, the
way in which Wittgenstein, from 1929 onwards, leans on Albert Einstein's clock-coordination as a metaphor for rule-following supports an
analysis of measuring in sociological rule-following terms (Kusch 2015).
The practice of measurement is communal. This illuminates an important
aspect of the simultaneity of the clock:

[C]ould we talk about minutes and hours, if we had no sense of time;
if there were no clocks, or could be none for physical reasons; if there
did not exist all the connexions that give our measure of time meaning and importance? In that case – we should say – the measure of
time would have lost its meaning (like the action of delivering check-
mate if the game of chess were to disappear) – or it would have some
quite different meaning.

(RFM, vii 18)

The clocks have to agree: only then can we use them for the activity that we call "measuring time". It is wrong to say that if there were no such agreement then the results of our measurements would be false. What we should say is that in that case there would be no such results.

(MS 123, 19v)

As Kusch points out, the concept of time is inseparable from the notion of simultaneity. Hence, we need to acknowledge that a single clock cannot be meaningfully said to measure time. Any given clock can measure time only if there is a protocol that links it to others (Kusch 2011).

Kusch's point is well taken. Indeed, as Wittgenstein's own comparison (in CV, 92) makes eminently clear, the concept of time is inseparable from the notion of simultaneity also for the auditory ear. The difference is precisely in the conception of simultaneity in music. It is not equivalent to the simultaneity of the clock. Comparing the two frameworks, the physical ear (pertaining to time-measuring and time-keeping by means of a clock or a metronome) and the auditory ear (pertaining to *musizieren*), we can say that the former can be seen as some sort of abstraction. On a common-sense level, chronometric time is the only adequate scheme we know of for synchronizing practical affairs, dating past events, and constructing some perspective of future ones (see Langer 1953, 111). Precision (for instance, in the sense prevalent in science) comes with a systematic refinement of this common-sense framework. However, as I argued earlier, the problem with the Augustinian picture of music is the insistence that the auditory ear "is incommensurable with the progress of common affairs" (ibid., 109), hence the tendency, which Wittgenstein was adamant to resist, to hold on to the picture of memory-time as "the source of cognition".

Wittgenstein's critique of the Augustinian picture of music, and the ensuing reversal of Augustinian priories, shift our focus to the "protocol" (*pace* Kusch), which enables the conception of simultaneity in music. My upshot is that, for Wittgenstein, such "protocol" inheres in *musizieren*, in the aptly collaborative quest for drawing in significance by means of the phrasing and re-phrasing of a passage in order to characterize it, enabling by means of such comparative investigation meaningful distinctions between right and wrong.

The musical example, which Wittgenstein suggested in parenthesis in both CV 85 and CV 92, seems to have been carefully chosen to bring out the philosophical peculiarity in the kind of music for which it would indeed be aesthetically "right" to play it exactly according to the metronome. The example alluded to by Wittgenstein is the opening theme of the second movement of Beethoven's eighth symphony in F major, op. 93. From a motivic perspective, the theme is structured in short figures, each of which consists of characteristic interval and characteristic rhythm. The theme itself is brief and sparse, consisting in dense repetition of the rhythmic figuration. Beethoven deliberately restricts the use of developmental devices, resorting mainly to transposition with hardly any digression from the original rhythmic pattern. From a formal perspective, there is also a deliberate restriction on development, which is actually quite atypical to Beethoven. He eliminates the development section of what should have been a sonatina form. In effect, the thematic density and these compositional restrictions undermine the musical dimensions of expressivity, flow, and structural flexibility. Merely repetitive adjacent musical statements with no hierarchy allow no escape from mechanical, rigid pulsation. So, this is truncated music, structurally coerced into metronomic precision by means of reducing musical elements, which would otherwise enliven musical performance. In other words, the peculiarity, which drew Wittgenstein's attention to this example, lies in the forced coinciding of the "now" of the physical ear and the "now" of the auditory ear, that is, the chronometric fixity of the "now" of the auditory ear, which is used in the movement to a particularly light-hearted, humorous effect. It is noteworthy that this movement is commonly regarded, with some biographic support, as some sort of musical parody on the expense of Johann Nepomuk Mälzel, the inventor of the metronome (and some other mechanical curiosities), who was a friend of Beethoven.

With this example in mind, one can see clearly what is so strikingly odd about Wittgenstein's suggestion to imagine "a language, which is spoken on the beat, so that you can also speak according to the *metronome*" (CV, 85). There are some fundamental differences between rhythm in spoken language and rhythm in music (see London 2001, II:2). Speech consists of phonological segments that have their own intrinsic durations and durational relationships. Segments and phrases are separated by pauses of variable length. Patterns of stress or accent are found only within the context of a breath group or subgroup. Normal speech is only locally rhythmic, whereas in music one normally fits successive motifs and phrases into a common, continuous metric framework. Thus, in Wittgenstein's imagined metered language, the normal rhythms of speech are bound to be seriously distorted, mainly by lengthening vowels but also by fitting the segmental pauses of speech within the constraints of the meter.

The analogy between such imagined metered language and the example from Beethoven's eighth symphony is clear. As in the musical example, also for the metered language to make sense (that is, to sound "right"), the various elements must be deliberately grouped and organized in such a way that non-metered speech would be incredulous – it would sound "wrong". The belabored strangeness of such metered language is a foil for appreciating Wittgenstein's contention that "it does not go without saying that music could be paced, like ours, at least occasionally, by a metronome" (CV, 85) and that the simultaneity of the clock and simultaneity in music are "by no means equivalent concepts" (CV, 92). In fact, elsewhere Wittgenstein put an emphasis precisely on the opposite type of cases: on the "meaningful irregularity" of "phenomena with speech-like character in music" (CV, 40; translation modified). Wittgenstein's example, again from Beethoven, is illuminating for our present discussion: the double bass recitative in the fourth movement of Beethoven's ninth symphony. Beethoven casts the recitative in triple meter (a strong beat followed by two weak beats with no further inner division), which tends to restrict, or perhaps overpower, the flow of the recitative much more than would a duple meter. To preserve the character of the recitative in performance, one would be inclined to "stretch" the notes that fall on the weak beats while running the risk of compromising the strict meter.

Ultimately, when the music is not truncated as in Wittgenstein's example from Beethoven's eighth symphony, "playing strictly according to the measure does not mean playing exactly according to the metronome" (CV, 92). Playing strictly according to the measure is couched in terms of the meter, not as a time signature for the metronome, but as a mode of attending (by the performers and the listeners), and in terms of rhythm as the ordered time attended. It is geared toward the auditory ear. The concept of simultaneity in musical performance is rough and vague in relation to our techniques of representation; yet as such it is needed to characterize our experience. Simultaneity in music requires from the musicians to attend aspects of music, which are not explicitly contained in the notation. They must attend complex aspects of timbral differences between instruments, and the different kinds of attack for different instruments, and the acoustics in actual spaces. They also need to exhibit sensitivity to the appropriate musical style, an understanding of the period and the appropriate performance practice for the period, as well as sensitivity to musical form and to pitch hierarchy within the musical language. The pacing of a metronome cannot guarantee the mutual alignment of all these elements. In fact, the use of a metronome can often disrupt an attempt to play strictly according to the measure (as in the aforementioned case of a rubato performance). Musicians may use the metronome "open-endedly" in order to verify or agree on a *tempo*. Once this goal has been achieved, the metronome is usually turned off so as not to obstruct the music.

One of the crucial elements in any successful management of musical time is achieving the "right" tempo in performance. The concept of tempo itself exhibits the Janus-face of musical time. Since the advent of the metronome, tempos have been indicated by correlating some durational unit (usually a quarter note) with a unit of clock-time (expressed as beats per minute). Yet a sense of tempo and motion is a hierarchically emergent property of the musical surface, and not simply a product of note-to-note transitions (London 2001, II:5). As David Epstein notes, its reduction into the element of speed per se notwithstanding, tempo "is a consequence of the sum of all factors within a piece – the overall sense of a work's themes, rhythms, articulations, 'breathing', motion, harmonic progressions, tonal movement, contrapuntal activity" (Epstein 1995, 99). The speed allows the overall, integrated bundle of musical elements to flow with a rightful sense. Thus, in the context of *musizieren*, achieving the right tempo becomes an elusive target, a matter of searching for a fitting characterization, even in musical styles that are familiar and whose performing practices are well documented. Indeed, the transition from late Baroque to early Classical music was marked by a greater sensitivity to "wrong" tempi to the extent that entire symphonic movements by Haydn, Beethoven and especially Mozart can be distorted by a poor choice of tempo (see Blume 1970, 33–35).

Achieving the right tempo is a perfect example for what Wittgenstein called an "aesthetic puzzle". It involves the possibility of hearing something differently, "just as you may find the head in a puzzle-picture" (M, 9:31). Consider one of Wittgenstein's own examples: the music score indicates the metronome marking of "quarter note = 88", but to play it right nowadays, he says, one must take a faster tempo, "quarter note = 94" (MS 110, 281; Z §37). When he asks "which is the tempo intended by the composer?" it is clear that the question is meant to sound bogus. Presumably, the composer intended that the music would sound "right". Yet merely setting the metronome will not solve the aesthetic puzzle: the proof is in the playing. This is true for different musicians playing the same piece, the same musician playing the same piece on different instruments, or the same musician playing the same piece on the same instrument at different occasions, and certainly when the same piece is played according to two very different performance practices (e.g., romantic versus historically-informed performances of Baroque music). This is even true in the case of clockwork pieces like the second movement of Beethoven's eighth symphony.

Making a choice about tempo is an instance of characterizing, of assembling in a specific field of valence and possibility and contrast. By characterizing we draw in significance, evincing a physiognomy. The attempt to characterize involves, as Juliet Floyd puts it, "the 'coming into view' of a scheme of possibilities available for characterization given a particular mode of characterization" (Floyd 2018, 368). The specificity of characterization means that by characterizing we can "get it just right", can meet or miss its mark, so we patently need to seek the right level and arrangement of elements in order to reveal something, to discover ways in which things and possibilities are. Wittgenstein wrote:

> I think it an important & remarkable fact that a musical theme, if it played \<at> (very) different tempi, changes its *character*. Transition from quantity to quality.
>
> (CV, 84)

The transition from quantity to quality is aesthetic: a transition from the physical ear conception of tempo as speed to the auditory ear conception of tempo as a hierarchically emergent "property" of the musical surface as situated in a culturally entrenched practice. Yet Wittgenstein's twofold point is that the aesthetically "right" pertains only to the latter, and that the transition from quantity to quality is non-reductive.

Searching for the right tempo, for the right characterization of a musical theme, is an example for what Wittgenstein described in his lectures on aesthetics in the 1930 as striving toward an "ideal": "Aesthetic reasons are given in the form: getting nearer to an ideal or farther from it" (M, 9:36). For Wittgenstein, ideals are facilitators of aesthetic discourse. They bring forth reasons that draw our attention to something which can assist us in finding a solution to an aesthetic puzzle (M, 9:33). An aesthetic ideal is not a simple representational standard, not simply a perceived token or a matter of fact that directs us and which we try to duplicate in our artistic activity. According to Wittgenstein, we identify an ideal due to a special role which it plays in the lives of certain people (M, 9:20); "the ideal is the tendency of people who create such a thing" (M, 9:22). It is a prototype (*Urbild*) in Wittgenstein's restricted sense of a merely regulative idea, the primacy of which is due to its heuristic use in providing the "logical space" for all possible relevant instances (Guter 2015). According to Wittgenstein, "you would need to describe the instances of the ideal in a sort of serial grouping" (AWL, 36). The ideal enables further descriptions, juxtaposing and grouping similar cases, both actual and possible, which collectively yield a "synopsis" or an "overview" (*Übersicht*) of a system – a collective arrangement, which may show us the point of a given practice. The ideal is precisely "an object of comparison – a measuring rod as it were – within our way of looking at things" (CV, 30).

The ideal, used as a measuring rod, enables and regulates a "protocol" for *musizieren* (AWL, 37). Yet this is a significantly open-ended protocol. "Aesthetic discussion is like discussion in a court of law," said Wittgenstein, "you don't say 'this is bad or good', but try to clear up circumstances" (M, 9:31–32). The circumstances are always particular. A reason in aesthetics is "a reason for having this word in this place rather than that; this musical phrase rather than that" (M, 9:30). The ideal, which facilitates the aesthetic discussion, is un-hypothetical in the sense of affording a mere picture as a useful device, which "enables [one] to overlook a system at a glance" (M, 9:38). It inheres in the particular case by means of paraphrasing, giving good similes, which result in a collective arrangement of (often surprisingly) similar cases (M, 9:37).

What compels us along with the reasons one begins to offer, set the parameters of the discussion – of what it makes sense to say. Yet these parameters are grammatically related to our ability to always "say much more" in giving reasons (M, 9:13). Wittgenstein insisted that it is hard to rule out anything *a priori* as it were, from potentially being (an aspect of) an aesthetic reason. According to Wittgenstein, the boundaries for giving reasons in aesthetics are set by means of the "verifying phenomena", which give the reasons adduced their meaning (M, 9:43). The aesthetically "right" hinges upon the possibility of being mutually attuned, and the multiform manner of manifesting appreciation, which involves, as Wittgenstein came to realize in his later writings, admitting concepts based on imponderable evidence – evidence that cannot be recognized or explained by reference to rules, yet accepted by those who are experienced with the infinite variation of human physiognomy (Guter 2017). "It is not only difficult to describe what appreciation consists in, but impossible," Wittgenstein reminds us, "To describe what it consists in we would have to describe the whole environment" (LC, I: 20). The verifying phenomena bring aesthetic reasoning to an end; they set a limit for language.

When Wittgenstein says that simultaneity in music is conceptually different from the simultaneity of the clock, this means that while simultaneity in music is geared toward the auditory ear, it is nonetheless casted in the language of informing and communicating. Yet there is a limit to this language: the verifying phenomena by which we determine what makes sense as we engage in *musizieren*. This is precisely the reason why the transition from tempo-as-quantity to tempo-as-quality is non-reductive. This is "the way music speaks", Wittgenstein noted – what is cast in the language of information (*Mitteilung*) "is not employed in the language-game of informing" (RPP I §888; Z §§160–161).

We may conclude that, ultimately, Wittgenstein's critique of the Augustinian picture of music can be seen as directed not only at the attempt to give rise to a bogus, nonsensical metaphysical language, which presupposes the primacy of the conceptual framework of memory-time, but also, and perhaps more poignantly, at the philosophical failure of such a view to acknowledge and appreciate the importance of the uniquely conversational, un-hypothetical, human immanence pertaining to the kind of aesthetic recalcitrance wherein the aesthetically "right" marks a limit for our most ordinary language.

Note

1.   In references to BT, page numbers refer to the pagination of the original typescript.

References

Augustine (1948) *Basic Writings of Saint Augustine*. Vol. 1. Edited by W. J. Oates. New York: Random House.
Berry, Wallace (1987) *Structural Functions in Music*. New York: Dover.
Broad, C. D. (1923) *Scientific Thought*. London: Kegan Paul.

Epstein, David (1995) *Shaping Time: Music, the Brain, and Performance.* New York: Schirmer.

Floyd, Juliet (2018) "Aspects of Aspects", in H. Sluga and D. G. Stern (eds), *The Cambridge Companion to Wittgenstein.* Second edition. Cambridge: Cambridge University Press, 361–388.

Gjerdingen, R. O. (1989) "Meter as a Mode of Attending: A Network Simulation of Attentional Rhythmicity in Music", *Integral* 3, 67–91.

Guter, Eran (2015) "The Good, the Bad and the Vacuous: Wittgenstein on Modern and Future Musics", *Journal of Aesthetics and Art Criticism* 73 (4), 427–439.

Guter, Eran (2017) "Wittgenstein on Musical Depth Music and Our Knowledge of Humankind", in G. Hagberg (ed), *Wittgenstein on Aesthetic Experience.* Basingstoke: Palgrave Macmillan, 217–247.

Hintikka, Jaakko (1996) *Ludwig Wittgenstein: Half-Truths and One-and-a-Half Truths*, Jaakko Hintikka Selected Papers. Vol. 1. Dordrecht: Kluwer Academic Publishers.

Husserl, Edmund (1964) *The Phenomenology of Internal Time-Consciousness.* Bloomington, IN: Indiana University Press.

Kusch, Martin (2011) "Wittgenstein and Einstein's Clocks", in E. Ramharter (ed), *Ungesellige Geselligkeiten/Unsocial Sociabilities: Wittgensteins Umgang mit anderen Denkern/Wittgenstein's Sources.* Berlin: Parerga, 203–218.

Kusch, Martin (2015) " 'A Branch of Human Natural History': Wittgenstein's Reflections on Metrology", in O. Schlaudt and L. Huber (eds), *Standardization in Measurement: Philosophical, Historical and Sociological Issues.* London: Pickering & Chatto, 11–24.

Langer, Susanne K. (1953) *Feeling and Form.* London: Routledge and Kegan Paul.

Levinson, Jerrold (1997) *Music in the Moment.* Ithaca, NY: Cornell University Press.

London, Justin (2001) "Rhythm", in *Grove Music Online*, accessed 10 September 2018, available at http:////www.oxfordmusiconline.com/grovemusic/view/10.1093/gmo/9781561592630.001.0001/omo-9781561592630-e-0000045963.

Mabbott, J. D. (1951) "Our Direct Experience of Time", *Mind* 60 (238), 153–167.

Schulte, Joachim (2006) "Wittgenstein on Time (1929–1933)", in F. Stadler and M. Stöltzner (eds), *Time and History. Zeit und Geschichte.* Frankfurt: Ontos Verlag, 557–567.

Scruton, Roger (1997) *The Aesthetics of Music.* Oxford: Oxford University Press.

Stern, David G. (1995) *Wittgenstein on Mind and Language.* New York: Oxford University Press.

Waite, William G. (1980) "Augustine of Hippo", in S. Sadie (ed), *The New Grove Dictionary of Music and Musicians.* Vol. 1. London: Palgrave Macmillan, 695–696.

12 Literature as the Measure of Our Lives

Danièle Moyal-Sharrock

In her Nobel Prize acceptance speech (1993), Toni Morrison said: "We die. That may be the meaning of life. But we do language. That may be the measure of our lives." With these words, Morrison may have captured the distinctive importance of language in the constitution and expression of human morality, sociality, psychology, science, and art; but this is not to say that, as the Tractarian Wittgenstein had it, "the limits of my language mean the limits of my world" (TLP 5.6). Whatever linguistic idealism may or may not have informed this Tractarian remark, the *later* Wittgenstein was no linguistic idealist: he did not share the view – as Bernard Williams (1973) would have us believe – that there is no reality independent of our conception of it.[1] What Wittgenstein groundbreakingly realises is that we do not read off our concepts from nature – as if nature could even be in the business of offering concepts. Our concepts do not track a conceptual ghost line in reality but rather create an order in reality – an order conditioned, but not dictated, by reality. Wittgenstein does not therefore preclude the existence of a language-independent reality to which our language connects; only the connection is not due to our *discovering* tracks in nature but to *making* them. The connection is not a correspondentist or empirical one, but a grammatical one: "The connection between 'language and reality' is made by definitions of words, and these belong to grammar" (PG, 97).

Nor does this grammatical or conceptual ordering preclude reality's impact on our ordering. Though we don't read off our concepts from nature, "[t]he rule we lay down is the one most strongly suggested by the facts of experience" (AWL, 84). And so our concepts are closely interwoven – though not inferentially – with what is most fundamental in our way of living (LW II, 43–44). The later Wittgenstein well understood that language is rooted in and *conditioned* by the extra-linguistic; by natural *facts* which are fundamental or salient for us: "very general facts of nature" such as the "common behaviour of mankind" (PI, 56; PI §206).[2] "Indeed" – he asks in *On Certainty* – "doesn't it seem obvious that the *possibility* of a language-game is conditioned by certain facts?" (OC §617; original emphasis).

I have elsewhere addressed the ways in which language is embedded in the extra-linguistic;[3] what I would like to do in this paper is explore how its being impacted by the extra-linguistic – how its being "reality-soaked" – makes language the vital and *autonomous* force that it is. I am *not* interested here in how we use language to describe and refer to the world, but in how we use language aesthetically to evoke what cannot be described or referred to veridically, and yet deeply generates or enhances understanding. Inasmuch as the most potent manifestations of language carrying life and conveying understanding are to be found in literature, I will use literature to help me flesh out how, in this non-referential and nonpropositional way, language is, immeasurably, "the measure of our lives".

The aim of the *Tractatus*, writes Wittgenstein in its Preface, is "to draw a limit to thought, or rather – not to thought, but to the expression of thoughts"; and that, he adds, can only be done by drawing the limit in language.[4] We might also put it this way: the *Tractatus* aims to demarcate "what can be said" from nonsense. That the limit of thought can only be drawn in language is not to say that the limit of thought coincides with that of language, for language exceeds "what can be said". Though the *Tractatus* narrows down what can be said or spoken about to a specific subgroup of propositions – the propositions of natural science (TLP 6.53) – language consists of far more than this. If what can be said, technically speaking, is narrowed down to what can be true or false – that is, what is verifiable: empirical propositions – there is much that cannot be said but is nevertheless dependent on language for its expression. When, at the close of the book, Wittgenstein writes: "What we cannot speak about we must pass over in silence" (TLP 7), he is alluding to 1) that which *can* be put into words, but is not strictly speaking sayable because not truth-evaluable; and 2) that which *cannot* be put into words but shows itself through the use of words. It is the latter ineffable that I am concerned with here: how some of the most acute and sensitive manifestations of "the measure of our lives" depend on language, though they cannot be formulated.

1. Language "Is in Order as It Is" (PI §98)

Wittgenstein writes that the ethical and the aesthetic are not sayable (TLP 6.421). Our words will give us "facts, facts, and facts but no Ethics" (LE, 40). The "mere description" of the facts of a murder, in all its physical and psychological detail, "will contain nothing which we could call an *ethical* proposition. The murder will be on exactly the same level as any other event, for instance the falling of a stone" (LE, 39; original emphasis). This is a version of the fact-value distinction. Value cannot be said because all that can be said is natural (or factual) meaning, and value is supernatural. This does not mean that value finds no expression;

only that its expression is not, and should not be confused with, empirical or natural/factual expression. The ethical value of the murder cannot be *said* for there are no ethical propositions; it can only *show* itself *in* what is said: "There are, indeed, things that cannot be put into words. They *make themselves manifest*" (TLP 6.522; original emphasis).

On the other hand, many of the things that *can* be put into words – such as tautologies (including propositions of logic) and contradictions – "say nothing" (TLP 4.461, 5.43, 6.1, 6.11). And so language can be misleading in that what looks like it *is* saying something – simply because it doesn't *look* as if lacking sense, (e.g., the propositions of logic) – in fact does lack sense and says nothing (TLP 4.461).[5] Indeed Wittgenstein regularly complains about "the misleading uniformity of language". From the *Tractatus* where he thanks Russell for "showing that the apparent logical form of a proposition need not be its real one" (TLP 4.0031), to the *Blue Book* where he notes the confusion provoked by "the outward similarity between a metaphysical proposition and an experiential one" (BB, 55f); or in *Philosophical Grammar*, "the confusion caused by the form of word-language, which makes everything uniform" (PG, 422); and the *Investigations*:

Of course, what confuses us is the uniform appearance of words when we hear them spoken or meet them in script and print. For their *application* is not presented to us so clearly. Especially when we are doing philosophy!

(PI §11; original emphasis)

This is why the philosopher's task is "[t]he clarification of the use of language" aimed at dismantling the "[t]raps of language" (PO, 183 /BT, 311). However, though the problems that arise through our misinterpreting the forms of our language go deep (PI §110), this cannot generate a desire for another language; it can only prompt the philosopher to alert us to instances of language going on holiday (PI §38) – as, for example, when philosophers say that radical "doubt" is possible. Here, language goes on holiday because philosophers use the word "doubt" in a way that transgresses its use in our ordinary language games and thereby confounds us; for, Wittgenstein reminds us, to speak of radical doubt is nonsense: "A doubt that doubted everything would not be a doubt" (OC §450); "Doubting and non-doubting behavior. There is the first only if there is the second" (OC §354). For in order even to doubt we must at least be certain of the meaning of our words (OC §370).

In spite of his wariness about the misleading uniformity of language, Wittgenstein does not fall into what Ben Ware calls "the modernist-linguistic impasse" (Ware 2015, 120). His acknowledgement of the "traps" that come with the nature of language – and which are compounded by our inattention to context, our misleading reifications, our violations of grammar – in no way betrays a dissatisfaction with ordinary language. Quite the contrary, Wittgenstein finds it perfectly in order as it is – and this, from the *Tractatus* onward:

> In fact, all the propositions of our everyday language, just as they stand, are in perfect logical order.
>
> (TLP 5.5563)

> On the one hand it is clear that every sentence in our language "is in order as it is". That is to say, we are not *striving after* an ideal, as if our ordinary vague sentences had not yet got a quite unexceptionable sense, and a perfect language awaited construction by us. – On the other hand it seems clear that where there is sense there must be perfect order. – So there must be perfect order even in the vaguest sentence.
>
> (PI §98; original emphasis)

These remarks are all on the side of ordinary language: not only is it in no need of interference or improvement, it *cannot* be improved, for it is – even in its vaguest sentences – in "perfect order". However, that "philosophy may in no way interfere with the actual use of language" (PI §124) does not mean that it should not correct *philosophical* use when it goes "on holiday". Conceptual elucidation is the philosopher's job:[6] she is responsible for discerning "differences" in "the misleading analogies in the use of language" (P, 163), and so ought not to use concepts indiscriminately. Though Wittgenstein refuses to admonish or correct the ordinary use of language when prey to misleading analogies, the philosopher must be corrected:

> For when Moore says "I know that that's a . . ." I want to reply "you don't *know* anything!" – and yet I would not say that to anyone who was speaking without philosophical intention.
>
> (OC §407; original emphasis)

Here Wittgenstein inveighs Moore for his carelessness; for the "wrong use" he made of the proposition "I know . . ." (OC §178).

As is well known, Wittgenstein himself struggled with language: "Here I am inclined to fight windmills, because I cannot yet say the thing I really want to say" (OC §400). However, Wittgenstein's struggle with language[7] is not a struggle with the limitations of language; it is a struggle with thought, a philosophical struggle. Language is perfectly adequate; it is the philosopher who may not be: "I do philosophy now like an old woman who is always mislaying something and having to look for it again: now her spectacles, now her keys" (OC §532). We should therefore take neither the incapacity of language to say "the supernatural" (i.e., the aesthetic, the ethical or the mystical generally), nor the philosopher's struggle with language, to be indications of any shortcoming in language. In the latter case, the philosopher's struggle, though it involves a struggle with language, is not due to any failing on the part of language, but to the philosopher's difficulty in apprehending and perspicuously relaying "something that already lies open to view and that becomes surveyable by a rearrangement" (PI §92). In the former case, it is simply that the *mode* of expression is not *saying*, but *showing*; language is perfectly adequate and indeed, where literature is concerned, essential to the evocation of the ineffable.

2. The Language of Literature: Showing, Not Saying

> For there is meaning that can be explained and meaning that does not come out in an explanation.
>
> (Z §156)

For Wittgenstein, the significance of aesthetics lies in the artist's ability to present objects, not as they exist in the empirical world, but *sub specie aeternitatis*.[8] Literally: "from the point of view of eternity"; that is atemporally, or non-contingently; from outside the world. This can mean something as metaphysically loaded as "from God's eye view" or more simply: "with detachment". Whereas the "usual way of looking at things sees objects . . . from the midst of them", the artist views them from outside, with aesthetic wonder ("*Künstlerische Wunder*") (NB, 86). This means that she views them with the kind of *detachment* that contemplates not facts, but the fact of existence: "Aesthetically, the miracle is that the world exists. That there is what there is" (NB, 86).

The world the artist sees is not factually different from the world we ordinarily see; it is her attitude to, and perspective of, that world that are different and transformative. For Wittgenstein, a kind of Gestalt switch takes place in artistic contemplation: where we "usually" see "the bare present image" as a "worthless momentary picture in the whole temporal world", the artist in aesthetic wonder sees it as "the true world among shadows" (NB, 83). It is the same "bare present" world for nothing has been added or removed from it, and yet an altogether different world, where the contingent and temporal fade out to allow the atemporal significance to emerge: "only an artist can represent an individual thing as to make it appear to us like a work of art. . . . A work of art forces us – as one might say – to see it in the right perspective but, in the absence of art, the object is just a fragment of nature like any other" (CV, 4–5).

And so the very same thing which had not otherwise made an impression on us will make one – indeed, the "right" one – when presented from an artistic perspective. This brings to mind Wittgenstein's notion of a "perspicuous presentation" – whereby something which had always been in plain view, and yet overlooked by us, when properly arranged (or *perspicuously presented*) is brought to our attention and strikes us significantly and as never before. There is something about the *artistic presentation* of a woman throwing herself under a train out of despair that a newspaper report of such an event cannot convey. Why is this? Many attempts have been made to explain it, but I find Wittgenstein's view (which he shares with F. R. Leavis) the most compelling. It is all in the term "presentation" – to be contrasted with report. If literature – the creative use of language – enables us to see in an event, a face or a gesture, a significance that the ordinary use of language is unable to evoke, it is because literature *presents* it so that we see it "in the right perspective"; but also because literature does not try to *say* what cannot be said. Wittgenstein is right, all that really matters in human life cannot be put into words, but it can be intimated or presented *through* language – particularly the language of literature:

> The poem by Uhland is really magnificent. And this is how it is: if only you do not try to utter what is unutterable then *nothing* gets lost. But the unutterable will be – unutterably – *contained* in what has been uttered.
>
> (EL, 7; original emphasis)

The poem does not make its point by what it literally says, but by what its words evoke or show – and *that* cannot be said. Wittgenstein's friend, Paul Engelmann, writes:

> The "positive" achievement of Wittgenstein, which has so far met with complete incomprehension, is his pointing to *what is manifest in a proposition*. And what is manifest in it, a proposition cannot also state explicitly. The poet's sentences, for instance, achieve their effect not through what they say but through what is manifest in them, and the same holds for music, which also says nothing.
>
> (EL, 83; original emphasis)

For Wittgenstein, literature – where words are used not naturalistically, but in a dance (CV, 37) – is capable of showing the ethical. It is (non-paradoxically) not through *saying*, but only through *showing* that it can do this. I have elsewhere made a rapprochement between Wittgenstein's "showing" or "presenting" and Leavis's "enactment" or "presentment", of the ethical in literature;[9] here, I want to flesh out what it means for language to present or show something.

Here is Leavis, defining a reader's task: "What we have to look for are the signs of something grasped and held, something presented in an ordering of words, not merely thought of or gestured towards" (Craig 2013, 24). And Wittgenstein:

> We speak of understanding a sentence in the sense in which it can be replaced by another which says the same; but also in the sense in which it cannot be replaced by any other. (Any more than one musical theme can be replaced by another.)
>
>   In the one case the thought in the sentence is something common to different sentences; in the other, something that is expressed only by these words in these positions. (Understanding a poem.)
>
> (PI §531)

Both Wittgenstein and Leavis are here acknowledging the inseparability of form and content in literature. Because the formal properties of a creative work essentially contribute to its meaning, attempting to prise apart meaning from its creative presentation will result in vacuous paraphrase. Garry Hagberg puts it well:

> The question what is the meaning of a work of art, where "meaning" carries an implicit analogy with language and where in turn language implies a fundamental separability of meaning from materials, is a question that ought to be treated with extreme caution.
>
> (Hagberg 1995, 74)

"Art is a kind of expression. Good art is complete expression" (NB, 83), writes Wittgenstein. Complete, in that nothing can be changed without sacrificing the expression. Yes, as Engelmann is right to point out, language is incalculably necessary, but the expression is equally dependent on the form: "[p]oetry can produce a profound artistic effect *beyond* (but never without) the immediate effect of its language. It is true that it needs a rare and felicitous conjuncture to bring off that effect" (EL, 84; original emphasis). Alluding to Wittgenstein's recitation "with a shudder of awe" of Mörike's *Mozart's Journey to Prague*, Engelmann remarks:

> In the rare cases where the venture succeeds . . . we are in the presence of sublime peaks of poetic language, and thus of verbal expression altogether. Here was one of the great passages in literature touching on Wittgenstein's most central language problem: that of the border of the unutterable and yet somehow expressible.
>
> (EL, 86)

This border where the unutterable somehow gets expressed is where meaning is not uttered or said but shown. *Saying* is not enough because the aesthetic and the ethical are not expressible in literal or naturalistic terms. We are not here in the realm of the verifiable but of what Wittgenstein calls "imponderable evidence" (LW I §§ 920–924): where the buzzing indeterminacy, spontaneity, and irreducibility of human life[10] hinges on its basic regularity and predictability so that though it is impossible to "put this indefiniteness, correctly and unfalsified, into words" (PI, 227), it is not impossible to *show* it. We have here to do with imponderable evidence – evidence that cannot be demonstrated, but can be "monstrated", as it were, or *shown*. Evidence that can only be apprehended non-discursively: through the blood, rather than the mind, would say D. H. Lawrence, for whom the novel, more than any other artistic medium, has this capacity for presentment or showing. Literature, and the novel in particular, gives us what philosophy, or any other discursive medium, cannot: "a passionate, implicit morality, not didactic. A morality which changes the blood, rather than the mind. Changes the blood first. The mind follows later, in the wake" (Lawrence 1964, 162). The idea here is to deintellectualize the ethical, to get us to see it as an attitude, a way of being and acting; and to deintellectualize, too, ethical understanding: morality reaches the mind through the blood – that is, through the immediacy of the aesthetic which is another kind of "perspicuous presentation". "A poet's words can pierce us" (Z §155) in a way a philosopher's cannot." For it is in the inextricable interrelatedness of form and content that meaning is made manifest; this is done by language that enacts rather than says: "Shakespeare displays the dance of human passions, one might say. . . . But he displays it to us in a dance, not naturalistically" (CV, 36–37).

For, meaning enacted in literature is grasped – as it is given – nondiscursively, with what Leavis calls "irresistible immediacy" (Leavis 1948, 204). The kind of grasp or understanding that requires no interpretation: we get the meaning or the point; we grasp it – the way we ordinarily grasp language, or the way we see an aspect emerging from a configuration, or the way we see emotion on a face. This is the *spontaneous, immediate intelligence* Christiane Chauviré recognizes as characterising much of what Wittgenstein means by "understanding":

> The relation of works of art or even musical phrases to the understanding we may have of them is not causal but internal, just as the relation of words that we read or hear in ordinary language is internal to our understanding of them. The drawback of interpretation is that it denotes an explicit verbal development that can engender others *ad infinitum*, each interpretation replacing the previous "as if we were content with one for the time being, until we thought of the next waiting immediately behind". And so, whether with regard to art or to rule-following, Wittgenstein reinstates spontaneous intelligence, immediate, silent at times, but always expressive.
>
> (Chauviré 2012, 338; my translation)

Wittgenstein clearly articulates this kind of nonpropositional under-standing prompted by music and literature: "If a theme, a phrase, sud-denly means something to you, you don't have to be able to explain it. Just *this* gesture has been made accessible to you" (Z §158; original emphasis); that is, you "understand it" (Z §159).[11] We can be impacted by, or "understand", the words of a poem, *directly*, which means without interpretation; for it speaks to us, writes Wittgenstein, "[t]he way music speaks. Do not forget that a poem, although it is composed in the lan-guage of information, is not used in the language-game of giving informa-tion" (Z §160). For there is meaning that can be explained and meaning that does not come out in an explanation (Z §156). I would now like to give an idea of how a novel can *show* us what I can only poorly explain.

3. The Perspicuous Presentations of Literature

In *Madame Bovary*, Gustave Flaubert depicts the life and state of a woman prey to *ennui*. To say that she finds herself engulfed in "a feeling of listlessness and dissatisfaction arising from a lack of occupation or excitement" (OED) would certainly summarize her state, but it would give you nothing of the texture of *ennui* or of the texture of Emma's life engulfed in it. Short of reading the novel, one cannot perceive and pene-trate the ways in which ennui in turn builds up and corrodes Emma's feel-ings, moods, expectations, dreams; how it comprises the recurring cycle of the fabrication of and luxuriating in what Baudelaire calls the "Ideal" and its slow, desperate consumption by the "Spleen". But perhaps these passages, albeit in translation, might give us a glimpse:

> [Charles] came home late – at ten o'clock, at midnight sometimes. Then he asked for something to eat, and as the servant had gone to bed, Emma waited on him. . . . He told her, one after the other, the people he had met, the villages where he had been, the prescrip-tions he had written, and, well pleased with himself, he finished the remainder of the boiled beef and onions, picked pieces off the cheese, munched an apple, emptied his water-bottle, and then went to bed, and lay on his back and snored. As he had been for a time accus-tomed to wear nightcaps, his handkerchief would not keep down over his ears, so that his hair in the morning was all tumbled pell-mell about his face and whitened with the feathers of the pillow, whose strings came untied during the night.
>
> . . . .
> She asked herself if by some other chance combination it would have not been possible to meet another man; and she tried to imag-ine what would have been these unrealised events, this different life, this unknown husband. All, surely, could not be like this one. He might have been handsome, witty, distinguished, attractive, such as,

no doubt, her old companions of the convent had married. What were they doing now? In town, with the noise of the streets, the buzz of the theatres and the lights of the ballroom, they were living lives where the heart expands, the senses bourgeon out. But she – her life was cold as a garret whose dormer window looks on the north, and ennui, the silent spider, was weaving its web in the darkness in every corner of her heart.

. . . .

As he grew older his manner grew heavier; . . . after eating he cleaned his teeth with his tongue; in taking soup he made a gurgling noise with every spoonful; and, as he was getting fatter, the puffed-out cheeks seemed to push the eyes, always small, up to the temples.

Sometimes . . . she told him of what she had read . . . for, after all, Charles was something, an ever-open ear, and ever-ready approbation. She confided many a thing to her greyhound. She would have done so to the logs in the fireplace or to the pendulum of the clock.

At the bottom of her heart, however, she was waiting for something to happen. Like shipwrecked sailors, she turned despairing eyes upon the solitude of her life, seeking afar off some white sail in the mists of the horizon. She did not know what this chance would be, what wind would bring it her, towards what shore it would drive her, if it would be a shallop or a three-decker, laden with anguish or full of bliss to the portholes. But each morning, as she awoke, she hoped it would come that day; she listened to every sound, sprang up with a start, wondered that it did not come; then at sunset, always more saddened, she longed for the morrow.

Scenes such as these penetratingly *show* the effect of ennui, with all the colour, light and shadow that language is capable of. To that effect, nonpropositional devices are used, such as image, metaphor, symbolism, juxtaposition, tension, mood, tone, cadence, irony etc. It is through the internal connectedness – or "subtle interrelatedness", as Lawrence puts it (Lawrence 1961, 528) – throughout the novel of these literary devices, as also of description, dialogue, action, enactment, that a nonpropositional, immediate, impact is made on us. As Leavis says: "The duly responsive reader cannot but *see* what it is that he has in front of him" (Leavis 1986, 63; original emphasis). And indeed we cannot but see the hopeless circularity that besets Emma's life through the novel as she perpetually fabricates an "ideal" only to watch it dissolve into vacuity. And beyond the force of individual passages, it is their being woven together to bolster, echo, and resonate from each other that gives the novel that structured, penetrating, coherence which is not of a discursive or philosophical kind. It leaves us with, as Leavis puts it, the "certitude" that we have "taken possession of . . . perceptions, intuitions and realizations communicated with consummate delicacy" to us in the creative work of a great writer. "Such certitude of possession is an ultimate; what could a proof, if proof were possible, add to it?" (Leavis 1982, 192). This immediate, irresistible, grasp of what literature *shows* resembles the certainty Wittgenstein describes in *On Certainty*. A certainty whose objects we take hold of, the way we directly take hold of a towel "without having doubts"; "And yet this direct taking-hold corresponds to a *sureness*, not to a knowing" (OC §§510– 511; original emphasis). An immediate nonpropositional certainty; a certainty where mistake is "logically excluded" (OC §194).

What great literature does is flesh out the density and texture of psychological and moral lives or experiences, thereby enhancing our understanding of what it means to be prey to ambition, remorse, alienation, jealousy, gnawing envy, and so on. So that, having read *Macbeth* and seen with exceptional clarity how the killing, spurred by ambition, of an innocent person can infect a life to the point of no return, sowing unbearable remorse, near-madness and the will to die, we are indubitably more perspicuously acquainted with the psychological and moral complexions of ambition and murder. Or, in Dostoevsky's *Crime and Punishment*, having observed how a man persuades himself of the permissibility of unprovoked murder, we close the book a couple of hundred pages later having witnessed in irrefutable clarity what it can be like to live the life of a murderer in its unrelenting existential reminders of the irreparability and consequences of a gratuitous act, and why it is not a life worth living. As also, having observed the vicissitudes of Emma Bovary's relentless aspirations, relentlessly crushed, we come to understand how an unquenchable thirst for the Ideal makes it impossible to see life in the every day.

In all these works, we live through the insidious, devastating, waste of a life. We are struck by the imponderable rightness of the narrative; its capturing, in wit-like acuity, what strikes us as not just *approximate*, but irrefutable. An irrefutability knitted in the intricate coherence of the whole work, so that, as Wittgenstein's certainty, what stands fast does so not on its own merit but because "it is held fast by what lies around it" (OC §144). And that is the power of the *story*, or what Aristotle called, the plot, and Amélie Rorty "a *structured* representation".[12] It is the importance of this *structured* or artistic representation that the words "not naturalistically" allude to in the following passage: "Shakespeare displays the dance of human passions. . . . But he displays it to us in a dance, not naturalistically" (CV, 36–37).

In *Madame Bovary*, Flaubert illuminates and extends our concept of boredom, showing how our mundane understanding of it as an occasional event cannot encompass the Existential malady Emma is continually prey to. Flaubert's original depiction of it takes us to the extreme, though not uncommon, manifestation of what we would call "boredom" and gives it more clarity and definition than, arguably, any other work preceding it.[13] And, of course, Flaubert does this through a struggle with language. Here is Maupassant's account of Flaubert's manner of composition:

Possessed of an absolute belief that there exists but one way of expressing one thing, one word to call it by, one adjective to qualify, one verb to animate it, he gave himself to super-human labour for the discovery, in every phrase of that word, that verb, that epithet.

(Maupassant 1884, 59)

We may find excessive, even when applied to literature, Flaubert's alleged belief that there exists but one way of expressing one thing. Although, as we shall see, Flaubert would by no means be the exception here, it may perhaps be better to say, as Richard Beardsmore does, that the writer's goal is "in some sense . . . to get things right" (Beardsmore 1971, 61). Or as we have seen Wittgenstein put it, to see things "in the right perspective" (CV, 4–5). But if Flaubert's concern is to get things right, "what does 'right' mean here?" it might be asked. As suggested earlier, the answer would not be: "a veridical concordance with reality or with a principle"; but rather something like: "you know it when you see it". However, in striking our psychological and moral chords, a great novel attunes or enhances, not our knowledge, but our understanding. It does this by presenting things in such a way that we "recognize" them as right, rather than "discover" them to be right because we are not aliens reading the novel, but human beings ensconced in human ways of living and responsive to the common behaviour of mankind. The language used by the creative writer is rooted and soaked in psychological and moral "promptings and potentialities" (Leavis 1976, 26) – as Leavis puts it – that have been "won or established in immemorial human living" (Leavis 1975, 68). It is human life that resonates in language, and the reader – the attentive and sensitive reader – will be "pierced" only by the right resonance – the one that coheres beyond (or rather beneath) explanation.

Flaubert had to wrestle with, and away from, the common conception of boredom to show us its Existential face: *ennui*. Thanks to Flaubert, and other writers, we are now more or less fluent with that new or revised concept: able to recognize its difference from mere boredom. In English, we mark that difference by adopting the French word; in French, when writing: we either italicise the word or capitalize its initial letter; when speaking, we qualify it somehow: "l'ennui existentiel" or use a near equivalent: "le spleen". The word "boredom" just won't do. However, what a creative writer does to our understanding is not always explicitly reflected by a change of word; and yet it behoves us to recognize it even where it is not thus flagged. Even when not signalled by a new word, the ongoing clarification and enrichment through writers of the concepts, virtues, vices that are most salient in our lives – love, ambition, jealousy, daughterliness, parenthood, friendship, sexuality, joie de vivre, faith, loyalty, deceit, war, depression, loss, death – are immense. Creative writing is a struggle with language in an effort to release from it an enhanced understanding of our basic and evolving humanness.

282 Danièle Moyal-Sharrock

Wittgenstein well understood this power of literature. For reasons that will immediately be obvious, I cannot resist mentioning yet another occasion which testifies to that. In 1945, Malcolm wrote a letter to Wittgenstein in which he alludes to the war as a "boredom". This is Wittgenstein's reply:

> I want to say something about the war being a "boredom". If a boy said that school was an intense boredom, one might answer him that, if he could only get himself to learn what can really be learned there, he would not find it so boring. Now forgive me for saying that I can't help believing that an enormous lot can be learned about human beings in this war – if you keep your eyes open. And the better you are at thinking the more you'll get out of what you see. For thinking is a digestion. If I'm writing in a preaching tone I'm just an ass. But the fact remains that if you're bored a lot it means that your mental digestion isn't what it should be. I think that a good remedy for this is sometimes opening your eyes wider. Sometimes a book helps a little, e.g., Tolstoi's *Hadshi Murat* wouldn't be bad.
>
> (Malcolm 1958, 41)

And here the philosopher hands over to literature. As Wittgenstein writes: "You cannot lead people to what is good: you can only lead them to some place or other. The good is outside the space of facts" (CV, 3). Well, literature leads us to some place or other, outside the space of facts, or what Wittgenstein calls "natural meaning", to a space of stories. And, there, *shows* us, not THE Good, but ways we ought to live and not live. In my attempt to understand how literature measures our lives, I was led to the active role of language in literary creation. Our moral being, as so much else, is embedded in language, and this is perhaps why in the same way that great creative literature cannot get away with stylistic blunders, it cannot get away with moral ones either. It is internally connected, as Wittgenstein rightly thought, to ethics.

"What expresses *itself* in language, *we* cannot express by means of language" (TLP 4.121; original emphasis). There is in this sentence a hint of language transcending any individual voice; of our shared language as an autonomous and irresistible force. The next and final section acknowledges language as a force whose measurement of human life which, though emerging from human life, we do not control.

4. The Irresistible Force of Language

> We are playing with elastic, indeed even flexible concepts. But this does not mean that they can be deformed *at will* and without offering resistance.
>
> (LW II, 24; original emphasis)

Language is public property and so it has a force and a life of its own – the life of generations of reality-embedded, reality-soaked, use. It carries shared concepts, feelings, meanings, emotions, and values, as well as density, precision, and a huge array of descriptive potential that the gifted user of language needs to wrestle with and interrogate, rather than manipulate. And of course we know – as Leavis and Wittgenstein have, in their different ways, enabled us to – that language is not a mere vehicle for thought but the *sine qua non* enabler of thought. Here is Leavis:

> Without the English language waiting quick and ready for him, Lawrence couldn't have communicated his thought: that is obvious enough. But it is also the case that he couldn't have thought it. English as he found it was a product of an immemorial sui generis collaboration on the part of its speakers and writers. It is alive with promptings and potentialities, and the great creative writer shows his genius in the way he responds.
>
> (Leavis 1976, 26)

Because language is a collaborative achievement, in using it, we tap into a collective source of meaning – that "apprehended totality of what, as registered in the language, has been won or established in immemorial human living" (Leavis 1975, 68). And inasmuch as "the fullest use of language is to be found in creative literature" (Leavis 1982, 143), it is there that we find the fullest engagement with the precipitate of immemorial human living, with human values, the human psyche and the question of how to live. If the creative writer is going to render us to ourselves with any acuity and depth, it will be through her confrontation with, and abandonment to, language. It is in the act of creation, in her intense and unimpeded head-to-head with language, her strenuous delving into its resources and potency for expression, that the artist finds she is not totally in control. In the "interplay" – as Leavis puts it – "between the living language and the creativity of individual genius" (Leavis 1975, 49), the writer finds not only the source of creativity but also her own limits. Language has fight and mettle: as she measures herself against language, the writer finds that she is "playing with elastic, indeed even flexible concepts. But this does not mean that they can be deformed *at will* and without offering resistance" (LW II, 24; original emphasis). Words cannot be manipulated without resistance; they can only be appealed to, interrogated, and acquiesced to. This is not to say that the creative writer does not also transform the language, but that she cannot do so without first abandoning herself to its deep-lying embeddedness in the reality of human living and fighting the fight from which both writer and language come out triumphant. As Bernard Harrison splendidly puts it: "The writer's occasional power to enlighten us comes, not from a special cognitive faculty, but rather from his power to ride the reality-gorged tiger of language" (ms, 19).

Creative writers often speak of themselves as the passive receptacles of an inspiration beyond their control. They say that the creative flow takes over, leads them; many of them speak of *watching* the characters in their novel develop and take on a life of their own; of *discovering* their characters' personalities and intentions; of *following* the morality of the plot as it *emerges*. In his study of "Creative Writers and Revision", David Calonne finds descriptions of "inspiration" by writers to be fairly consistent: "The writing seems to take place almost 'against the writer's will' – it is 'automatic' in a sense, or autonomous" (Calonne 2006, 156). Although it is also clear that inspiration does not exclude perspiration – or, as Ionesco puts it: "spontaneous creation does not exclude the pursuit and consciousness of style" (in Weiss 1991, 96), the autonomy of language prevails in the following extracts from Calonne's study:

> in writing a draft, writers often speak of finding what they have to say in the process of trying to say it. They find their way to their true thoughts about a subject only through wrestling through the fierce struggle of putting words down on paper. In the search for expression, one finds out that to which one is really committed. And there is often great surprise for the writer as he/she discovers in the act of writing what lies dormant within the self.
>
> (Calonne 2006, 144)

> The author himself/ herself clearly often does not know where the trail will lead as they embark on a poem, play or novel.
>
> (ibid., 173)

> The writer is the caretaker of an indwelling genius, an inner daimon/demon which speaks in riddles like an oracle – speaks sometimes seemingly unintelligibly but in the pure language of the poetic unconscious.
>
> (ibid., 156)

"Not I, but the wind that blows through me", writes D. H. Lawrence.[14] Such accounts of inspiration have often been given a metaphysical or spiritual reading, but they needn't have. What is in play here is the autonomous force of *language*. Inspiration is the active participation of language in a writer's attempt to bring something to clarity, and yes it also involves perspiration: it is the mysterious welling-up and laborious harnessing through language of notions, feelings, apprehensions unformed. It is only through language that the writer can achieve the perspicuous presentation of her unformed notions and perceptions in all of their subtle interrelatedness. As their testimonies make clear, writers feel that creation and revelation are brought about *in the process of* composition; as *resulting* from their immersion in, and struggle with, words. In an interview, Ernest Hemingway said "I rewrote the ending to *Farewell to Arms*, the last page of it, thirty-nine times before I was satisfied." When asked by the interviewer "Was there some technical problem there? What was it that had stumped you?" Hemingway replied "Getting the words right" (Calonne 2006, 149). This struggle of the writer with language signals both the *potency* of language and its *autonomy*: language has, as it were, a life of its own.

The creative imagination is really creative; it doesn't stage the ethical, but allows it to emerge from the artistic fabric. The morality is in the novel, not in the novelist: "Never trust the artist. Trust the tale", writes Lawrence (Lawrence 1964, 8). This perhaps clarifying what Wittgenstein means by "What expresses *itself* in language, *we* cannot express by means of language" (TLP 4.121; original emphasis). And so the important things don't get expressed by our *saying* them; it is when language is used in a creative way that the important things get expressed. This dovetails with what Leavis calls "creative impersonality" (Leavis 1986, 67). None of this is meant, as post-modernists have tried, to "kill" the author: writers are the writers they are because of the individuals they are, but this has to include an acutely sensitive attention to, and engagement with, language.

The way literature enlightens us is not through *saying* but through *showing*. Of course words are used, but the insight they evoke is not of the propositional kind; it cannot be said. And so we conclude this journey in the realisation that when we reach the power of language at its peak – in literature – we have simultaneously also returned to its limits. And yet those limits – literature's inability to *say* the most important things – should not blind us to its unlimited ability to *show* what can never be demonstrated, neither by the language of science nor by that of philosophy.[15]

Notes

1. For a fully-fledged argument, see Moyal-Sharrock 2016a.
2. I have not adopted the 2009 translation of PI because I find its rendering of several passages either less pertinent (e.g., "shared human behaviour" rather than "the common behaviour of mankind" for "*die gemeinsame menschliche Handlungsweise*" (PI §206)) or less felicitous (e.g., "marshalling recollections" rather than "assembling reminders" (PI §127)) than its predecessor. References are to the 1997 edition.
3. See, for example, Moyal-Sharrock (forthcoming).
4. "[T]he aim of the book is to draw a limit to thought, or rather – not to thought, but to the expression of thoughts: for in order to be able to draw a limit to thought, we should have to find both sides of the limit thinkable (i.e. we should have to be able to think what cannot be thought). It will therefore only be in language that the limit can be drawn" (TLP, 3).
5. For a more in-depth discussion, see Moyal-Sharrock (2007).
6. "The philosophical problem is an awareness of disorder in our concepts, and can be solved by ordering them" (BT, 309).
7. This struggle is also manifest in the multiple times Wittgenstein begins his sentences with: "I want to say."

8. "The work of art is the object seen *sub specie aeternitatis*; and the good life is the world seen *sub specie aeternitatis*. This is the connexion between art and ethics" (NB, 83).
9. See Moyal-Sharrock (2016b).
10. "What is . . . difficult here is to put this indefiniteness, correctly and unfalsified, into words" (PI, 227).
11. "But you do speak of *understanding* music. You understand it, surely, while you hear it! Ought we to say this is an experience which accompanies the hearing?" (Z §159; original emphasis).
12. Alluding to Aristotle's notion of tragedy in the *Poetics*, Rorty writes: "While there is sorrow, grief, loss, pain in life, there is *tragedy* only when the actions and events that compose a life are organized into a story, a structured representation of that life" (Rorty 1992, 3–4; my emphasis).
13. Including Chateaubriand's *René* (1802) which was hailed as the first to diagnose this French *mal du siècle*. *Madame Bovary* was published in 1856, one year before Baudelaire's *Les Fleurs du Mal*, which starts off its section on *Spleen et Idéal* with a poem referring to "l'Ennui, ce monster délicat".
14. This is the first verse of Lawrence's poem: "Song of a man who has come through".
15. I am grateful to Constantine Sandis and Keith Farman for their valuable and sensitive comments on the final draft of this chapter. I feel prompted by these to dispel the impression that I do not value the role of *saying*, or indeed of philosophy, in moral understanding. In fact, having argued against Cora Diamond for the importance of philosophical ethics for moral understanding (Moyal-Sharrock 2012), my aim in this chapter was to highlight and flesh out the important difference of *showing* and of literature for moral understanding. The "perspicuous presentations" of philosophy are of a different kind from those of literature; because philosophy's mode is *saying* rather than *showing*, it lacks the tools to transmit the fine-grained texture of being. However, philosophy has other tools. Take, for instance, Russell's sentence – "I cannot see how to refute the arguments for the subjectivity of ethical values, but I find myself incapable of believing that all that is wrong with wanton cruelty is that I don't like it" (Russell 1999, 165). It summarizes in a nutshell one of the deepest and most persistent problems of ethics; and if one were to replace the ethical values in that passage with aesthetic ones, it would be a brilliant summary of Kant's *Third Critique*. Literature is not able to do this: it takes philosophy to make perspicuous presentations of that kind. Russell's sentence describes, without literary texture, the problem we have with ethical objectivity or intersubjectivity, and elucidates beautifully in articulating the problem simply.

References

Beardsmore, Richard W. (1971) "Art and Understanding", in J. Haldane and L. Lloyd (eds), *Art, Morality and Human Nature: Writings by Richard W. Beardsmore*. Exeter: Imprint Academic, 2017, 55–79.
Calonne, David S. (2006) "Creative Writers and Revision", in A. Horning and A. Becker (eds), *Revision: History, Theory, and Practice*. Indiana: Parlor Press, 142–176.
Chauviré, Christiane (2012) "L'Art Incorporé: A propos des réactions esthétiques", in C. Romano (ed), *Wittgenstein*. Paris: Cerf, 225–251.
Craig, David (2013) "Thank God for the Leavisites", *London Review of Books* 35 (20), 24. www.lrb.co.uk/v35/n20/letters#letter9

Hagberg, Garry L. (1995) *Art as Language: Wittgenstein, Meaning and Aesthetic Theory*. Ithaca, NY: Cornell University Press.

Harrison, Bernard (ms) "Making Room for the Human: On the Unity of a Philosophical Project", 1–25.

Lawrence, D. H. (1961) *Phoenix I: The Posthumous Papers of D.H. Lawrence*. Edited by Edward D. McDonald. London: Heinemann.

Lawrence, D. H. (1964) *Studies in Classic American Literature*. London: Heinemann.

Leavis, F. R. (1948) *The Great Tradition*. London: Chatto and Windus.

Leavis, F. R. (1975) *The Living Principle: 'English' as a Discipline of Thought*. London: Chatto & Windus.

Leavis, F. R. (1976) *Thought, Words and Creativity: Art and Thought in Lawrence*. London: Chatto & Windus.

Leavis, F. R. (1982) *The Critic as Anti-Philosopher*. Edited by G. Singh. London: Chatto & Windus.

Leavis, F. R. (1986) *Valuation in Criticism and other Essays* (posth.). Edited by G. Singh. Cambridge: Cambridge University Press.

Malcolm, Norman (1958) *Ludwig Wittgenstein: A Memoir*. Oxford: Oxford University Press.

Maupassant, de, Guy (1884) *Etude sur Gustave Flaubert* in *La Revue bleue*. Quoted in and translated by Walter Pater in *Appreciations*. London: Palgrave Macmillan, 1910.

Moyal-Sharrock, Danièle (2007) "The Good Sense of Nonsense: A Reading of Wittgenstein's *Tractatus* as Nonself-Repudiating", *Philosophy* 82 (1), 147–177.

Moyal-Sharrock, Danièle (2012) "Cora Diamond and the Ethical Imagination", *British Journal of Aesthetics* 52 (3), 223–240.

Moyal-Sharrock, Danièle (2016a) "Wittgenstein, No Linguistic Idealist", in S. Greve and J. Mácha (eds), *Wittgenstein and the Creativity of Language*. Basingstoke: Palgrave Macmillan, 117–140.

Moyal-Sharrock, Danièle (2016b) "Wittgenstein and Leavis: Literature and the Enactment of the Ethical", *Philosophy and Literature* 40 (1), 24–64.

Moyal-Sharrock, Danièle (forthcoming) "Through Thick and Thin: Wittgenstein's Grammar", in S. Wuppuluri (ed), *wittgensteinian (adj.): Looking at Things from the Viewpoint of Wittgenstein's Philosophy*. Berlin: Springer.

Rorty, Amélie (1992) "The Psychology of Aristotelian Tragedy", in A. Rorty (ed), *Essays on Aristotle's Poetics*. Princeton, NJ: Princeton University Press, 1–22.

Russell, B. (1999) *Russell on Ethics: Selections from the Writings of Bertrand Russell*. Edited by C. Pigden. London: Routledge.

Ware, Ben (2015) *Dialectic of the Ladder: Wittgenstein, the* Tractatus *and Modernism*. London: Bloomsbury.

Weiss, Jason (1991) *Writing at Risk: Interviews in Paris With Uncommon Writers*. Iowa City IA: University of Iowa Press.

Williams, Bernard (1974) "Wittgenstein and Idealism", in G. Vesey (ed), *Understanding Wittgenstein* (Royal Institute of Philosophy Lectures 7, 1972–1973). London: Palgrave Macmillan, reprinted in his *Moral Luck*. Cambridge: Cambridge University Press, 1981, 144–163.

Contributors

Hanne Appelqvist is Docent of Theoretical Philosophy at the University of Helsinki and the University of Turku and Editor-in-Chief of *Estetika: The Central European Journal of Aesthetics*. Currently she works as the Deputy Director of the Helsinki Collegium for Advanced Studies. In her publications, Appelqvist has explored the affinities between Wittgenstein and Kant especially from the viewpoint of aesthetics.

William Child is Professor of Philosophy at the University of Oxford and Fellow in Philosophy at University College, Oxford. He is the author of *Causality, Interpretation, and the Mind* (OUP, 1994) and *Wittgenstein* (Routledge, 2011) and of papers on many topics in philosophy of mind and the philosophy of Wittgenstein.

Hans-Johann Glock is Professor of Philosophy at the University of Zurich and Visiting Professor at the University of Reading (UK). His recent publications include *The Blackwell Companion to Wittgenstein* (2017, co-edited with John Hyman), as well as several articles on the philosophy of animal minds, the normativity of meaning and the dominance of English as the medium of (analytic) philosophy. He gave the 2019 Francis Bacon Lecture of the Royal Institute of Philosophy on the topic of "Animal Minds and Animal Ethics".

Eran Guter has a PhD in philosophy from Boston University. He is currently a Senior Lecturer in philosophy at the Max Stern Yezreel Valley College, and a researcher at the Department of Philosophy, University of Haifa, Israel. He is the author of *Aesthetics A-Z* (Edinburgh University Press, 2010) as well as a number of articles on Wittgenstein, philosophy of music, and new media aesthetics. He has received a Joint Excellence in Science and Humanities (JESH) grant from the Austrian Academy of Sciences for his research project on "Wittgenstein's reversal in the philosophy of music".

Leila Haaparanta is Professor Emerita of Philosophy at the University of Tampere and Docent of Theoretical Philosophy at the University of Helsinki. She has published widely on the history of logic, early twentieth-century analytic philosophy and phenomenology, epistemology, philosophy of mind and language, philosophy of religion, and pragmatism. For the last few years, she has focused on epistemology of testimony and theories of judgment and assertion. Her recent edited works include *The Development of Modern Logic* (OUP, 2009) and *Categories of Being* (with Heikki J. Koskinen, OUP, 2012).

Colin Johnston is Senior Lecturer in Philosophy, University of Stirling. Johnston's historical concerns centre around Frege and the early Wittgenstein's views on truth and judgment. Key papers on this topic include "Frege on syntax, ontology, and truth's pride of place" (*European Journal of Philosophy*), "The picture theory" (*Blackwell Companion to Wittgenstein*), "Judgment and the identity theory of truth" (*Philosophical Studies*), and "Symbols in Wittgenstein's Tractatus" (*European Journal of Philosophy*).

A. W. Moore is Professor of Philosophy at the University of Oxford and Tutorial Fellow at St Hugh's College Oxford, where he is also Vice-Principal. His publications include: *Points of View* (OUP, 1997), *Noble in Reason, Infinite in Faculty: Themes and Variations in Kant's Moral and Religious Philosophy* (Routledge, 2003), *The Evolution of Modern Metaphysics: Making Sense of Things* (OUP, 2012), *The Infinite* (Routledge, 3rd edition 2019), and *Language, World, and Limits: Essays in the Philosophy of Language and Metaphysics* (OUP, 2019). He is joint editor, with Lucy O'Brien, of *MIND*.

Danièle Moyal-Sharrock is Professor in Philosophy at the University of Hertfordshire (UK). Her work focuses on "hinge epistemology" and on applying Wittgenstein's philosophy to disciplines outside philosophy, such as psychology, primatology, language acquisition, and literature. Her publications include *Understanding Wittgenstein's On Certainty* (Palgrave, 2007), *The Third Wittgenstein* (Ashgate, 2004), *Perspicuous Presentations* (Palgrave, 2007), *Hinge Epistemology* (with Annalisa Coliva, Brill, 2016), and *F. R. Leavis: Critic, Teacher, Philosopher* (*Philosophy and Literature*, 2016). She is President of the British Wittgenstein Society.

Yrsa Neuman received her doctoral degree from Åbo Akademi University in 2015. She is the former Editor-in-Chief and current editorial board member of *Nordic Wittgenstein Review* and a member of the steering group of the von Wright and Wittgenstein Archives at the University of Helsinki. Currently she works as the Open Science Project Manager at Åbo Akademi University. Her philosophical work has focused on the methods of philosophizing after the later Wittgenstein and the history of attention to language use in philosophy.

Sami Pihlström is Professor of Philosophy of Religion at the University of Helsinki, Finland, and President of the Philosophical Society of Finland. He has published widely on pragmatism, philosophy of religion, transcendental philosophy, and metaphilosophy. His recent books include *Taking Evil Seriously* (Palgrave, 2014), *Death and Finitude* (Rowman and Littlefield, 2016), and *Kantian Antitheodicy* (with Sari Kivistö, Palgrave, 2016).

Panu-Matti Pöykkö is Doctoral Candidate in Philosophy of Religion at the Faculty of Theology, University of Helsinki, and a member of the Academy of Finland's Centre of Excellence *Reason and Religious Recognition*. He is currently finishing his doctoral thesis on Emmanuel Levinas's philosophy of religion and phenomenology.

Constantine Sandis is Professor of Philosophy at the University of Hertfordshire, Fellow of the Royal Society of Arts, and Secretary of the British Wittgenstein Society. In recent publications, Sandis has explored Wittgenstein's views on understanding others. He is currently writing a book on "If a Lion Could Speak . . .".

Paul Standish is Professor of Philosophy of Education at UCL Institute of Education, Visiting Professor at Kyoto University, and Chair of the Philosophy of Education Society of Great Britain (2017–2020). His work is characterised by a broadly phenomenological approach to questions of education, with particular regard to language. He is the author or editor of some twenty books – ranging from *Beyond the Self: Wittgenstein, Heidegger, and the Limits of* Language (Avebury, 1992) to *Stanley Cavell and Philosophy as* Translation (Rowman and Littlefield, 2017), and *Democracy and Education from Dewey to Cavell* (Wiley, 2020), the last two in collaboration with Naoko Saito.

Index